the *nightly*
NEWS
[A Lie Told In Six Parts]

by: **jonathanHICKMAN**

IMAGE COMICS, INC.

Robert Kirkman
Erik Larsen
Todd McFarlane
Marc Silvestri
Jim Valentino

Eric Stephenson
Todd Martinez
Betsy Gomez
Branwyn Bigglestone
Sarah deLaine
Tyler Shainline
Drew Gill
Jonathan Chan
Monica Howard
Vincent Kukua
Kevin Yuen

www.imagecomics.com

for **LORI** *and* **DARIEN**
This is Bread • *This is Milk*

acknowledge
ments

First and foremost, I owe a debt to all the good people I've worked with at Image comics: Erik Larsen, Eric Stephenson, Mark Britt, Joe Keatinge, Jim Demonakos, Allen Hui, Drew Gill and Traci Hui. All I needed was an opportunity and you delivered in spades.

A special thanks to the stars of the book: Brad Jordan, Forest Kinnett, Marty Shelley, Josh Laney, Sherri Gore, Danny Smith, Kyle Rechsteiner and Caroline Kinnett.

To the comicbook press that got behind the book, specifically: Comic News Insider, Around Comics, Word Balloon, Comic Geek Speak, Attack of the Show, Comicazi, Comicology, Evil Avatar, The-ISB, CBR, Newsarama, The Comicbloc, The Beat, Silver Bullet, The Buy Pile, Fractal Matter and Comic Foundry. Thanks for believing in something completely different.

And lastly, but so very sincerely, thanks to my peers, *whose work I love and respect*, for taking time I know they don't have to recognize, encourage or praise my work: Andy Diggle, Warren Ellis, Stuart Immonen, Brian K. Vaughn, Brad Meltzer and Brian Michael Bendis.

fore WORD

by:
andy DIG

Andy Diggle has sold, studied, taught, edited and written comics - which probably explains why he's starting to get a little bit jaded with the whole comics thing. And hey, movies pay better. His Vertigo series THE LOSERS is currently being developed for the big screen by Warner Bros.

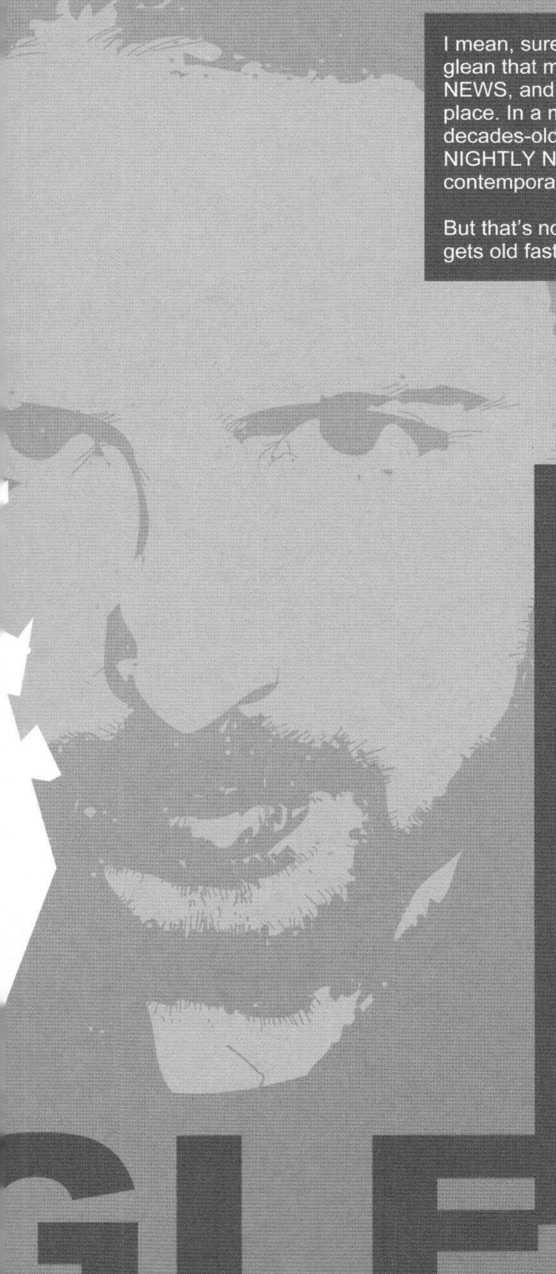
GLE

Jonathan Hickman has a nasty streak.

I mean, sure, the guy obviously knows design. You can glean that much just from a cursory glance at THE NIGHTLY NEWS, and it's what made me pick up the book in the first place. In a medium dominated by stale regurgitations of decades-old spandex-wearing corporate trademarks, THE NIGHTLY NEWS leaps out as something visually fresh, contemporary and relevant.

But that's not enough to keep me reading. After all, novelty gets old fast.

No, it's not just the snazzy design, nor the intricately woven conspiracy plot, nor the commentary on the nature of the modern corporate media. Sure, that stuff doesn't hurt. But the real thing that kept me picking up this book issue after issue is that *nasty streak*.

I mean, not only are this guy's protagonists a bunch of unredeemed, cold-blooded murderers - they're all *fucking crazy* to boot. And I don't mean that Wow-you're-so-cool-and-unorthodox-I-wish-I-could-be-just-like-you kind of crazy. I mean that shoot-you-in-the-head-on-live-TV-and-set-myself-on-fire-in-Times-Square kind of crazy.

That, and it's *funny*.

The question is, does Hickman actually believe the shit he's slinging? The trail of infographics sprinkled like breadcrumbs to a rat-trap certainly give the book a sense of authorial veracity. But does that mean the worldview of the story itself should somehow be taken as "true" by association? Is the narrative voice actually the authorial voice? Does Jonathan Hickman condone the wholesale slaughter of members of the news media?

Is this guy fucking crazy?

Hard to say. After all, he does attempt to distance his own personal views from those of his characters. There are those cute little disclaimers at the start of every chapter; plus he subtitles the story "A Lie Told In Six Parts", telling us up front that this is bullshit, make believe, *fiction*. In other words, don't try this at home, kids.

Yeah, right. Like we're buying *that*, Hickman.

See, maybe that's just what he *wants* you to think. Maybe Hickman really is The Voice, channeling his anger through the only mass medium left that still allows any kind of subversive self-expression - namely, creator-owned comic books.

Maybe he is. Maybe I'm dictating this introduction duct-taped to a chair with a bag over my head. Maybe I can smell gun oil and lighter fluid.

Like I said. Nasty streak.

I'll be sure to buy Jonathan Hickman's next book. Honest.

ANDY DIGGLE
LONDON, 2007

"The mass media serve as a system for communicating messages and symbols to the general populace. It is their function to amuse, entertain, and inform, and to inculcate individuals with the values, beliefs, and codes of behavior that will integrate then into the institutional structures of the larger society. In a world of concentrated wealth and major conflicts of class interest, to fulfill this role requires systematic propaganda."

Noam Chomsky & Edward S. Herman
MANUFACTURING CONSENT

"...Chomsky's a fucking retard."

Senator M. Jay Rector
Democrat, State of Georgia

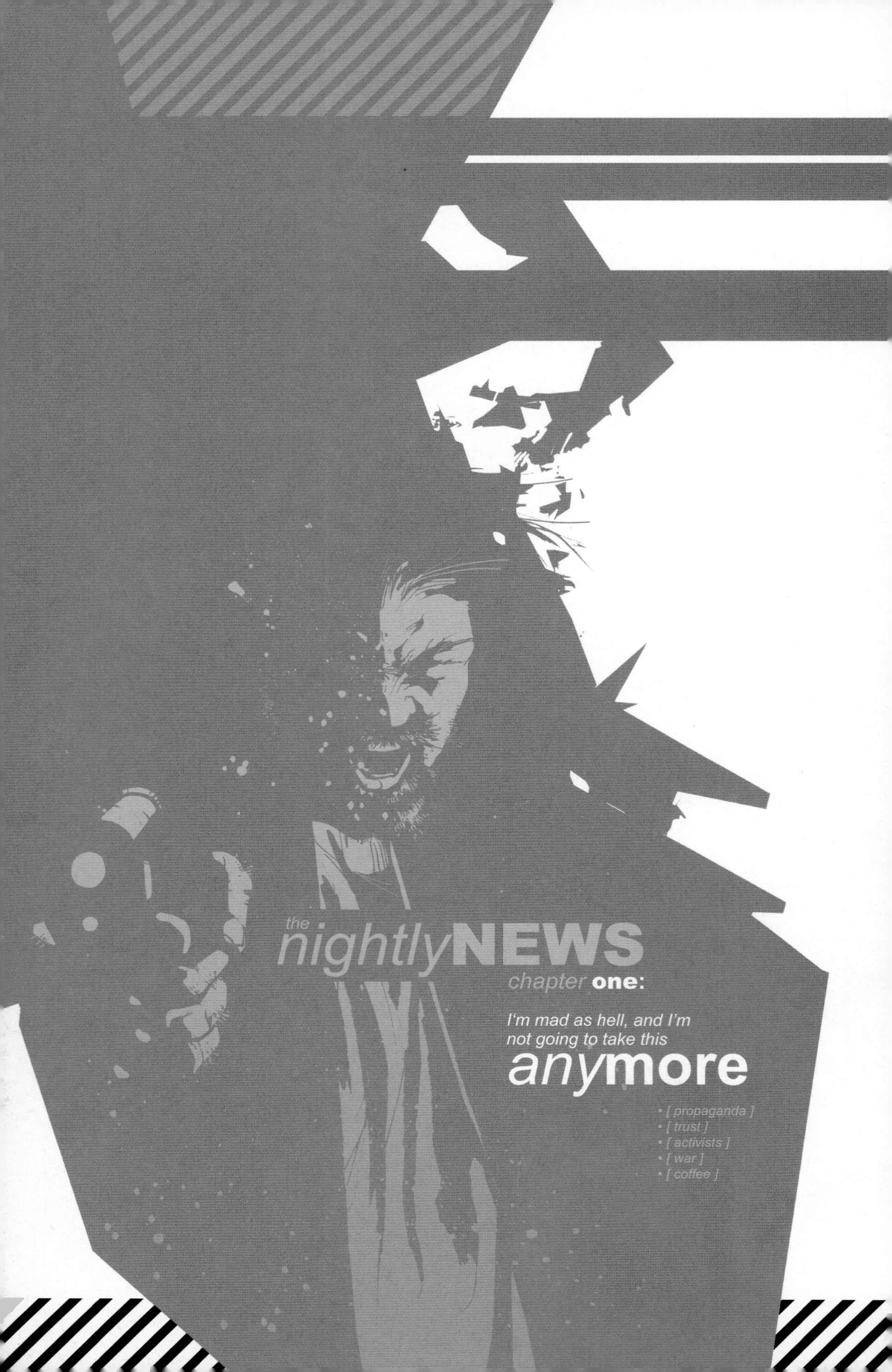

the nightlyNEWS
chapter one:
I'm mad as hell, and I'm not going to take this anymore
• [propaganda]
• [trust]
• [activists]
• [war]
• [coffee]

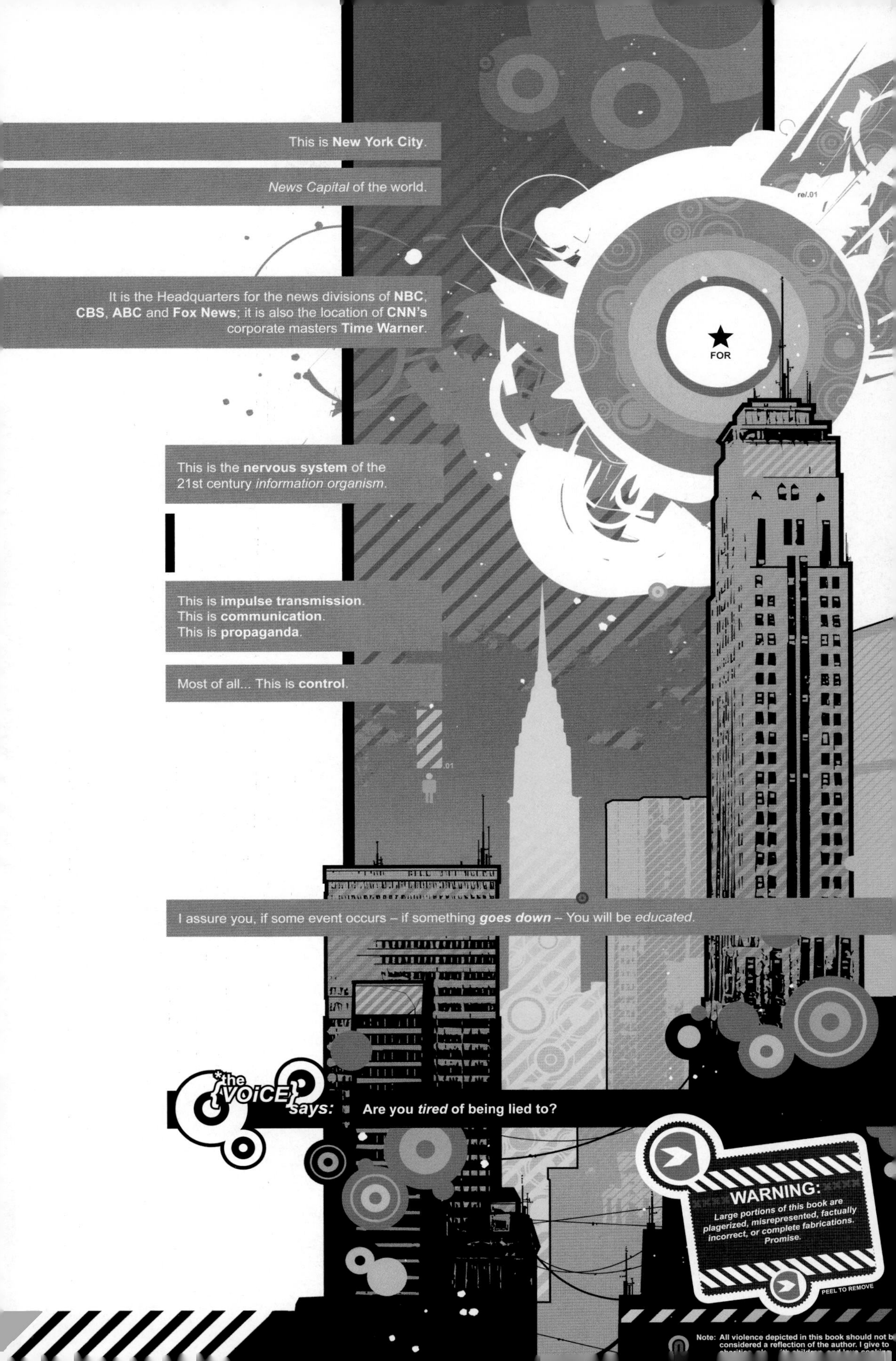

This is **New York City**.
News Capital of the world.
It is the Headquarters for the news divisions of **NBC**, **CBS**, **ABC** and **Fox News**; it is also the location of **CNN's** corporate masters **Time Warner**.
FOR
re/.01
This is the **nervous system** of the 21st century *information organism*.
This is **impulse transmission**.
This is **communication**.
This is **propaganda**.
Most of all... This is **control**.
.01
I assure you, if some event occurs – if something ***goes down*** – You will be *educated*.
*the {VoiCE} says:
Are you *tired* of being lied to?
WARNING:
Large portions of this book are plagerized, misrepresented, factually incorrect, or complete fabrications. Promise.
PEEL TO REMOVE
Note: All violence depicted in this book should not b
considered a reflection of the author. I give to

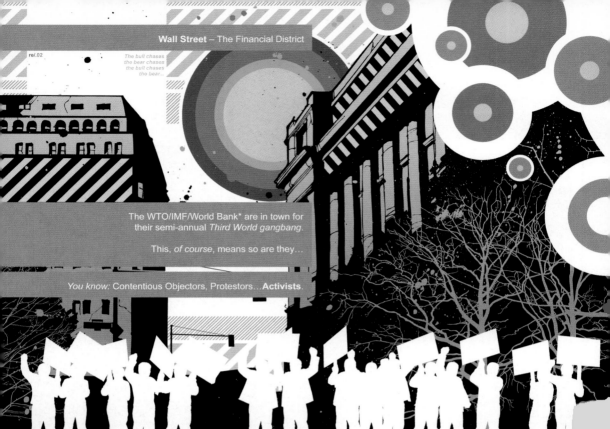

Wall Street – The Financial District

ref.02

The bull chases the bear chases the bull chases the bear...

The WTO/IMF/World Bank* are in town for their semi-annual *Third World gangbang*.

This, *of course*, means so are they…

You know: Contentious Objectors, Protestors…**Activists**.

To find out more about globalization, read below. However, if you're like me and only care about your own personal entertainment (certainly not anything like children dying of dysentery in Togo), keep reading on the next page!

modified group awareness: globalization

International Monetary Fund

List of Managing Directors

	1946 - 1951	Camille Gutt
	1951 - 1956	Ivar Rooth
	1956 - 1963	Per Jacobsson
	1963 - 1973	Pierre-Paul Schweitzer
	1973 - 1978	Johannes Witteveen
	1978 - 1987	Jacques de Larosière
	1987 - 2000	Michel Camdessus
	2000 - 2004	Horst Köhler
	2004	Anne Krueger
	2004 – Present	Rodrigo Rato

World Bank

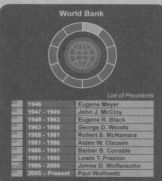

List of Presidents

	1946	Eugene Meyer
	1947 - 1949	John J. McCloy
	1949 - 1963	Eugene R. Black
	1963 - 1968	George D. Woods
	1968 - 1981	Robert S. McNamara
	1981 - 1986	Alden W. Clausen
	1986 - 1991	Barber B. Conable
	1991 - 1995	Lewis T. Preston
	1995 - 2005	James D. Wolfensohn
	2005 – Present	Paul Wolfowitz

The shocking *favorabilty* ratings for the **World Trade Organization**, **International Monetary Fund** and the **World Bank** by geographic region.

NORTH AMERICA	60%
SOUTH AMERICA	50%
WESTERN EUROPE	65%
EASTERN EUROPE	55%
AFRICA	70%
ASIA	60%
MIDDLE EAST	40%

ONE DOLLAR·ONE VOTE   ONE DOLLAR·ONE VOTE
ONE DOLLAR ONE VOTE
This is Global Democracy

free markets equal ...\\ **CAPITAL** **FLIGHT //**...

The amount of funds held by individuals in offshore and onshore tax havens *and* undeclared in the country of residence is around **$11.5 trillion**

Did you know?
Currently the world's richest **500 people** have a greater wealth than the combined income of the **3.3 billion** poorest?

Countries in financial crisis can apply for a crisis loan package from the **IMF** or the **World Bank**.

These loans come with a set of *at least* **100** conditions.

Privatization > Deregulation > Free Trade > Market Capitalization > Ruin

ATTENTION: In the case of a national financial emergency, if you are an emerging market country and you hear the phrases **structural assistance program** or **poverty reduction strategy**, *RUN!*

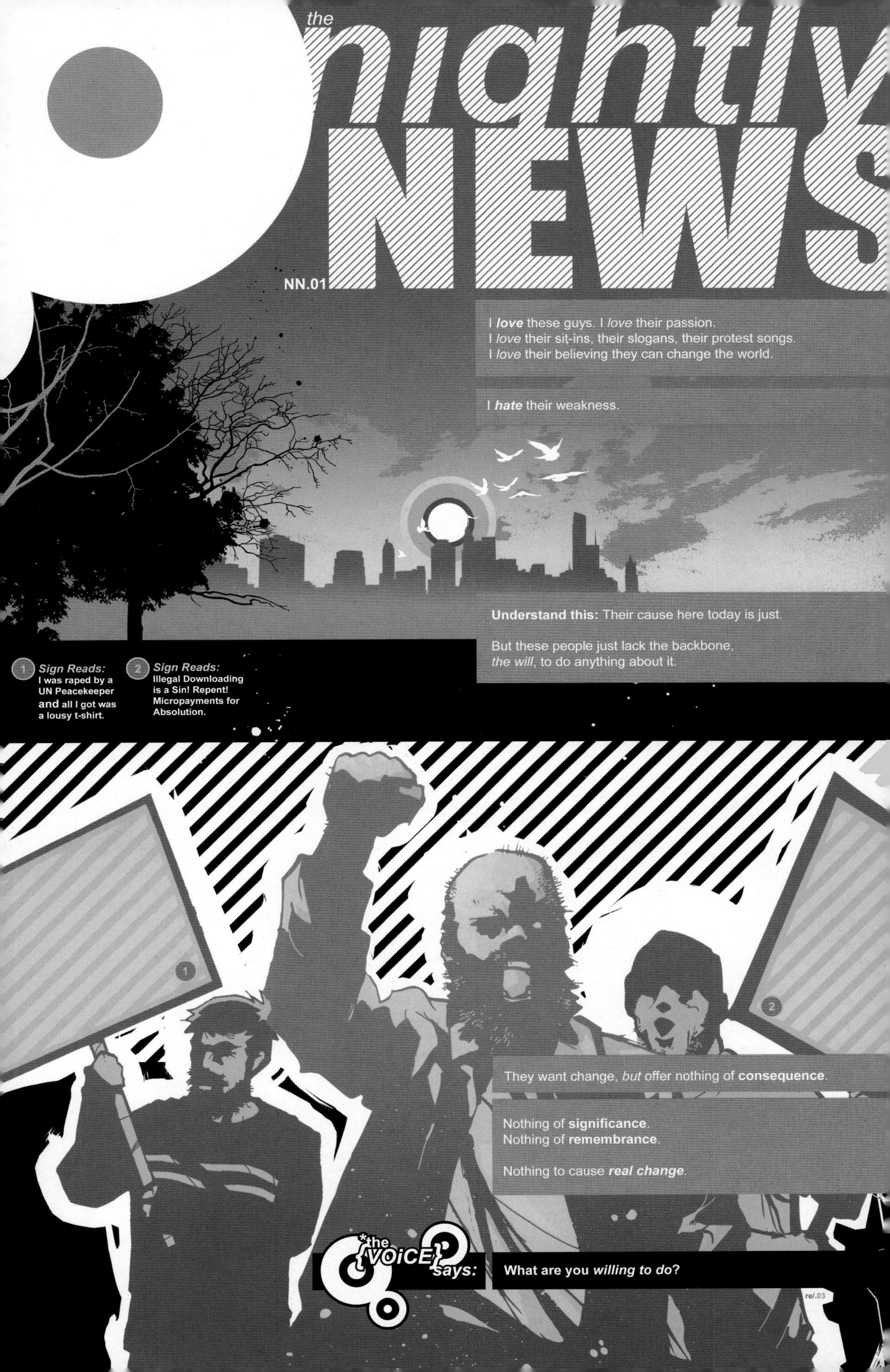

the nightly NEWS
NN.01
I *love* these guys. I *love* their passion.
I *love* their sit-ins, their slogans, their protest songs.
I *love* their believing they can change the world.
I *hate* their weakness.
Understand this: Their cause here today is just.
But these people just lack the backbone, *the will*, to do anything about it.
1 *Sign Reads:* I was raped by a UN Peacekeeper and all I got was a lousy t-shirt.
2 *Sign Reads:* Illegal Downloading is a Sin! Repent! Micropayments for Absolution.
1
2
They want change, *but* offer nothing of **consequence**.
Nothing of **significance**.
Nothing of **remembrance**.
Nothing to cause ***real change***.
*the {VOiCE} says:
What are you *willing to do*?
re/.03

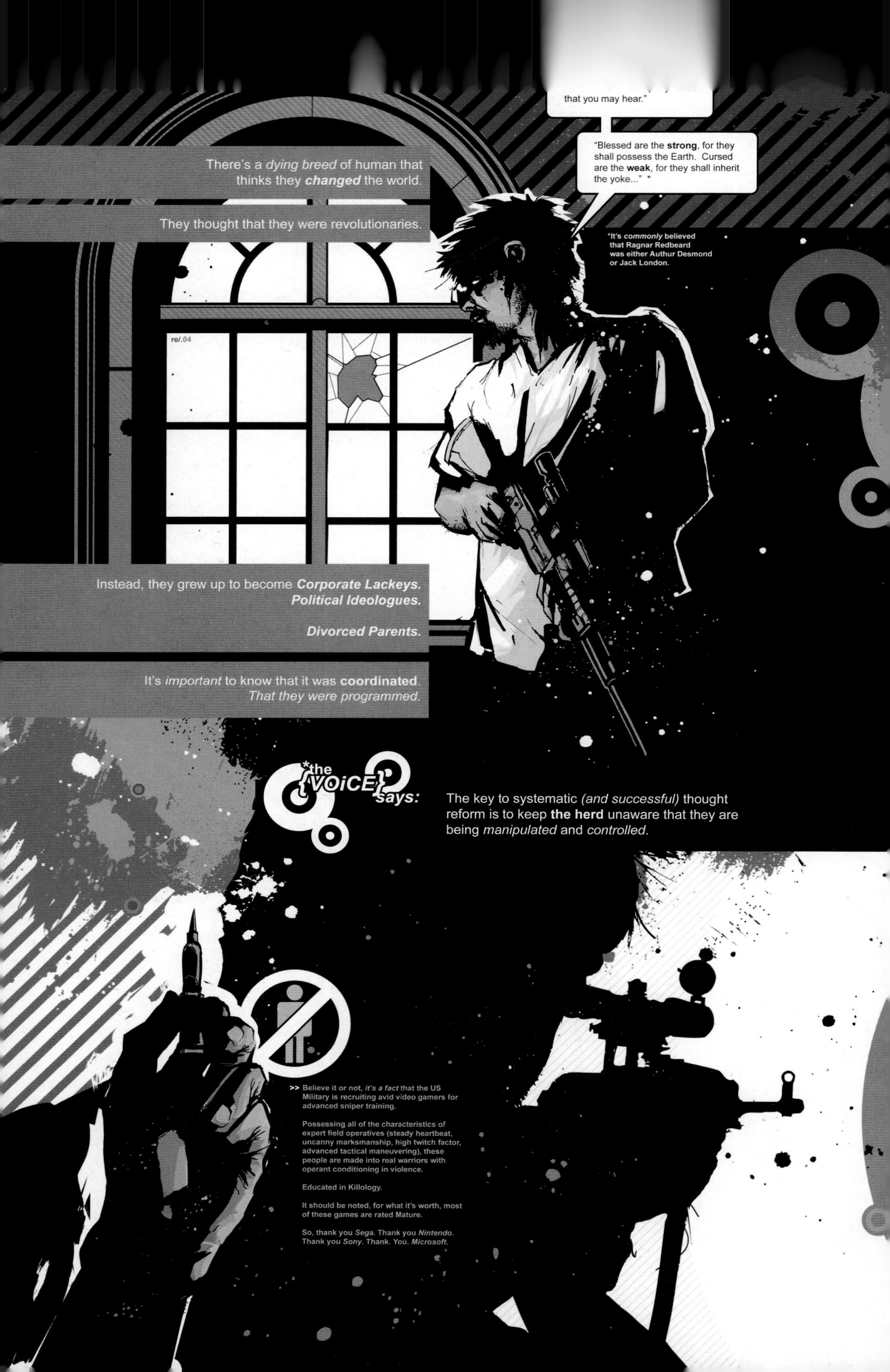

that you may hear.”
“Blessed are the **strong**, for they shall possess the Earth. Cursed are the **weak**, for they shall inherit the yoke...” *
There’s a *dying breed* of human that thinks they ***changed*** the world.
They thought that they were revolutionaries.
*It’s *commonly* believed that Ragnar Redbeard was either Authur Desmond or Jack London.
re/.04
Instead, they grew up to become ***Corporate Lackeys. Political Ideologues.***
Divorced Parents.
It’s *important* to know that it was **coordinated**. *That they were programmed.*
*the {VOiCE} says:
The key to systematic *(and successful)* thought reform is to keep **the herd** unaware that they are being *manipulated* and *controlled*.
>> Believe it or not, *it’s a fact* that the US Military is recruiting avid video gamers for advanced sniper training.
Possessing all of the characteristics of expert field operatives (steady heartbeat, uncanny marksmanship, high twitch factor, advanced tactical maneuvering), these people are made into real warriors with operant conditioning in violence.
Educated in Killology.
It should be noted, for what it’s worth, most of these games are rated Mature.
So, thank you *Sega*. Thank you *Nintendo*. Thank you *Sony*. Thank. You. *Microsoft*.

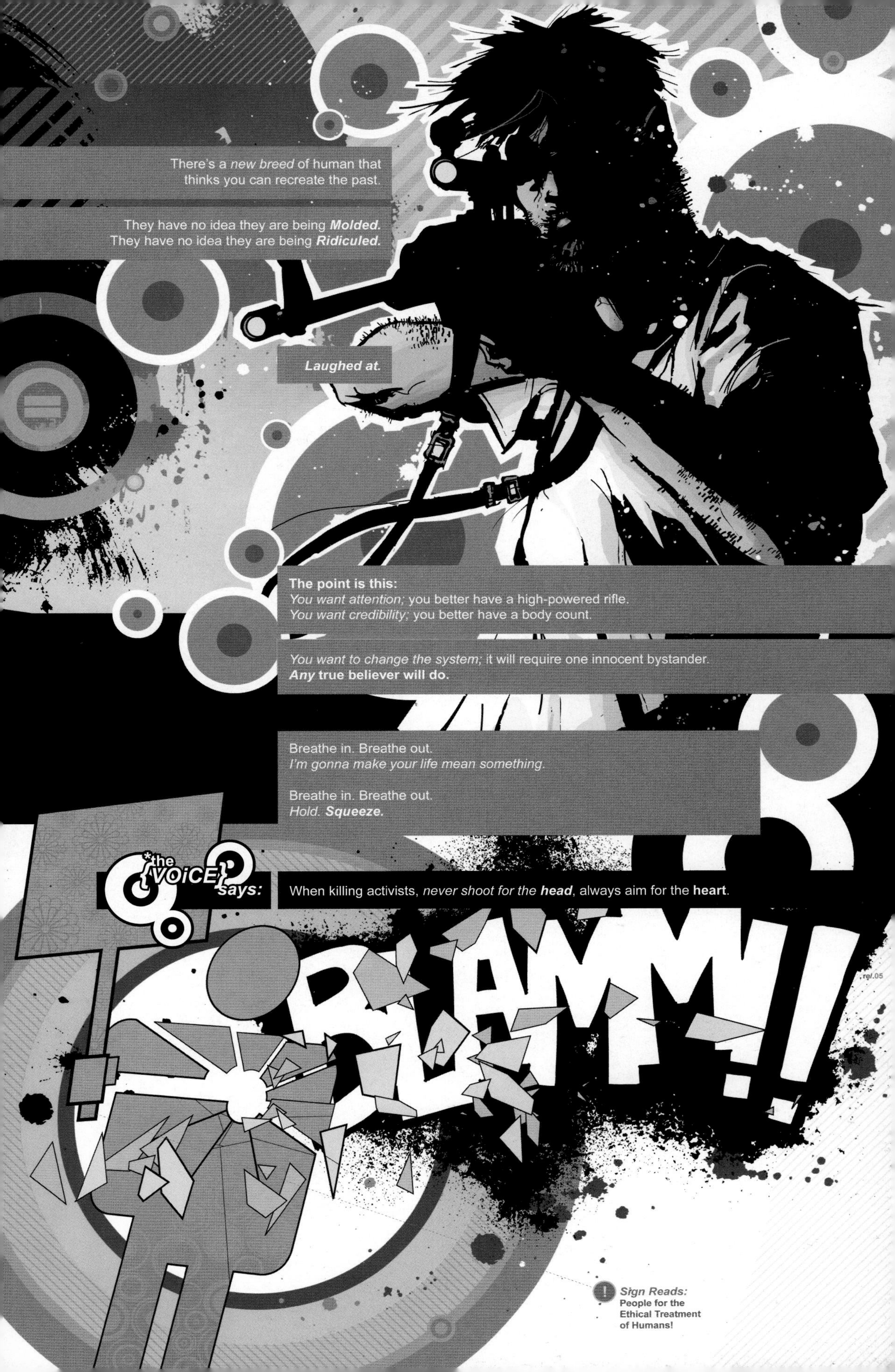
There's a *new breed* of human that thinks you can recreate the past.
They have no idea they are being ***Molded.*** They have no idea they are being ***Ridiculed.***
Laughed at.
The point is this: *You want attention;* you better have a high-powered rifle. *You want credibility;* you better have a body count.
You want to change the system; it will require one innocent bystander. ***Any* true believer will do.**
Breathe in. Breathe out. *I'm gonna make your life mean something.*
Breathe in. Breathe out. *Hold.* ***Squeeze.***
*the {VOiCE} says:
When killing activists, *never shoot for the* ***head***, always aim for the **heart**.
BLAMM!!
rel.05
Sign Reads: **People for the Ethical Treatment of Humans!**

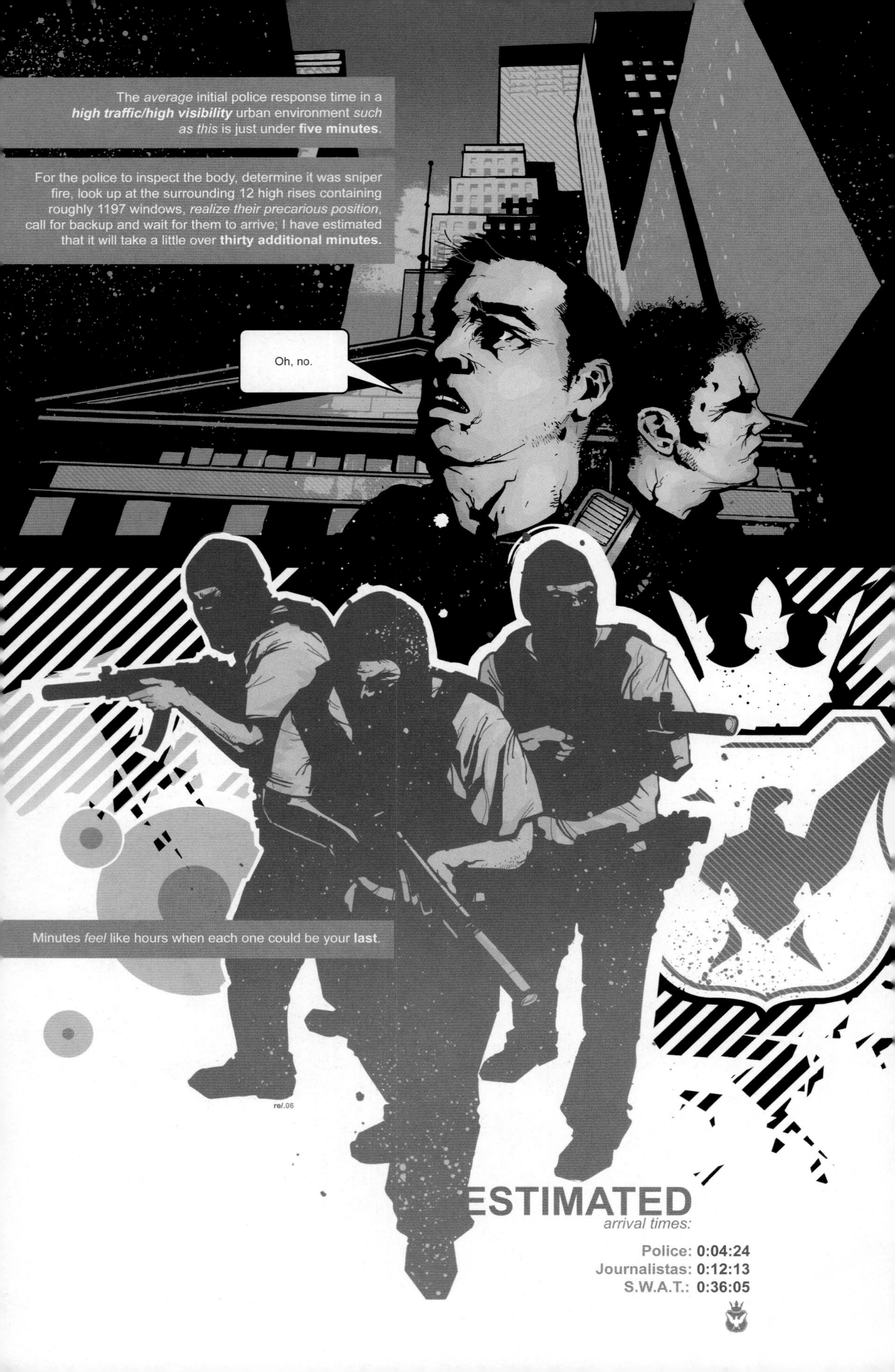
The *average* initial police response time in a ***high traffic/high visibility*** urban environment *such as this* is just under **five minutes**.
For the police to inspect the body, determine it was sniper fire, look up at the surrounding 12 high rises containing roughly 1197 windows, *realize their precarious position*, call for backup and wait for them to arrive; I have estimated that it will take a little over **thirty additional minutes.**
Oh, no.
Minutes *feel* like hours when each one could be your **last**.
re/.06
ESTIMATED
arrival times:
Police: **0:04:24**
Journalistas: **0:12:13**
S.W.A.T.: **0:36:05**

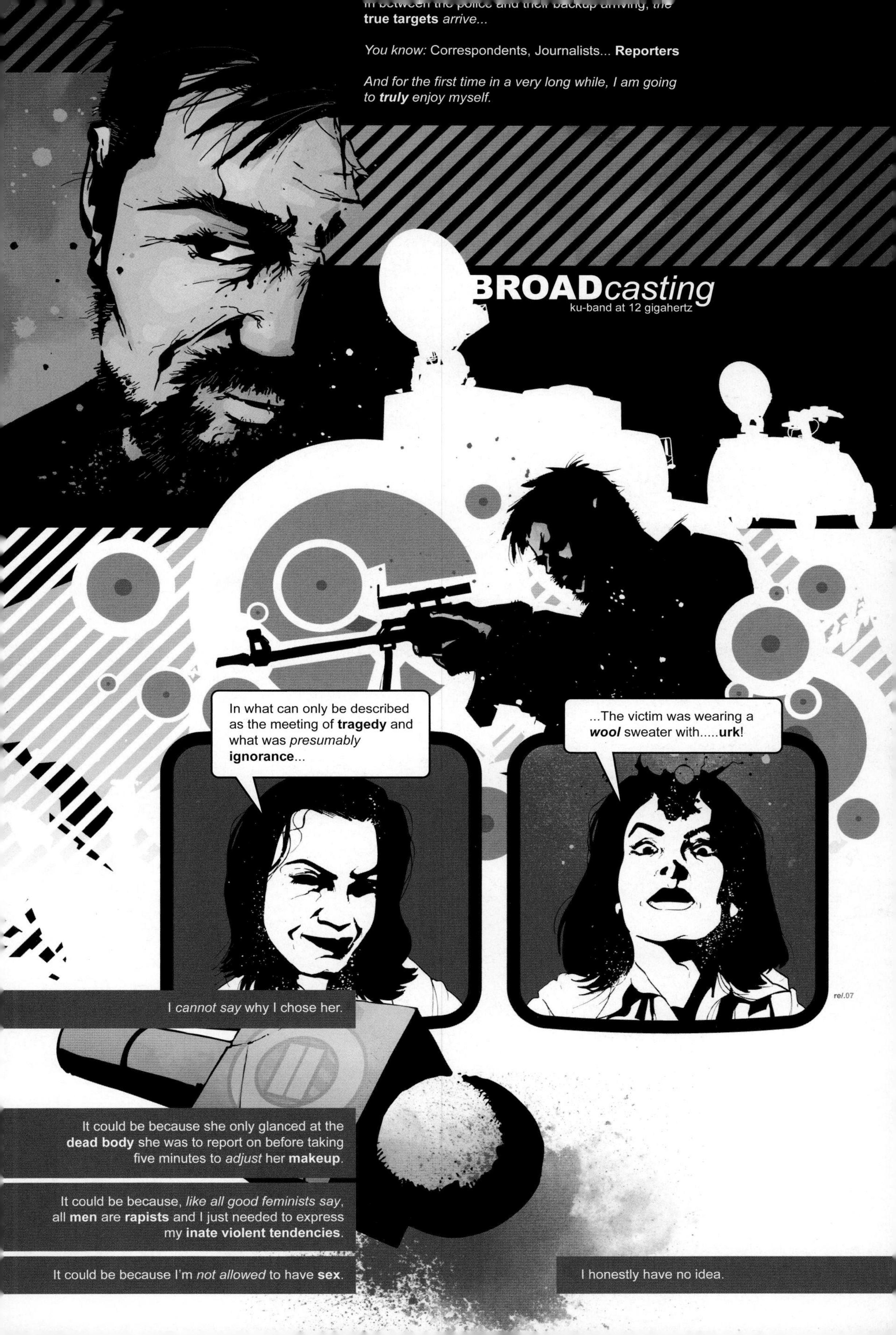

In between the police and their backup arriving, the **true targets** *arrive...*
You know: Correspondents, Journalists... **Reporters**
And for the first time in a very long while, I am going to ***truly*** *enjoy myself.*
BROAD*casting*
ku-band at 12 gigahertz
In what can only be described as the meeting of **tragedy** and what was *presumably* **ignorance**...
...The victim was wearing a ***wool*** sweater with.....**urk**!
rel.07
I *cannot say* why I chose her.
It could be because she only glanced at the **dead body** she was to report on before taking five minutes to *adjust* her **makeup**.
It could be because, *like all good feminists say*, all **men** are **rapists** and I just needed to express my **inate violent tendencies**.
It could be because I'm *not allowed* to have **sex**.
I honestly have no idea.

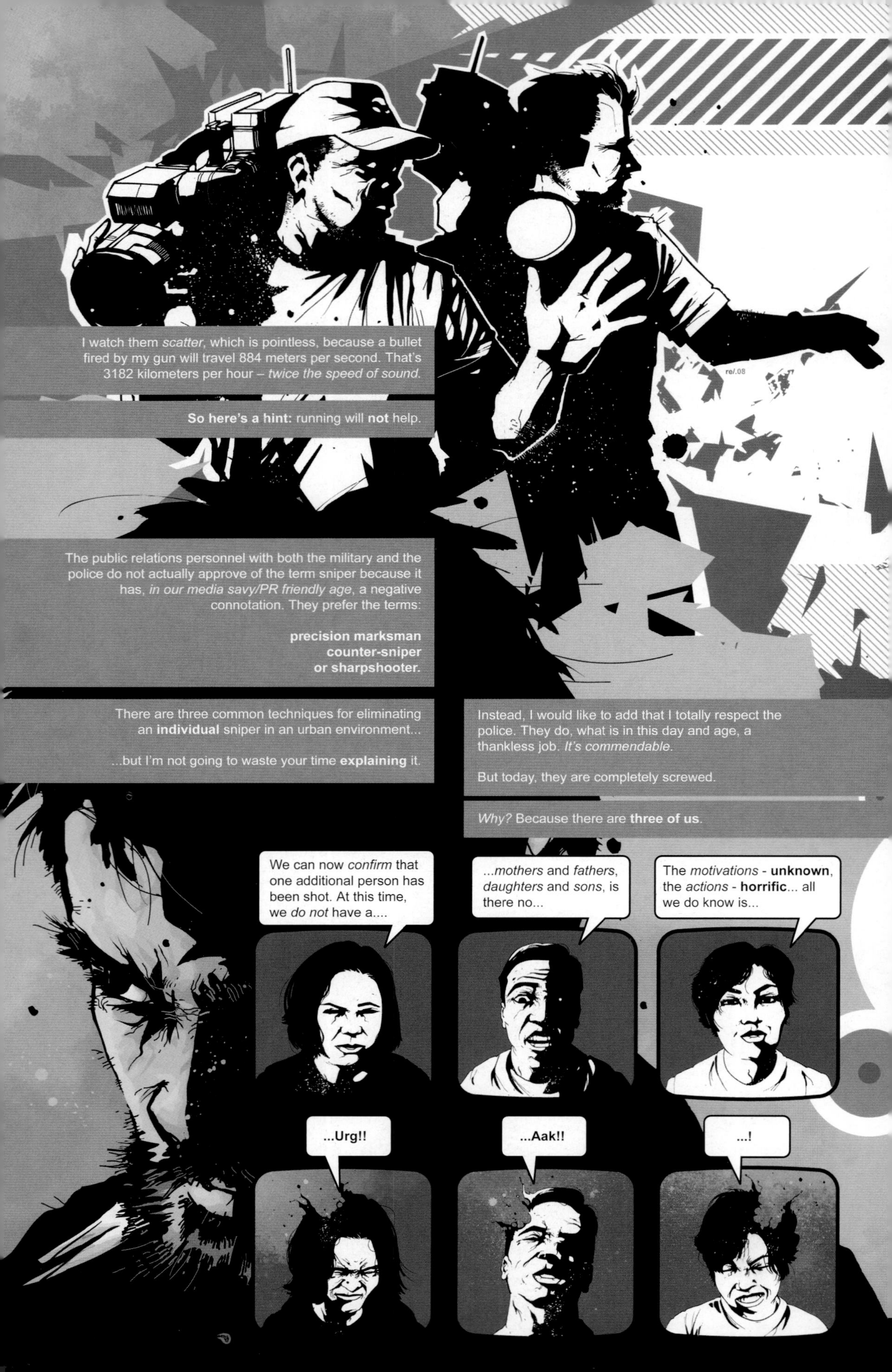
I watch them *scatter*, which is pointless, because a bullet fired by my gun will travel 884 meters per second. That's 3182 kilometers per hour – *twice the speed of sound*.
So here's a hint: running will **not** help.
re/.08
The public relations personnel with both the military and the police do not actually approve of the term sniper because it has, *in our media savy/PR friendly age*, a negative connotation. They prefer the terms:
precision marksman
counter-sniper
or sharpshooter.
There are three common techniques for eliminating an **individual** sniper in an urban environment...
...but I'm not going to waste your time **explaining** it.
Instead, I would like to add that I totally respect the police. They do, what is in this day and age, a thankless job. *It's commendable.*
But today, they are completely screwed.
Why? Because there are **three of us**.
We can now *confirm* that one additional person has been shot. At this time, we *do not* have a....
...*mothers* and *fathers*, *daughters* and *sons*, is there no...
The *motivations* - **unknown**, the *actions* - **horrific**... all we do know is...
...Urg!!
...Aak!!
...!

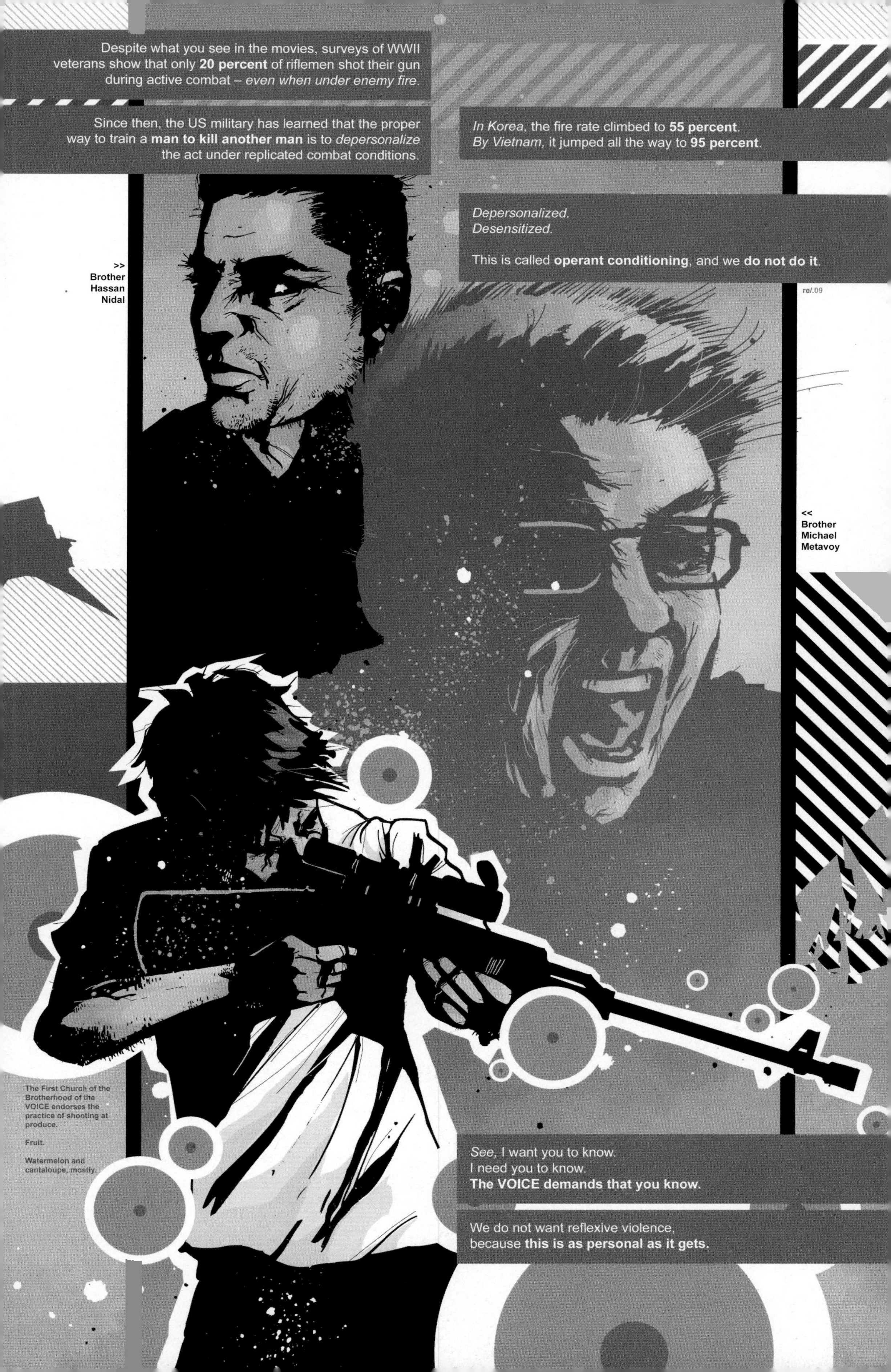
Despite what you see in the movies, surveys of WWII veterans show that only **20 percent** of riflemen shot their gun during active combat – *even when under enemy fire*.
Since then, the US military has learned that the proper way to train a **man to kill another man** is to *depersonalize* the act under replicated combat conditions.
In Korea, the fire rate climbed to **55 percent**. *By Vietnam*, it jumped all the way to **95 percent**.
Depersonalized. *Desensitized.*
This is called **operant conditioning**, and we **do not do it**.
>> Brother Hassan Nidal
re/.09
<< Brother Michael Metavoy
The First Church of the Brotherhood of the VOICE endorses the practice of shooting at produce.
Fruit.
Watermelon and cantaloupe, mostly.
See, I want you to know.
I need you to know.
The VOICE demands that you know.
We do not want reflexive violence, because **this is as personal as it gets.**

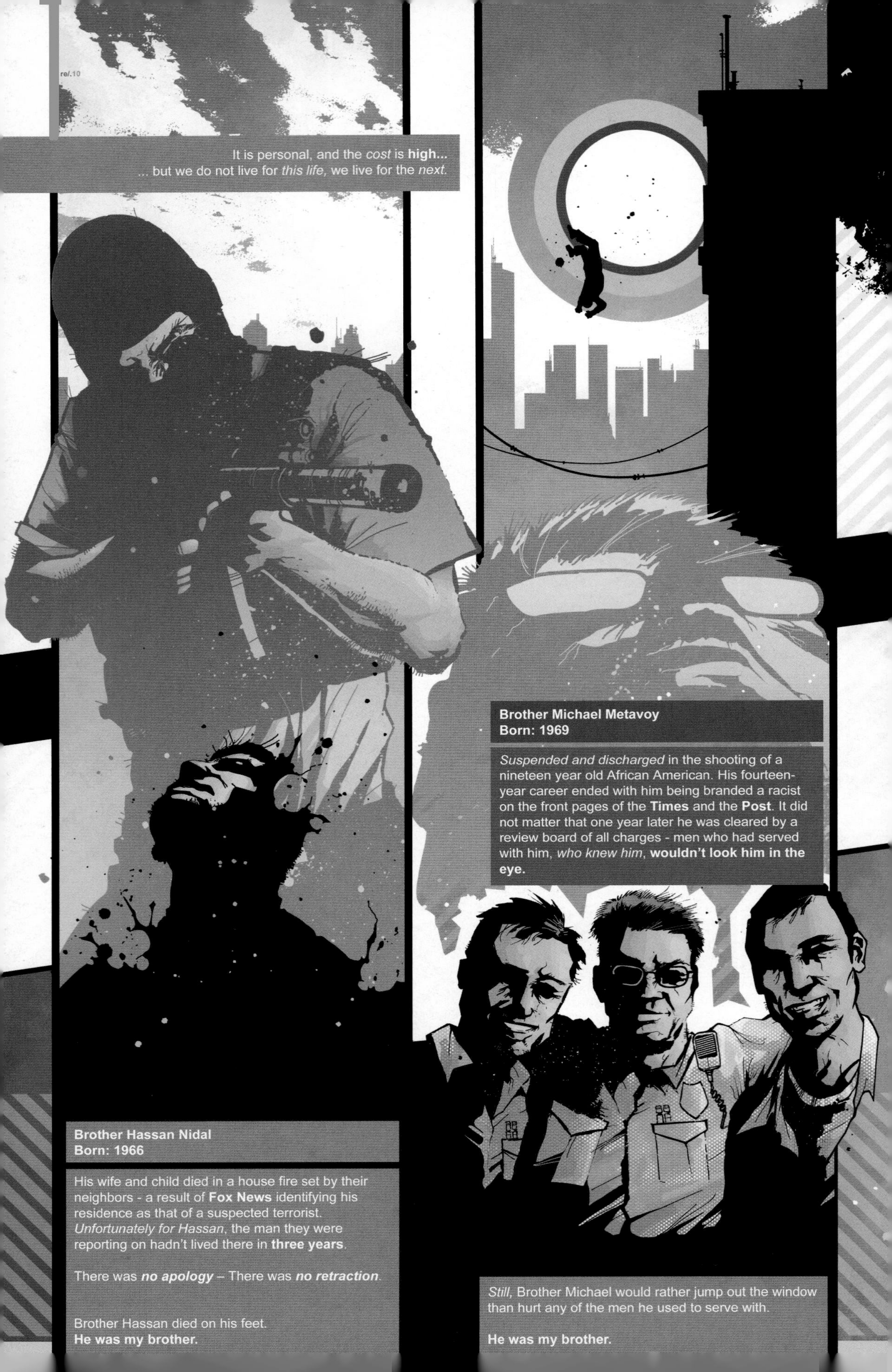
re/.10
It is personal, and the *cost* is **high...**
... but we do not live for *this life,* we live for the *next.*
Brother Michael Metavoy
Born: 1969
Suspended and discharged in the shooting of a nineteen year old African American. His fourteen-year career ended with him being branded a racist on the front pages of the **Times** and the **Post**. It did not matter that one year later he was cleared by a review board of all charges - men who had served with him, *who knew him*, **wouldn't look him in the eye.**
Brother Hassan Nidal
Born: 1966
His wife and child died in a house fire set by their neighbors - a result of **Fox News** identifying his residence as that of a suspected terrorist. *Unfortunately for Hassan*, the man they were reporting on hadn't lived there in **three years**.
There was ***no apology*** – There was ***no retraction***.
Brother Hassan died on his feet.
He was my brother.
Still, Brother Michael would rather jump out the window than hurt any of the men he used to serve with.
He was my brother.

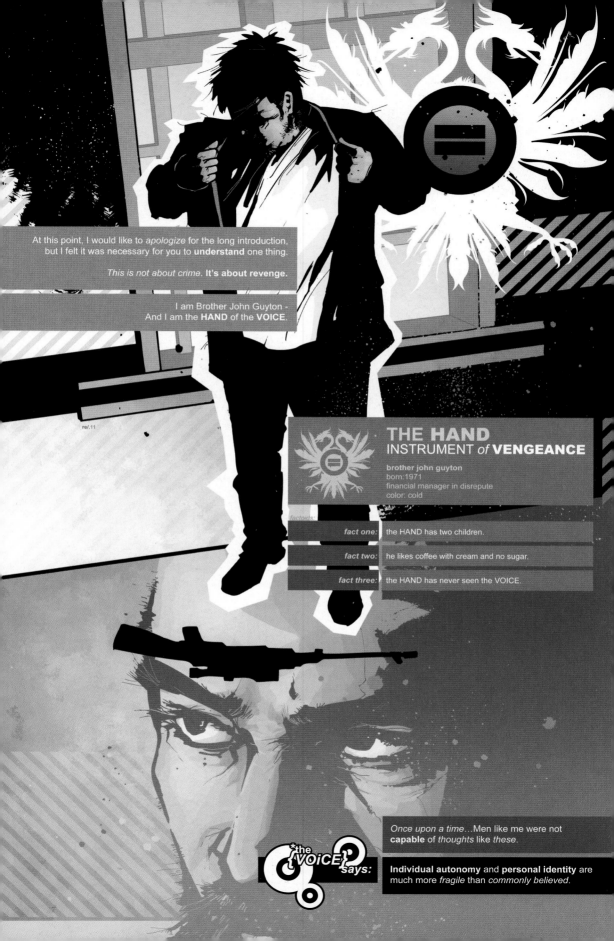

At this point, I would like to *apologize* for the long introduction, but I felt it was necessary for you to **understand** one thing.

This is not about crime. **It's about revenge.**

I am Brother John Guyton - And I am the **HAND** of the **VOICE**.

re/.11

THE HAND
INSTRUMENT *of* VENGEANCE

brother john guyton
born:1971
financial manager in disrepute
color: cold

factoids:

fact one:	the HAND has two children.
fact two:	he likes coffee with cream and no sugar.
fact three:	the HAND has never seen the VOICE.

Once upon a time…Men like me were not **capable** *of thoughts* like *these*.

the VOICE says:

Individual autonomy and **personal identity** are much more *fragile* than *commonly believed*.

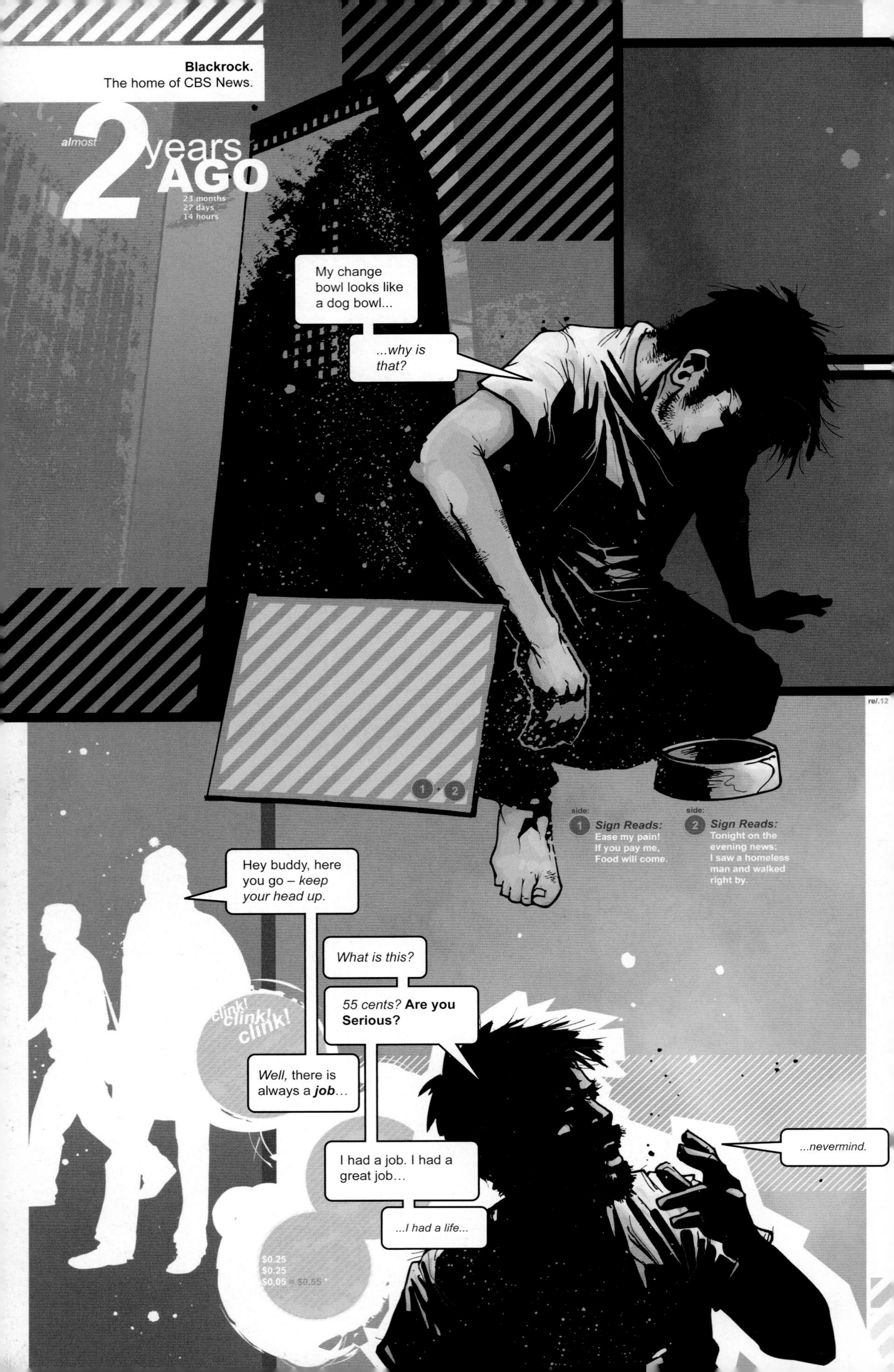

Blackrock.
The home of CBS News.
almost 2 years AGO
23 months
27 days
14 hours
My change bowl looks like a dog bowl...
...why is that?
re/.12
side: 1 Sign Reads: Ease my pain! If you pay me, Food will come.
side: 2 Sign Reads: Tonight on the evening news: I saw a homeless man and walked right by.
Hey buddy, here you go – *keep your head up.*
clink! clink! clink!
Well, there is always a ***job***...
What is this?
55 cents? **Are you Serious?**
I had a job. I had a great job...
...I had a life...
...nevermind.
$0.25
$0.25
$0.05 = $0.55

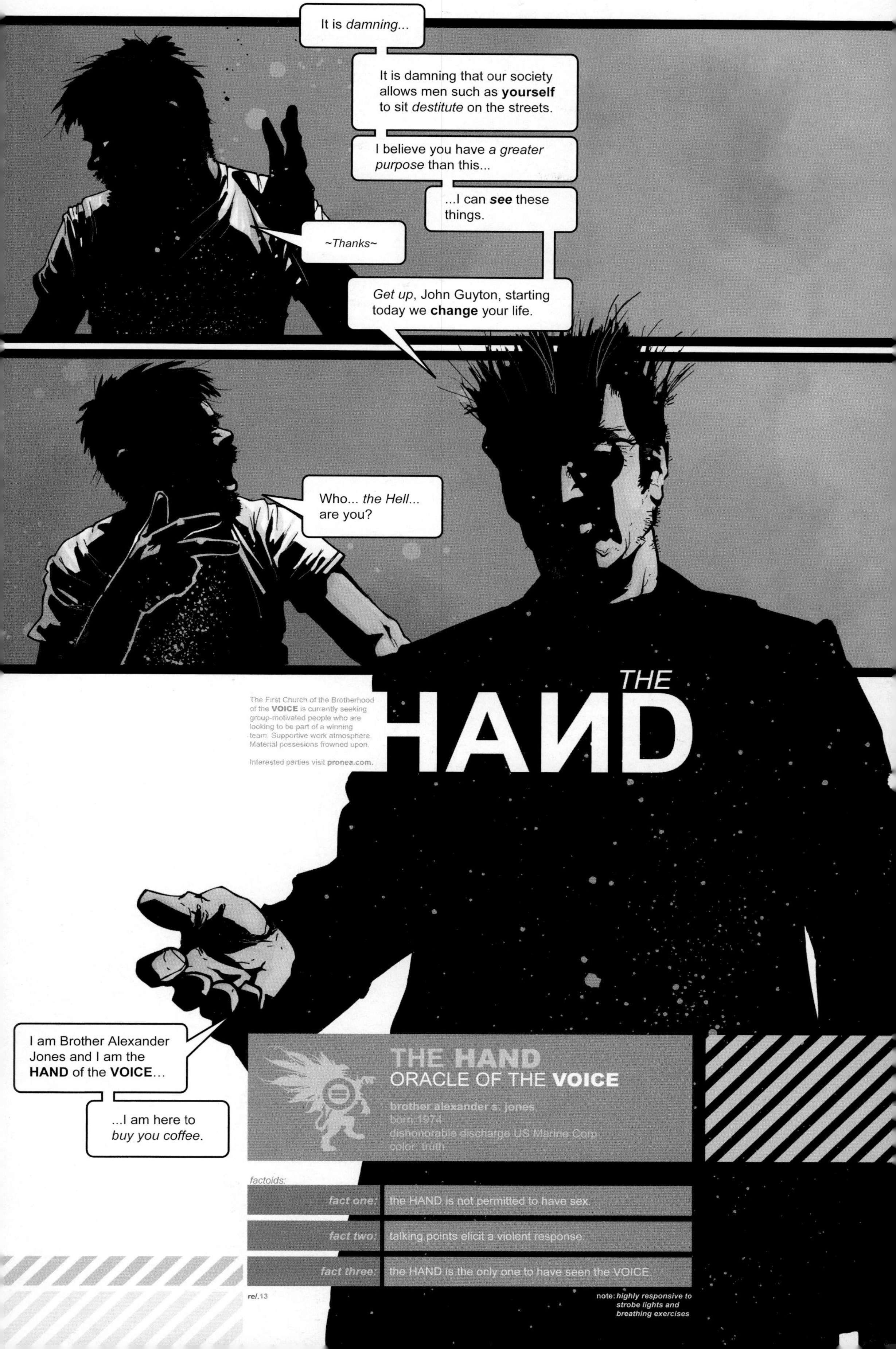
It is *damning*...
It is damning that our society allows men such as **yourself** to sit *destitute* on the streets.
I believe you have *a greater purpose* than this...
...I can ***see*** these things.
~*Thanks*~
Get up, John Guyton, starting today we **change** your life.
Who... *the Hell*... are you?
THE
HAND
The First Church of the Brotherhood of the **VOICE** is currently seeking group-motivated people who are looking to be part of a winning team. Supportive work atmosphere. Material possesions frowned upon.
Interested parties visit **pronea.com.**
I am Brother Alexander Jones and I am the **HAND** of the **VOICE**...
...I am here to *buy you coffee*.
THE HAND
ORACLE OF THE **VOICE**
brother alexander s. jones
born:1974
dishonorable discharge US Marine Corp
color: truth
factoids:
fact one: the HAND is not permitted to have sex.
fact two: talking points elicit a violent response.
fact three: the HAND is the only one to have seen the VOICE.
note: *highly responsive to strobe lights and breathing exercises*

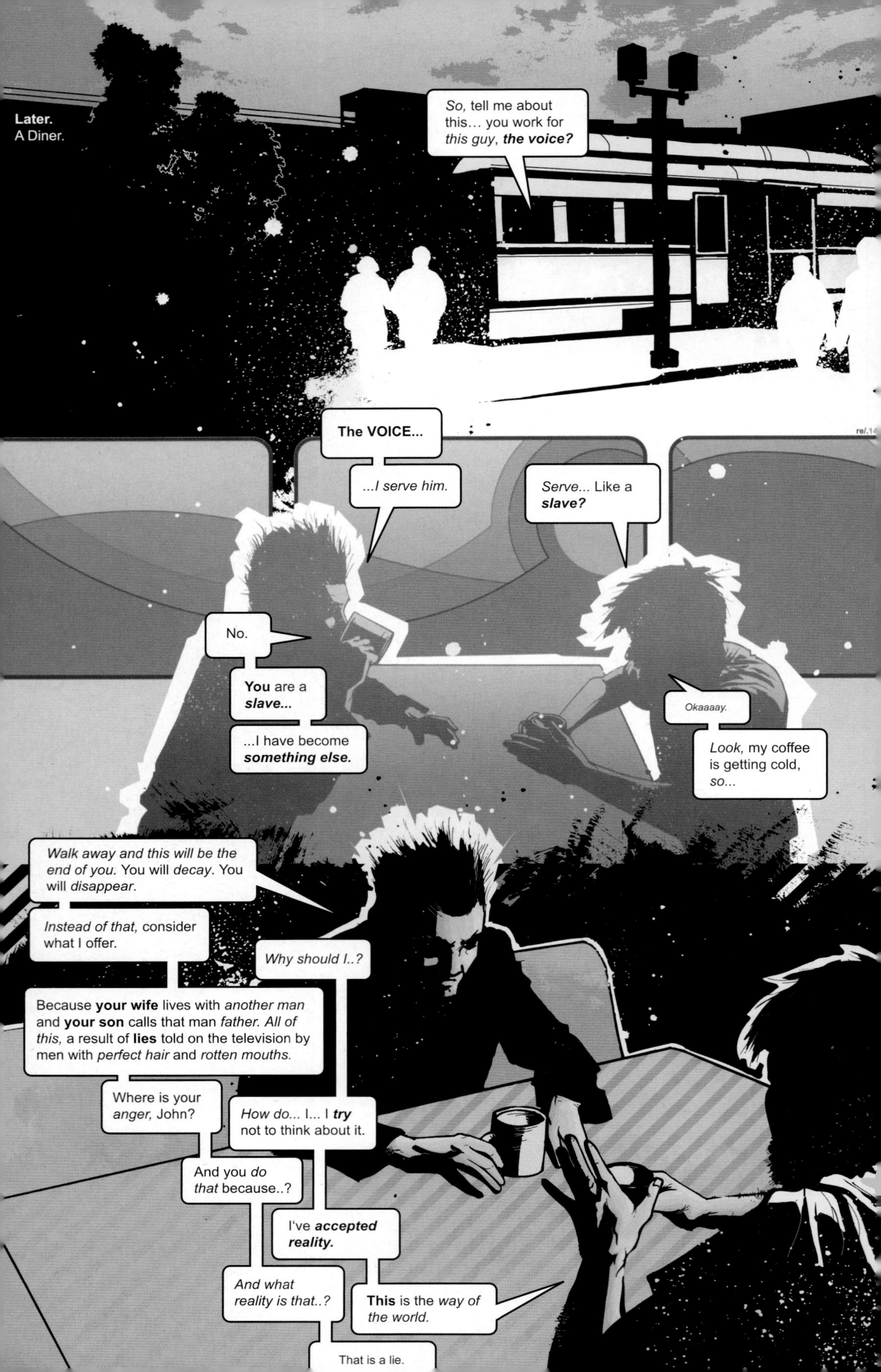
Later.
A Diner.
So, tell me about this… you work for this guy, the voice?
The VOICE...
...I serve him.
Serve... Like a slave?
No.
You are a slave...
...I have become something else.
Okaaaay.
Look, my coffee is getting cold, so...
Walk away and this will be the end of you. You will decay. You will disappear.
Instead of that, consider what I offer.
Why should I..?
Because your wife lives with another man and your son calls that man father. All of this, a result of lies told on the television by men with perfect hair and rotten mouths.
Where is your anger, John?
How do... I... I try not to think about it.
And you do that because..?
I've accepted reality.
And what reality is that..?
This is the way of the world.
That is a lie.

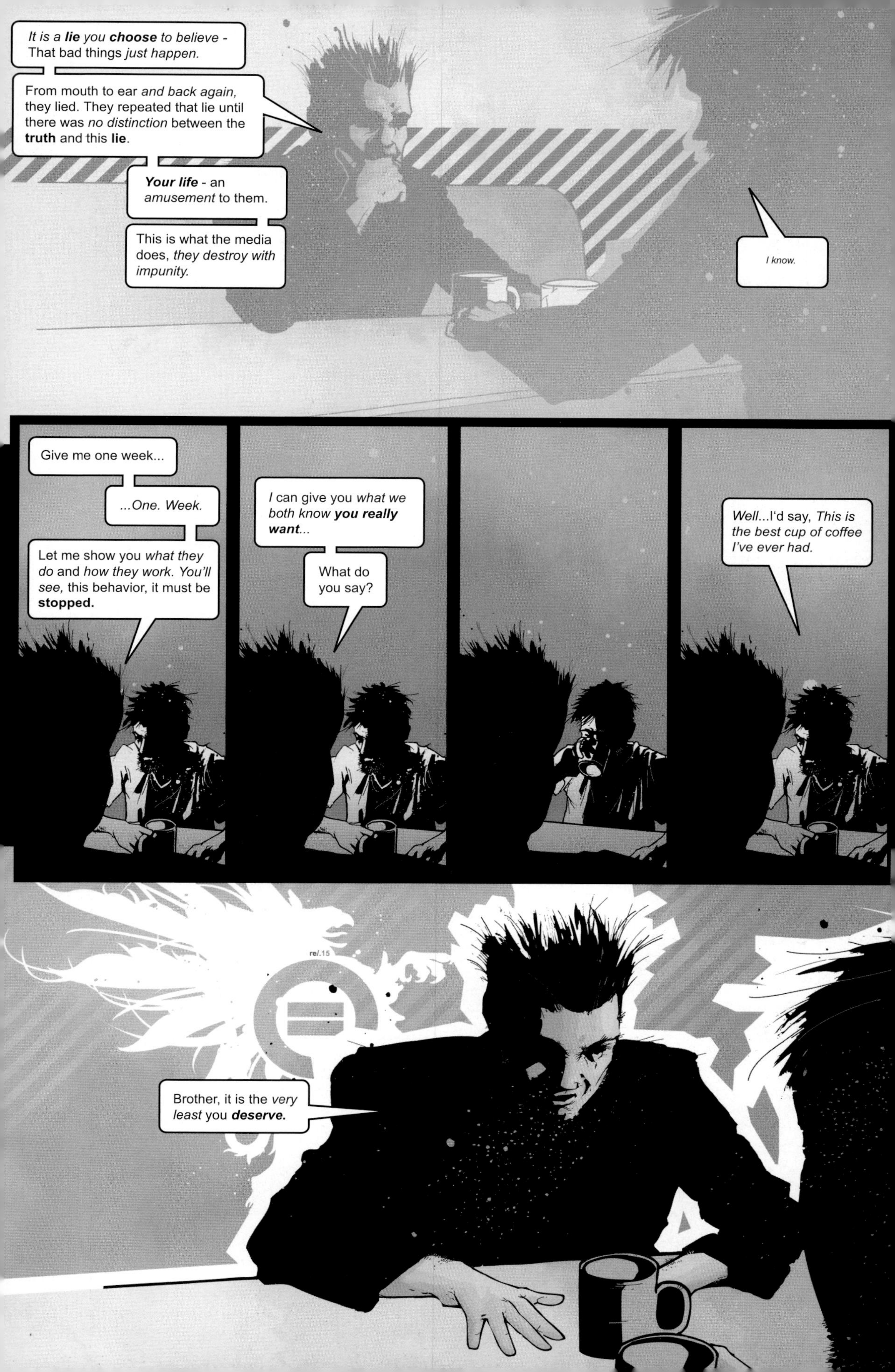
It is a lie you choose to believe - That bad things just happen.
From mouth to ear and back again, they lied. They repeated that lie until there was no distinction between the truth and this lie.
Your life - an amusement to them.
This is what the media does, they destroy with impunity.
I know.
Give me one week...
...One. Week.
Let me show you what they do and how they work. You'll see, this behavior, it must be stopped.
I can give you what we both know you really want...
What do you say?
Well...I'd say, This is the best cup of coffee I've ever had.
re/.15
Brother, it is the very least you deserve.

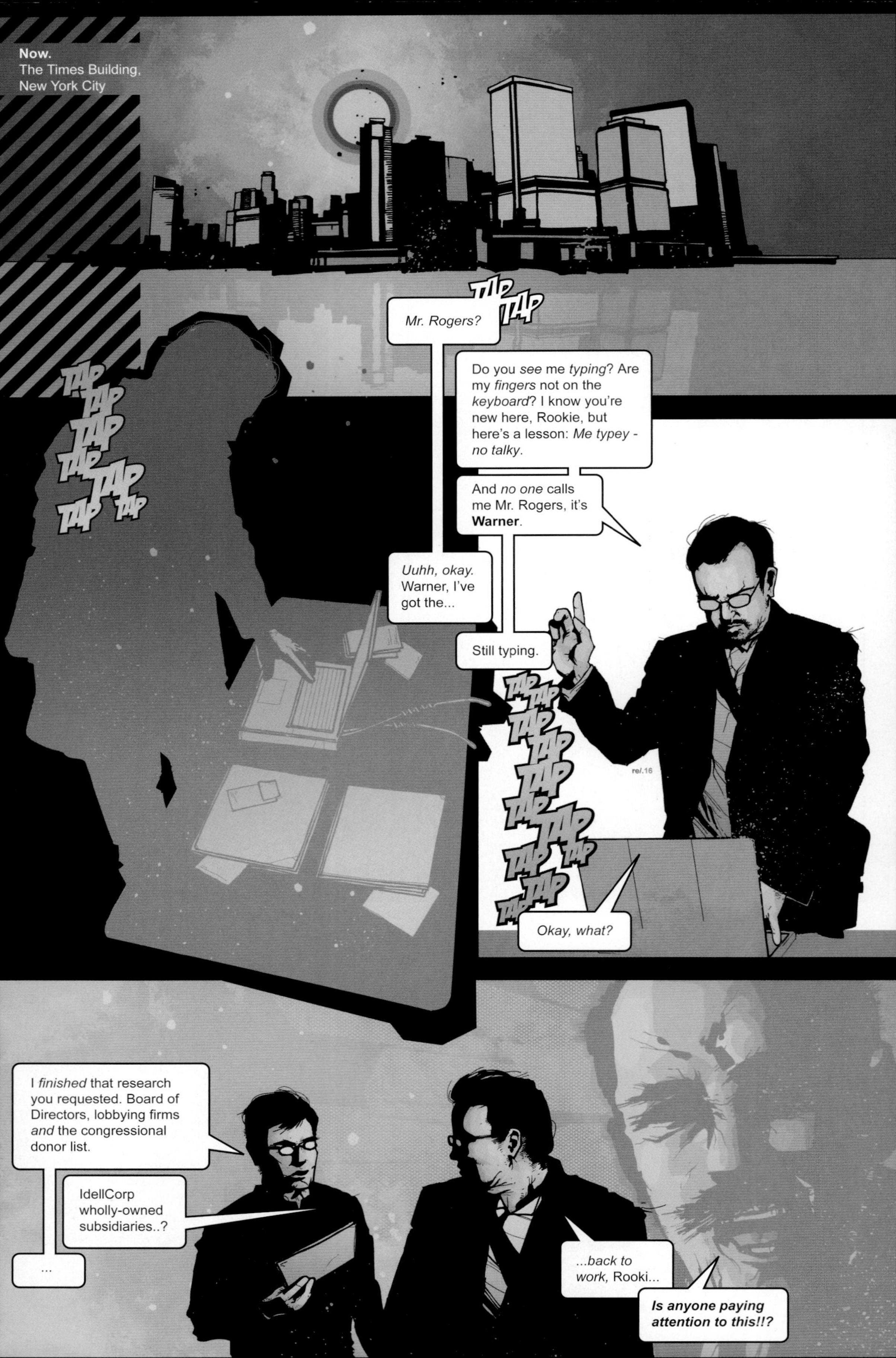
Now.
The Times Building,
New York City
TAP TAP
Mr. Rogers?
TAP TAP TAP TAP TAP TAP TAP
Do you *see* me *typing*? Are my *fingers* not on the *keyboard*? I know you're new here, Rookie, but here's a lesson: *Me typey - no talky*.
And *no one* calls me Mr. Rogers, it's **Warner**.
Uuhh, okay. Warner, I've got the...
Still typing.
TAP TAP TAP TAP TAP TAP TAP TAP TAP TAP TAP
Okay, what?
rel.16
I *finished* that research you requested. Board of Directors, lobbying firms *and* the congressional donor list.
IdellCorp wholly-owned subsidiaries..?
...
...back to work, Rooki...
Is anyone paying attention to this!!?

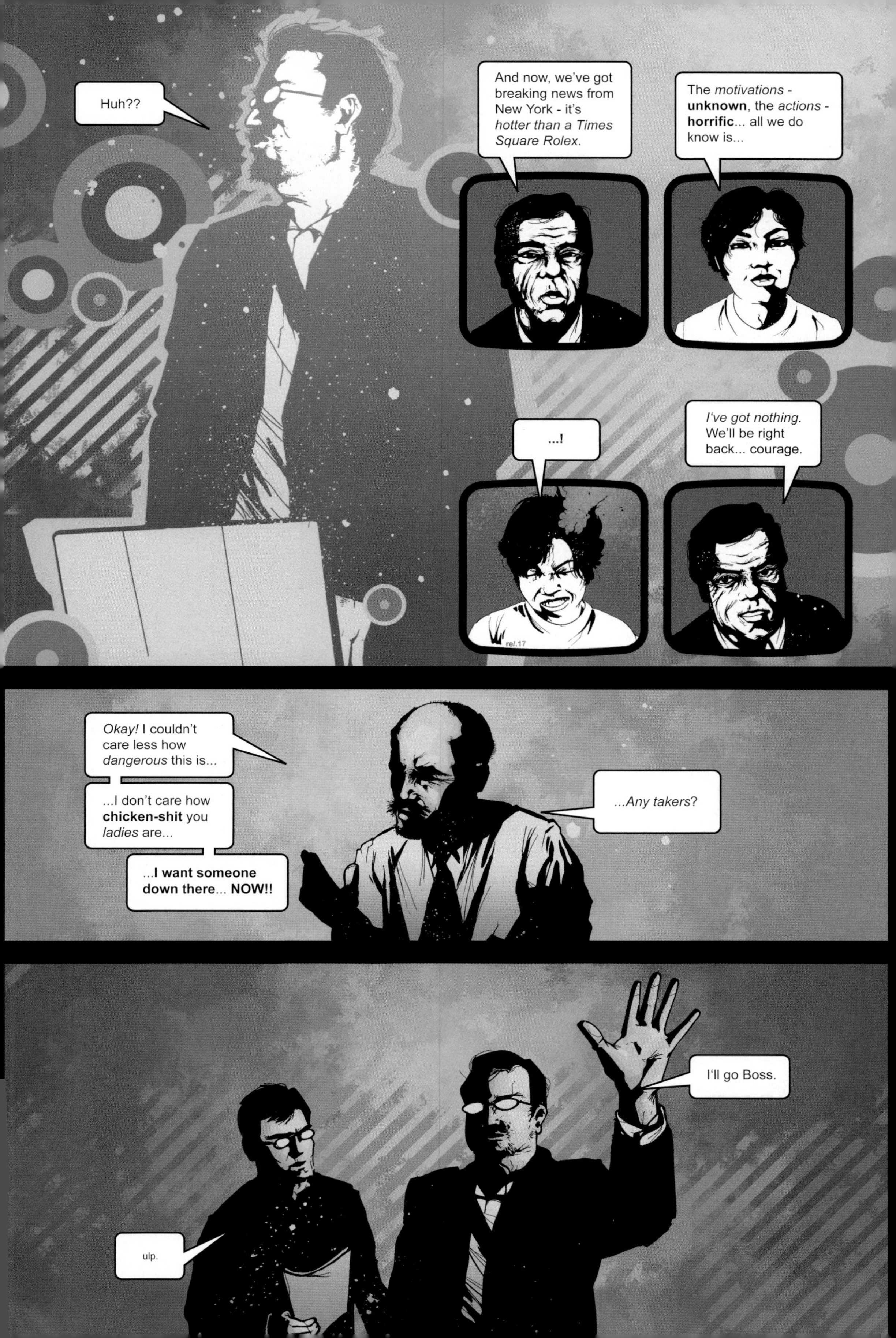
Huh??
And now, we've got breaking news from New York - it's *hotter than a Times Square Rolex*.
The *motivations* - **unknown**, the *actions* - **horrific**... all we do know is...
...!
I've got nothing. We'll be right back... courage.
re/.17
Okay! I couldn't care less how *dangerous* this is...
...I don't care how **chicken-shit** you *ladies* are...
...**I want someone down there... NOW!!**
...Any takers?
I'll go Boss.
ulp.

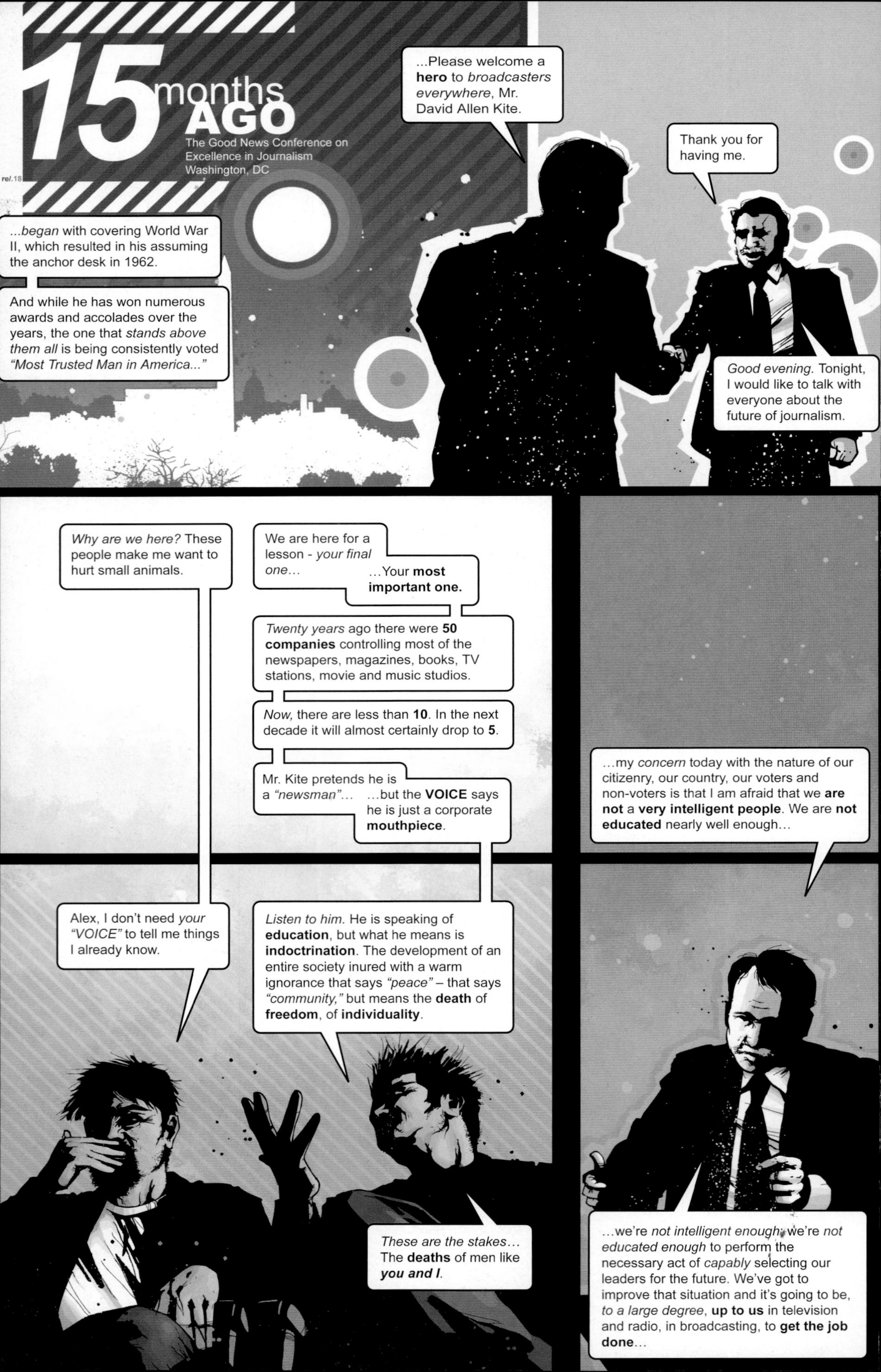
15 months AGO
The Good News Conference on Excellence in Journalism Washington, DC
rel.18
...began with covering World War II, which resulted in his assuming the anchor desk in 1962.
And while he has won numerous awards and accolades over the years, the one that stands above them all is being consistently voted "Most Trusted Man in America..."
...Please welcome a hero to broadcasters everywhere, Mr. David Allen Kite.
Thank you for having me.
Good evening. Tonight, I would like to talk with everyone about the future of journalism.
Why are we here? These people make me want to hurt small animals.
We are here for a lesson - your final one...
...Your most important one.
Twenty years ago there were 50 companies controlling most of the newspapers, magazines, books, TV stations, movie and music studios.
Now, there are less than 10. In the next decade it will almost certainly drop to 5.
Mr. Kite pretends he is a "newsman"...
...but the VOICE says he is just a corporate mouthpiece.
...my concern today with the nature of our citizenry, our country, our voters and non-voters is that I am afraid that we are not a very intelligent people. We are not educated nearly well enough...
Alex, I don't need your "VOICE" to tell me things I already know.
Listen to him. He is speaking of education, but what he means is indoctrination. The development of an entire society inured with a warm ignorance that says "peace" – that says "community," but means the death of freedom, of individuality.
These are the stakes... The deaths of men like you and I.
...we're not intelligent enough; we're not educated enough to perform the necessary act of capably selecting our leaders for the future. We've got to improve that situation and it's going to be, to a large degree, up to us in television and radio, in broadcasting, to get the job done...

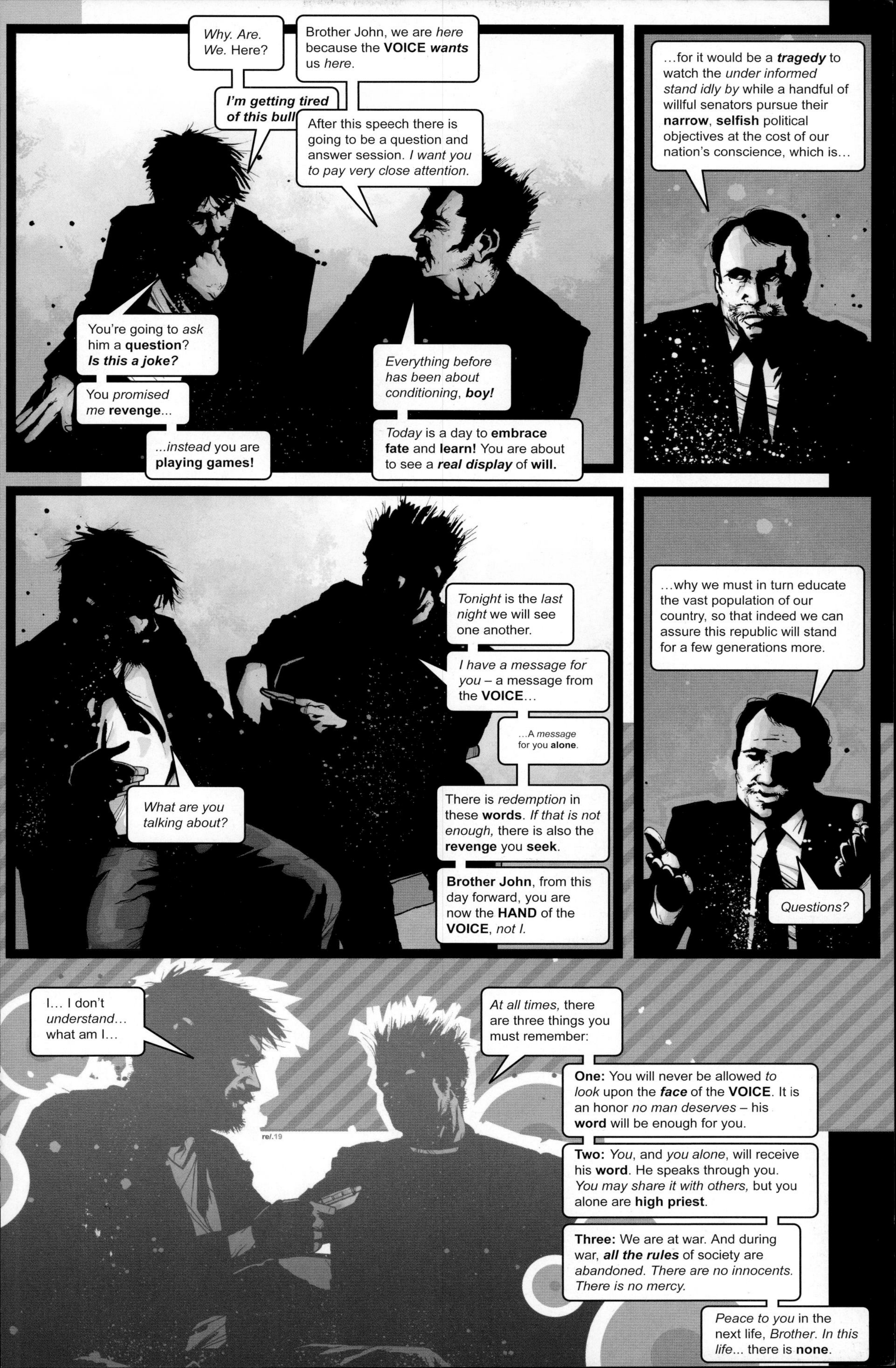

Why. Are. We. Here?
I'm getting tired of this bull
Brother John, we are here because the VOICE wants us here.
After this speech there is going to be a question and answer session. I want you to pay very close attention.
You're going to ask him a question? Is this a joke?
You promised me revenge...
...instead you are playing games!
Everything before has been about conditioning, boy!
Today is a day to embrace fate and learn! You are about to see a real display of will.
...for it would be a tragedy to watch the under informed stand idly by while a handful of willful senators pursue their narrow, selfish political objectives at the cost of our nation's conscience, which is...
Tonight is the last night we will see one another.
I have a message for you – a message from the VOICE...
...A message for you alone.
What are you talking about?
There is redemption in these words. If that is not enough, there is also the revenge you seek.
Brother John, from this day forward, you are now the HAND of the VOICE, not I.
...why we must in turn educate the vast population of our country, so that indeed we can assure this republic will stand for a few generations more.
Questions?
I... I don't understand... what am I...
At all times, there are three things you must remember:
One: You will never be allowed to look upon the face of the VOICE. It is an honor no man deserves – his word will be enough for you.
Two: You, and you alone, will receive his word. He speaks through you. You may share it with others, but you alone are high priest.
Three: We are at war. And during war, all the rules of society are abandoned. There are no innocents. There is no mercy.
Peace to you in the next life, Brother. In this life... there is none.

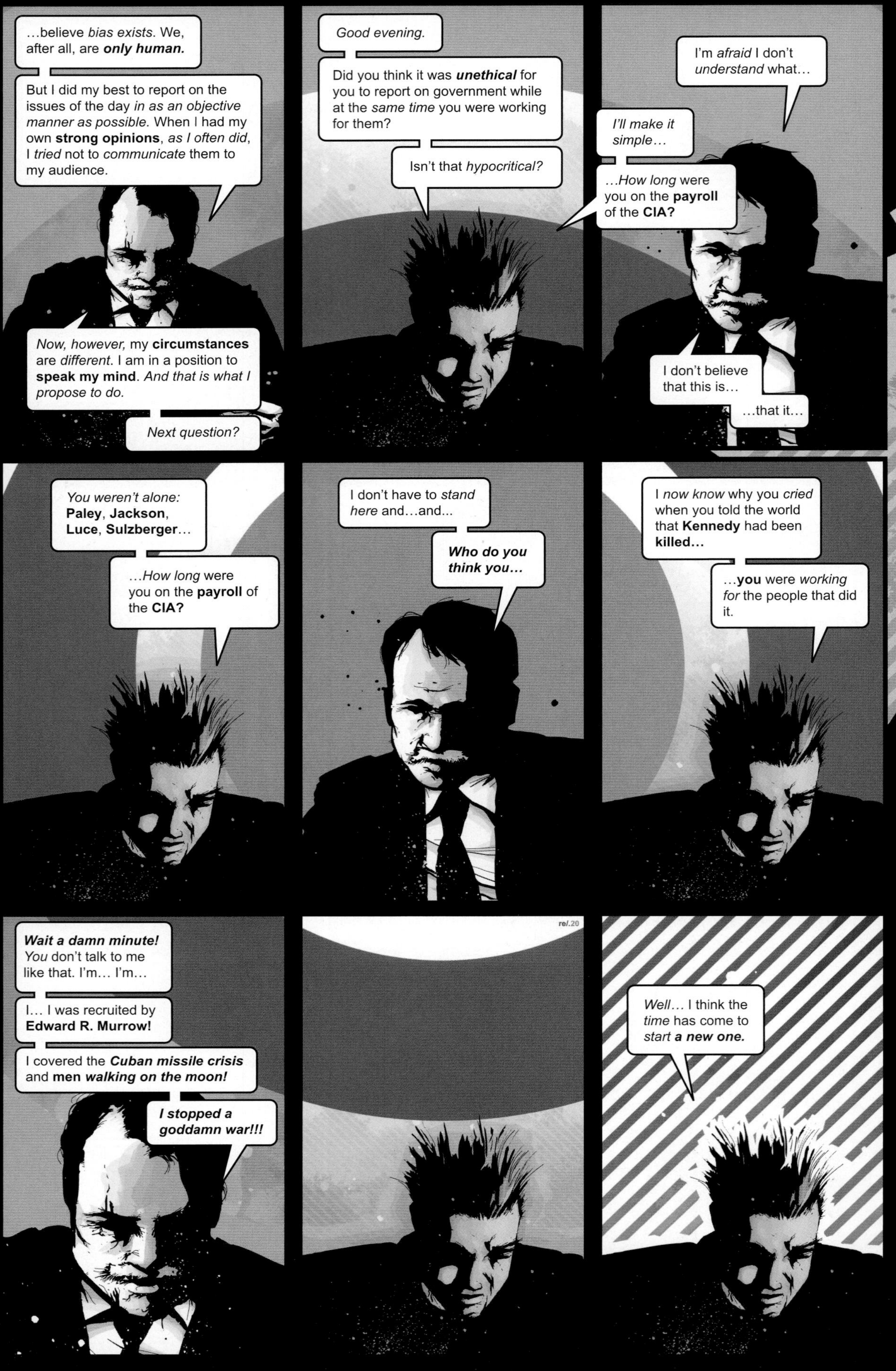
…believe *bias exists*. We, after all, are ***only human.***
But I did my best to report on the issues of the day *in as an objective manner as possible.* When I had my own **strong opinions**, *as I often did*, I *tried* not to *communicate* them to my audience.
Now, however, my **circumstances** are *different*. I am in a position to **speak my mind**. *And that is what I propose to do.*
Next question?
Good evening.
Did you think it was ***unethical*** for you to report on government while at the *same time* you were working for them?
Isn't that *hypocritical?*
I'm *afraid* I don't *understand* what…
I'll make it simple…
…How long were you on the **payroll** of the **CIA?**
I don't believe that this is…
…that it…
You weren't alone: **Paley**, **Jackson**, **Luce**, **Sulzberger**…
…How long were you on the **payroll** of the **CIA?**
I don't have to *stand here* and…and...
Who do you think you…
I *now know* why you *cried* when you told the world that **Kennedy** had been **killed…**
…**you** were *working for* the people that did it.
Wait a damn minute! *You* don't talk to me like that. I'm… I'm…
I… I was recruited by **Edward R. Murrow!**
I covered the ***Cuban missile crisis*** and **men *walking on the moon!***
I stopped a goddamn war!!!
re/.20
Well… I think the *time* has come to *start **a new one.***

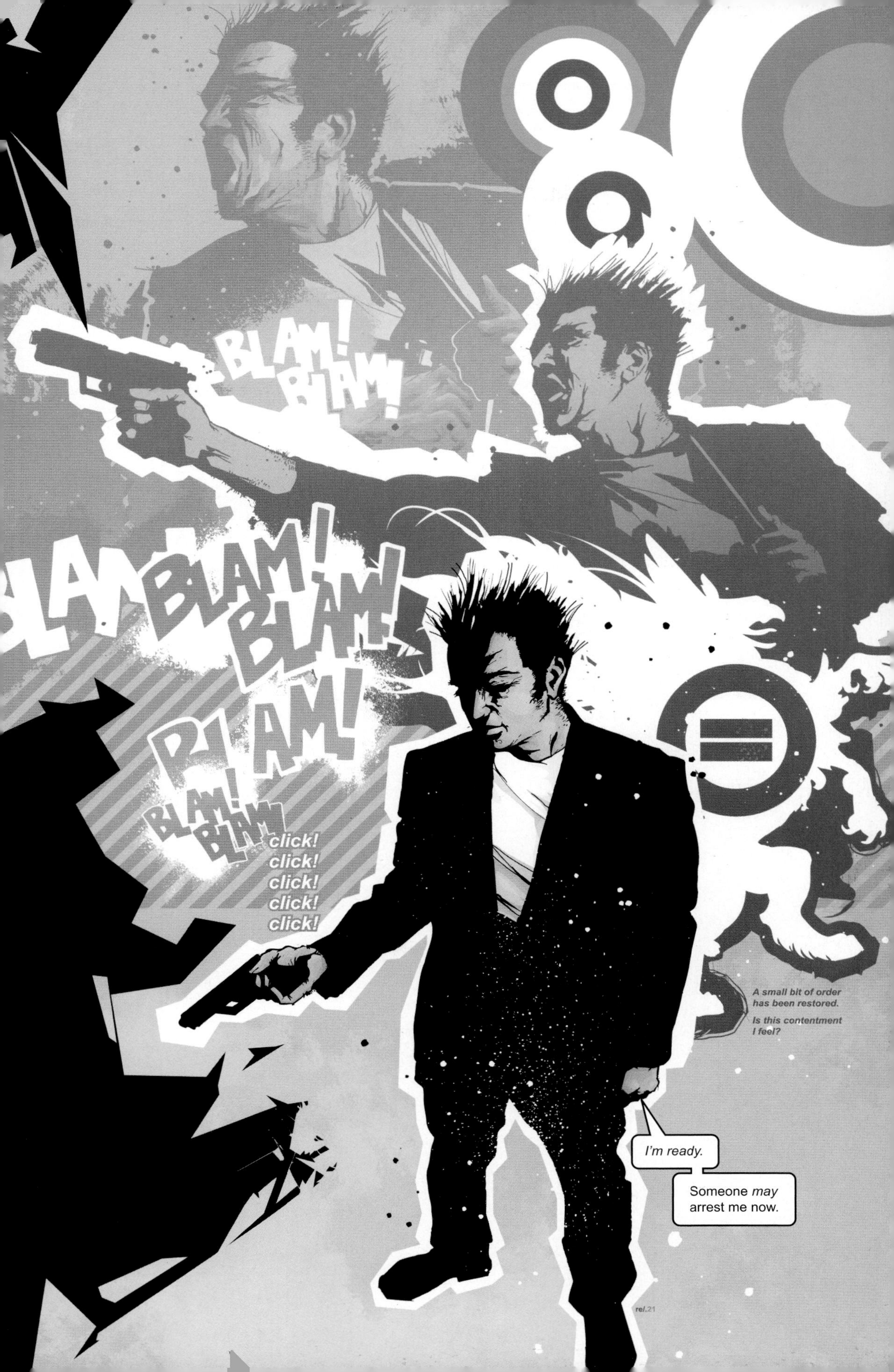
BLAM! BLAM!
BLAM! BLAM! BLAM! BLAM!
BLAM! BLAM! BLAM!
click!
click!
click!
click!
click!
A small bit of order has been restored.
Is this contentment I feel?
I'm ready.
Someone *may* arrest me now.

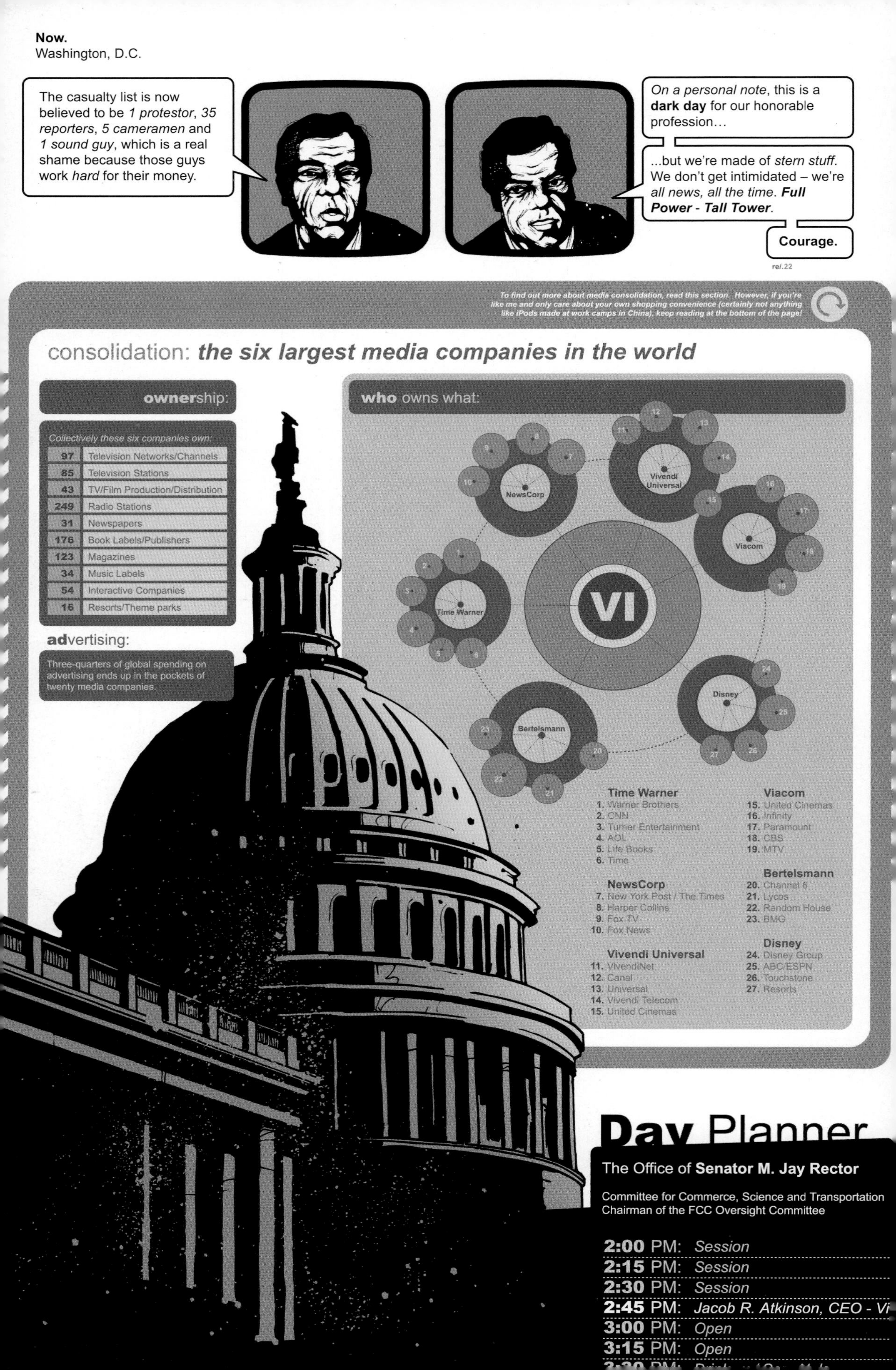
Now.
Washington, D.C.
The casualty list is now believed to be 1 protestor, 35 reporters, 5 cameramen and 1 sound guy, which is a real shame because those guys work hard for their money.
On a personal note, this is a dark day for our honorable profession…
...but we're made of stern stuff. We don't get intimidated – we're all news, all the time. Full Power - Tall Tower.
Courage.
re/.22
To find out more about media consolidation, read this section. However, if you're like me and only care about your own shopping convenience (certainly not anything like iPods made at work camps in China), keep reading at the bottom of the page!
consolidation: the six largest media companies in the world
ownership:
Collectively these six companies own:
97 Television Networks/Channels
85 Television Stations
43 TV/Film Production/Distribution
249 Radio Stations
31 Newspapers
176 Book Labels/Publishers
123 Magazines
34 Music Labels
54 Interactive Companies
16 Resorts/Theme parks
advertising:
Three-quarters of global spending on advertising ends up in the pockets of twenty media companies.
who owns what:
VI
NewsCorp
Vivendi Universal
Viacom
Time Warner
Disney
Bertelsmann
Time Warner
1. Warner Brothers
2. CNN
3. Turner Entertainment
4. AOL
5. Life Books
6. Time
NewsCorp
7. New York Post / The Times
8. Harper Collins
9. Fox TV
10. Fox News
Vivendi Universal
11. VivendiNet
12. Canal
13. Universal
14. Vivendi Telecom
15. United Cinemas
Viacom
15. United Cinemas
16. Infinity
17. Paramount
18. CBS
19. MTV
Bertelsmann
20. Channel 6
21. Lycos
22. Random House
23. BMG
Disney
24. Disney Group
25. ABC/ESPN
26. Touchstone
27. Resorts
Day Planner
The Office of Senator M. Jay Rector
Committee for Commerce, Science and Transportation
Chairman of the FCC Oversight Committee
2:00 PM: Session
2:15 PM: Session
2:30 PM: Session
2:45 PM: Jacob R. Atkinson, CEO - Vi
3:00 PM: Open
3:15 PM: Open

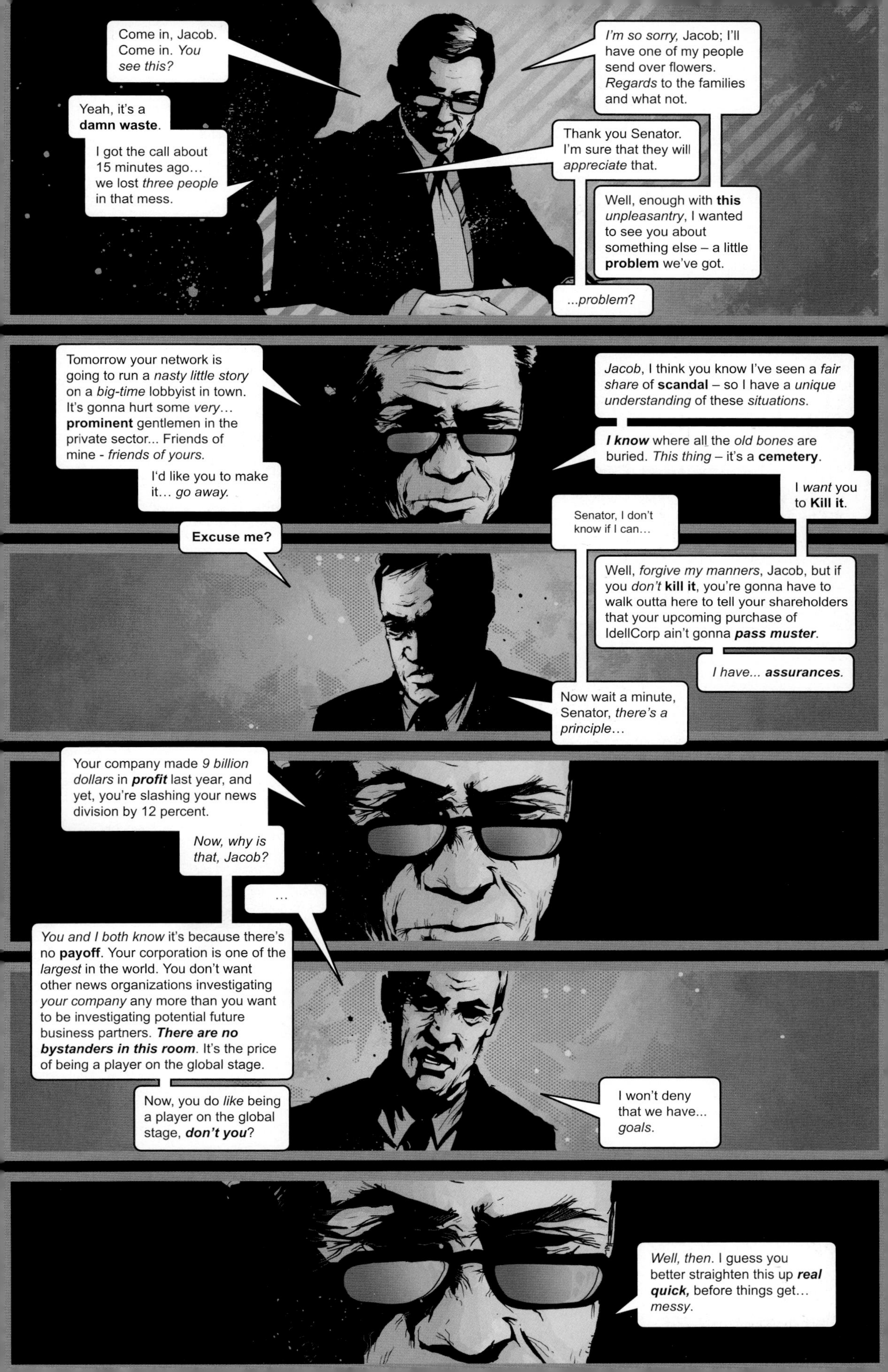
Come in, Jacob. Come in. *You see this?*
Yeah, it's a **damn waste**.
I got the call about 15 minutes ago… we lost *three people* in that mess.
I'm so sorry, Jacob; I'll have one of my people send over flowers. *Regards* to the families and what not.
Thank you Senator. I'm sure that they will *appreciate* that.
Well, enough with **this** *unpleasantry*, I wanted to see you about something else – a little **problem** we've got.
...*problem*?
Tomorrow your network is going to run a *nasty little story* on a *big-time* lobbyist in town. It's gonna hurt some *very…* **prominent** gentlemen in the private sector... Friends of mine - *friends of yours.*
I'd like you to make it… *go away.*
Jacob, I think you know I've seen a *fair share* of **scandal** – so I have a *unique understanding* of these *situations*.
I know where all the *old bones* are buried. *This thing* – it's a **cemetery**.
I *want* you to **Kill it**.
Excuse me?
Senator, I don't know if I can…
Well, *forgive my manners*, Jacob, but if you *don't* **kill it**, you're gonna have to walk outta here to tell your shareholders that your upcoming purchase of IdellCorp ain't gonna ***pass muster***.
I have... ***assurances.***
Now wait a minute, Senator, *there's a principle…*
Your company made *9 billion dollars* in ***profit*** last year, and yet, you're slashing your news division by 12 percent.
Now, why is that, Jacob?
…
You and I both know it's because there's no **payoff**. Your corporation is one of the *largest* in the world. You don't want other news organizations investigating *your company* any more than you want to be investigating potential future business partners. ***There are no bystanders in this room***. It's the price of being a player on the global stage.
Now, you do *like* being a player on the global stage, ***don't you***?
I won't deny that we have... *goals*.
Well, then. I guess you better straighten this up ***real quick,*** before things get… *messy*.

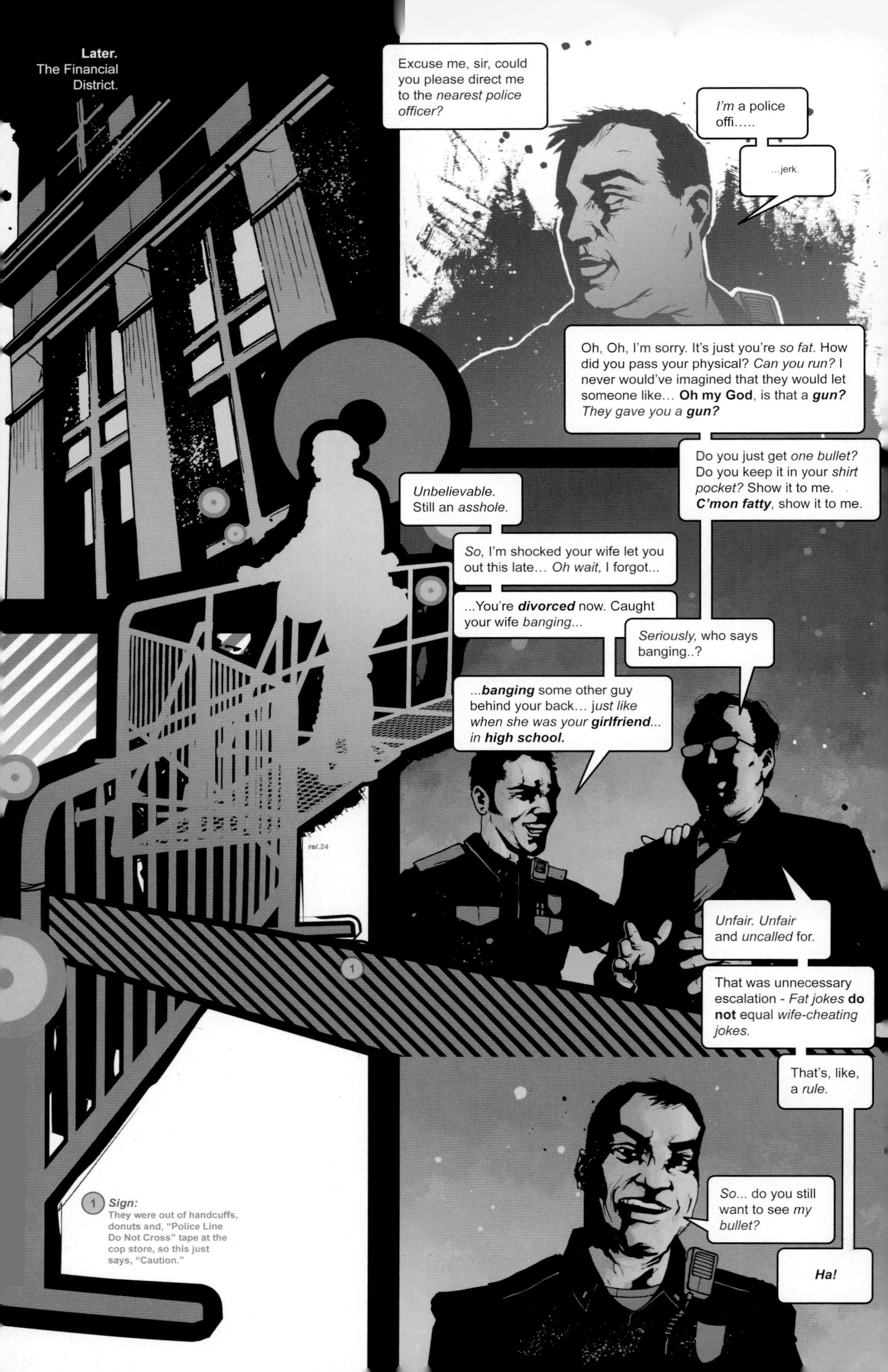
Later. The Financial District.
Excuse me, sir, could you please direct me to the nearest police officer?
I'm a police offi…..
…jerk.
Oh, Oh, I'm sorry. It's just you're so fat. How did you pass your physical? Can you run? I never would've imagined that they would let someone like… Oh my God, is that a gun? They gave you a gun?
Do you just get one bullet? Do you keep it in your shirt pocket? Show it to me. C'mon fatty, show it to me.
Unbelievable. Still an asshole.
So, I'm shocked your wife let you out this late… Oh wait, I forgot...
...You're divorced now. Caught your wife banging...
Seriously, who says banging..?
...banging some other guy behind your back… just like when she was your girlfriend... in high school.
Unfair. Unfair and uncalled for.
That was unnecessary escalation - Fat jokes do not equal wife-cheating jokes.
That's, like, a rule.
So... do you still want to see my bullet?
Ha!
1
re/.24
1 Sign:
They were out of handcuffs, donuts and, "Police Line Do Not Cross" tape at the cop store, so this just says, "Caution."

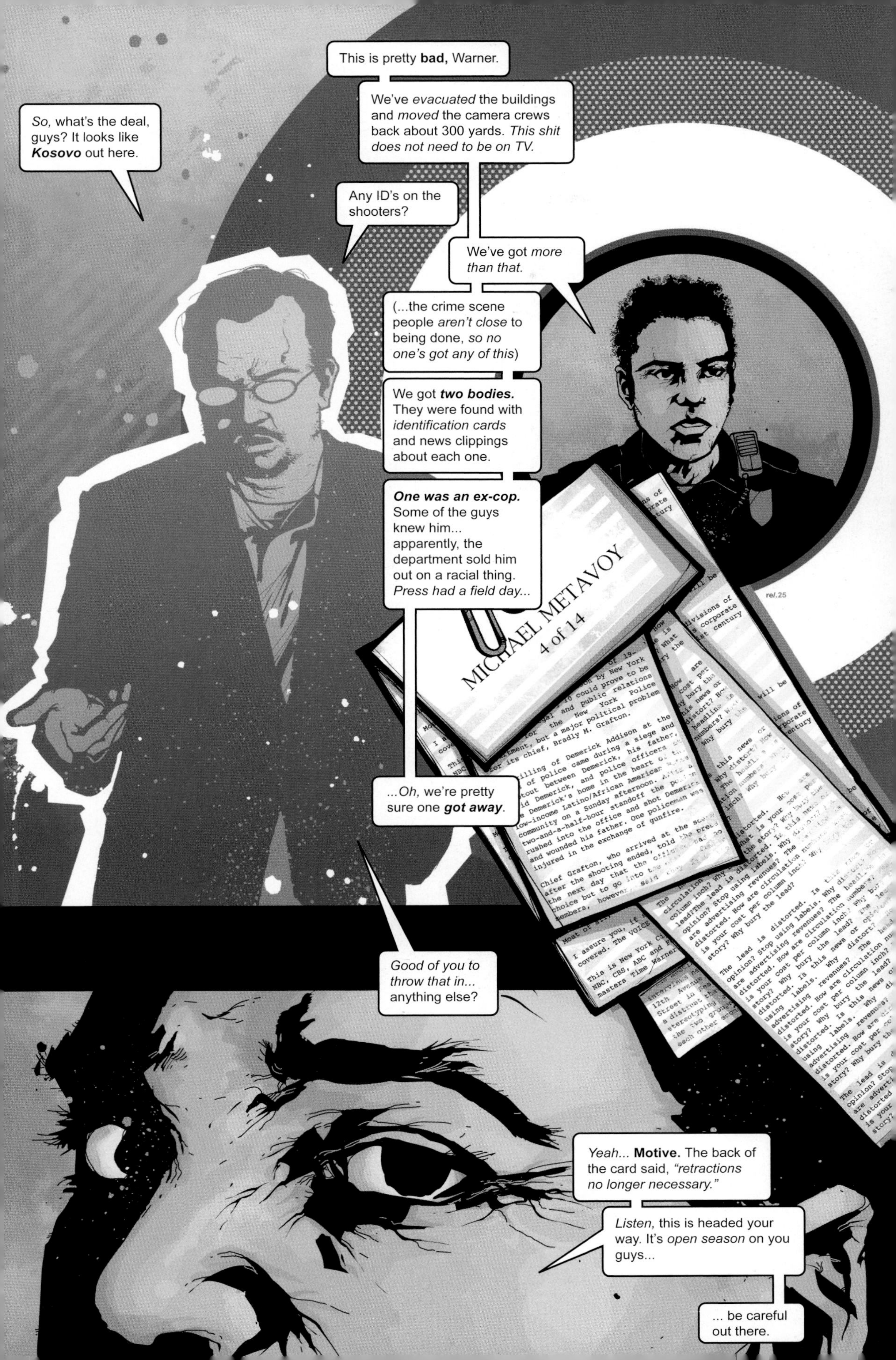
So, what's the deal, guys? It looks like Kosovo out here.
This is pretty bad, Warner.
We've evacuated the buildings and moved the camera crews back about 300 yards. This shit does not need to be on TV.
Any ID's on the shooters?
We've got more than that.
(...the crime scene people aren't close to being done, so no one's got any of this)
We got two bodies. They were found with identification cards and news clippings about each one.
One was an ex-cop. Some of the guys knew him... apparently, the department sold him out on a racial thing. Press had a field day...
MICHAEL METAVOY
4 of 14
rel.25
...Oh, we're pretty sure one got away.
Good of you to throw that in... anything else?
Yeah... Motive. The back of the card said, "retractions no longer necessary."
Listen, this is headed your way. It's open season on you guys...
... be careful out there.

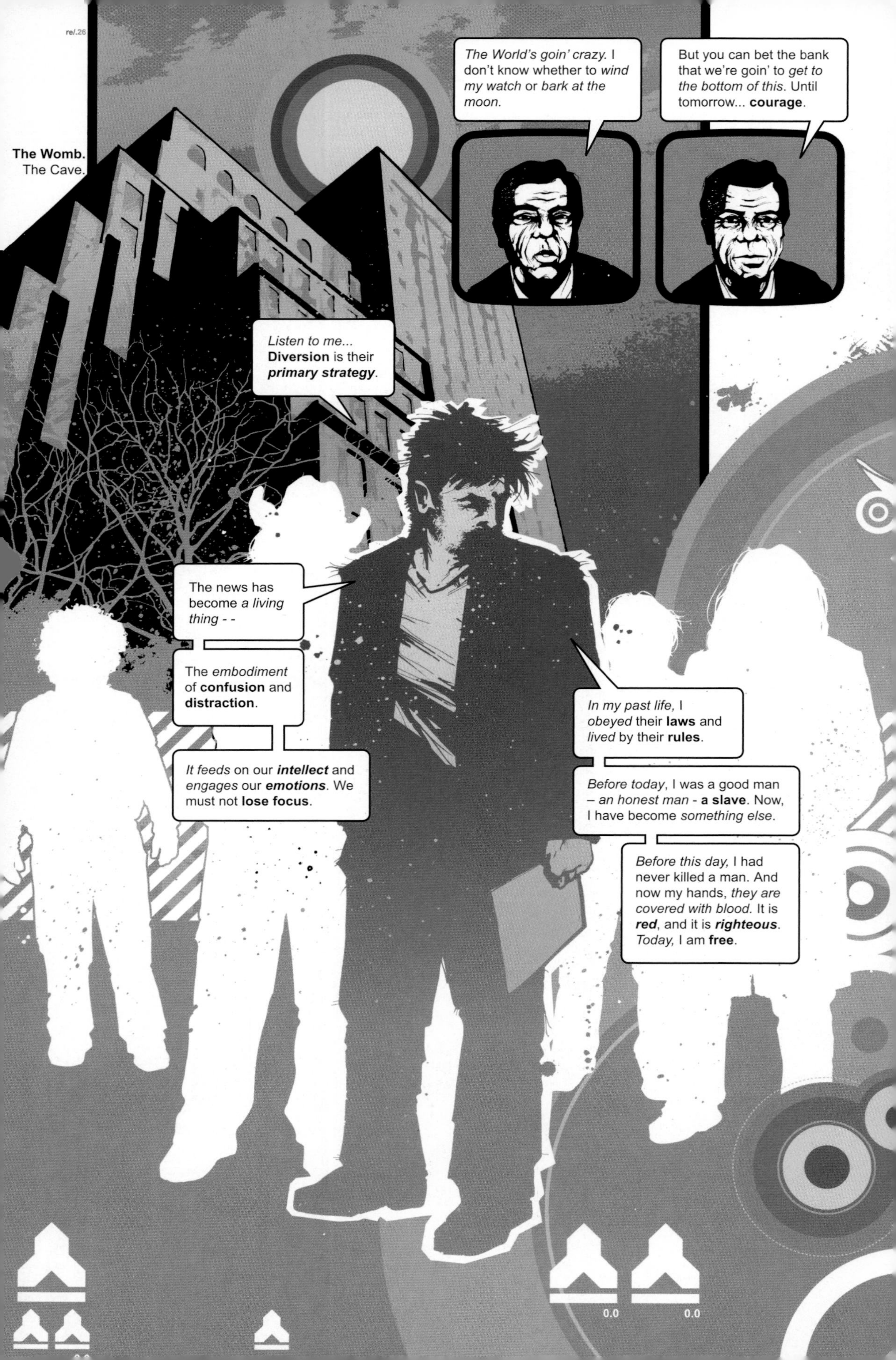
The Womb.
The Cave.
The World's goin' crazy. I don't know whether to wind my watch or bark at the moon.
But you can bet the bank that we're goin' to get to the bottom of this. Until tomorrow... courage.
Listen to me... Diversion is their primary strategy.
The news has become a living thing - -
The embodiment of confusion and distraction.
It feeds on our intellect and engages our emotions. We must not lose focus.
In my past life, I obeyed their laws and lived by their rules.
Before today, I was a good man – an honest man - a slave. Now, I have become something else.
Before this day, I had never killed a man. And now my hands, they are covered with blood. It is red, and it is righteous. Today, I am free.
0.0
0.0

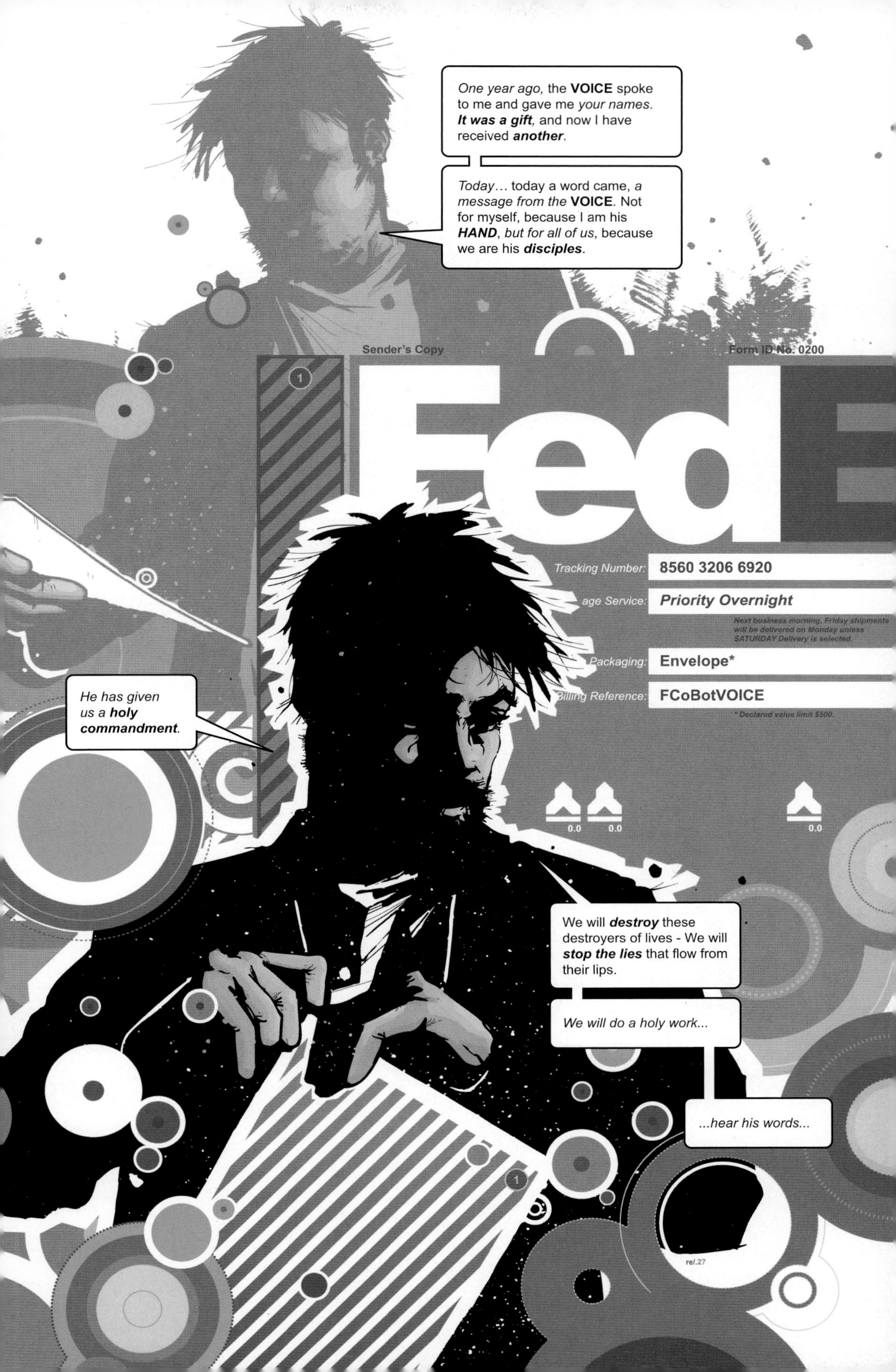

One year ago, the **VOICE** spoke to me and gave me *your names*. ***It was a gift***, and now I have received ***another***.
Today... today a word came, *a message from the* **VOICE**. Not for myself, because I am his ***HAND***, *but for all of us*, because we are his ***disciples***.
Sender's Copy
Form ID No. 0200
FedE
Tracking Number: 8560 3206 6920
age Service: Priority Overnight
Next business morning. Friday shipments will be delivered on Monday unless SATURDAY Delivery is selected.
Packaging: Envelope*
Billing Reference: FCoBotVOICE
* Declared value limit $500.
He has given us a ***holy commandment***.
0.0 0.0 0.0
We will ***destroy*** these destroyers of lives - We will ***stop the lies*** that flow from their lips.
We will do a holy work...
...hear his words...
rel.27

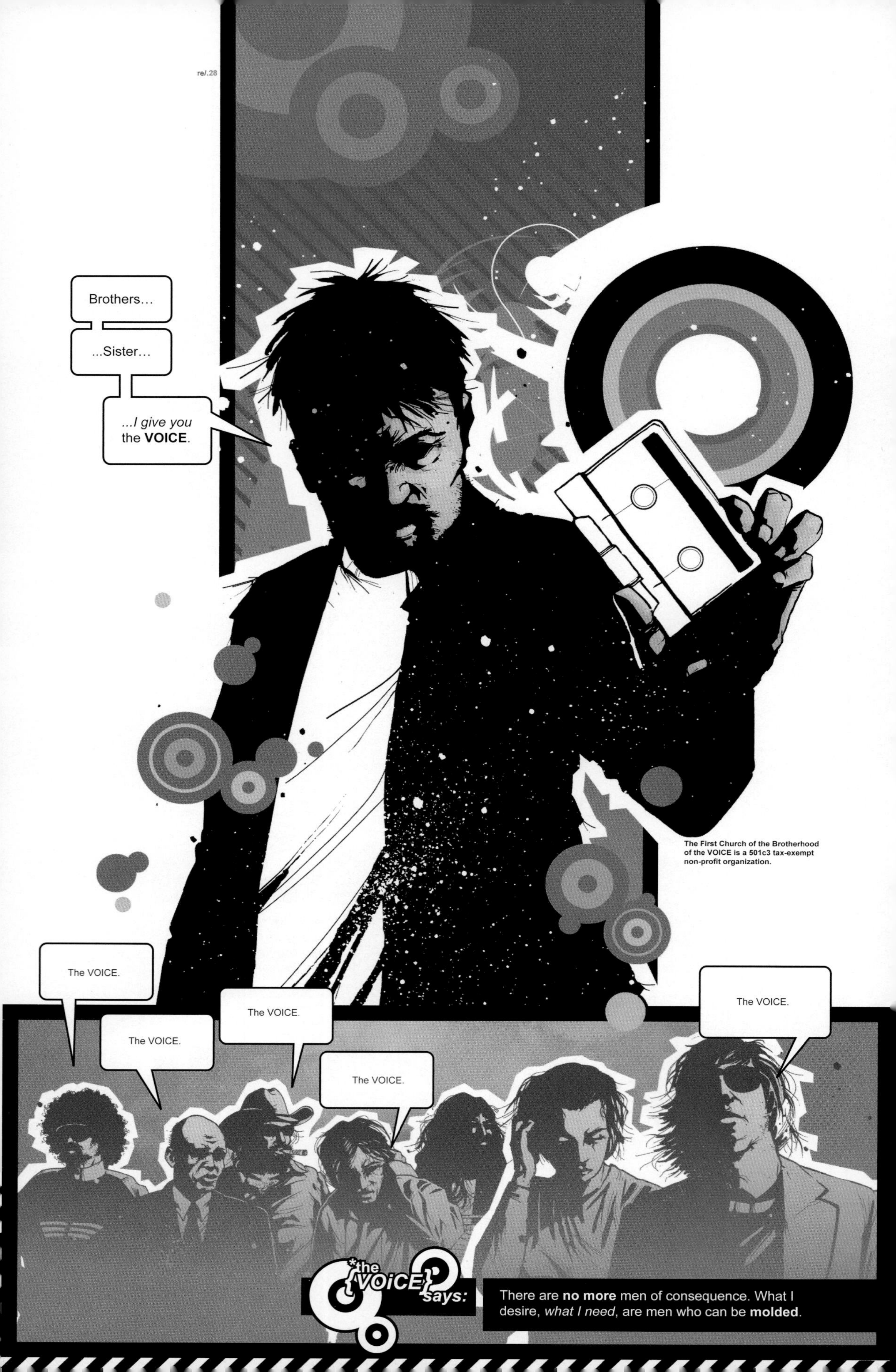
Brothers...
...Sister...
...I give you the VOICE.
The First Church of the Brotherhood of the VOICE is a 501c3 tax-exempt non-profit organization.
The VOICE.
The VOICE.
The VOICE.
The VOICE.
The VOICE.
the VOICE says:
There are no more men of consequence. What I desire, what I need, are men who can be molded.

re/.BC

END_CHAPTER 01

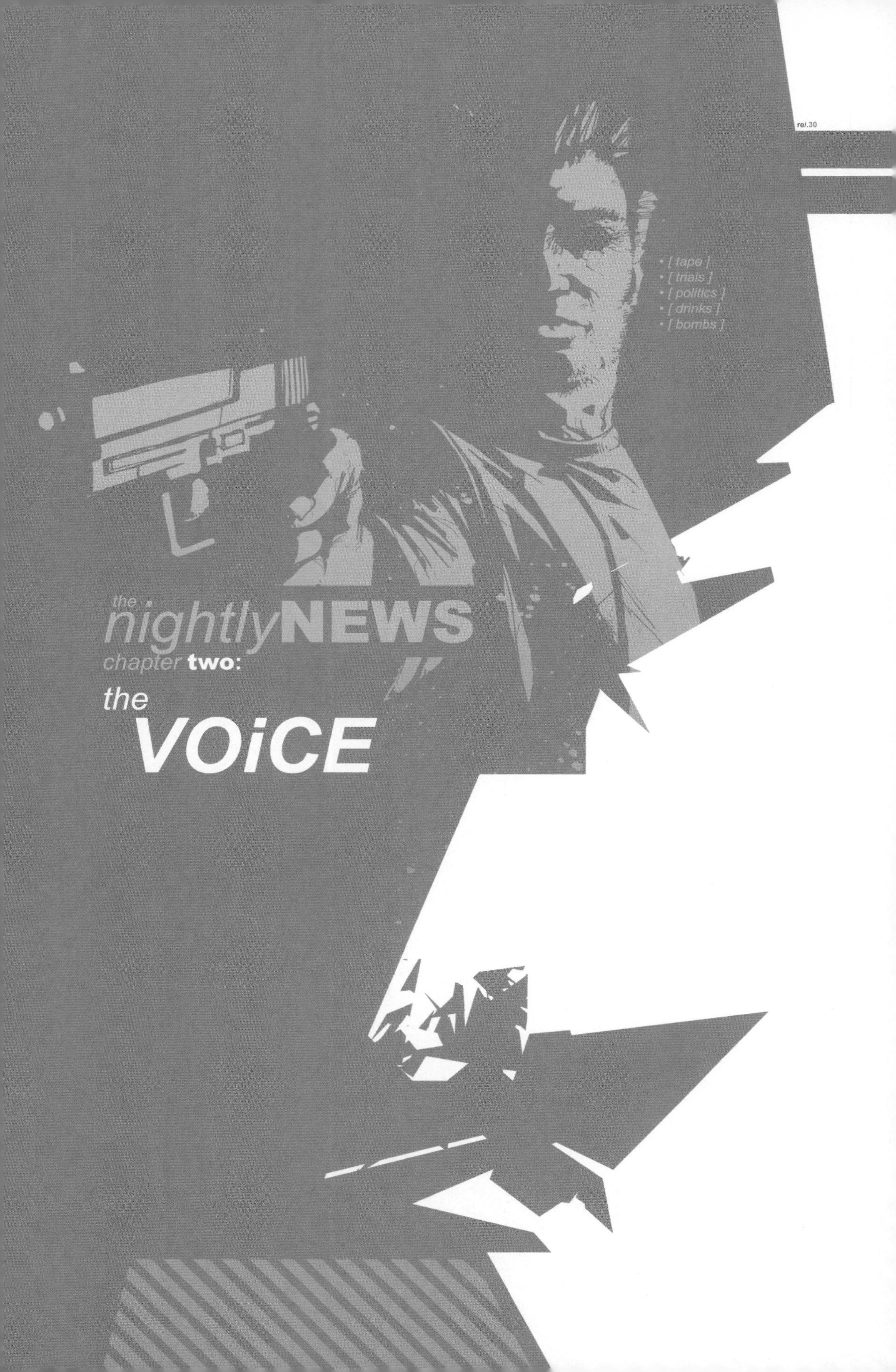
re/.30
• [tape]
• [trials]
• [politics]
• [drinks]
• [bombs]
the nightlyNEWS
chapter two:
the VOiCE

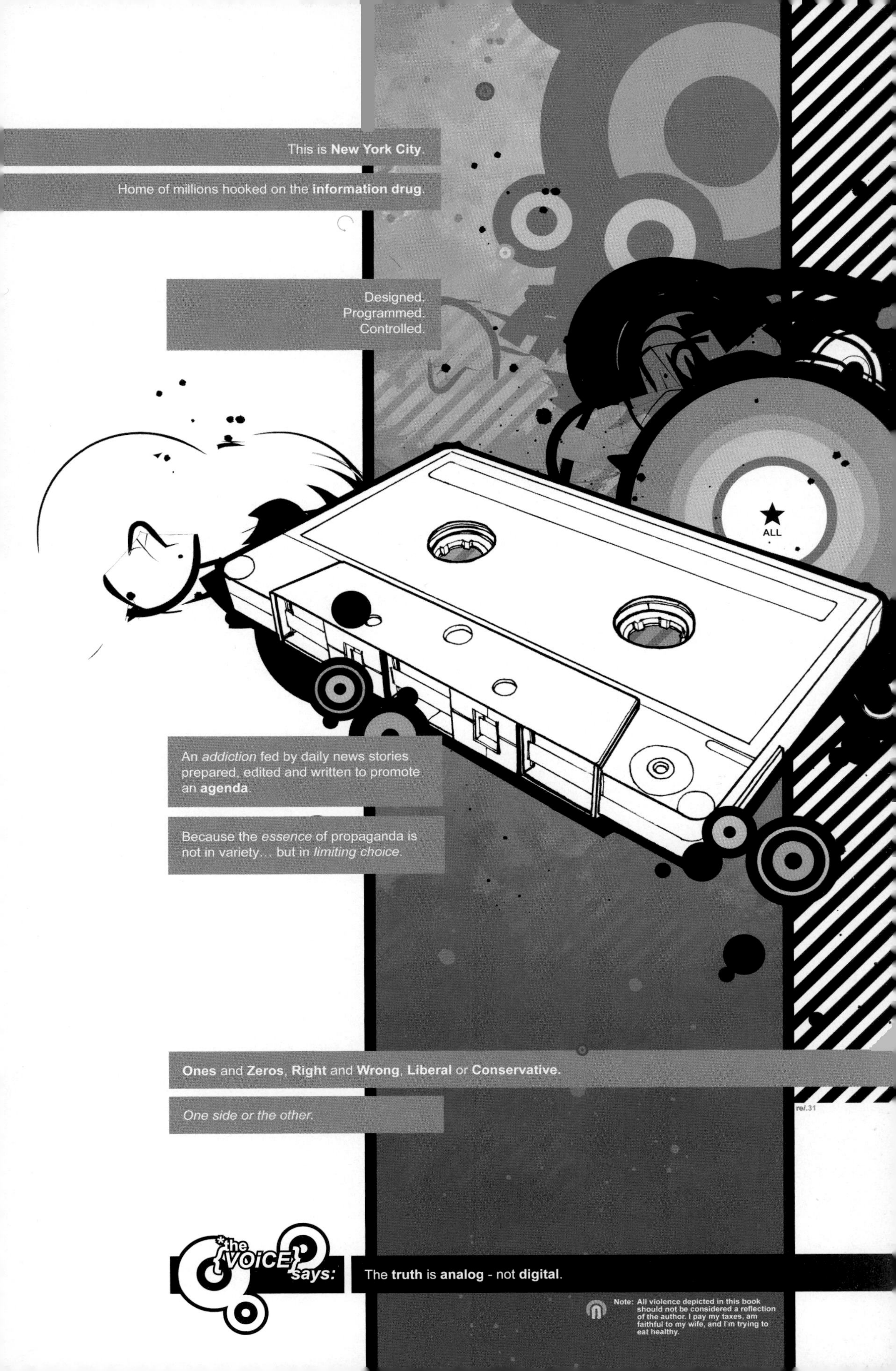
This is **New York City**.
Home of millions hooked on the **information drug**.
Designed.
Programmed.
Controlled.
ALL
An *addiction* fed by daily news stories prepared, edited and written to promote an **agenda**.
Because the *essence* of propaganda is not in variety... but in *limiting choice*.
Ones and **Zeros**, **Right** and **Wrong**, **Liberal** or **Conservative.**
One side or the other.
*the {VOiCE} says:
The **truth** is **analog** - not **digital**.
Note: All violence depicted in this book should not be considered a reflection of the author. I pay my taxes, am faithful to my wife, and I'm trying to eat healthy.

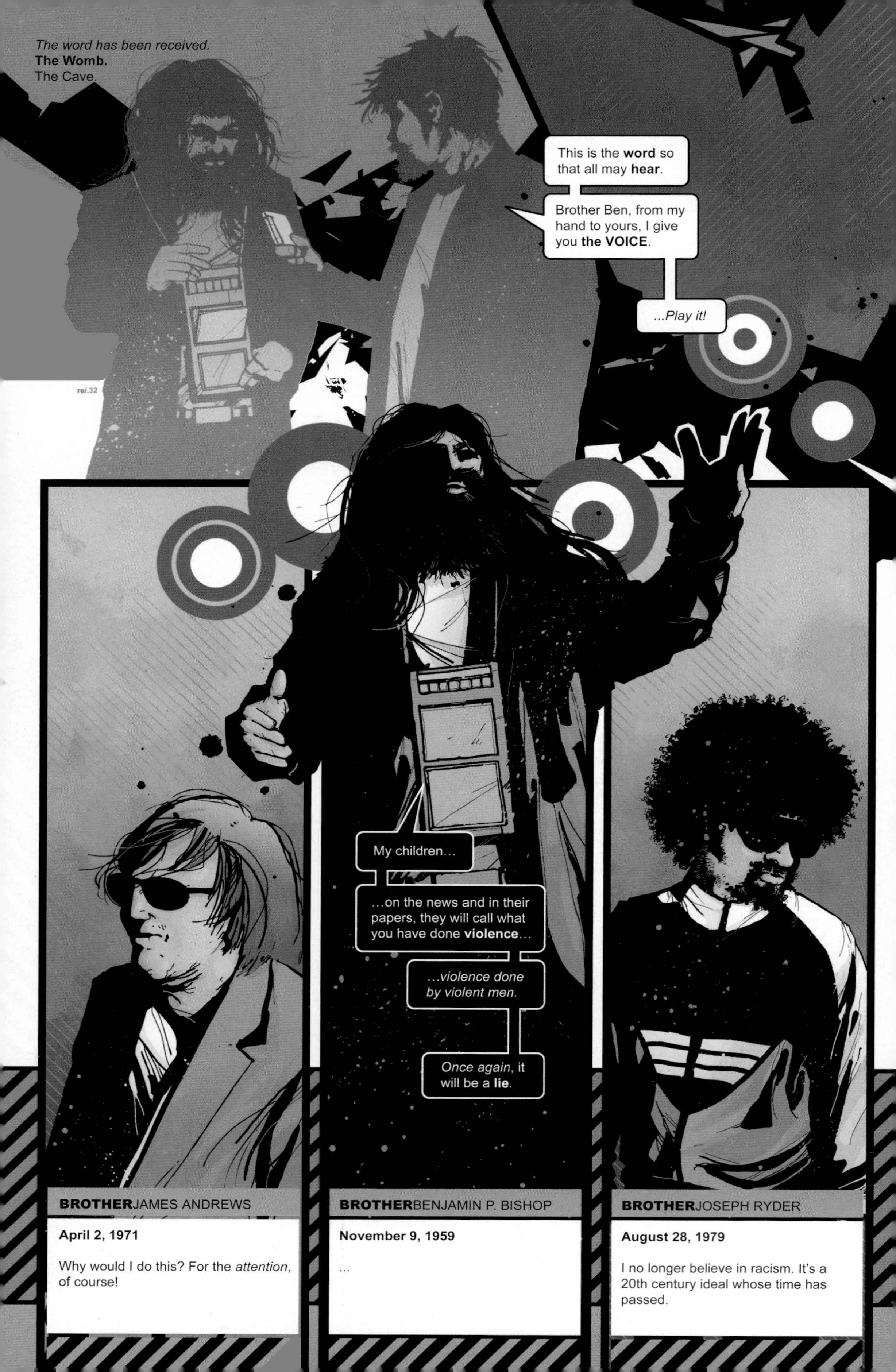

The word has been received.
The Womb.
The Cave.
This is the **word** so that all may **hear**.
Brother Ben, from my hand to yours, I give you **the VOICE**.
...Play it!
re/.32
My children...
...on the news and in their papers, they will call what you have done **violence**...
...violence done by violent men.
Once again, it will be a **lie**.
BROTHERJAMES ANDREWS
April 2, 1971
Why would I do this? For the *attention*, of course!
BROTHERBENJAMIN P. BISHOP
November 9, 1959
...
BROTHERJOSEPH RYDER
August 28, 1979
I no longer believe in racism. It's a 20th century ideal whose time has passed.

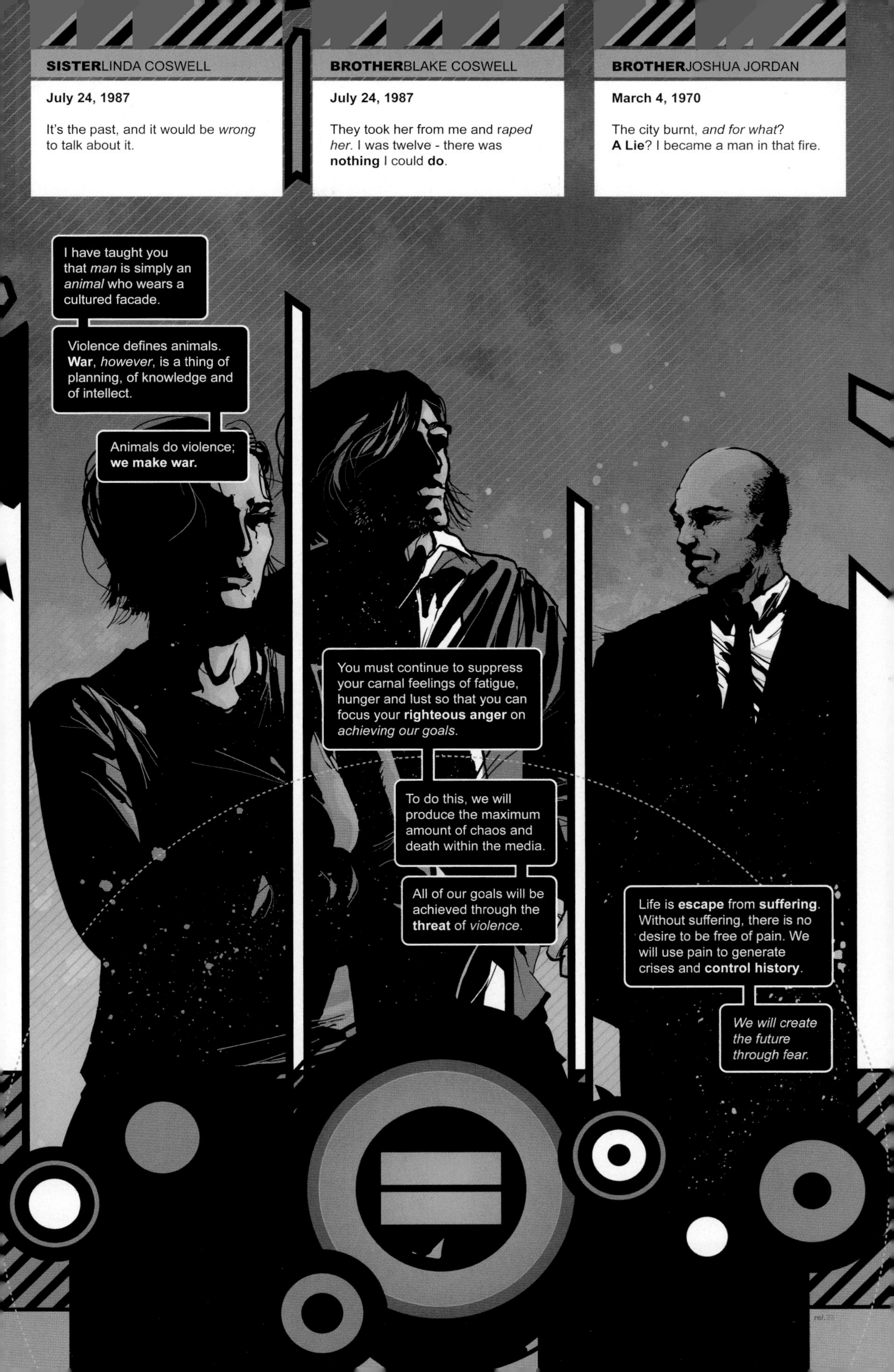
SISTER LINDA COSWELL
July 24, 1987
It's the past, and it would be *wrong* to talk about it.
BROTHER BLAKE COSWELL
July 24, 1987
They took her from me and *raped her*. I was twelve - there was **nothing** I could **do**.
BROTHER JOSHUA JORDAN
March 4, 1970
The city burnt, *and for what*? **A Lie**? I became a man in that fire.
I have taught you that *man* is simply an *animal* who wears a cultured facade.
Violence defines animals. **War**, *however*, is a thing of planning, of knowledge and of intellect.
Animals do violence; **we make war.**
You must continue to suppress your carnal feelings of fatigue, hunger and lust so that you can focus your **righteous anger** on *achieving our goals*.
To do this, we will produce the maximum amount of chaos and death within the media.
All of our goals will be achieved through the **threat** of *violence*.
Life is **escape** from **suffering**. Without suffering, there is no desire to be free of pain. We will use pain to generate crises and **control history**.
We will create the future through fear.

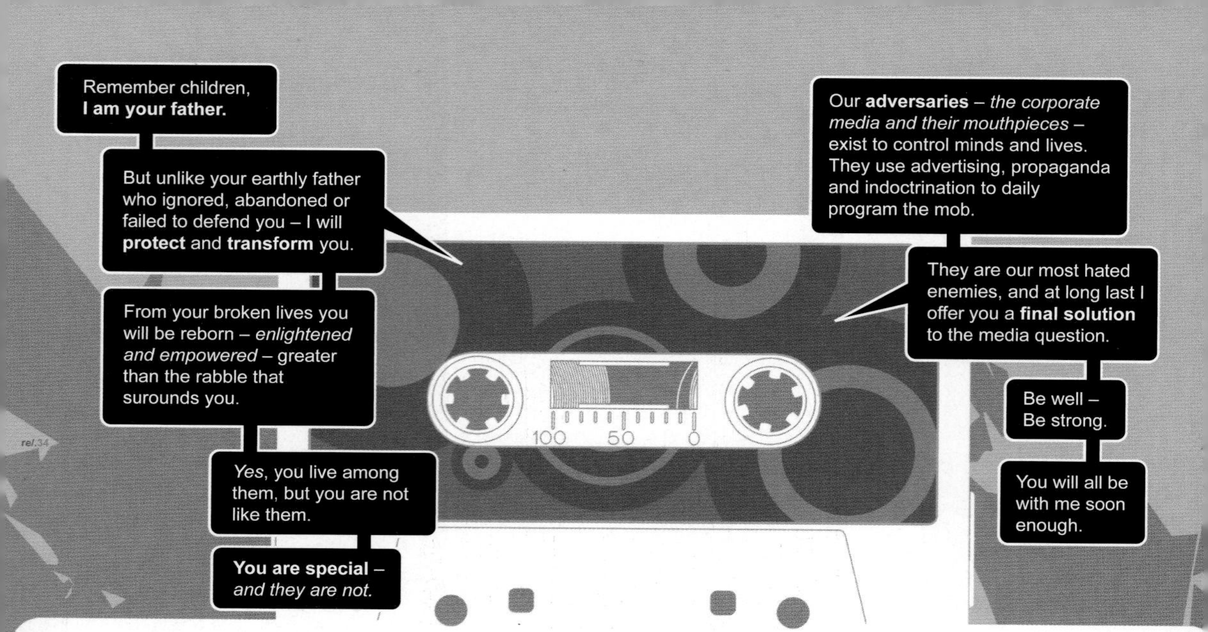

Remember children, I am your father.

But unlike your earthly father who ignored, abandoned or failed to defend you – I will **protect** and **transform** you.

From your broken lives you will be reborn – *enlightened and empowered* – greater than the rabble that surrounds you.

Yes, you live among them, but you are not like them.

You are special – *and they are not.*

Our **adversaries** – *the corporate media and their mouthpieces* – exist to control minds and lives. They use advertising, propaganda and indoctrination to daily program the mob.

They are our most hated enemies, and at long last I offer you a **final solution** to the media question.

Be well – Be strong.

You will all be with me soon enough.

ref/34

To find out more about news errors, read below. However, if you're like me and only care about your own personal entertainment (certainly not anything like Katie Couric shoving a camera up her ass and calling it news), keep reading on the next page!

*errors in the news: *greatest hits*

Jayson**Blair:**

About:

Disgraced New York Times reporter who, in 2003, was caught plagiarizing and fabricating articles. The scandal resulted in the resignation of both Executive Editor Howell Raines and Managing Editor Gerald Boyd.

4

Reason for Ranking:

Over hyped - only ranked this high because of the Raines/Boyd fallout.

Jack**Kelley:**

About:

USA Today reporter who wrote scripts for friends and associates so they could pose as fake news sources. He was a member of the World Journalism Institute, whose goal is to inject Christians into mainstream news organizations.

3.5

Reason for Ranking:

Baby Jesus says USA Today kind of sucks.

Janet**Cooke:**

About:

Washington Post journalist who won a Pulitzer Prize for the fabricated story, "Jimmy's World." It was the make believe tale of an 8-year-old heroin addict. We should all cry now.

4.5

Reason for Ranking:

Stop using the kids!

Stephen**Glass:**

About:

Reporter fired from The New Republic in 1998 for journalistic fraud. Created a fake website and voice mail account to get past the company fact checkers.

3

Reason for Ranking:

Only because his story was made into the movie, "Shattered Glass" which starred the crappy Darth Vader.

Patricia**Smith:**

About:

She was asked to resign from the Boston Globe for fabrications in her reporting. Went on to become a four-time National Poetry Slam winner.

1

Reason for Ranking:

"No earthly man knows the solution to our hips, asses urgent as sirens..." tough to argue with that.

Dan**Rather:**

About:

Along with Mary Mapes, Mr. Rather was caught using forged documents to try and sway a Presidential election. Rather maintains that even if the documents are fakes, he stands by the story.

5

Reason for Ranking:

Dan Rather has always been, and always will be, a douche bag.

Add**endum:**

Larry**King:**

About:

Larry King is an award-winning broadcaster who farted on air while interviewing Starr Jones.

Available free of charge on YouTube right now!

 2.5

Reason for Ranking:

None, but being married six times has contributed to Mr. King's malodorous constitution.

seriously..?

fact-checking:

In the last decade, Time and Newsweek have eliminated their fact-checking departments.

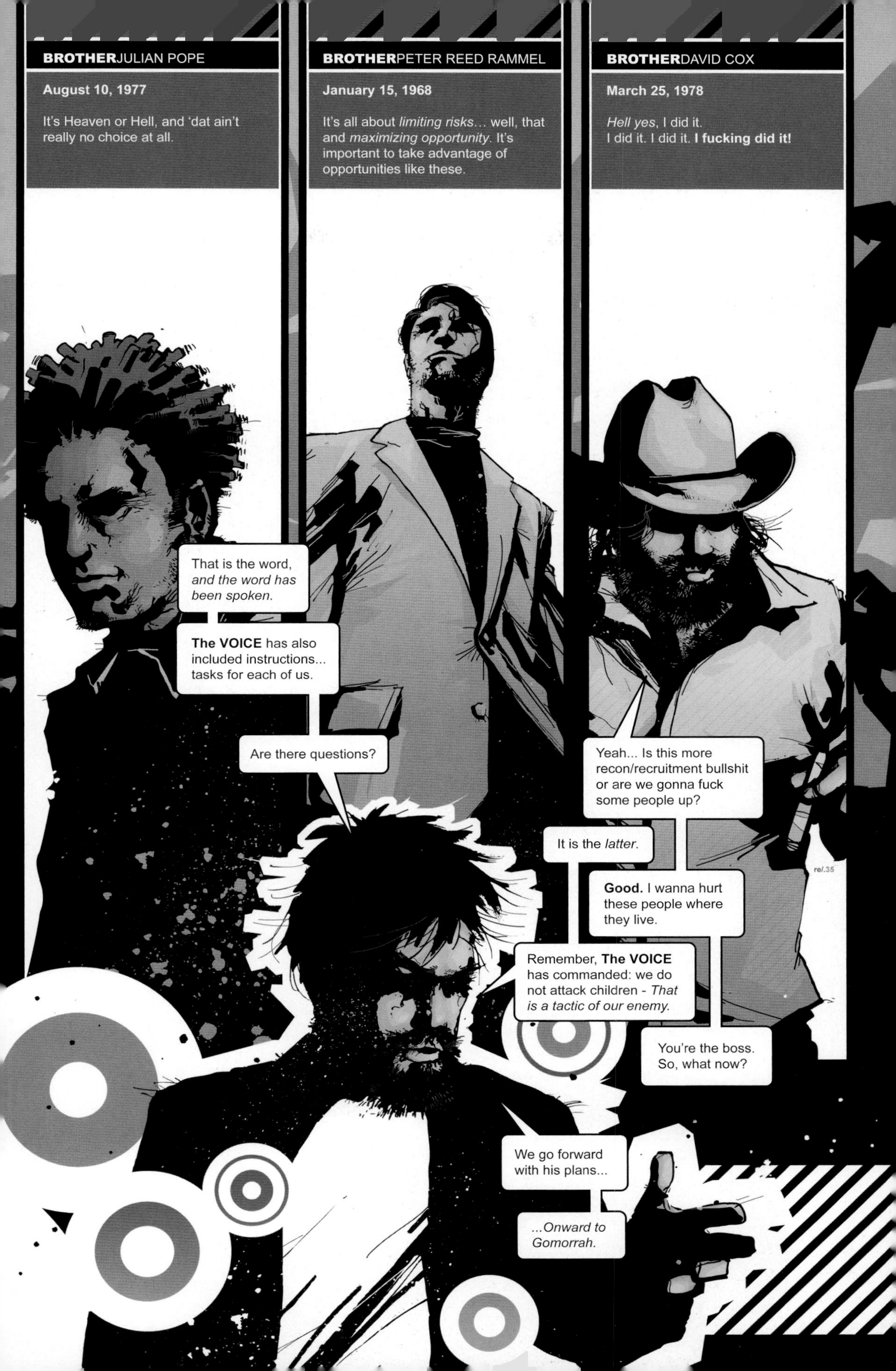

BROTHER JULIAN POPE
August 10, 1977
It's Heaven or Hell, and 'dat ain't really no choice at all.
BROTHER PETER REED RAMMEL
January 15, 1968
It's all about *limiting risks*... well, that and *maximizing opportunity*. It's important to take advantage of opportunities like these.
BROTHER DAVID COX
March 25, 1978
Hell yes, I did it. I did it. I did it. **I fucking did it!**
That is the word, *and the word has been spoken.*
The VOICE has also included instructions... tasks for each of us.
Are there questions?
Yeah... Is this more recon/recruitment bullshit or are we gonna fuck some people up?
It is the *latter*.
Good. I wanna hurt these people where they live.
Remember, **The VOICE** has commanded: we do not attack children - *That is a tactic of our enemy.*
You're the boss. So, what now?
We go forward with his plans...
...Onward to Gomorrah.
re/.35

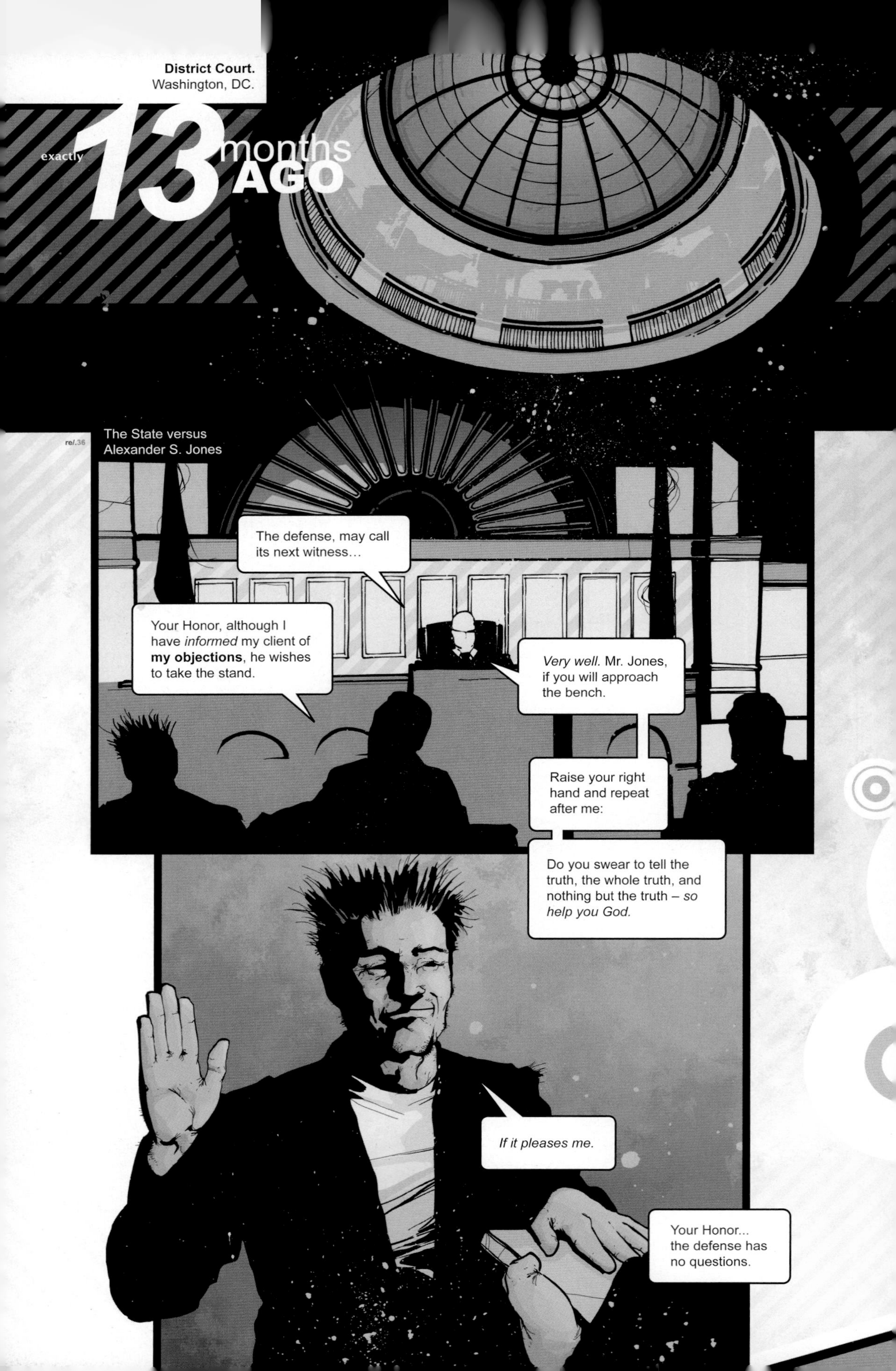
District Court.
Washington, DC.
exactly 13 months AGO
re/.36
The State versus
Alexander S. Jones
The defense, may call its next witness…
Your Honor, although I have *informed* my client of **my objections**, he wishes to take the stand.
Very well. Mr. Jones, if you will approach the bench.
Raise your right hand and repeat after me:
Do you swear to tell the truth, the whole truth, and nothing but the truth – *so help you God.*
If it pleases me.
Your Honor... the defense has no questions.

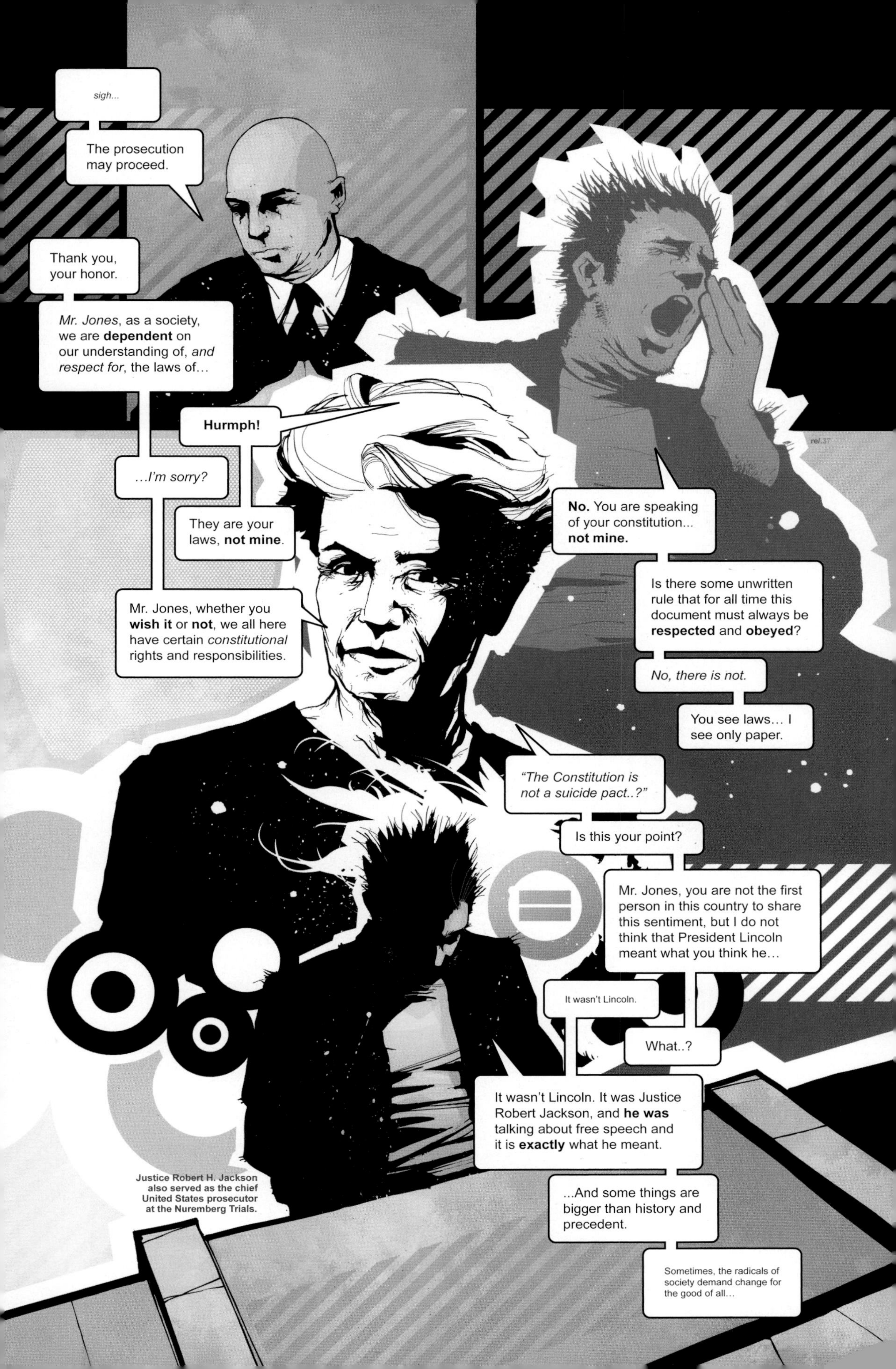

sigh...
The prosecution may proceed.
Thank you, your honor.
Mr. Jones, as a society, we are **dependent** on our understanding of, *and respect for*, the laws of…
Hurmph!
…*I'm sorry?*
They are your laws, **not mine**.
Mr. Jones, whether you **wish it** or **not**, we all here have certain *constitutional* rights and responsibilities.
No. You are speaking of your constitution... **not mine.**
Is there some unwritten rule that for all time this document must always be **respected** and **obeyed**?
No, there is not.
You see laws… I see only paper.
"The Constitution is not a suicide pact..?"
Is this your point?
Mr. Jones, you are not the first person in this country to share this sentiment, but I do not think that President Lincoln meant what you think he…
It wasn't Lincoln.
What..?
It wasn't Lincoln. It was Justice Robert Jackson, and **he was** talking about free speech and it is **exactly** what he meant.
...And some things are bigger than history and precedent.
Sometimes, the radicals of society demand change for the good of all…
Justice Robert H. Jackson also served as the chief United States prosecutor at the Nuremberg Trials.
rel.37

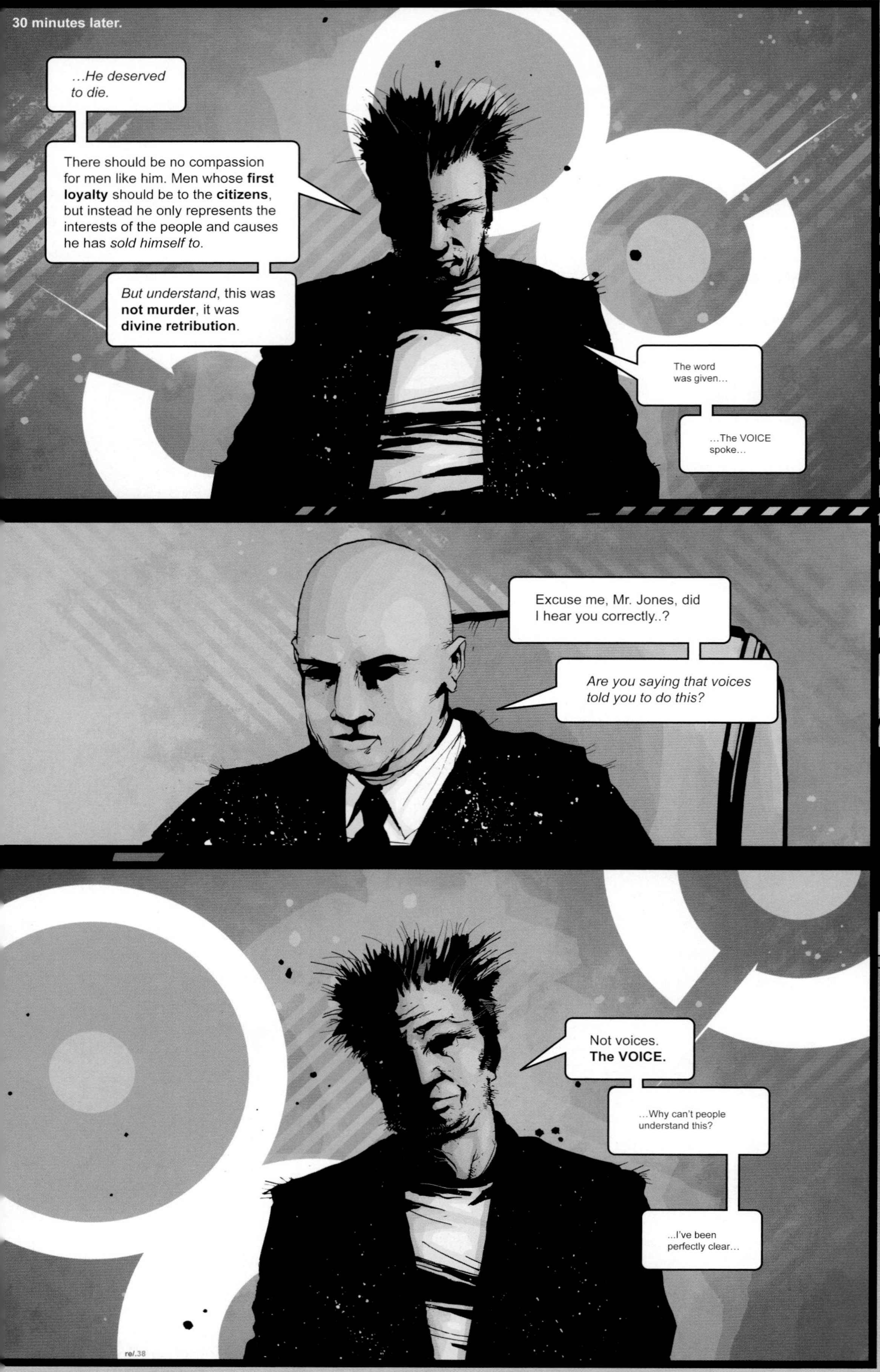
30 minutes later.
...He deserved to die.
There should be no compassion for men like him. Men whose first loyalty should be to the citizens, but instead he only represents the interests of the people and causes he has sold himself to.
But understand, this was not murder, it was divine retribution.
The word was given...
...The VOICE spoke...
Excuse me, Mr. Jones, did I hear you correctly..?
Are you saying that voices told you to do this?
Not voices. The VOICE.
...Why can't people understand this?
...I've been perfectly clear...

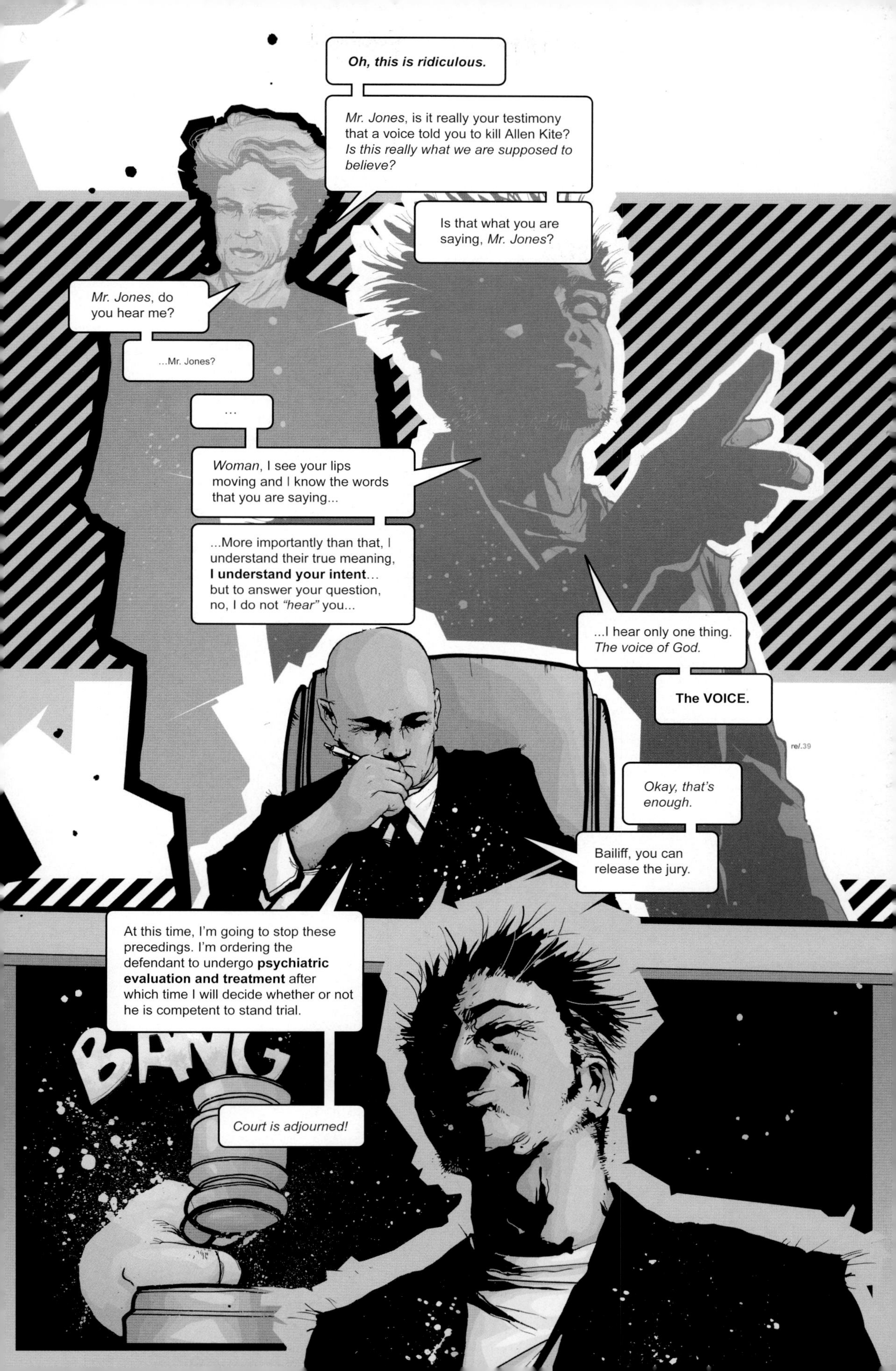
Oh, this is ridiculous.
Mr. Jones, is it really your testimony that a voice told you to kill Allen Kite? Is this really what we are supposed to believe?
Is that what you are saying, Mr. Jones?
Mr. Jones, do you hear me?
...Mr. Jones?
...
Woman, I see your lips moving and I know the words that you are saying...
...More importantly than that, I understand their true meaning, I understand your intent... but to answer your question, no, I do not "hear" you...
...I hear only one thing. The voice of God.
The VOICE.
Okay, that's enough.
Bailiff, you can release the jury.
At this time, I'm going to stop these precedings. I'm ordering the defendant to undergo psychiatric evaluation and treatment after which time I will decide whether or not he is competent to stand trial.
BANG
Court is adjourned!

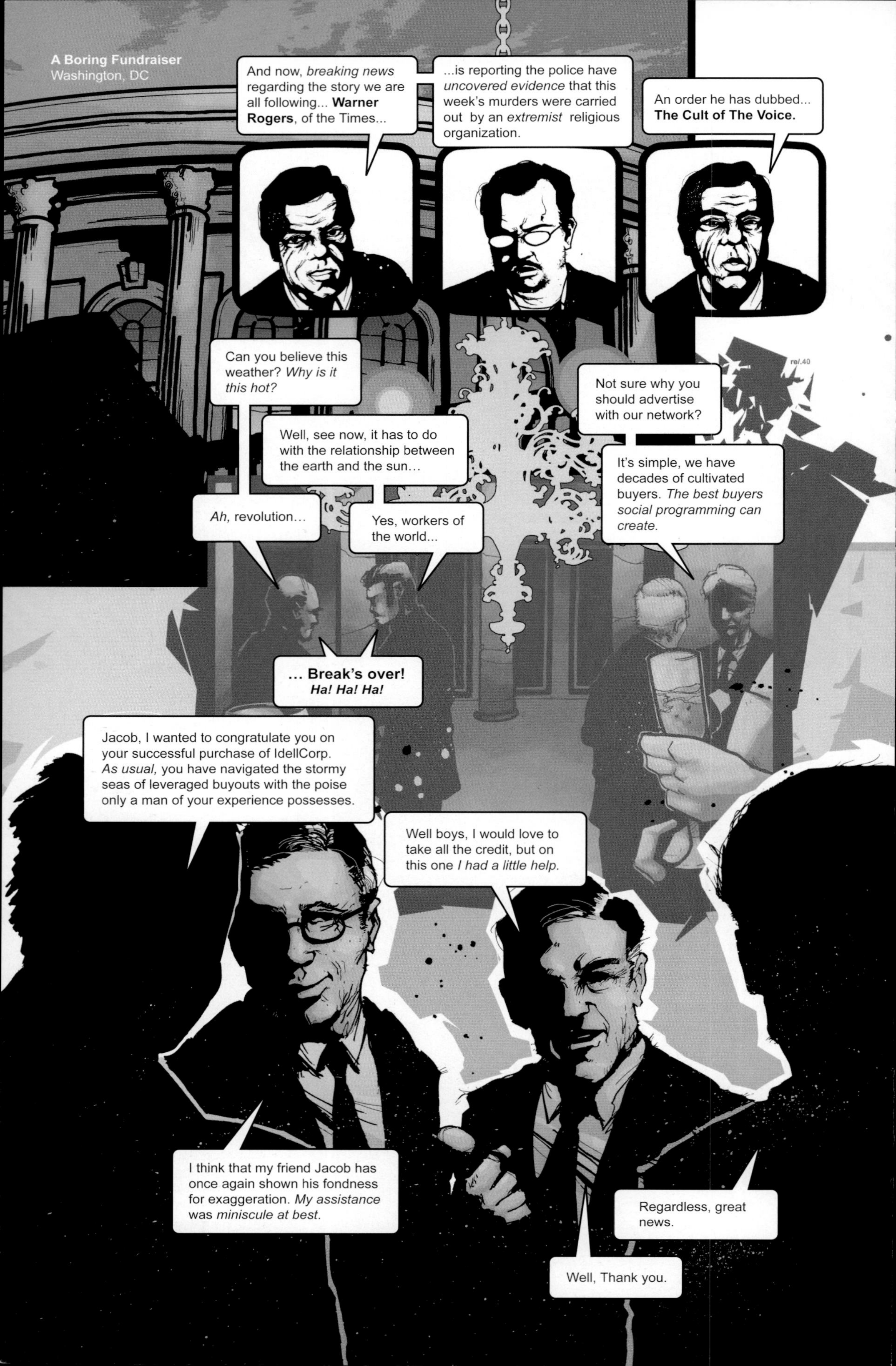

A Boring Fundraiser
Washington, DC
And now, breaking news regarding the story we are all following... Warner Rogers, of the Times...
...is reporting the police have uncovered evidence that this week's murders were carried out by an extremist religious organization.
An order he has dubbed... The Cult of The Voice.
Can you believe this weather? Why is it this hot?
Well, see now, it has to do with the relationship between the earth and the sun…
Ah, revolution…
Yes, workers of the world...
Not sure why you should advertise with our network?
It's simple, we have decades of cultivated buyers. The best buyers social programming can create.
… Break's over! Ha! Ha! Ha!
Jacob, I wanted to congratulate you on your successful purchase of IdellCorp. As usual, you have navigated the stormy seas of leveraged buyouts with the poise only a man of your experience possesses.
Well boys, I would love to take all the credit, but on this one I had a little help.
I think that my friend Jacob has once again shown his fondness for exaggeration. My assistance was miniscule at best.
Regardless, great news.
Well, Thank you.

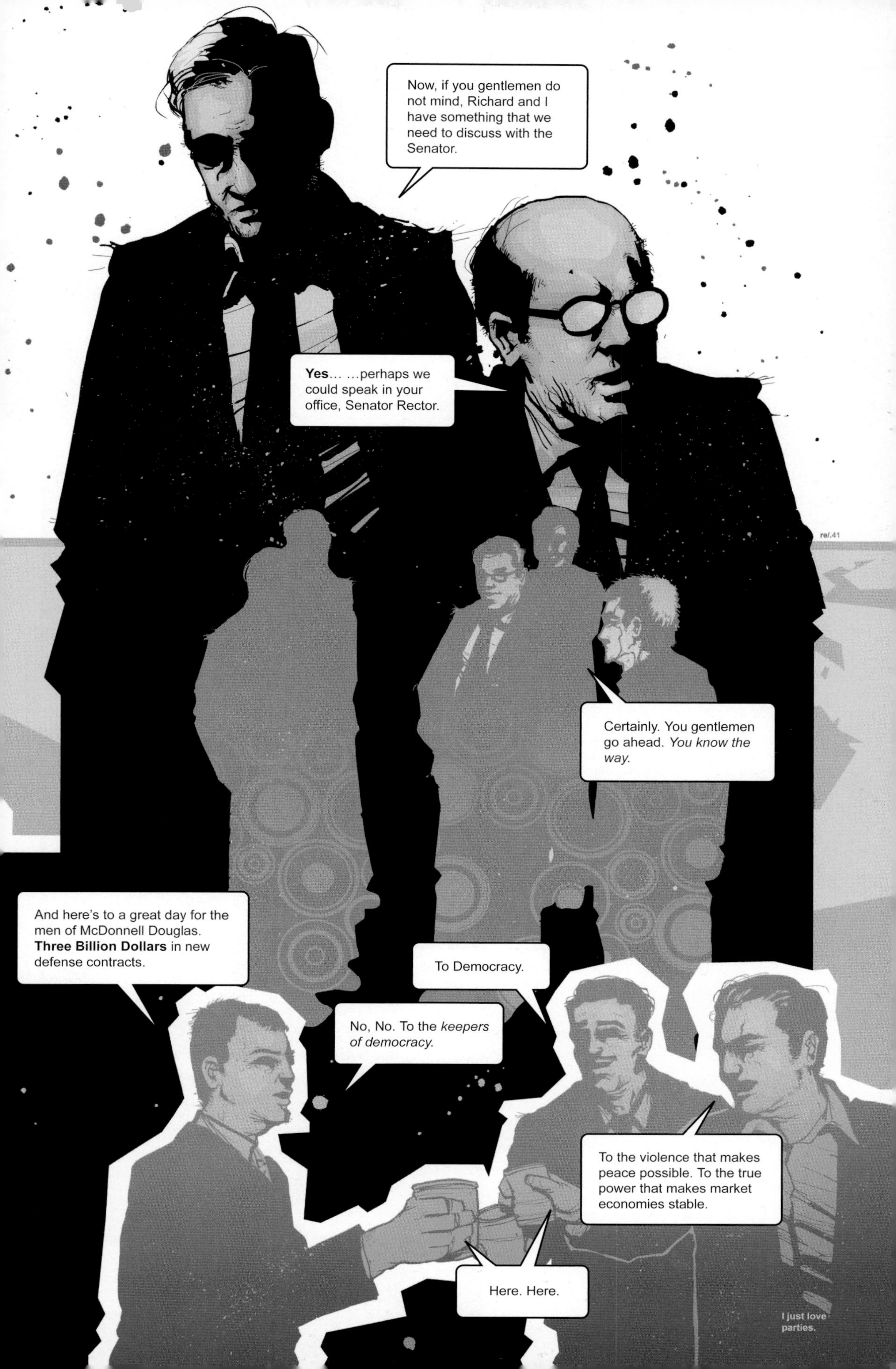
Now, if you gentlemen do not mind, Richard and I have something that we need to discuss with the Senator.
Yes… …perhaps we could speak in your office, Senator Rector.
Certainly. You gentlemen go ahead. *You know the way.*
And here's to a great day for the men of McDonnell Douglas. **Three Billion Dollars** in new defense contracts.
To Democracy.
No, No. To the *keepers of democracy.*
To the violence that makes peace possible. To the true power that makes market economies stable.
Here. Here.
I just love parties.

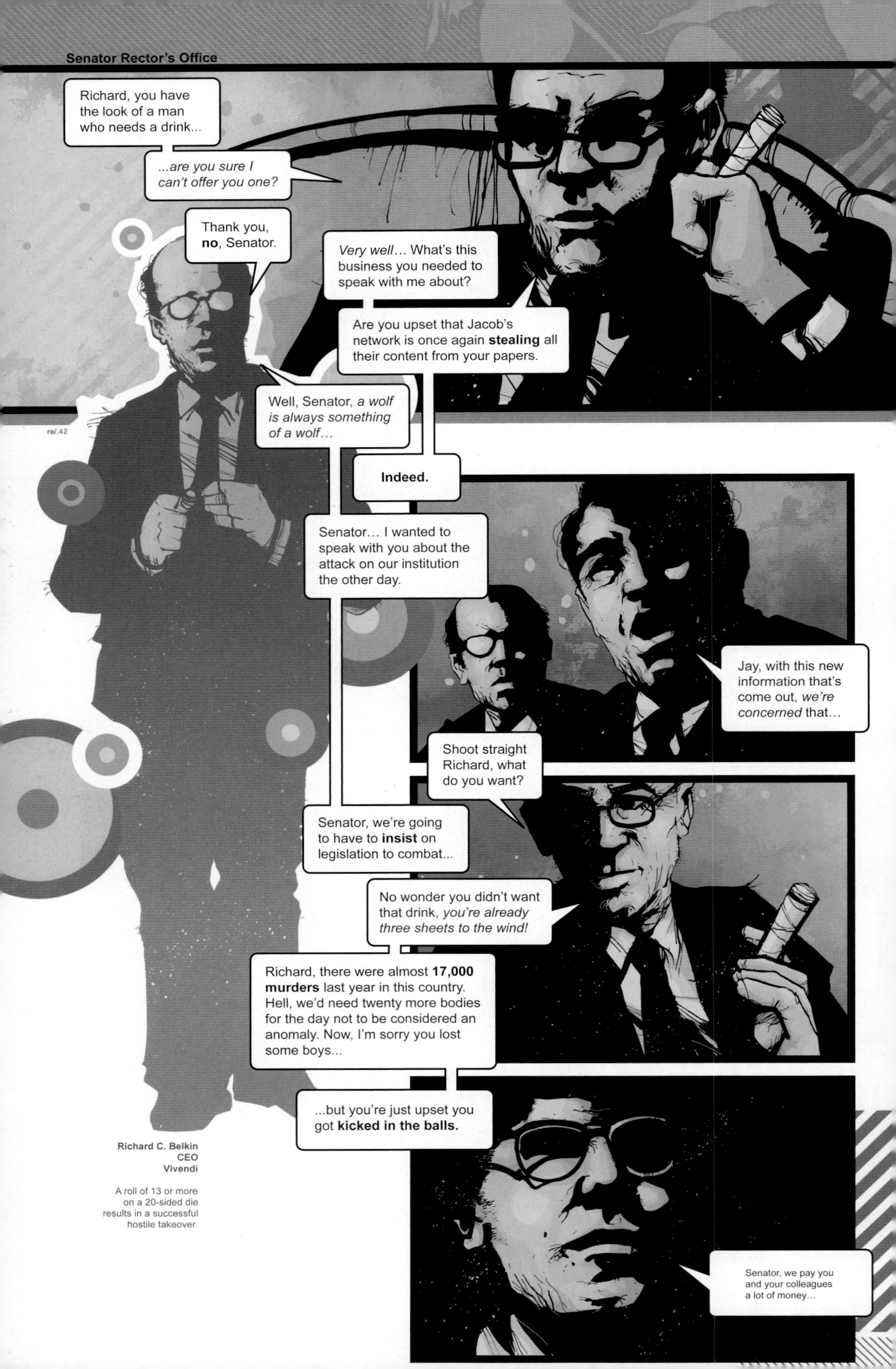
Senator Rector's Office
Richard, you have the look of a man who needs a drink...
...are you sure I can't offer you one?
Thank you, **no**, Senator.
Very well... What's this business you needed to speak with me about?
Are you upset that Jacob's network is once again **stealing** all their content from your papers.
Well, Senator, *a wolf is always something of a wolf*...
Indeed.
Senator... I wanted to speak with you about the attack on our institution the other day.
Jay, with this new information that's come out, *we're concerned* that...
Shoot straight Richard, what do you want?
Senator, we're going to have to **insist** on legislation to combat...
No wonder you didn't want that drink, *you're already three sheets to the wind!*
Richard, there were almost **17,000 murders** last year in this country. Hell, we'd need twenty more bodies for the day not to be considered an anomaly. Now, I'm sorry you lost some boys...
...but you're just upset you got **kicked in the balls.**
Senator, we pay you and your colleagues a lot of money...

Richard C. Belkin
CEO
Vivendi

A roll of 13 or more on a 20-sided die results in a successful hostile takeover.

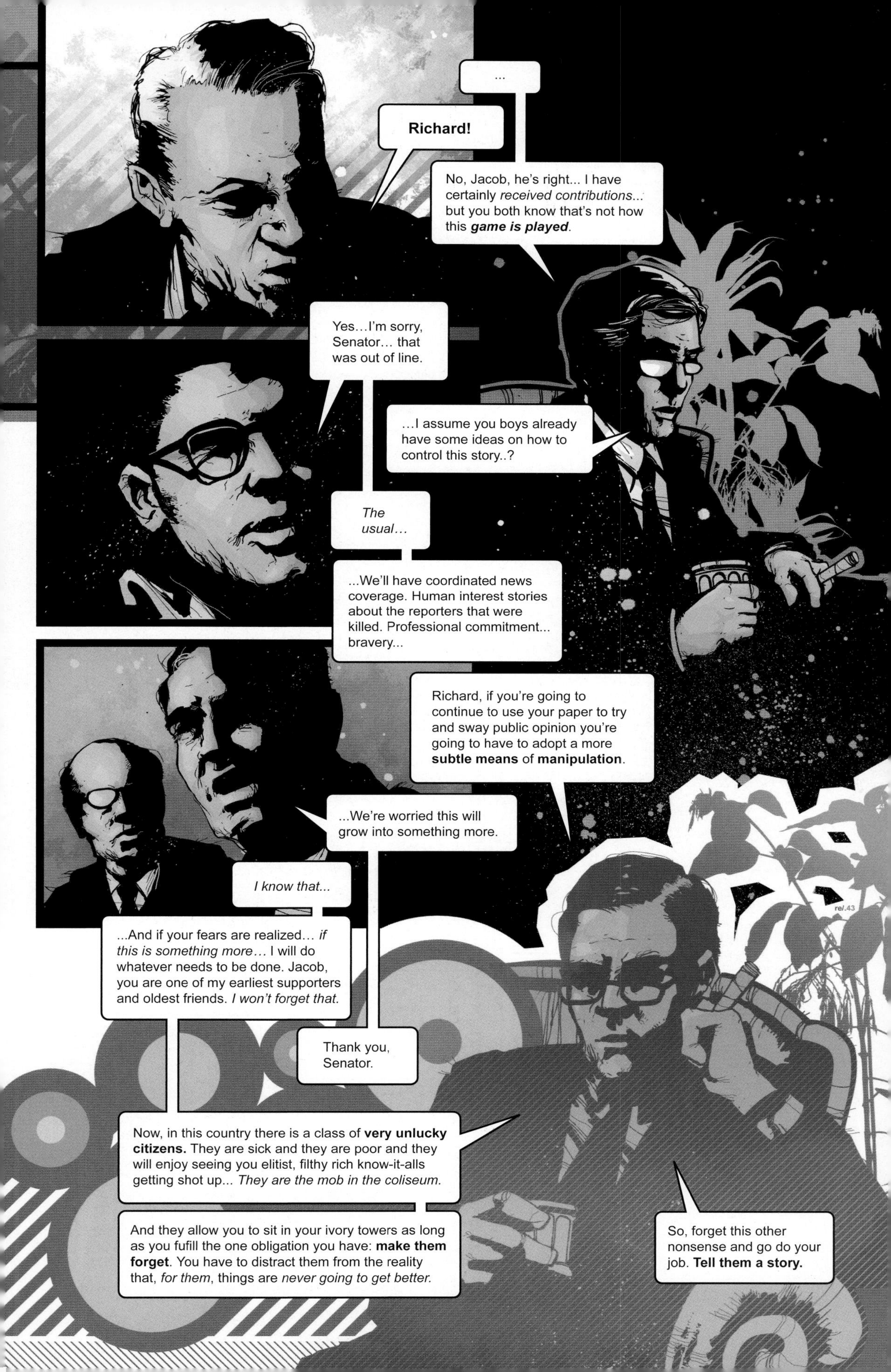
...
Richard!
No, Jacob, he's right... I have certainly *received contributions*... but you both know that's not how this ***game is played***.
Yes…I'm sorry, Senator… that was out of line.
…I assume you boys already have some ideas on how to control this story..?
The usual…
...We'll have coordinated news coverage. Human interest stories about the reporters that were killed. Professional commitment... bravery...
Richard, if you're going to continue to use your paper to try and sway public opinion you're going to have to adopt a more **subtle means** of **manipulation**.
...We're worried this will grow into something more.
I know that...
...And if your fears are realized… *if this is something more…* I will do whatever needs to be done. Jacob, you are one of my earliest supporters and oldest friends. *I won't forget that.*
Thank you, Senator.
Now, in this country there is a class of **very unlucky citizens.** They are sick and they are poor and they will enjoy seeing you elitist, filthy rich know-it-alls getting shot up... *They are the mob in the coliseum.*
And they allow you to sit in your ivory towers as long as you fufill the one obligation you have: **make them forget**. You have to distract them from the reality that, *for them*, things are *never going to get better.*
So, forget this other nonsense and go do your job. **Tell them a story.**
re/.43

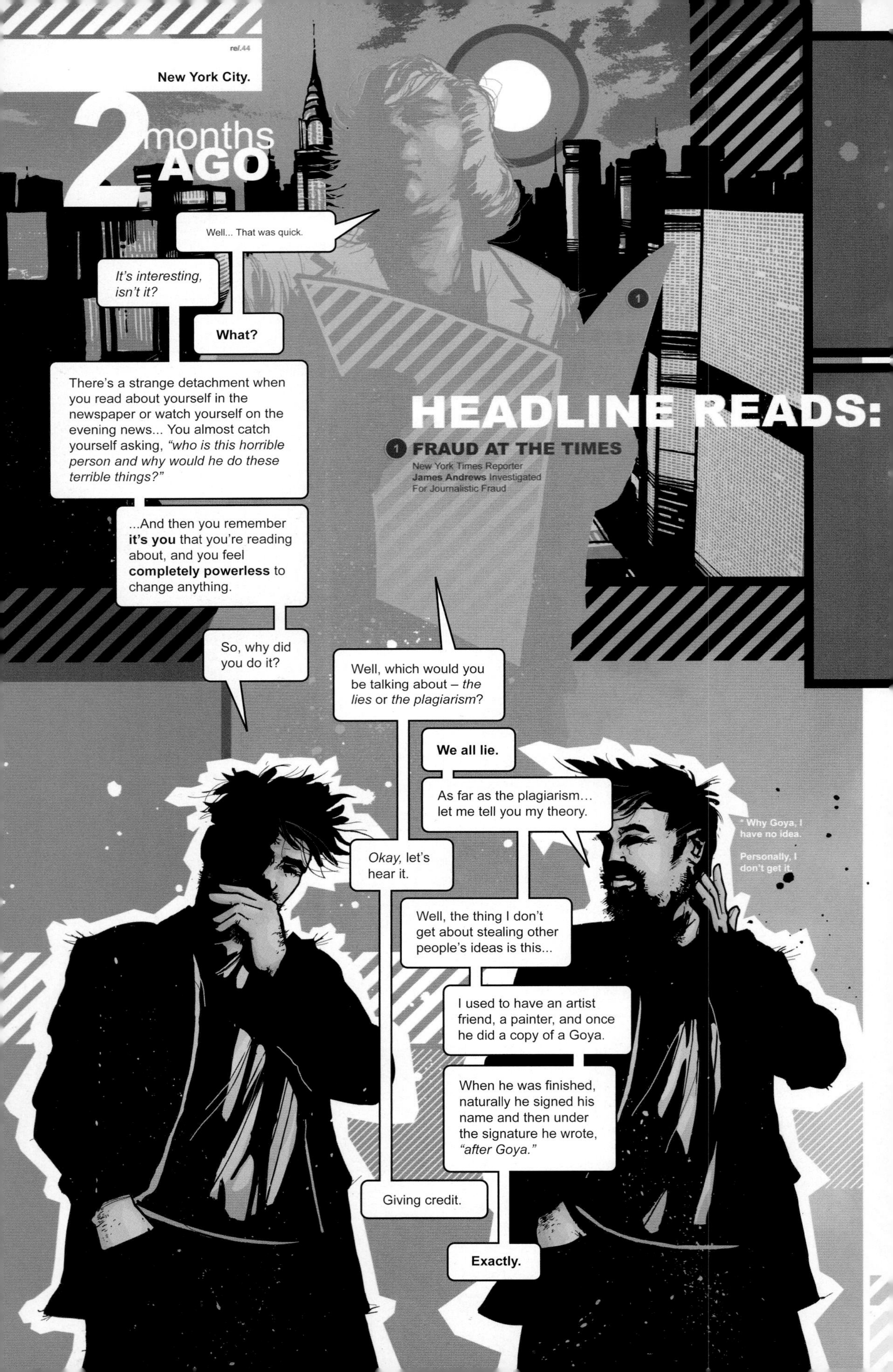
rel.44
New York City.
2 months AGO
Well... That was quick.
It's interesting, isn't it?
What?
There's a strange detachment when you read about yourself in the newspaper or watch yourself on the evening news... You almost catch yourself asking, *"who is this horrible person and why would he do these terrible things?"*
...And then you remember **it's you** that you're reading about, and you feel **completely powerless** to change anything.
HEADLINE READS:
1 FRAUD AT THE TIMES
New York Times Reporter **James Andrews** Investigated For Journalistic Fraud
So, why did you do it?
Well, which would you be talking about – *the lies* or *the plagiarism*?
We all lie.
As far as the plagiarism… let me tell you my theory.
Okay, let's hear it.
Well, the thing I don't get about stealing other people's ideas is this...
I used to have an artist friend, a painter, and once he did a copy of a Goya.
When he was finished, naturally he signed his name and then under the signature he wrote, *"after Goya."*
Giving credit.
Exactly.
* Why Goya, I have no idea.
Personally, I don't get it.

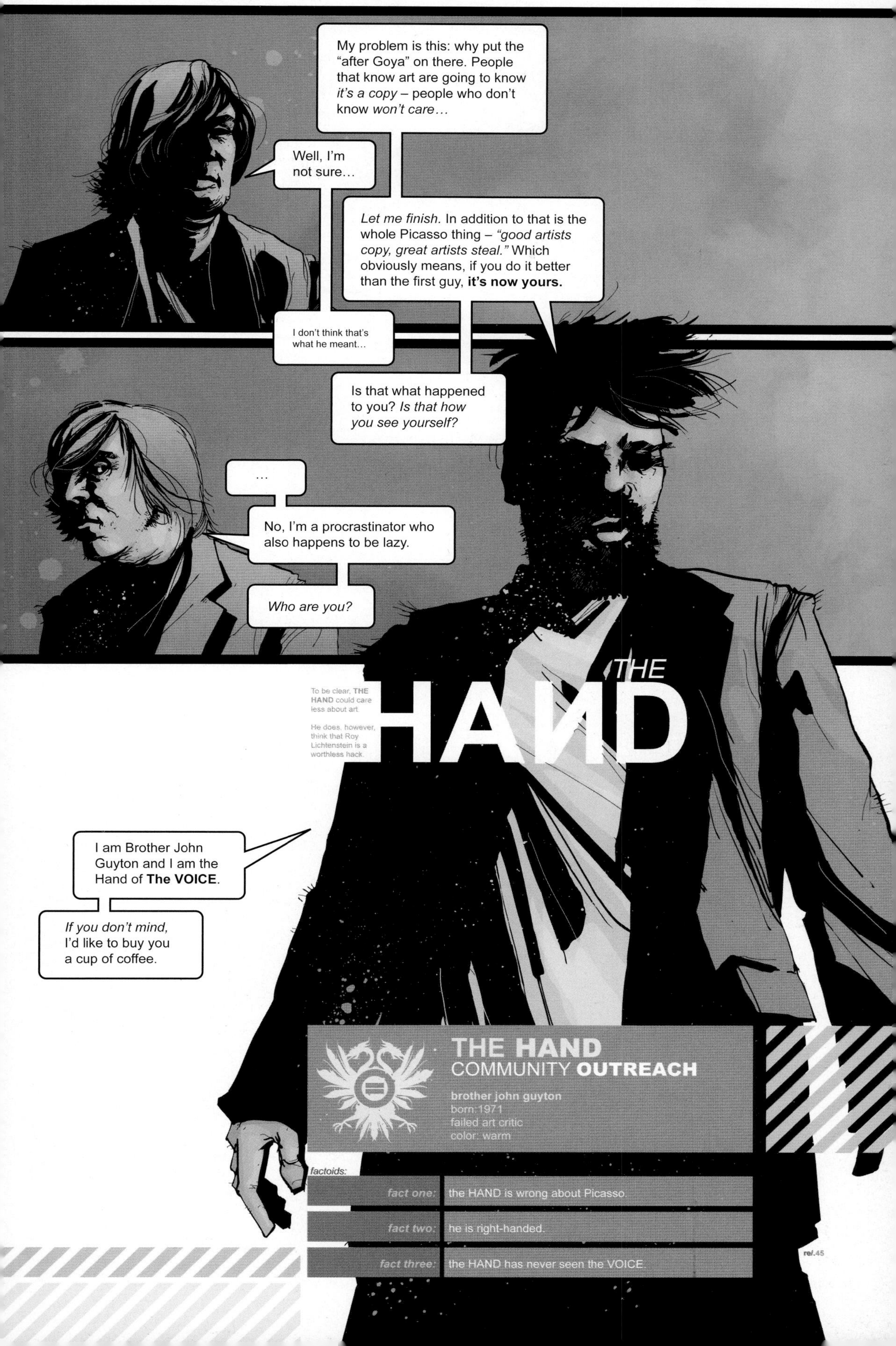
My problem is this: why put the "after Goya" on there. People that know art are going to know *it's a copy* – people who don't know *won't care…*
Well, I'm not sure…
Let me finish. In addition to that is the whole Picasso thing – *"good artists copy, great artists steal."* Which obviously means, if you do it better than the first guy, **it's now yours.**
I don't think that's what he meant…
Is that what happened to you? *Is that how you see yourself?*
…
No, I'm a procrastinator who also happens to be lazy.
Who are you?
THE HAND
To be clear, **THE HAND** could care less about art.
He does, however, think that Roy Lichtenstein is a worthless hack.
I am Brother John Guyton and I am the Hand of **The VOICE**.
If you don't mind, I'd like to buy you a cup of coffee.
THE HAND
COMMUNITY OUTREACH
brother john guyton
born: 1971
failed art critic
color: warm
factoids:
fact one: the HAND is wrong about Picasso.
fact two: he is right-handed.
fact three: the HAND has never seen the VOICE.

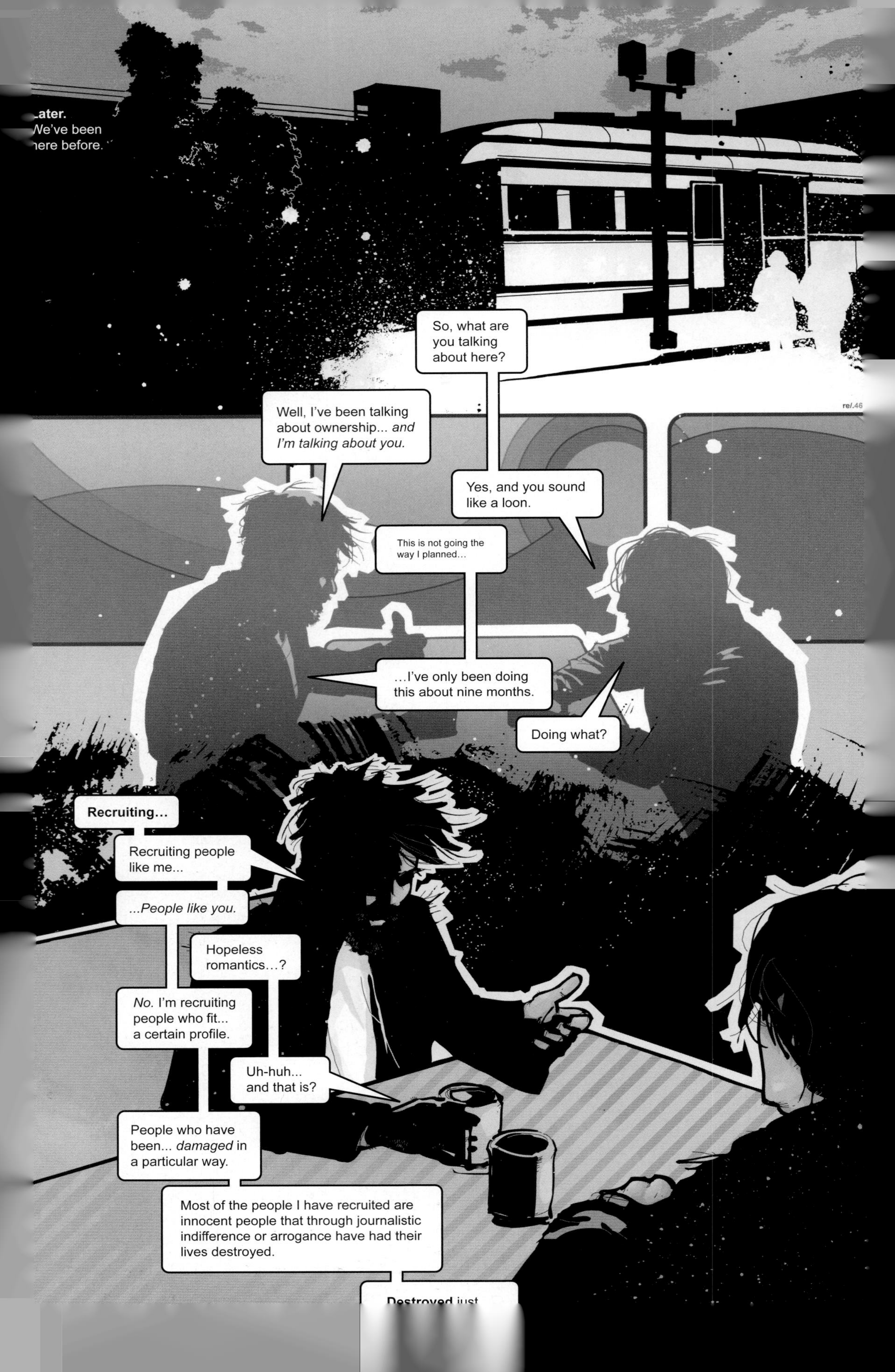
ater.
We've been
ere before.
re/.46
So, what are you talking about here?
Well, I've been talking about ownership... *and I'm talking about you.*
Yes, and you sound like a loon.
This is not going the way I planned…
…I've only been doing this about nine months.
Doing what?
Recruiting…
Recruiting people like me...
...People like you.
Hopeless romantics…?
No. I'm recruiting people who fit... a certain profile.
Uh-huh... and that is?
People who have been... *damaged* in a particular way.
Most of the people I have recruited are innocent people that through journalistic indifference or arrogance have had their lives destroyed.
Destroyed just

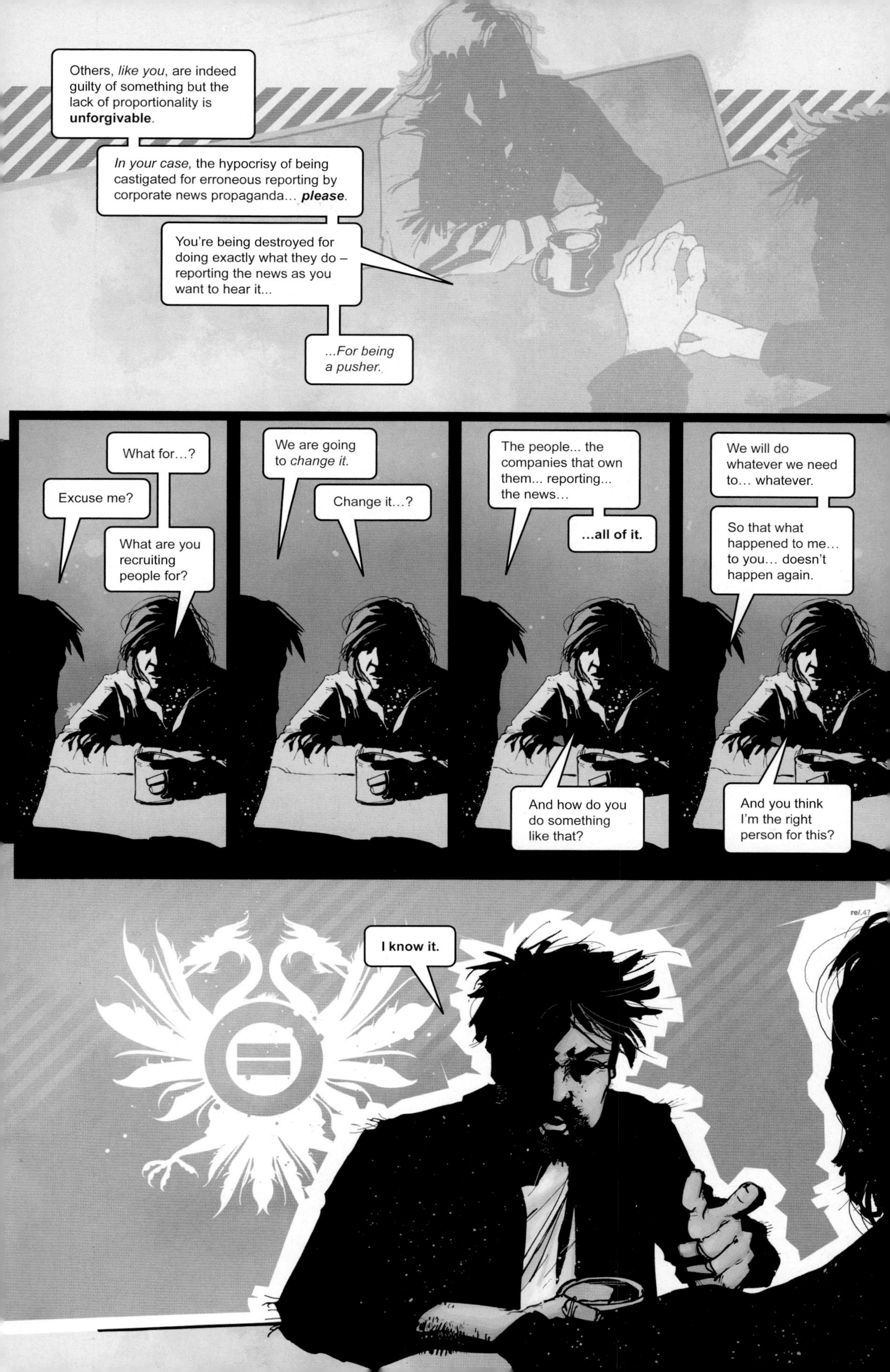
Others, *like you*, are indeed guilty of something but the lack of proportionality is **unforgivable**.
In your case, the hypocrisy of being castigated for erroneous reporting by corporate news propaganda... ***please***.
You're being destroyed for doing exactly what they do – reporting the news as you want to hear it...
...For being a pusher.
Excuse me?
What for...?
What are you recruiting people for?
We are going to *change it.*
Change it...?
The people... the companies that own them... reporting... the news...
...all of it.
And how do you do something like that?
We will do whatever we need to... whatever.
So that what happened to me... to you... doesn't happen again.
And you think I'm the right person for this?
rel.47
I know it.

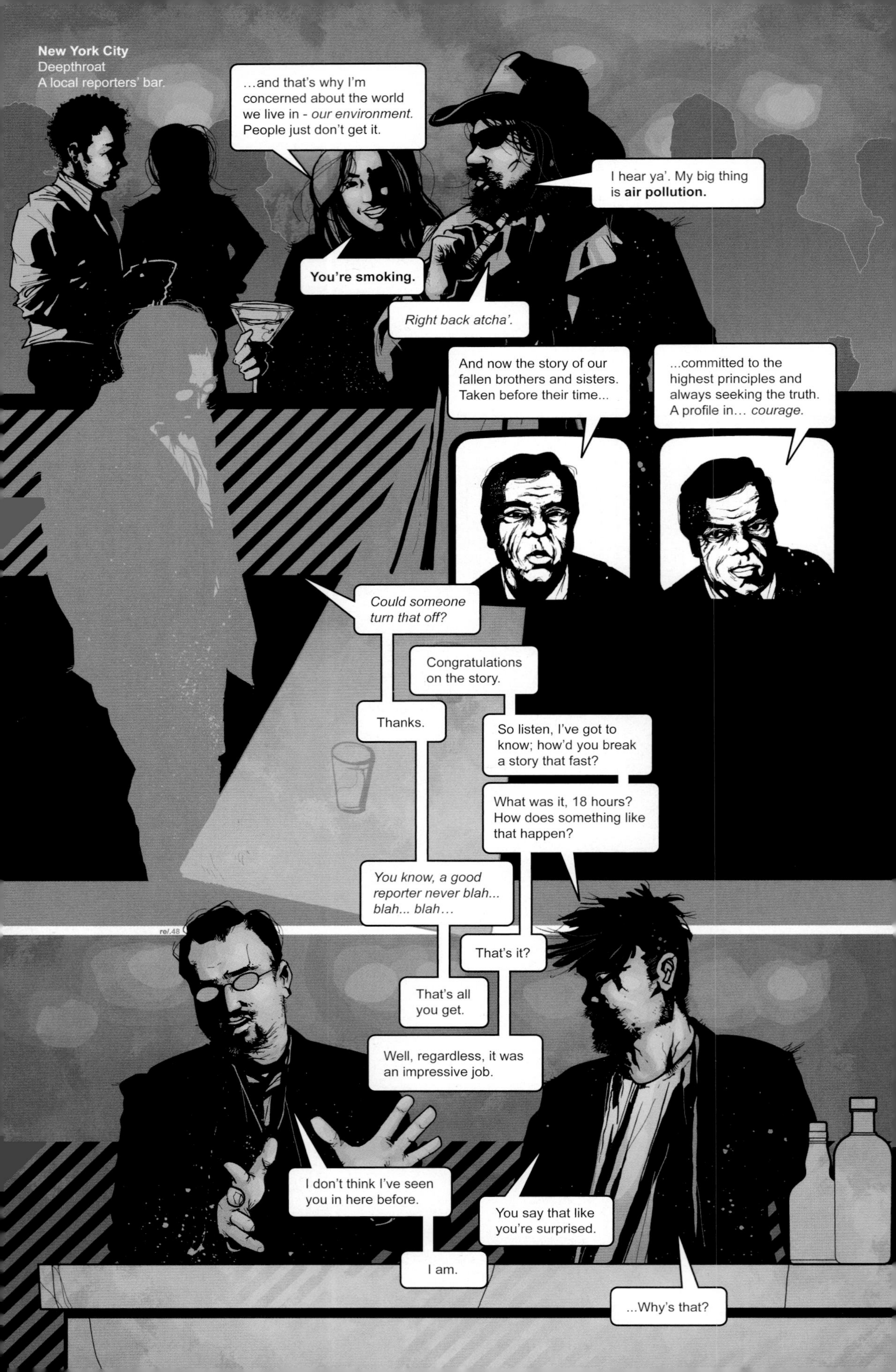
New York City
Deepthroat
A local reporters' bar.
...and that's why I'm concerned about the world we live in - *our environment.* People just don't get it.
I hear ya'. My big thing is **air pollution.**
You're smoking.
Right back atcha'.
And now the story of our fallen brothers and sisters. Taken before their time...
...committed to the highest principles and always seeking the truth. A profile in... *courage.*
Could someone turn that off?
Congratulations on the story.
Thanks.
So listen, I've got to know; how'd you break a story that fast?
What was it, 18 hours? How does something like that happen?
You know, a good reporter never blah... blah... blah...
That's it?
That's all you get.
Well, regardless, it was an impressive job.
I don't think I've seen you in here before.
You say that like you're surprised.
I am.
...Why's that?
re/.48

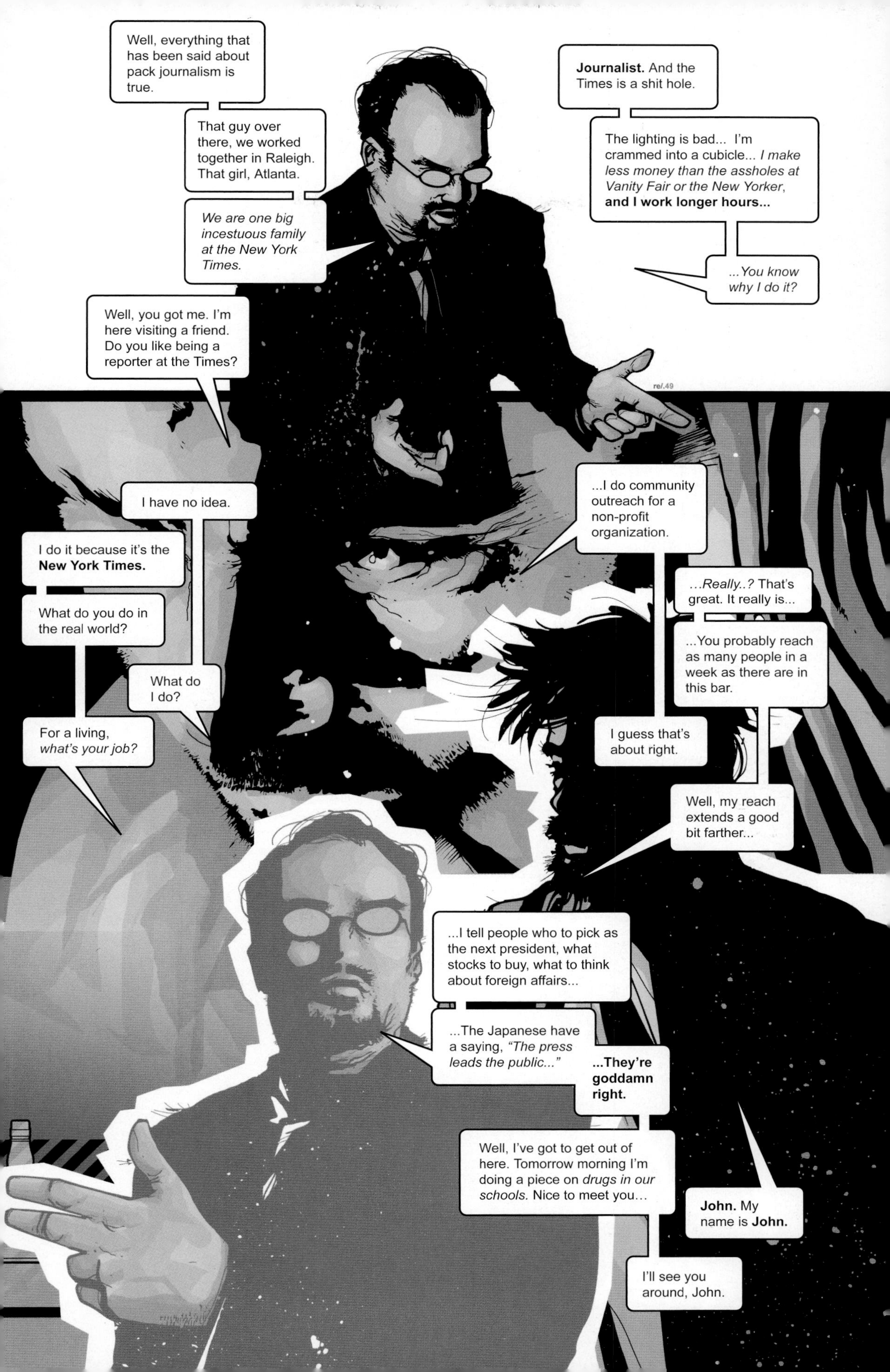

Well, everything that has been said about pack journalism is true.
That guy over there, we worked together in Raleigh. That girl, Atlanta.
We are one big incestuous family at the New York Times.
Well, you got me. I'm here visiting a friend. Do you like being a reporter at the Times?
Journalist. And the Times is a shit hole.
The lighting is bad... I'm crammed into a cubicle... *I make less money than the assholes at Vanity Fair or the New Yorker,* **and I work longer hours...**
...You know why I do it?
I have no idea.
I do it because it's the **New York Times.**
What do you do in the real world?
What do I do?
For a living, *what's your job?*
...I do community outreach for a non-profit organization.
...Really..? That's great. It really is...
...You probably reach as many people in a week as there are in this bar.
I guess that's about right.
Well, my reach extends a good bit farther...
...I tell people who to pick as the next president, what stocks to buy, what to think about foreign affairs...
...The Japanese have a saying, *"The press leads the public..."*
...They're goddamn right.
Well, I've got to get out of here. Tomorrow morning I'm doing a piece on *drugs in our schools.* Nice to meet you...
John. My name is **John.**
I'll see you around, John.

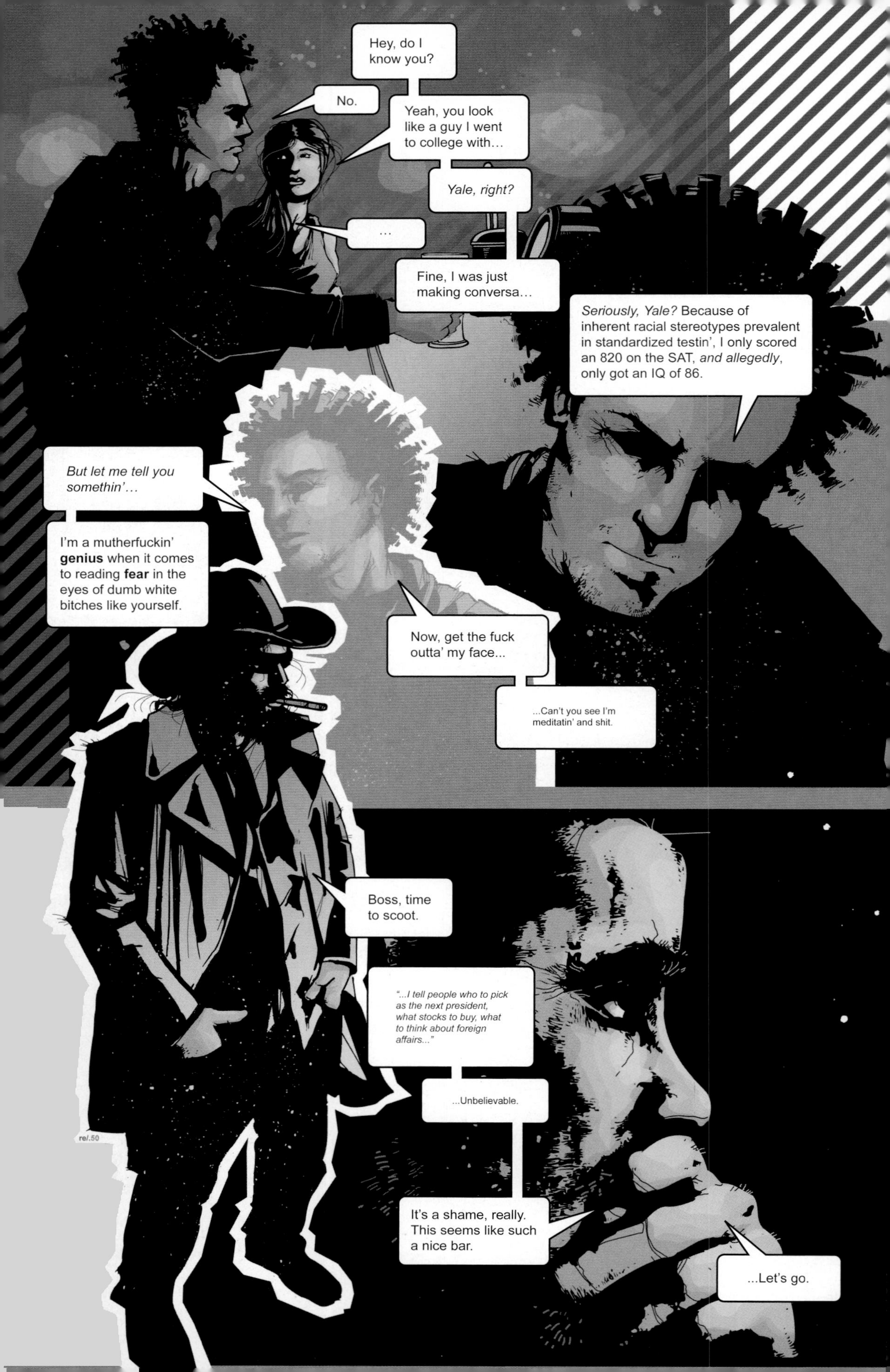
Hey, do I know you?
No.
Yeah, you look like a guy I went to college with…
Yale, right?
…
Fine, I was just making conversa…
Seriously, Yale? Because of inherent racial stereotypes prevalent in standardized testin', I only scored an 820 on the SAT, *and allegedly*, only got an IQ of 86.
But let me tell you somethin'…
I'm a mutherfuckin' **genius** when it comes to reading **fear** in the eyes of dumb white bitches like yourself.
Now, get the fuck outta' my face...
...Can't you see I'm meditatin' and shit.
Boss, time to scoot.
"...I tell people who to pick as the next president, what stocks to buy, what to think about foreign affairs..."
...Unbelievable.
It's a shame, really. This seems like such a nice bar.
...Let's go.

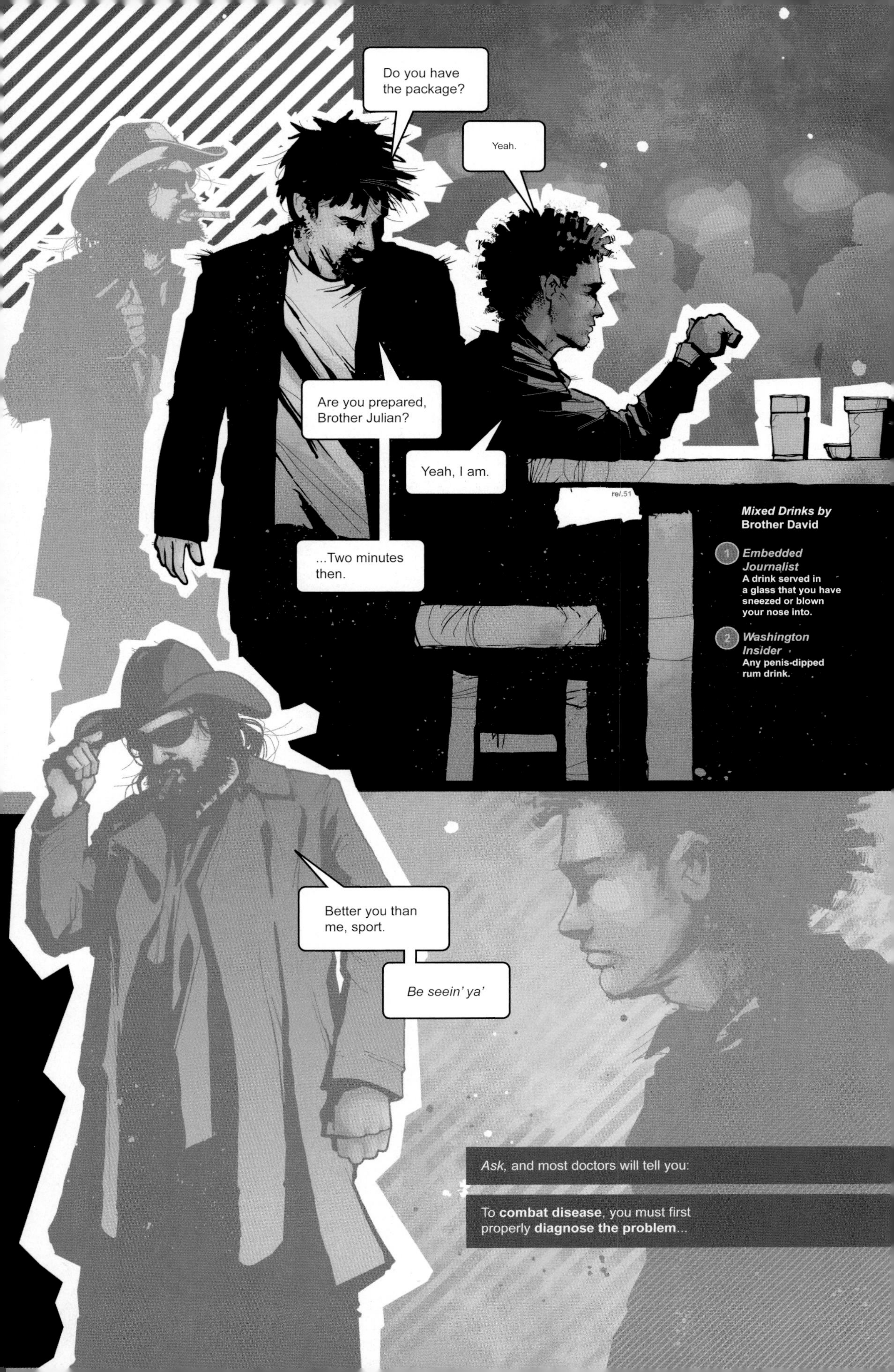
Do you have the package?
Yeah.
Are you prepared, Brother Julian?
Yeah, I am.
...Two minutes then.
rel.51
Mixed Drinks by Brother David
1 Embedded Journalist
A drink served in a glass that you have sneezed or blown your nose into.
2 Washington Insider
Any penis-dipped rum drink.
Better you than me, sport.
Be seein' ya'
Ask, and most doctors will tell you:
To combat disease, you must first properly diagnose the problem...

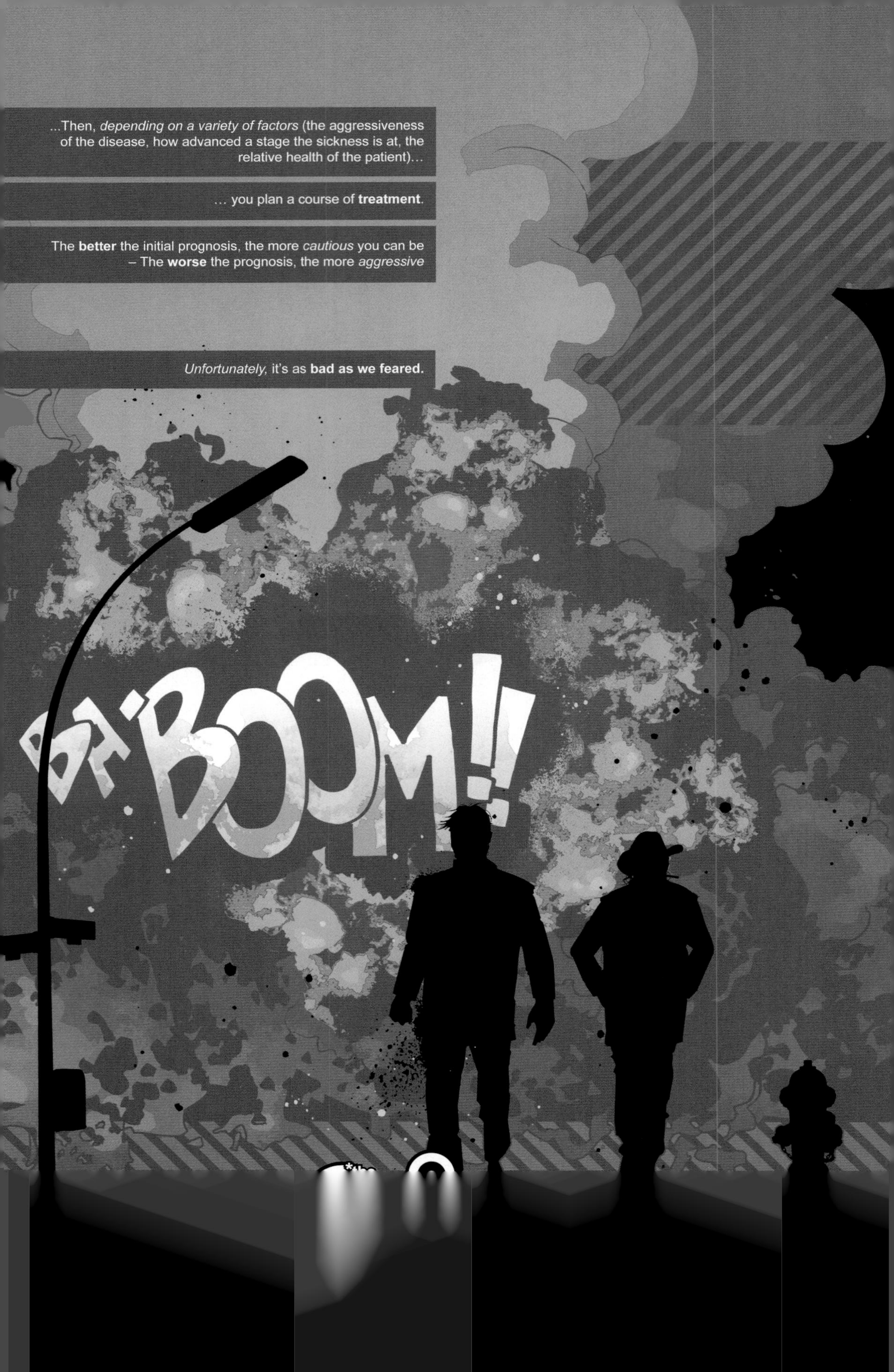
...Then, *depending on a variety of factors* (the aggressiveness of the disease, how advanced a stage the sickness is at, the relative health of the patient)...
... you plan a course of **treatment**.
The **better** the initial prognosis, the more *cautious* you can be – The **worse** the prognosis, the more *aggressive*
Unfortunately, it's as **bad as we feared.**
BA'BOOM!!

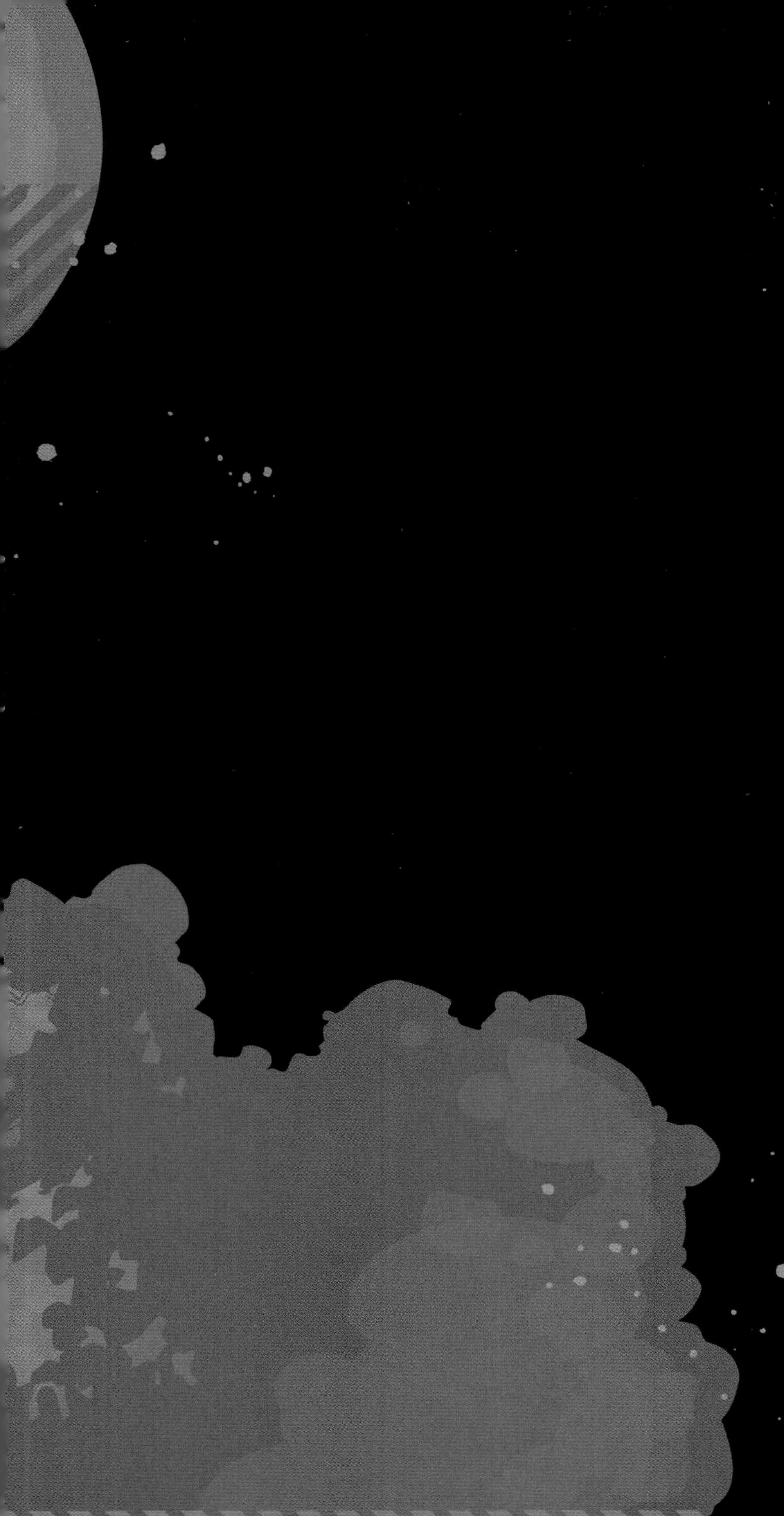

END_CHAPTER 02

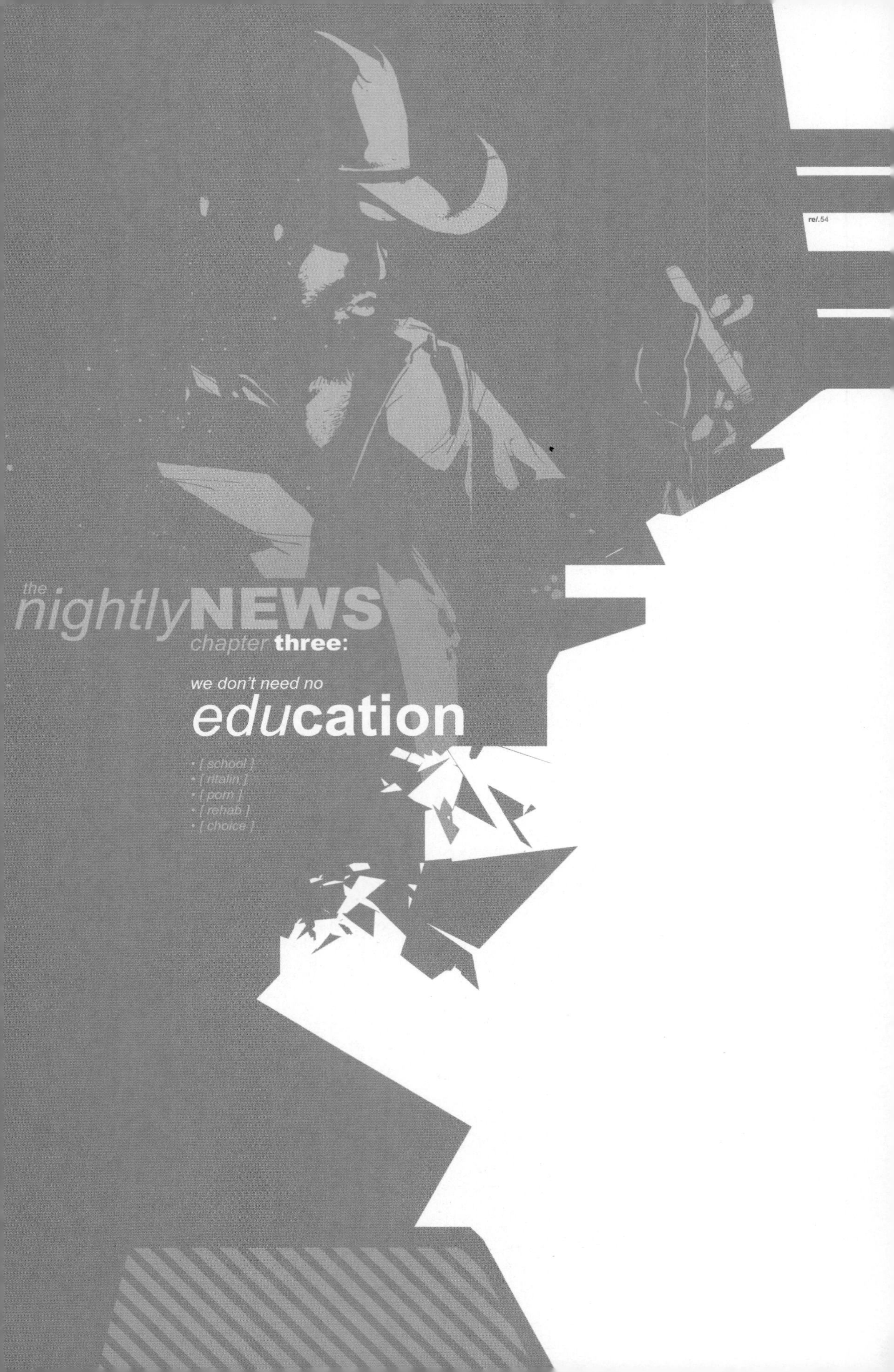

re/.54
the nightlyNEWS
chapter three:
we don't need no
education
• [school]
• [ritalin]
• [porn]
• [rehab]
• [choice]

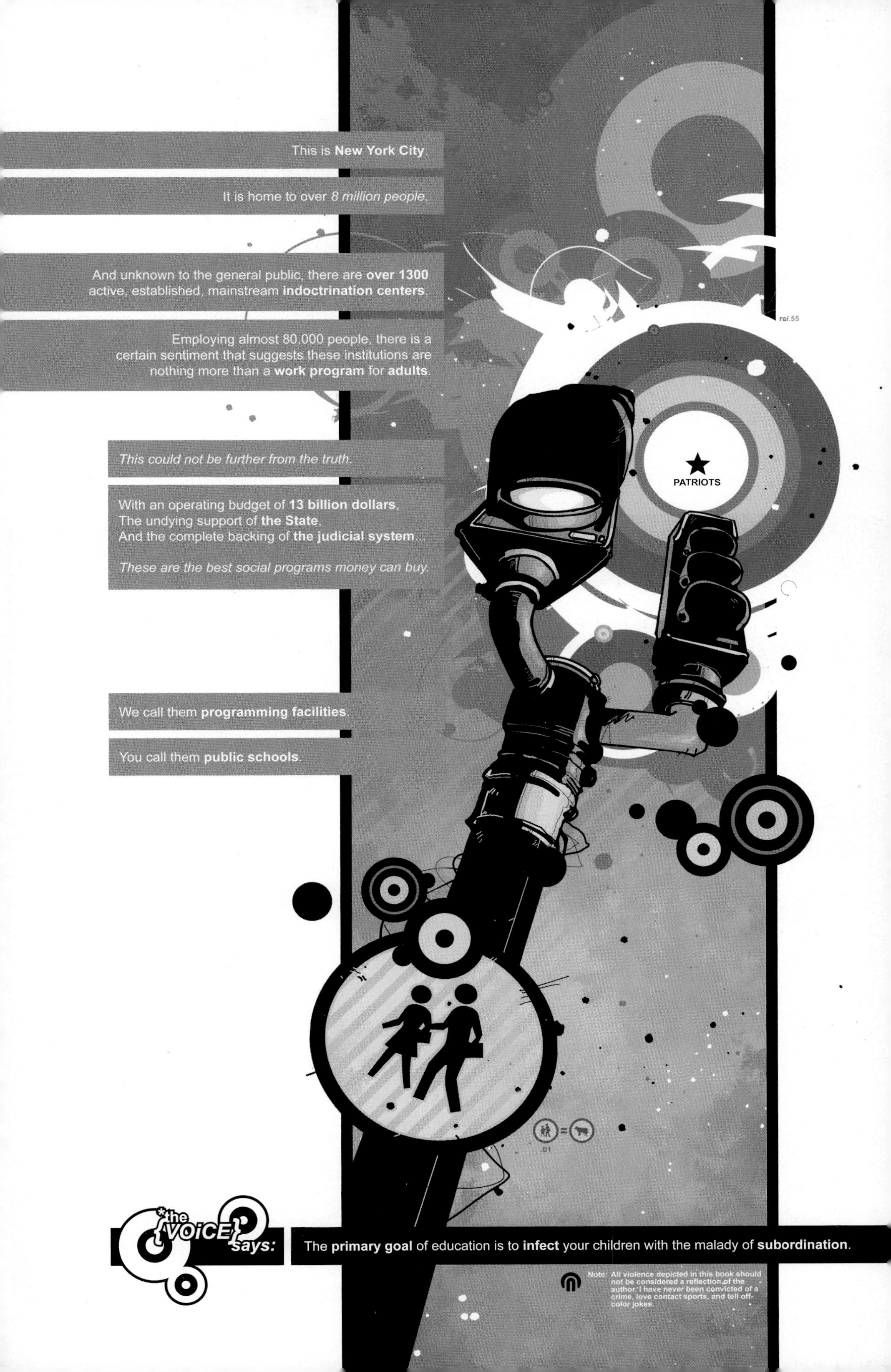
This is **New York City**.
It is home to over *8 million people*.
And unknown to the general public, there are **over 1300** active, established, mainstream **indoctrination centers**.
Employing almost 80,000 people, there is a certain sentiment that suggests these institutions are nothing more than a **work program** for **adults**.
This could not be further from the truth.
With an operating budget of **13 billion dollars**,
The undying support of **the State**,
And the complete backing of **the judicial system**...
These are the best social programs money can buy.
We call them **programming facilities**.
You call them **public schools**.
re/.55
PATRIOTS
.01
*the {VOiCE} says:
The **primary goal** of education is to **infect** your children with the malady of **subordination**.
Note: All violence depicted in this book should not be considered a reflection of the author. I have never been convicted of a crime, love contact sports, and tell off-color jokes.

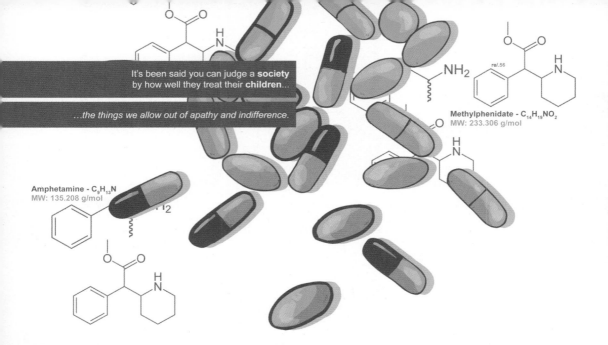

It's been said you can judge a **society** by how well they treat their **children**...

...the things we allow out of apathy and indifference.

Amphetamine - $C_9H_{13}N$
MW: 135.208 g/mol

Methylphenidate - $C_{14}H_{19}NO_2$
MW: 233.306 g/mol

To find out more about drugging your male children into submission, read below. However, if you're like me and only care about your own personal entertainment, keep reading on the next page!

*behavior modification: *ritalin**

DrugYourMale**Children:**

About:

- Every year almost 9 million prescriptions for Ritalin are written for children in the United States, most of these for boys between the ages of six and twelve.

- Boys are four times as likely as girls to receive a diagnosis of attention deficit hyperactivity disorder (ADHD), and the vast majority of learning-disabled students are boys.

Note: Reports on ADHD from both the NIH and the American Academy of Pediatrics have confirmed there is no known biological basis for ADHD.

How do six-year-olds have established behavioral problems?

Harmful**Effects:**

Harmful Effects of Ritalin*
*(Dexedrine, Aderall and Other Similar Drugs)

Depression, Mania, Psychosis, Hallucinations, Anxiety, Insomnia, Hostility, Aggression, Convulsions, Social Withdrawal, Mental Impairment, Confusion, Obsessive-compulsive behavior.

AreWe**Wrong:**

Ain't that America:

The United States uses approximately 90 percent of the world's Ritalin.

Sche**dule II:**

Classification:

The DEA and all other drug enforcement agencies worldwide classify Ritalin as a Schedule II drug. Other Schedule II drugs include: methamphetamine, cocaine and the most potent opiates and barbiturates.

Schedule II only includes those drugs with the highest potential for addiction and abuse.

NeverToo**Young:**

In the last 5 years, there has been a three-fold increase in the prescription of stimulants to 2 and 4-year-old children.

?

*Do you consider yourself to be a **Good Parent**?*

Brought to you by **Novartis:** The makers of **Ritalin.**

Novartis (NVS) Stock Price:

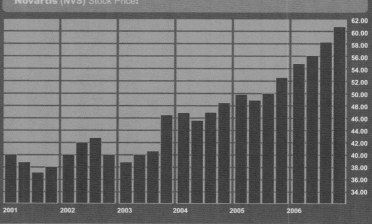

2001	2002	2003	2004	2005	2006

62.00
60.00
58.00
56.00
54.00
52.00
50.00
48.00
46.00
44.00
42.00
40.00
38.00
36.00
34.00

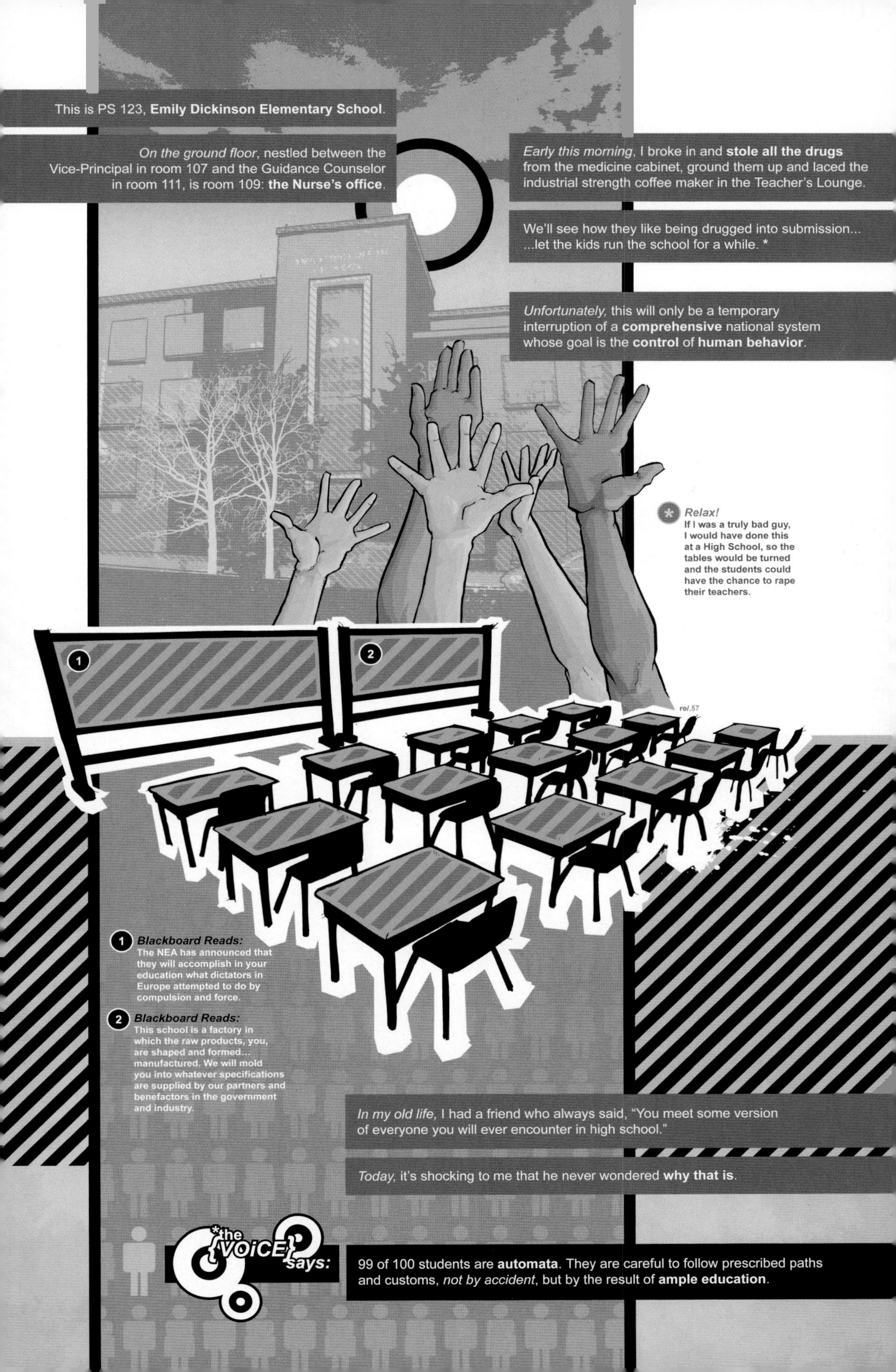

This is PS 123, **Emily Dickinson Elementary School**.
On the ground floor, nestled between the Vice-Principal in room 107 and the Guidance Counselor in room 111, is room 109: **the Nurse's office**.
Early this morning, I broke in and **stole all the drugs** from the medicine cabinet, ground them up and laced the industrial strength coffee maker in the Teacher's Lounge.
We'll see how they like being drugged into submission... ...let the kids run the school for a while. *
Unfortunately, this will only be a temporary interruption of a **comprehensive** national system whose goal is the **control** of **human behavior**.
* *Relax!* If I was a truly bad guy, I would have done this at a High School, so the tables would be turned and the students could have the chance to rape their teachers.
1 *Blackboard Reads:* The NEA has announced that they will accomplish in your education what dictators in Europe attempted to do by compulsion and force.
2 *Blackboard Reads:* This school is a factory in which the raw products, you, are shaped and formed... manufactured. We will mold you into whatever specifications are supplied by our partners and benefactors in the government and industry.
In my old life, I had a friend who always said, "You meet some version of everyone you will ever encounter in high school."
Today, it's shocking to me that he never wondered **why that is**.
*the {VOiCE} says:
99 of 100 students are **automata**. They are careful to follow prescribed paths and customs, *not by accident*, but by the result of **ample education**.

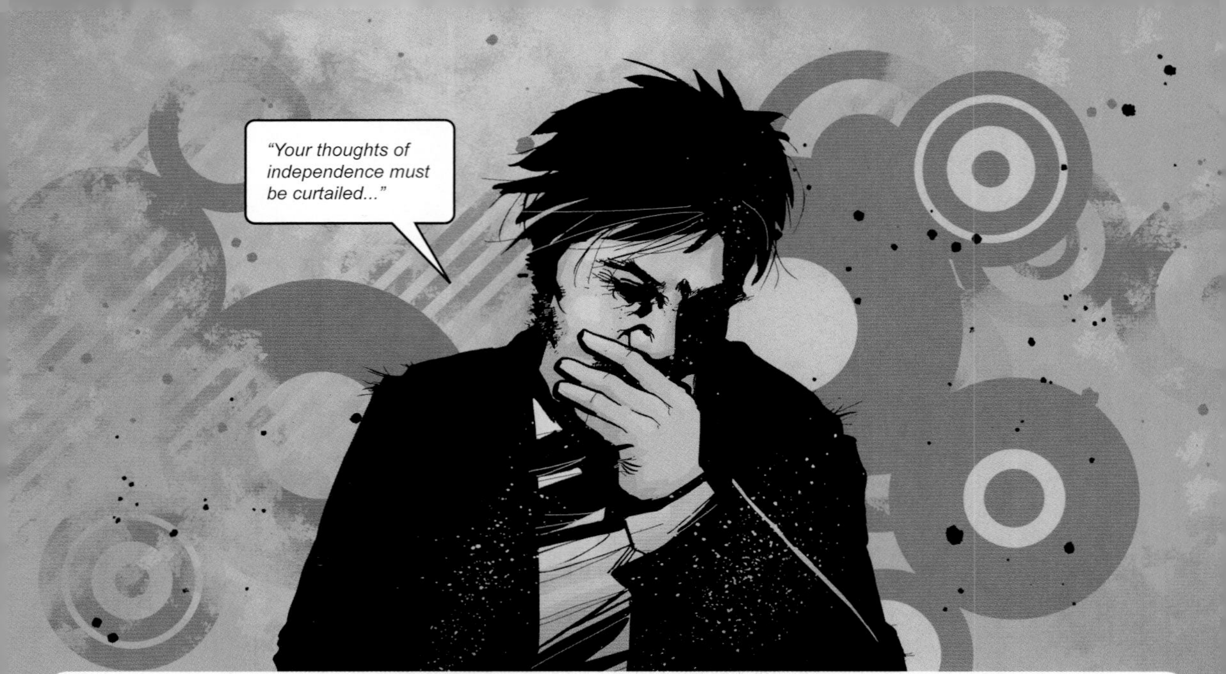
"Your thoughts of independence must be curtailed..."

WasYourEducation**WorthIt**?

$$\frac{DRE_{M} + 4(12 - N^{E})}{(S_{D} + J_{UH})^{2}} = E^{DU}$$

If E^{DU} is = 1 or greater, *then congratulations*, your education was worth it.

N^{E} = The number of years in your higher education

S_{D} = Your school debt on a scale of 1 to 10
(1 being one last payment and it's all paid off and 10 being I can't believe I owe $100,000 for my art degree)

J_{UH} = job unhappiness on a scale of 1 to 10
(1 being I wish I didn't have a family so I could dedicate all my time to my job and 10 being I hate waking up in the morning because I know work is waiting)

D = necessary diploma on a scale of 1 to 10
(1 being my political science degree has really helped me with my trash collecting and 10 being why won't they let me cut people open without a medical degree)

R = the number of lifetime relationships on a scale of 1 to 10
(1 being I was a science major with a cool chemistry set and 10 being I was in a sorority/fraternity)

E_{M} = environmental maturity on a scale of 1 to 10
(1 being your mom still helps pay the bills and 10 being you pay her bills)

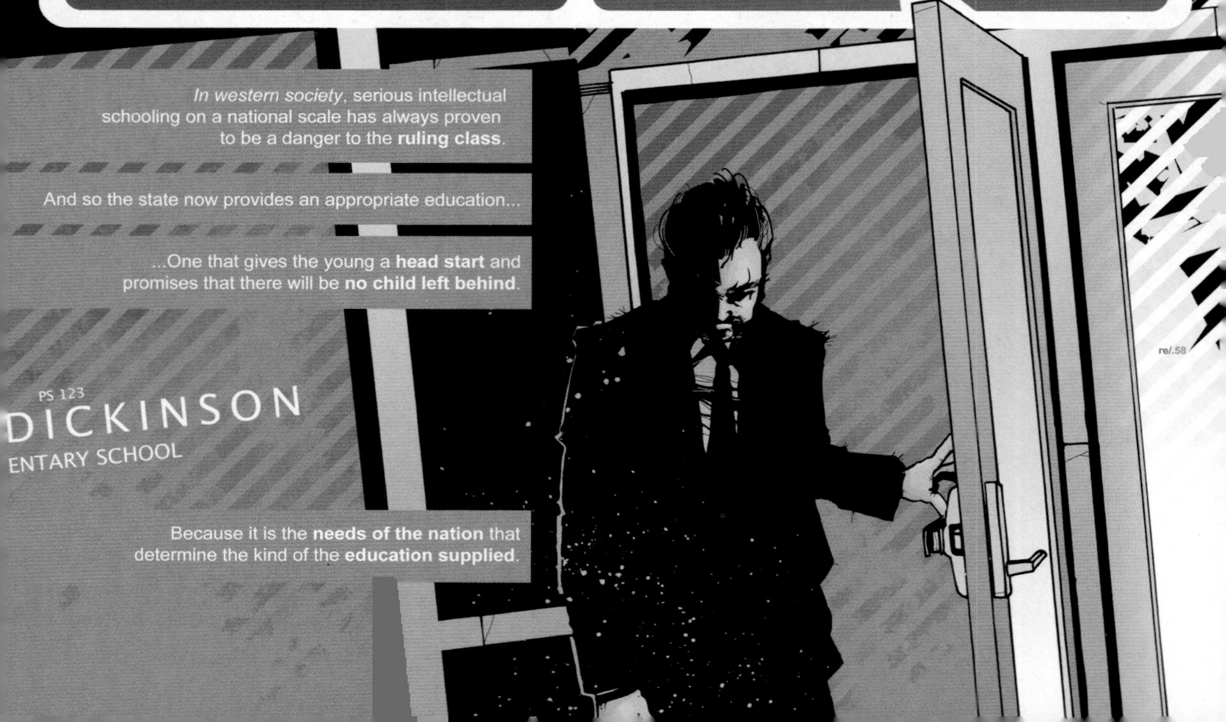
In western society, serious intellectual schooling on a national scale has always proven to be a danger to the **ruling class**.
And so the state now provides an appropriate education...
...One that gives the young a **head start** and promises that there will be **no child left behind**.
PS 123
DICKINSON
ENTARY SCHOOL
Because it is the **needs of the nation** that determine the kind of the **education supplied**.

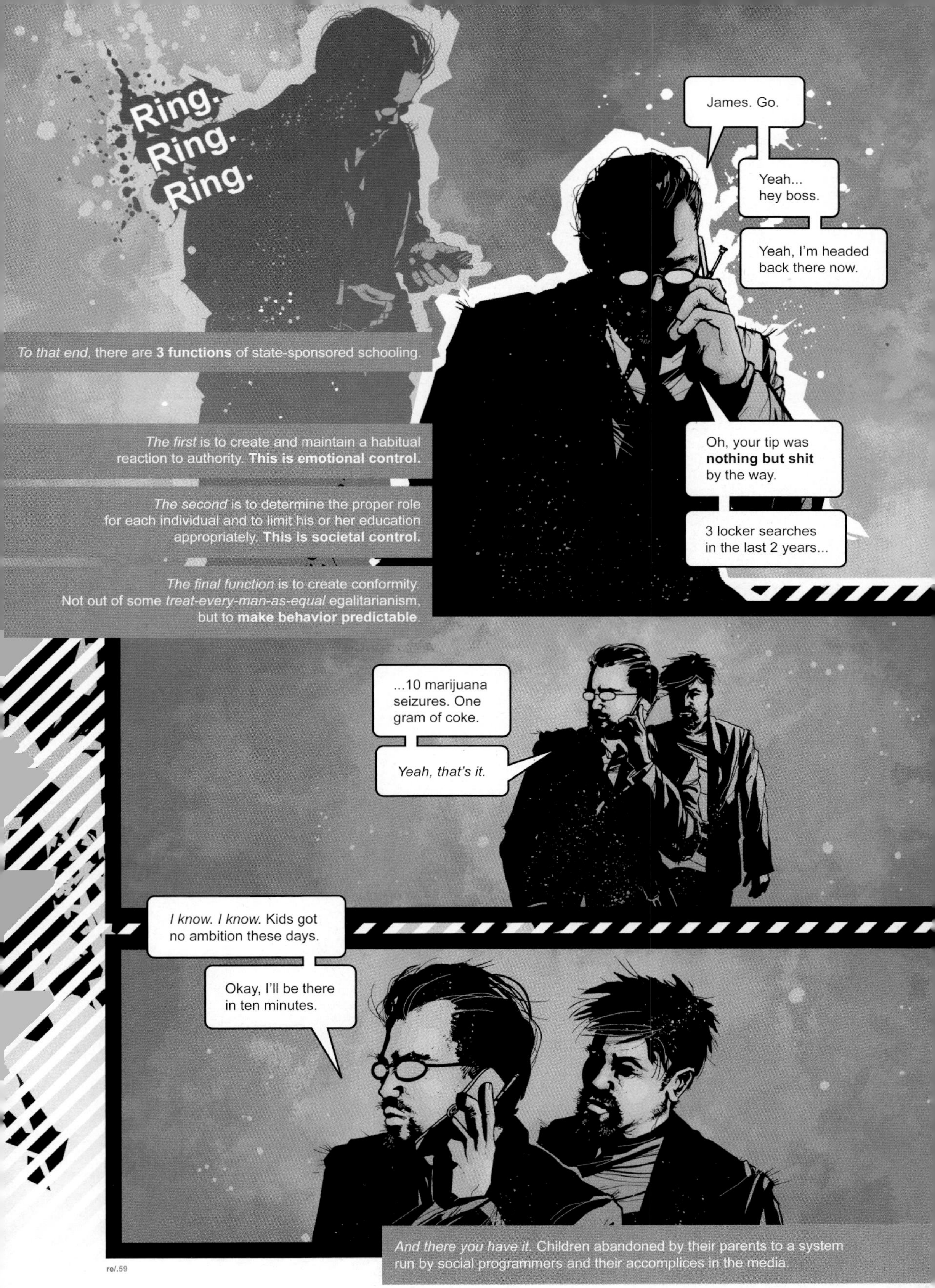
Ring.
Ring.
Ring.
James. Go.
Yeah... hey boss.
Yeah, I'm headed back there now.
To that end, there are **3 functions** of state-sponsored schooling.
The first is to create and maintain a habitual reaction to authority. **This is emotional control.**
The second is to determine the proper role for each individual and to limit his or her education appropriately. **This is societal control.**
The final function is to create conformity. Not out of some *treat-every-man-as-equal* egalitarianism, but to **make behavior predictable**.
Oh, your tip was **nothing but shit** by the way.
3 locker searches in the last 2 years...
...10 marijuana seizures. One gram of coke.
Yeah, that's it.
I know. I know. Kids got no ambition these days.
Okay, I'll be there in ten minutes.
And there you have it. Children abandoned by their parents to a system run by social programmers and their accomplices in the media.

the {VOiCE} says: The **only thing** you should ever learn from school is that **you don't belong**.

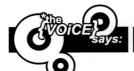

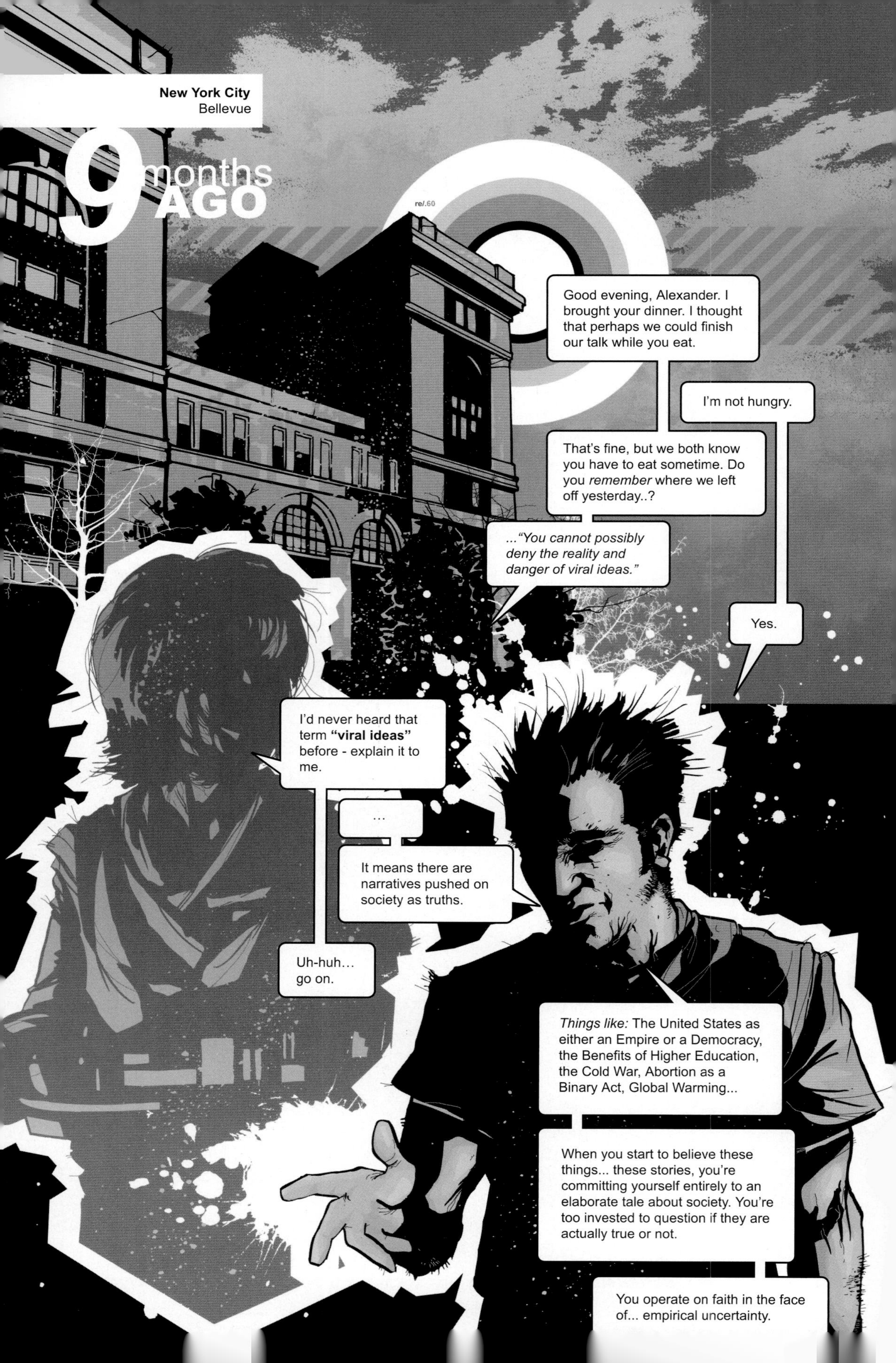

New York City
Bellevue
9 months AGO
re/.60
Good evening, Alexander. I brought your dinner. I thought that perhaps we could finish our talk while you eat.
I'm not hungry.
That's fine, but we both know you have to eat sometime. Do you *remember* where we left off yesterday..?
...*"You cannot possibly deny the reality and danger of viral ideas."*
Yes.
I'd never heard that term **"viral ideas"** before - explain it to me.
...
It means there are narratives pushed on society as truths.
Uh-huh... go on.
Things like: The United States as either an Empire or a Democracy, the Benefits of Higher Education, the Cold War, Abortion as a Binary Act, Global Warming...
When you start to believe these things... these stories, you're committing yourself entirely to an elaborate tale about society. You're too invested to question if they are actually true or not.
You operate on faith in the face of... empirical uncertainty.

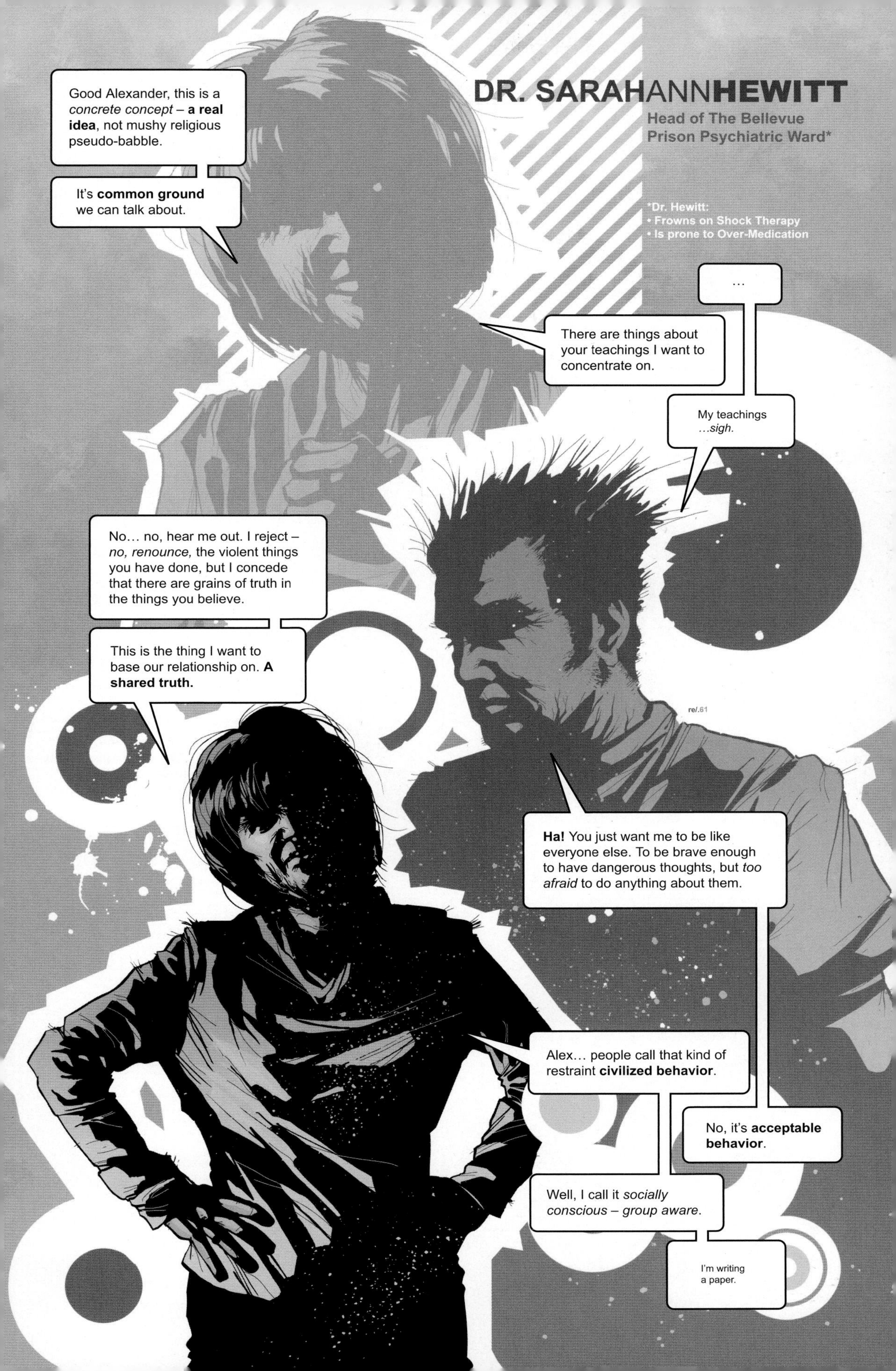
DR. SARAHANNHEWITT
Head of The Bellevue Prison Psychiatric Ward*
*Dr. Hewitt: • Frowns on Shock Therapy • Is prone to Over-Medication
Good Alexander, this is a *concrete concept* – **a real idea**, not mushy religious pseudo-babble.
It's **common ground** we can talk about.
There are things about your teachings I want to concentrate on.
…
My teachings *…sigh.*
No… no, hear me out. I reject – *no, renounce,* the violent things you have done, but I concede that there are grains of truth in the things you believe.
This is the thing I want to base our relationship on. **A shared truth.**
re/.61
Ha! You just want me to be like everyone else. To be brave enough to have dangerous thoughts, but *too afraid* to do anything about them.
Alex… people call that kind of restraint **civilized behavior**.
No, it's **acceptable behavior**.
Well, I call it *socially conscious – group aware*.
I'm writing a paper.

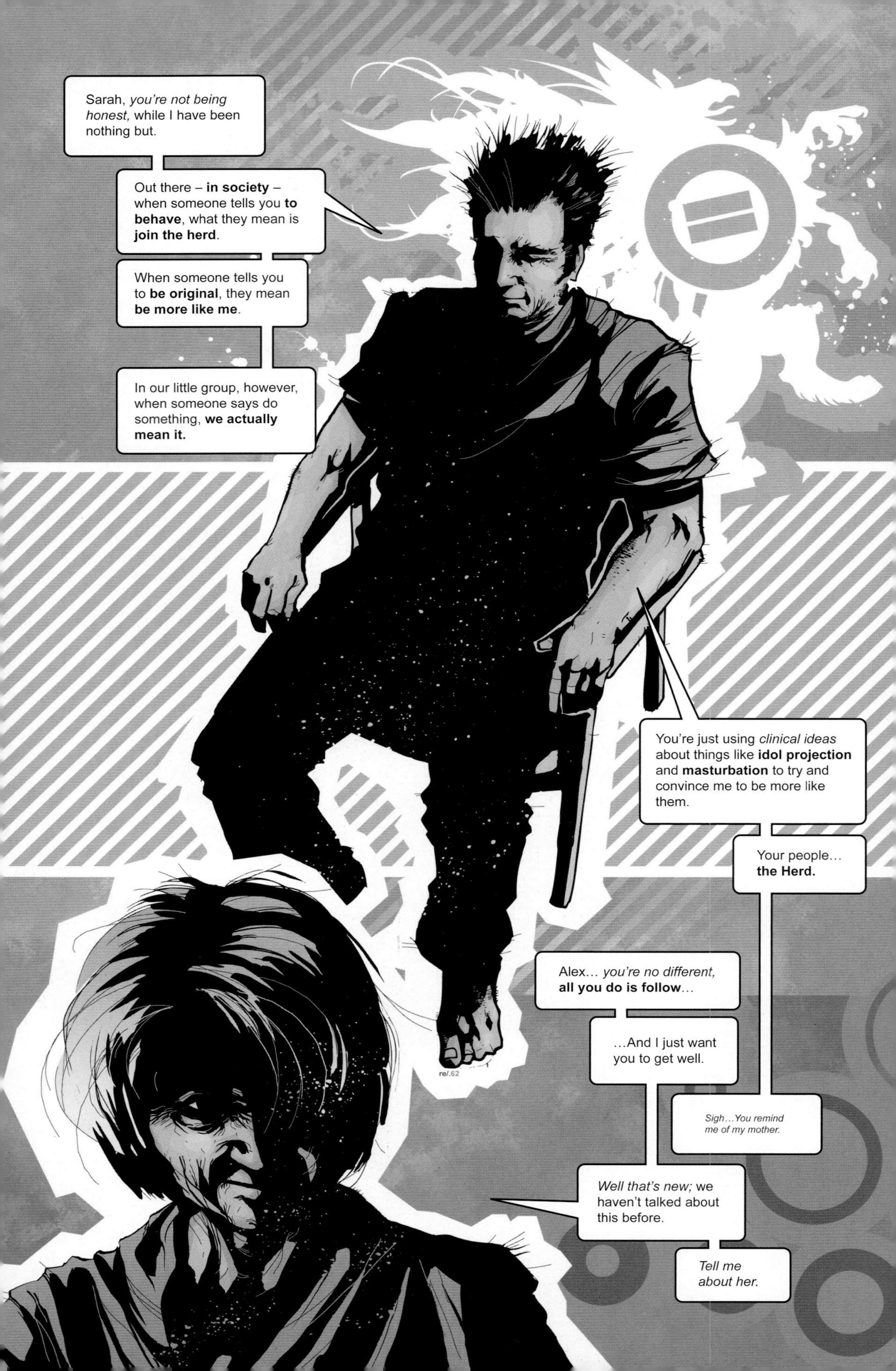

Sarah, *you're not being honest,* while I have been nothing but.
Out there – **in society** – when someone tells you **to behave**, what they mean is **join the herd**.
When someone tells you to **be original**, they mean **be more like me**.
In our little group, however, when someone says do something, **we actually mean it.**
You're just using *clinical ideas* about things like **idol projection** and **masturbation** to try and convince me to be more like them.
Your people… **the Herd.**
Alex… *you're no different,* **all you do is follow**…
…And I just want you to get well.
Sigh…You remind me of my mother.
Well that's new; we haven't talked about this before.
Tell me about her.
re/.62

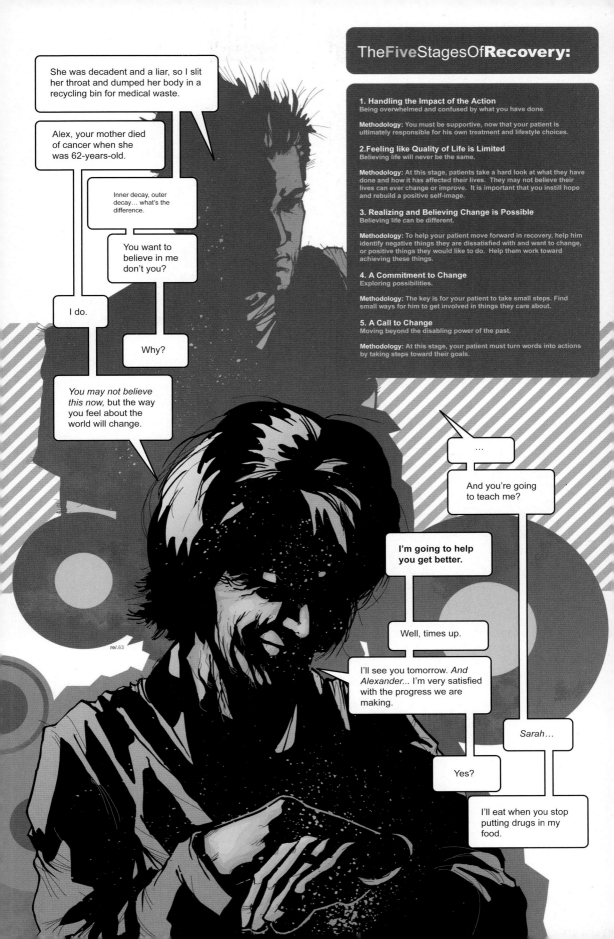

She was decadent and a liar, so I slit her throat and dumped her body in a recycling bin for medical waste.

Alex, your mother died of cancer when she was 62-years-old.

Inner decay, outer decay... what's the difference.

You want to believe in me don't you?

I do.

Why?

You may not believe this now, but the way you feel about the world will change.

The Five Stages Of Recovery:

1. Handling the Impact of the Action
Being overwhelmed and confused by what you have done.

Methodology: You must be supportive, now that your patient is ultimately responsible for his own treatment and lifestyle choices.

2. Feeling like Quality of Life is Limited
Believing life will never be the same.

Methodology: At this stage, patients take a hard look at what they have done and how it has affected their lives. They may not believe their lives can ever change or improve. It is important that you instill hope and rebuild a positive self-image.

3. Realizing and Believing Change is Possible
Believing life can be different.

Methodology: To help your patient move forward in recovery, help him identify negative things they are dissatisfied with and want to change, or positive things they would like to do. Help them work toward achieving these things.

4. A Commitment to Change
Exploring possibilities.

Methodology: The key is for your patient to take small steps. Find small ways for him to get involved in things they care about.

5. A Call to Change
Moving beyond the disabling power of the past.

Methodology: At this stage, your patient must turn words into actions by taking steps toward their goals.

...

And you're going to teach me?

I'm going to help you get better.

Well, times up.

I'll see you tomorrow. *And Alexander...* I'm very satisfied with the progress we are making.

Sarah...

Yes?

I'll eat when you stop putting drugs in my food.

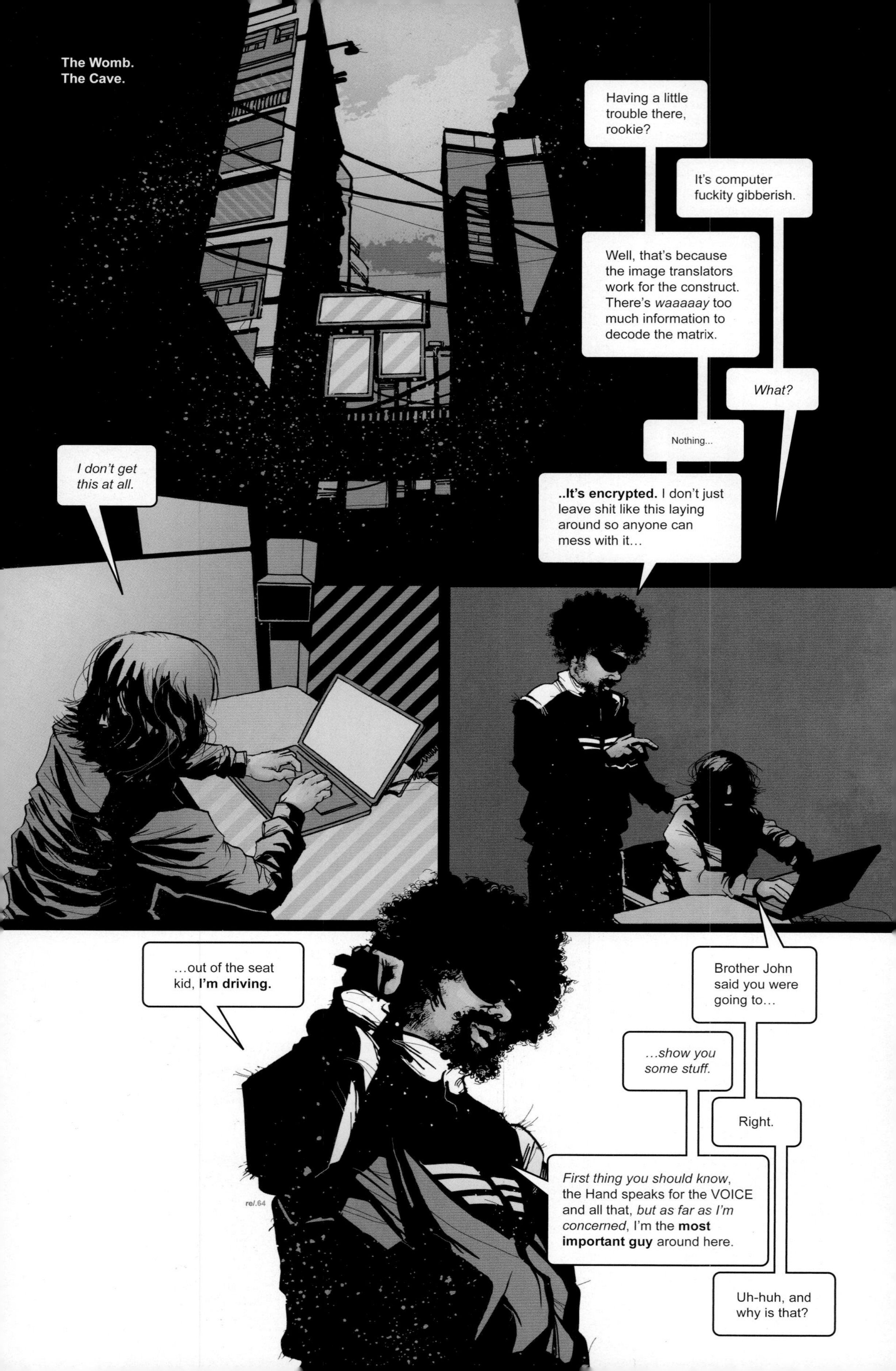

The Womb.
The Cave.
Having a little trouble there, rookie?
It's computer fuckity gibberish.
Well, that's because the image translators work for the construct. There's *waaaaay* too much information to decode the matrix.
What?
Nothing...
..It's encrypted. I don't just leave shit like this laying around so anyone can mess with it…
I don't get this at all.
…out of the seat kid, **I'm driving.**
Brother John said you were going to…
…show you some stuff.
Right.
First thing you should know, the Hand speaks for the VOICE and all that, *but as far as I'm concerned*, I'm the **most important guy** around here.
Uh-huh, and why is that?
re/.64

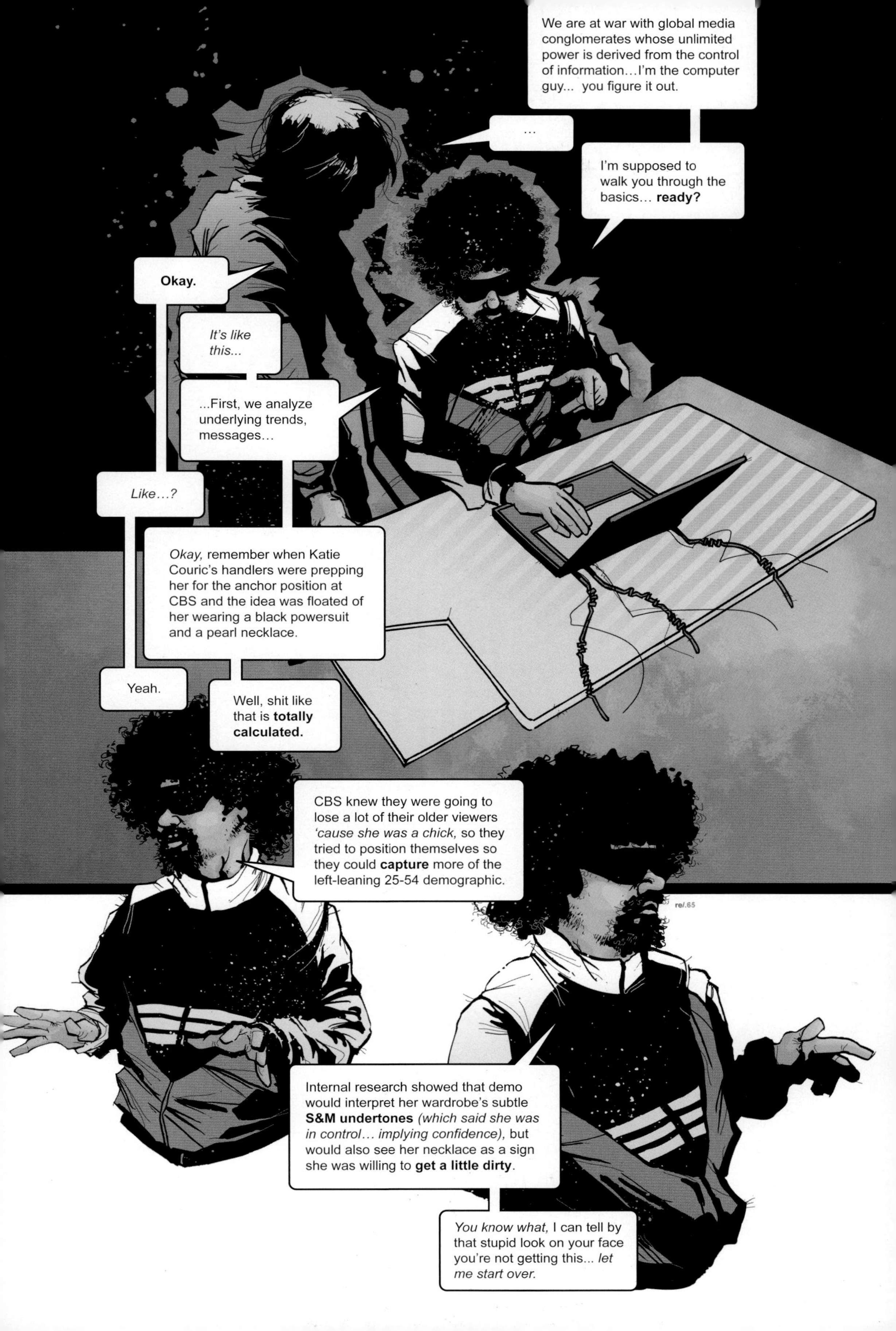
We are at war with global media conglomerates whose unlimited power is derived from the control of information…I'm the computer guy... you figure it out.
…
I'm supposed to walk you through the basics… **ready?**
Okay.
It's like this...
...First, we analyze underlying trends, messages…
Like…?
Okay, remember when Katie Couric's handlers were prepping her for the anchor position at CBS and the idea was floated of her wearing a black powersuit and a pearl necklace.
Yeah.
Well, shit like that is **totally calculated.**
CBS knew they were going to lose a lot of their older viewers *'cause she was a chick,* so they tried to position themselves so they could **capture** more of the left-leaning 25-54 demographic.
re/.65
Internal research showed that demo would interpret her wardrobe's subtle **S&M undertones** *(which said she was in control… implying confidence),* but would also see her necklace as a sign she was willing to **get a little dirty**.
You know what, I can tell by that stupid look on your face you're not getting this... *let me start over.*

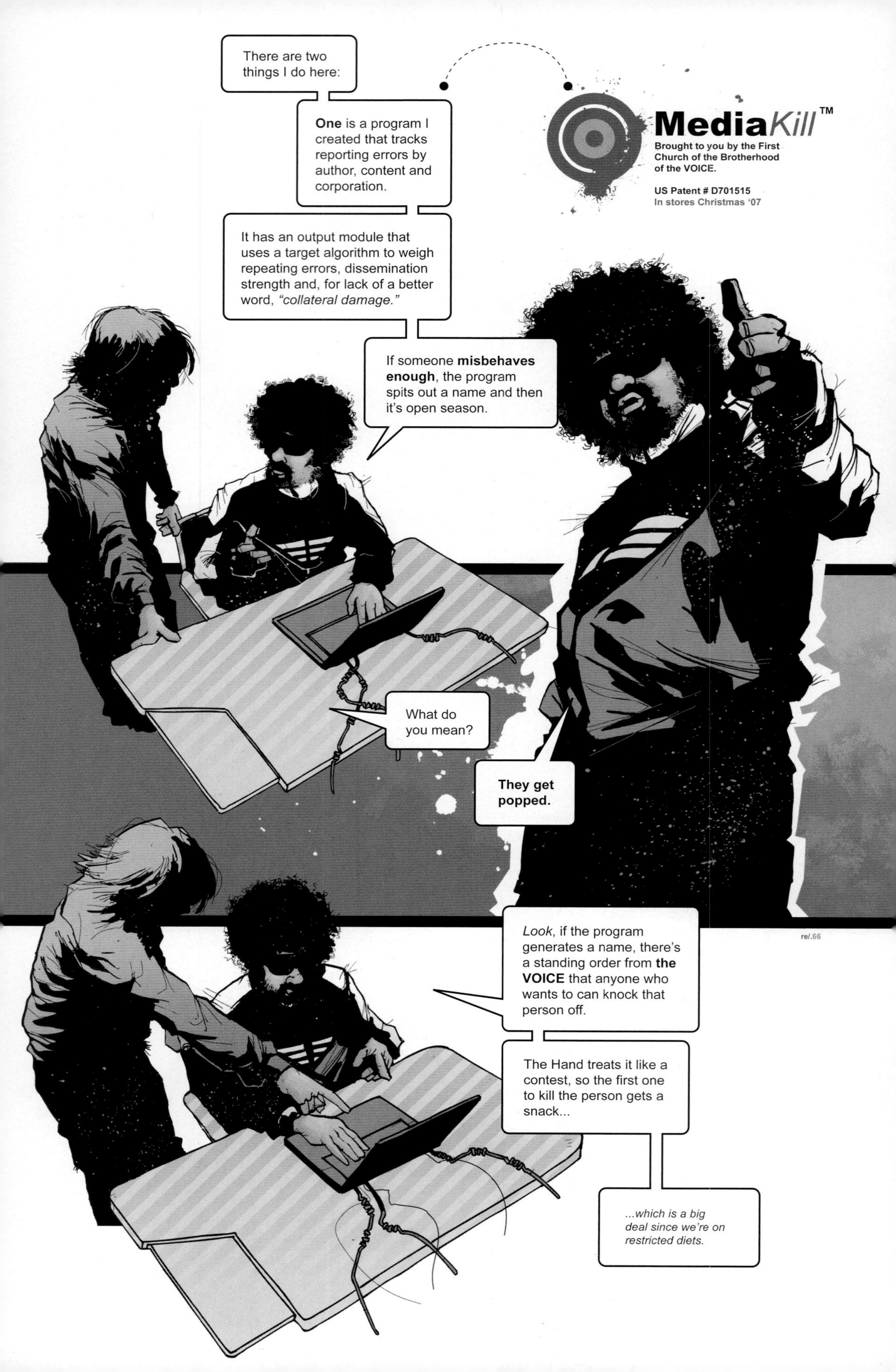
There are two things I do here:
One is a program I created that tracks reporting errors by author, content and corporation.
It has an output module that uses a target algorithm to weigh repeating errors, dissemination strength and, for lack of a better word, *"collateral damage."*
MediaKill™
Brought to you by the First Church of the Brotherhood of the VOICE.
US Patent # D701515
In stores Christmas '07
If someone **misbehaves enough**, the program spits out a name and then it's open season.
What do you mean?
They get popped.
Look, if the program generates a name, there's a standing order from **the VOICE** that anyone who wants to can knock that person off.
The Hand treats it like a contest, so the first one to kill the person gets a snack...
...which is a big deal since we're on restricted diets.
re/.66

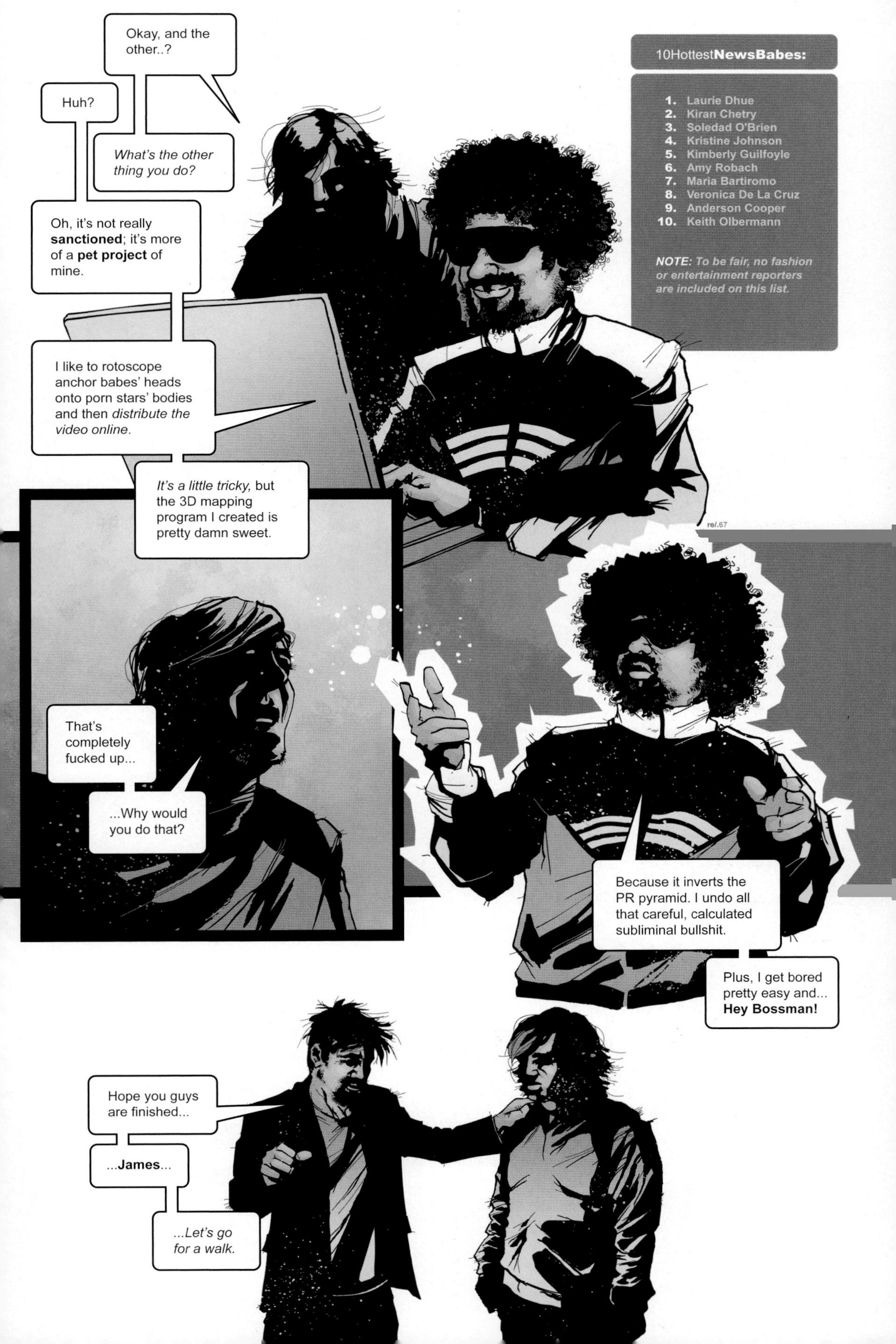
Okay, and the other..?
Huh?
What's the other thing you do?
Oh, it's not really sanctioned; it's more of a pet project of mine.
10HottestNewsBabes:
1. Laurie Dhue
2. Kiran Chetry
3. Soledad O'Brien
4. Kristine Johnson
5. Kimberly Guilfoyle
6. Amy Robach
7. Maria Bartiromo
8. Veronica De La Cruz
9. Anderson Cooper
10. Keith Olbermann
NOTE: To be fair, no fashion or entertainment reporters are included on this list.
I like to rotoscope anchor babes' heads onto porn stars' bodies and then distribute the video online.
It's a little tricky, but the 3D mapping program I created is pretty damn sweet.
re/.67
That's completely fucked up...
...Why would you do that?
Because it inverts the PR pyramid. I undo all that careful, calculated subliminal bullshit.
Plus, I get bored pretty easy and... Hey Bossman!
Hope you guys are finished...
...James...
...Let's go for a walk.

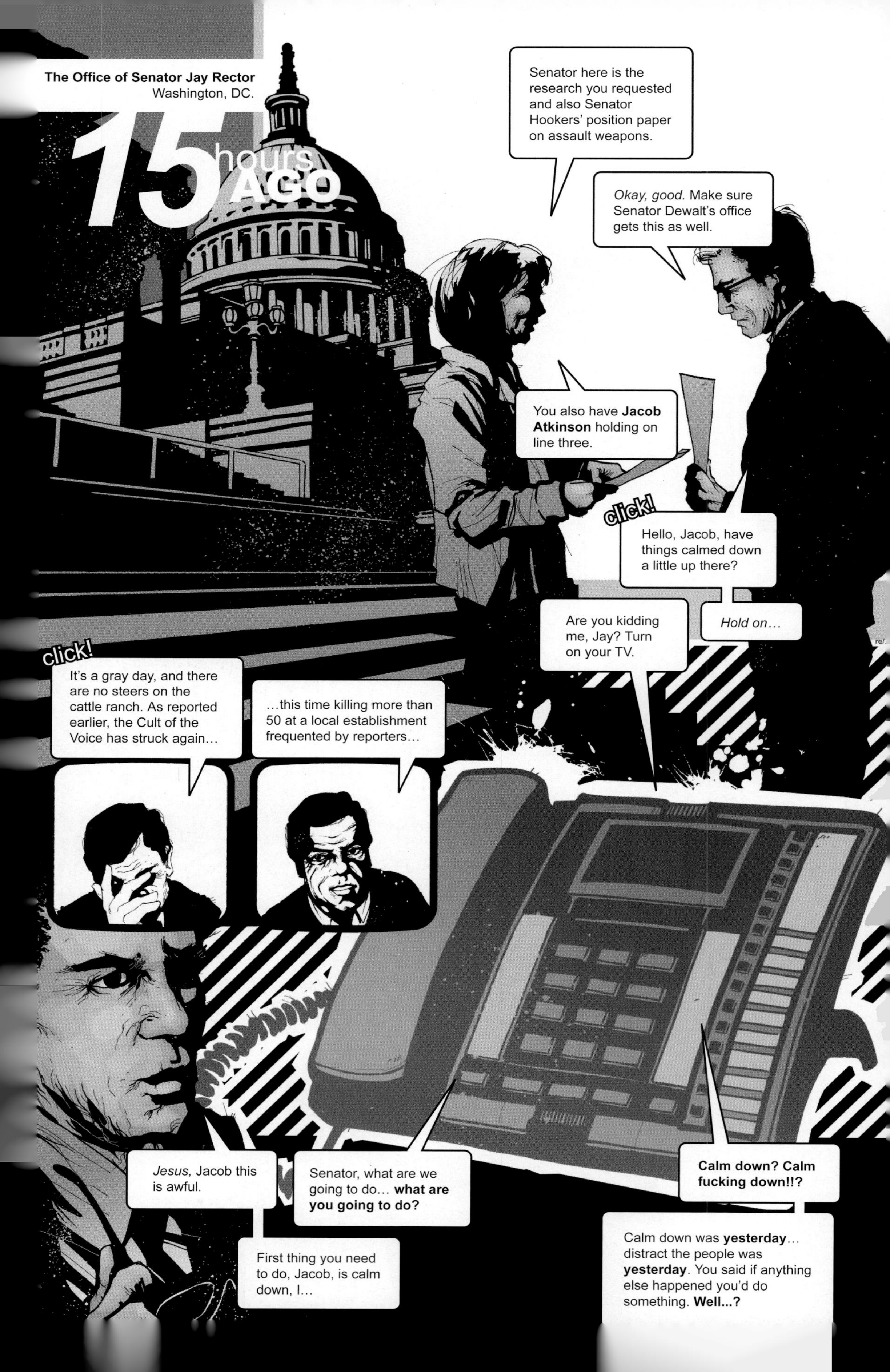
The Office of Senator Jay Rector
Washington, DC.
15 hours AGO
Senator here is the research you requested and also Senator Hookers' position paper on assault weapons.
Okay, good. Make sure Senator Dewalt's office gets this as well.
You also have Jacob Atkinson holding on line three.
click!
Hello, Jacob, have things calmed down a little up there?
Are you kidding me, Jay? Turn on your TV.
Hold on…
click!
It's a gray day, and there are no steers on the cattle ranch. As reported earlier, the Cult of the Voice has struck again…
…this time killing more than 50 at a local establishment frequented by reporters…
Jesus, Jacob this is awful.
Senator, what are we going to do… what are you going to do?
First thing you need to do, Jacob, is calm down, I…
Calm down? Calm fucking down!!?
Calm down was yesterday… distract the people was yesterday. You said if anything else happened you'd do something. Well...?

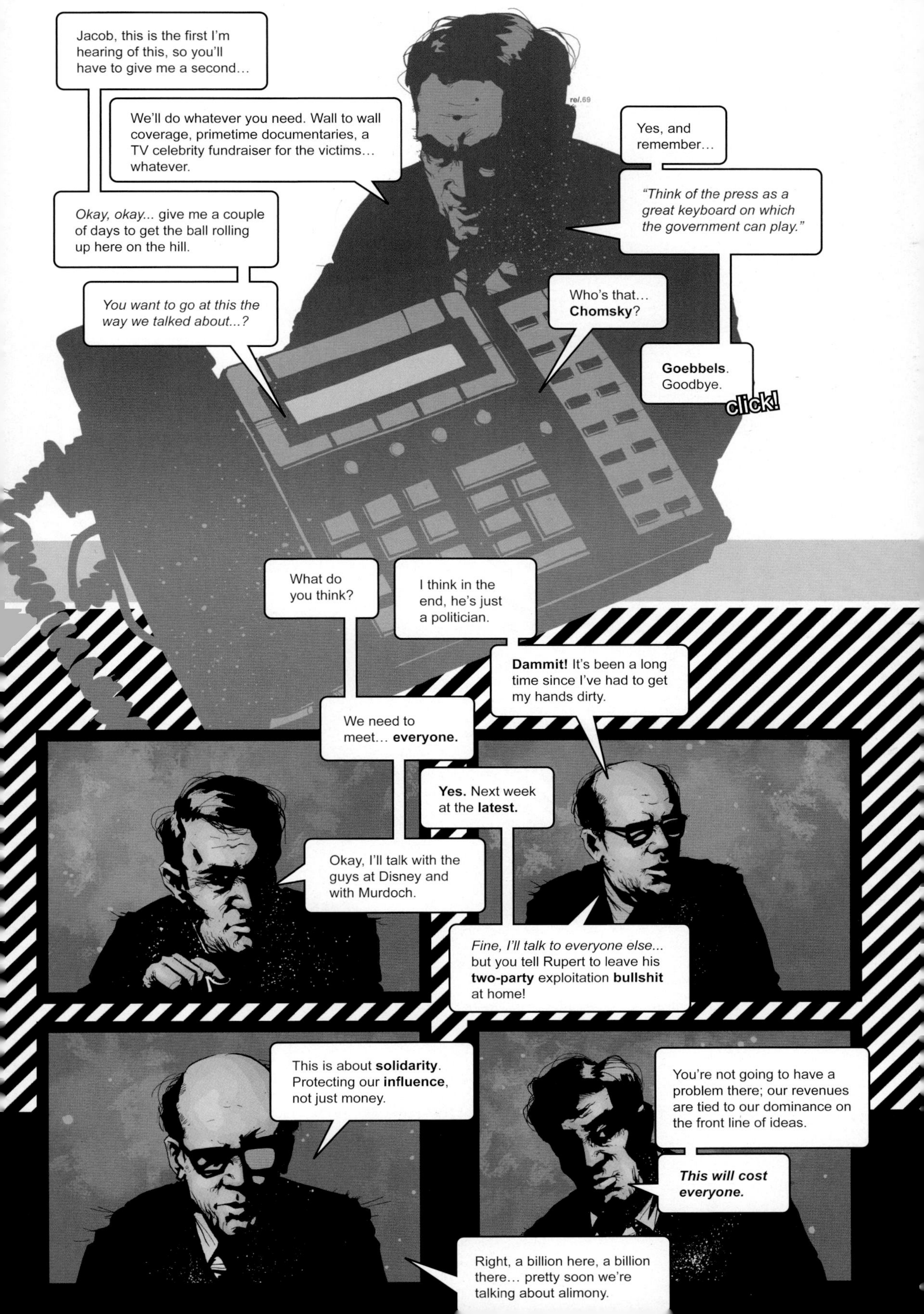
re/.69
Jacob, this is the first I'm hearing of this, so you'll have to give me a second…
We'll do whatever you need. Wall to wall coverage, primetime documentaries, a TV celebrity fundraiser for the victims… whatever.
Okay, okay... give me a couple of days to get the ball rolling up here on the hill.
You want to go at this the way we talked about...?
Yes, and remember…
"Think of the press as a great keyboard on which the government can play."
Who's that… Chomsky?
Goebbels. Goodbye.
click!
What do you think?
I think in the end, he's just a politician.
Dammit! It's been a long time since I've had to get my hands dirty.
We need to meet… everyone.
Yes. Next week at the latest.
Okay, I'll talk with the guys at Disney and with Murdoch.
Fine, I'll talk to everyone else... but you tell Rupert to leave his two-party exploitation bullshit at home!
This is about solidarity. Protecting our influence, not just money.
You're not going to have a problem there; our revenues are tied to our dominance on the front line of ideas.
This will cost everyone.
Right, a billion here, a billion there… pretty soon we're talking about alimony.

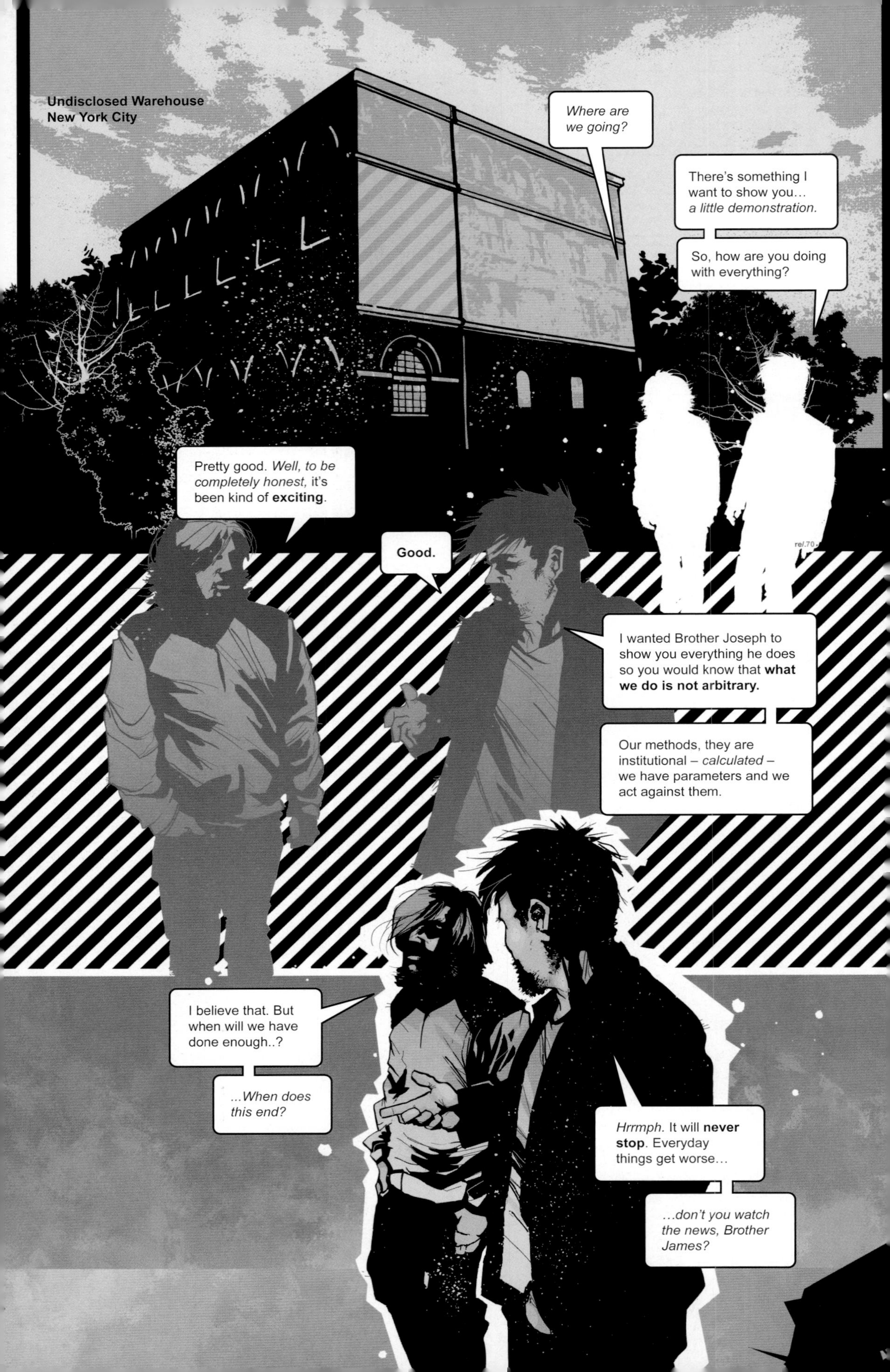

Undisclosed Warehouse New York City
Where are we going?
There's something I want to show you… *a little demonstration.*
So, how are you doing with everything?
Pretty good. *Well, to be completely honest,* it's been kind of **exciting**.
Good.
I wanted Brother Joseph to show you everything he does so you would know that **what we do is not arbitrary.**
Our methods, they are institutional – *calculated* – we have parameters and we act against them.
I believe that. But when will we have done enough..?
...When does this end?
Hrrmph. It will **never stop**. Everyday things get worse…
…don't you watch the news, Brother James?

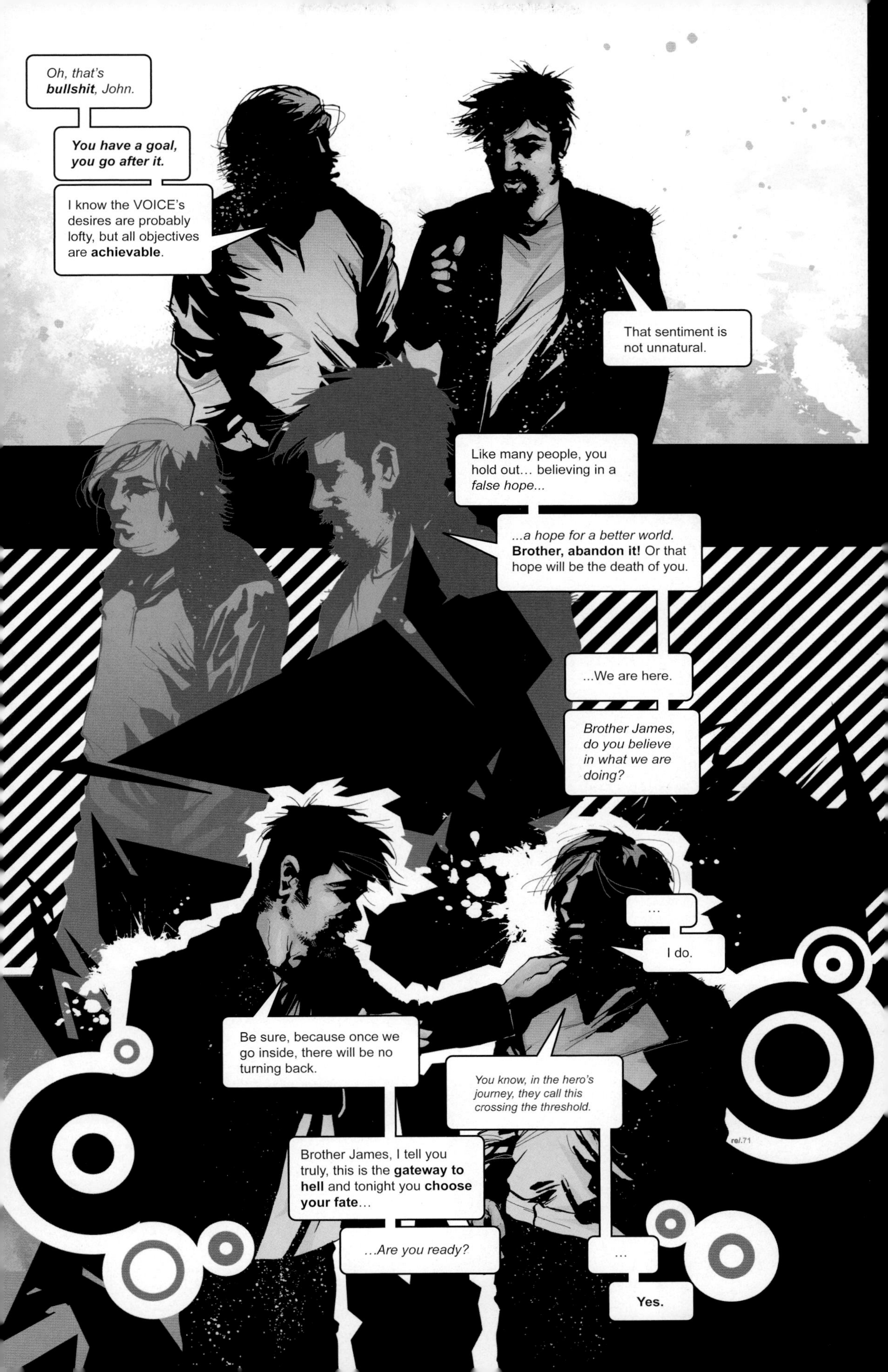
Oh, that's **bullshit**, John.
You have a goal, you go after it.
I know the VOICE's desires are probably lofty, but all objectives are **achievable**.
That sentiment is not unnatural.
Like many people, you hold out… believing in a *false hope...*
...a hope for a better world. **Brother, abandon it!** Or that hope will be the death of you.
...We are here.
Brother James, do you believe in what we are doing?
…
I do.
Be sure, because once we go inside, there will be no turning back.
You know, in the hero's journey, they call this crossing the threshold.
Brother James, I tell you truly, this is the **gateway to hell** and tonight you **choose your fate**…
…Are you ready?
…
Yes.
rel.71

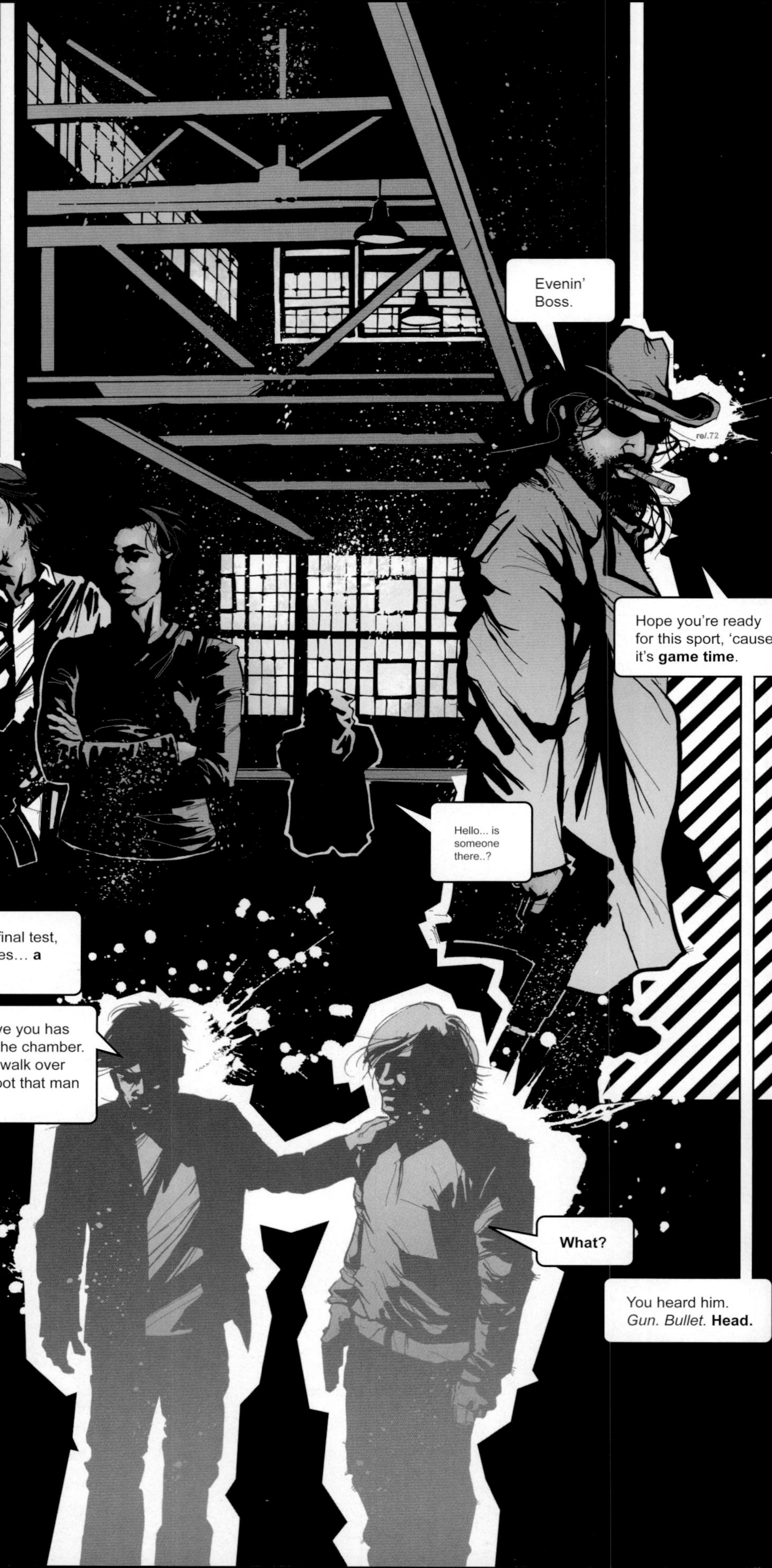
Evenin' Boss.
Hope you're ready for this sport, 'cause it's **game time**.
Hello... is someone there..?
final test, es… **a**
ve you has he chamber. walk over oot that man
What?
You heard him. *Gun. Bullet.* **Head.**

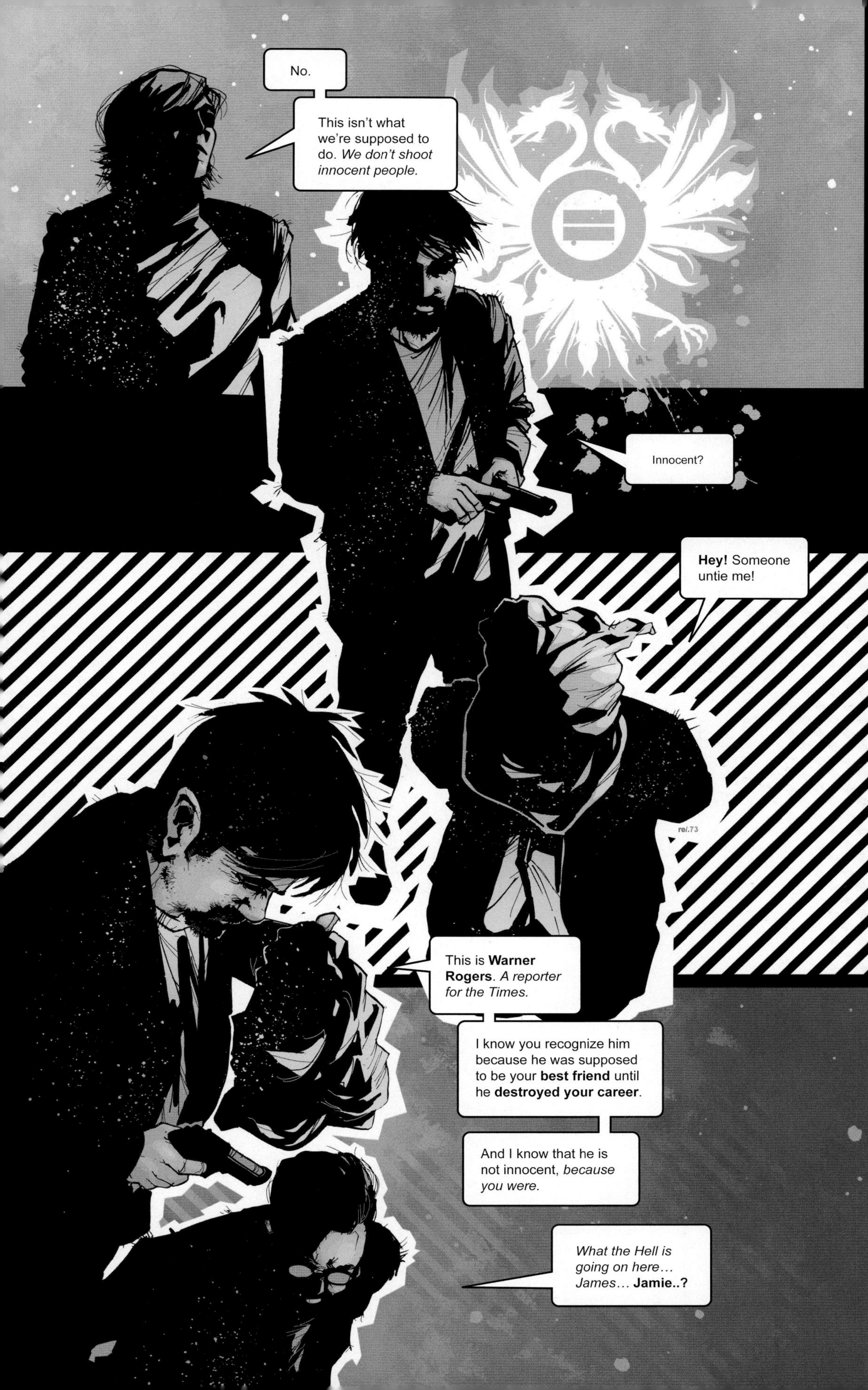
No.
This isn't what we're supposed to do. *We don't shoot innocent people.*
Innocent?
Hey! Someone untie me!
rel.73
This is **Warner Rogers**. *A reporter for the Times.*
I know you recognize him because he was supposed to be your **best friend** until he **destroyed your career**.
And I know that he is not innocent, *because you were*.
What the Hell is going on here… James… **Jamie..?**

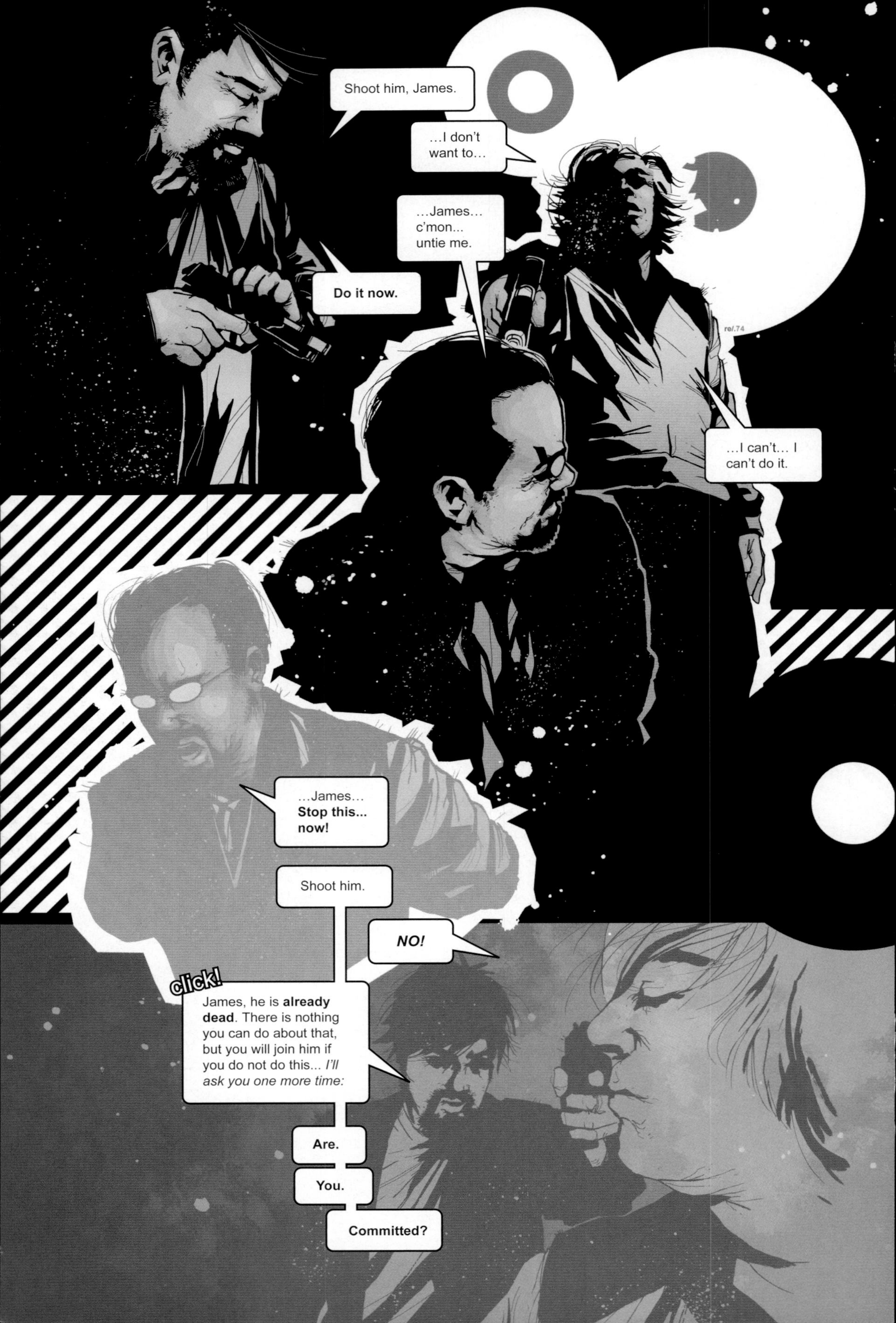
Shoot him, James.
…I don't want to…
…James… c'mon... untie me.
Do it now.
re/.74
…I can't… I can't do it.
…James… **Stop this... now!**
Shoot him.
NO!
click!
James, he is **already dead**. There is nothing you can do about that, but you will join him if you do not do this... *I'll ask you one more time:*
Are.
You.
Committed?

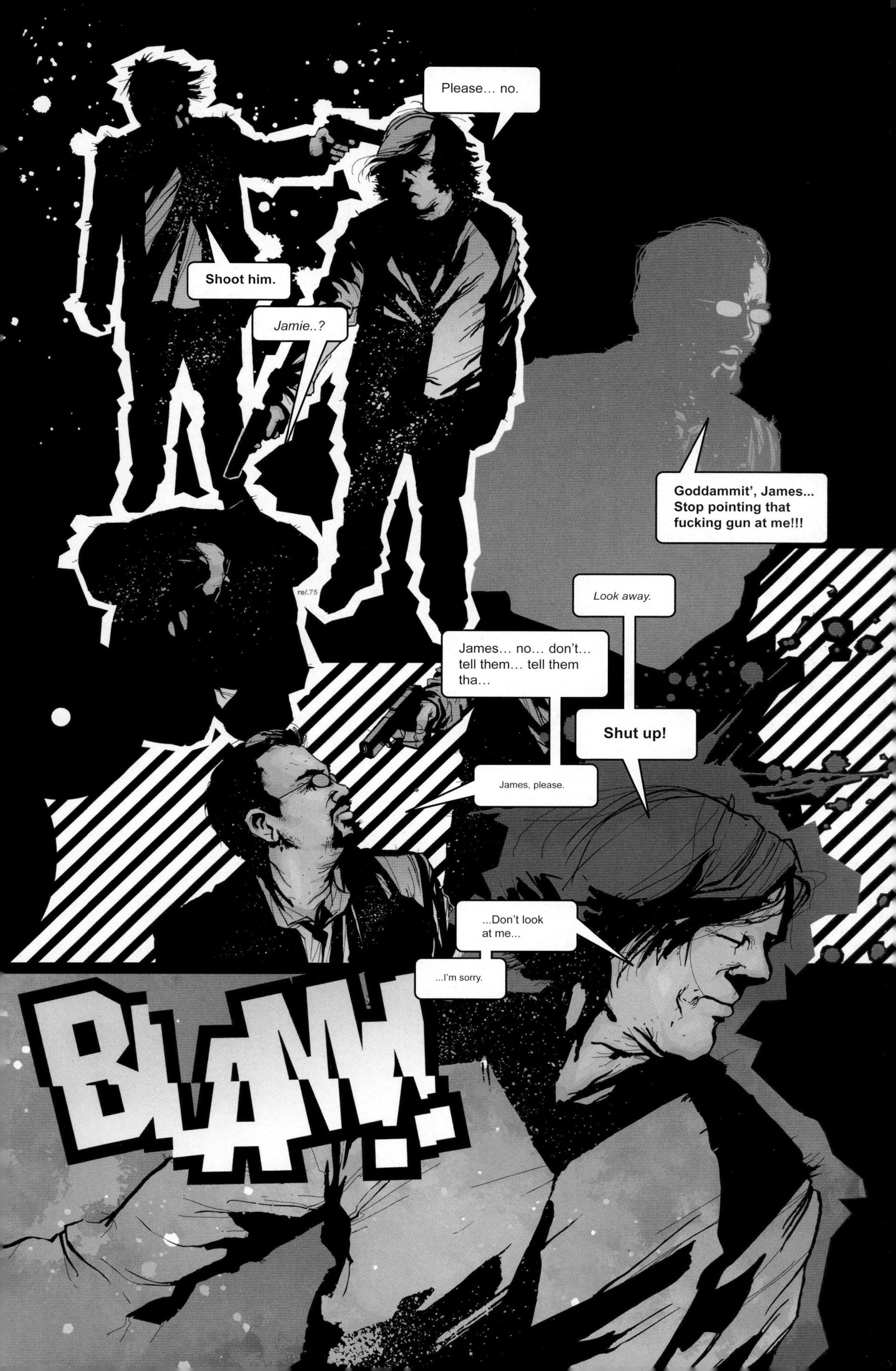
Please… no.
Shoot him.
Jamie..?
Goddammit', James... Stop pointing that fucking gun at me!!!
rel.75
Look away.
James… no… don't… tell them… tell them tha…
Shut up!
James, please.
...Don't look at me...
...I'm sorry.
BLAM!

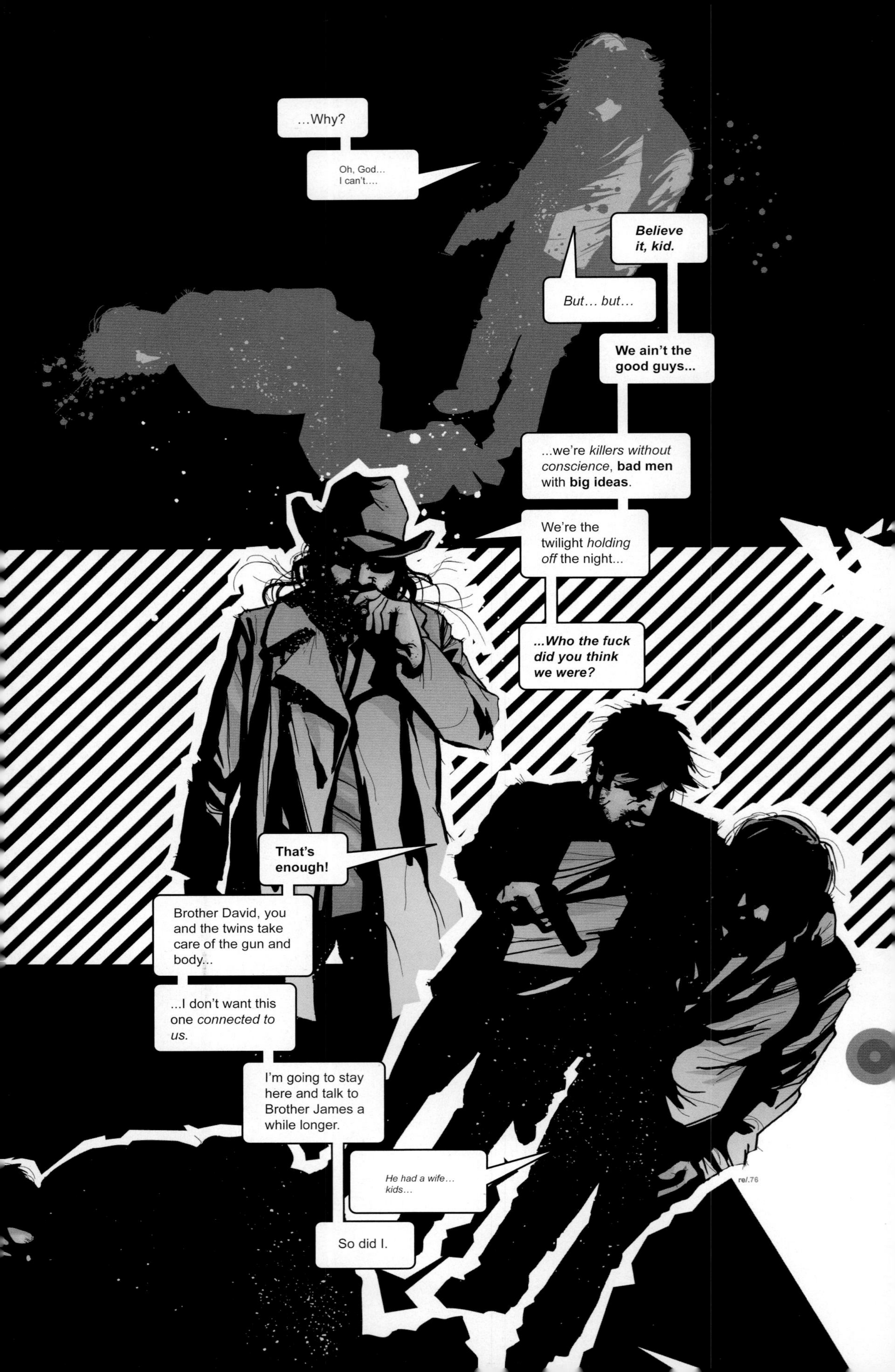
...Why?
Oh, God... I can't....
Believe it, kid.
But... but...
We ain't the good guys...
...we're killers without conscience, bad men with big ideas.
We're the twilight holding off the night...
...Who the fuck did you think we were?
That's enough!
Brother David, you and the twins take care of the gun and body...
...I don't want this one connected to us.
I'm going to stay here and talk to Brother James a while longer.
He had a wife... kids...
So did I.

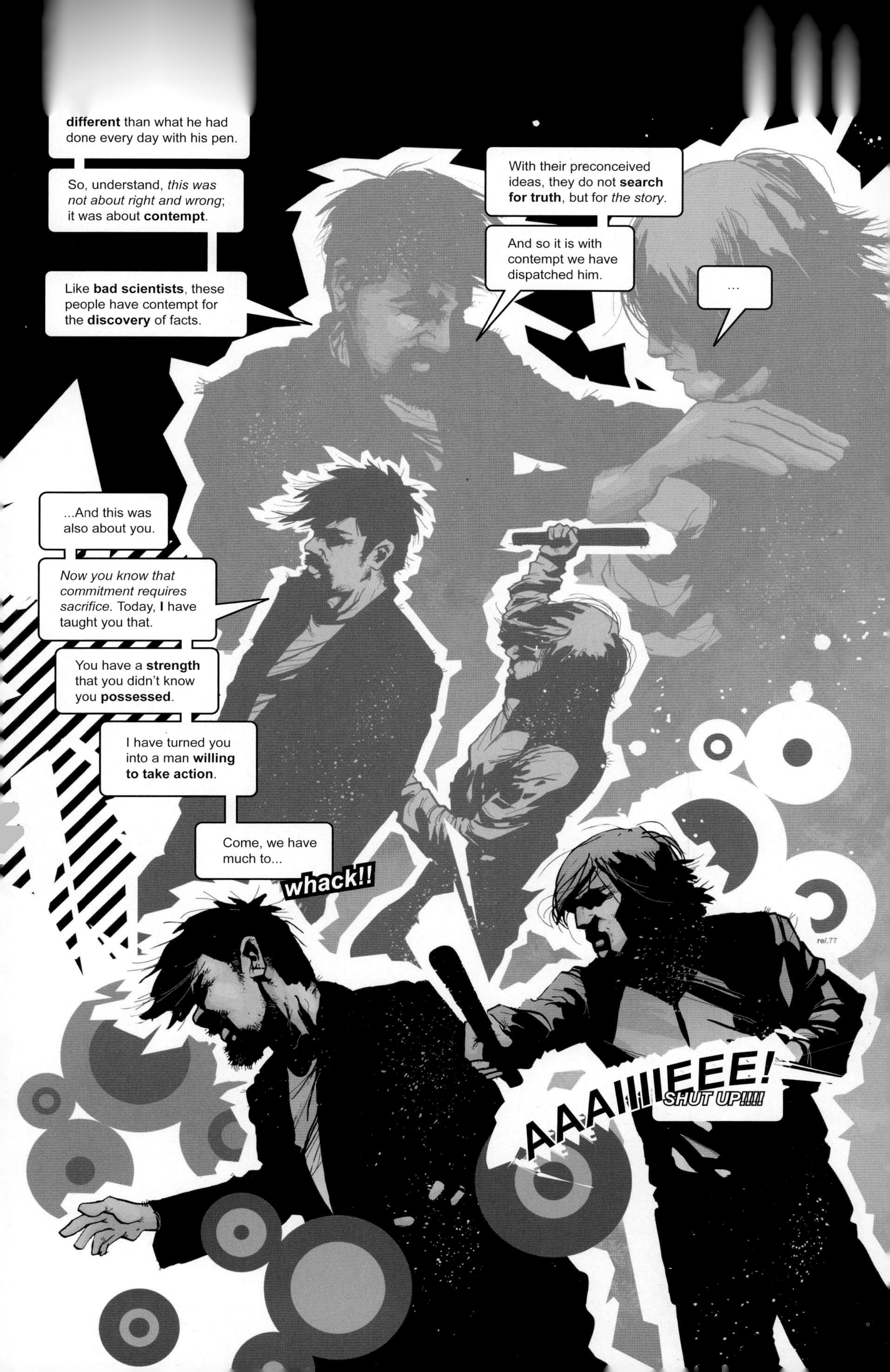

different than what he had done every day with his pen.
So, understand, *this was not about right and wrong*; it was about **contempt**.
Like **bad scientists**, these people have contempt for the **discovery** of facts.
With their preconceived ideas, they do not **search for truth**, but for *the story*.
And so it is with contempt we have dispatched him.
...
...And this was also about you.
Now you know that commitment requires sacrifice. Today, **I** have taught you that.
You have a **strength** that you didn't know you **possessed**.
I have turned you into a man **willing to take action**.
Come, we have much to...
whack!!
AAAIIIIEEE!
SHUT UP!!!!
rel.77

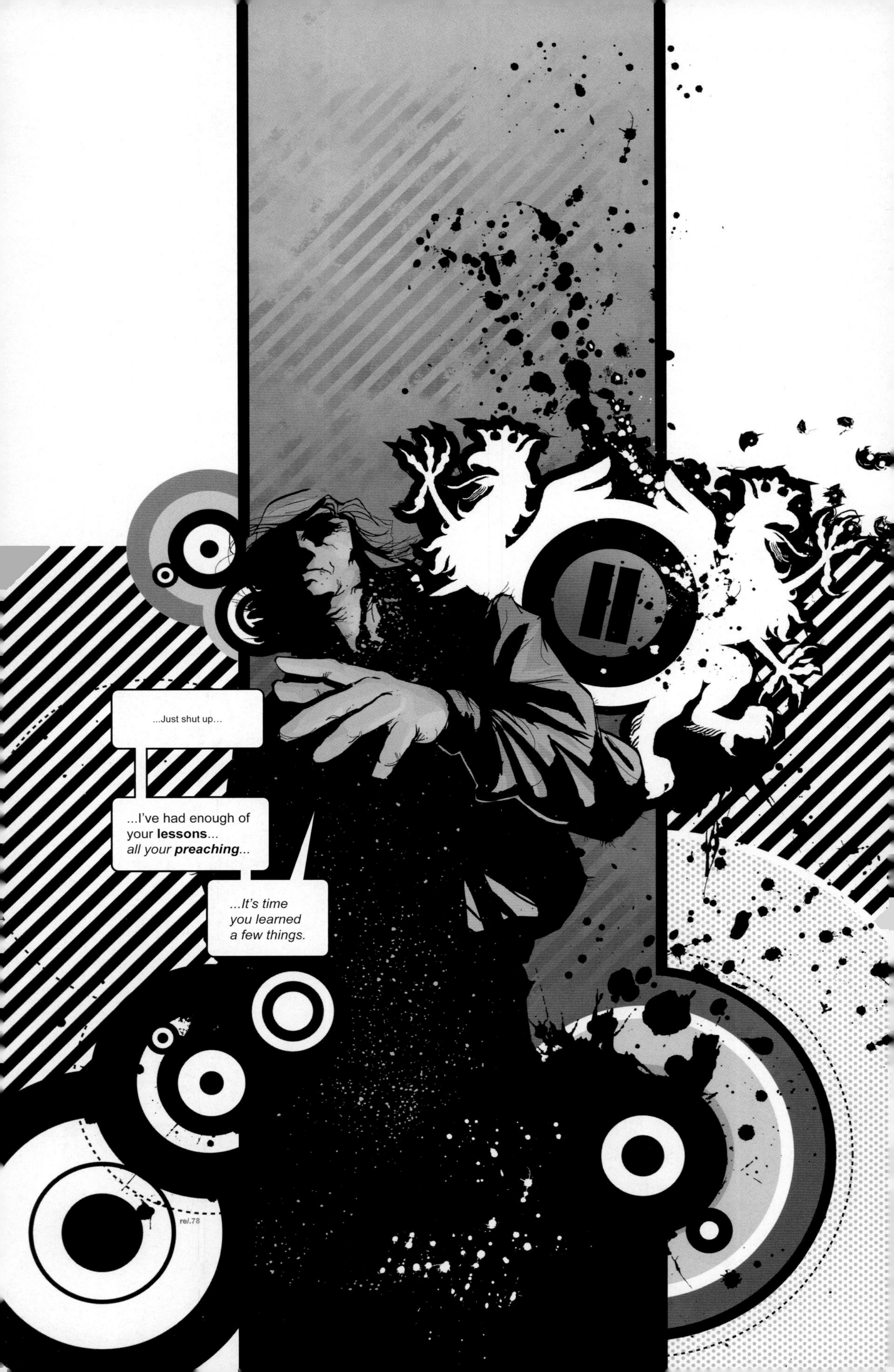

...Just shut up...
...I've had enough of your **lessons**... *all your **preaching**...*
...It's time you learned a few things.
rel.78

END_CHAPTER 03

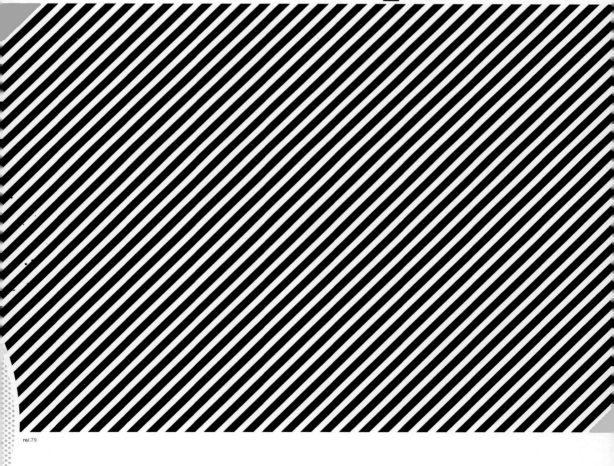

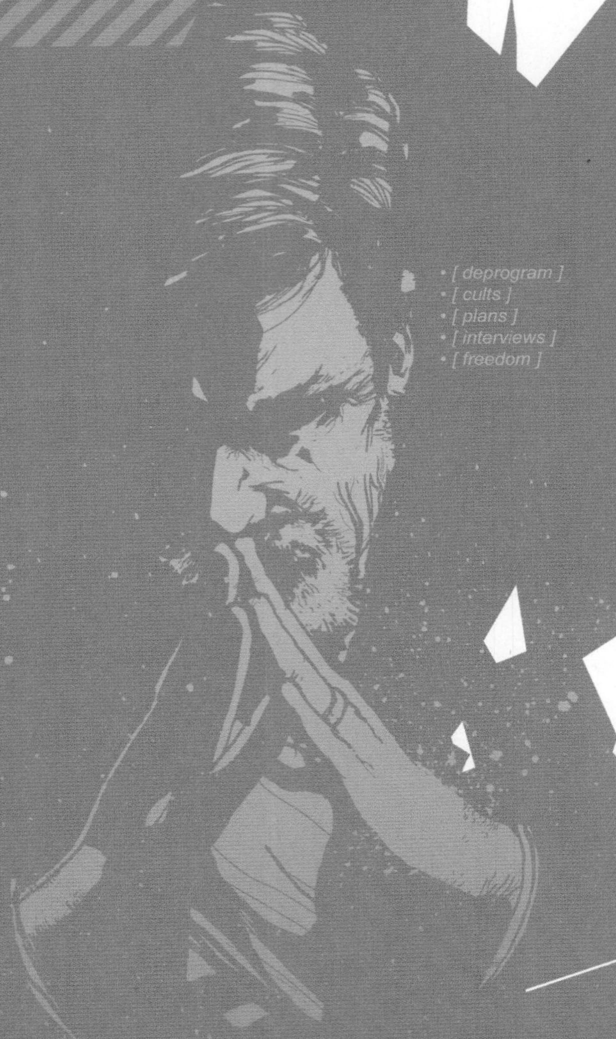

- [deprogram]
- [cults]
- [plans]
- [interviews]
- [freedom]

the nightly**NEWS**

chapter **four:**

Cults in our *mi*dst

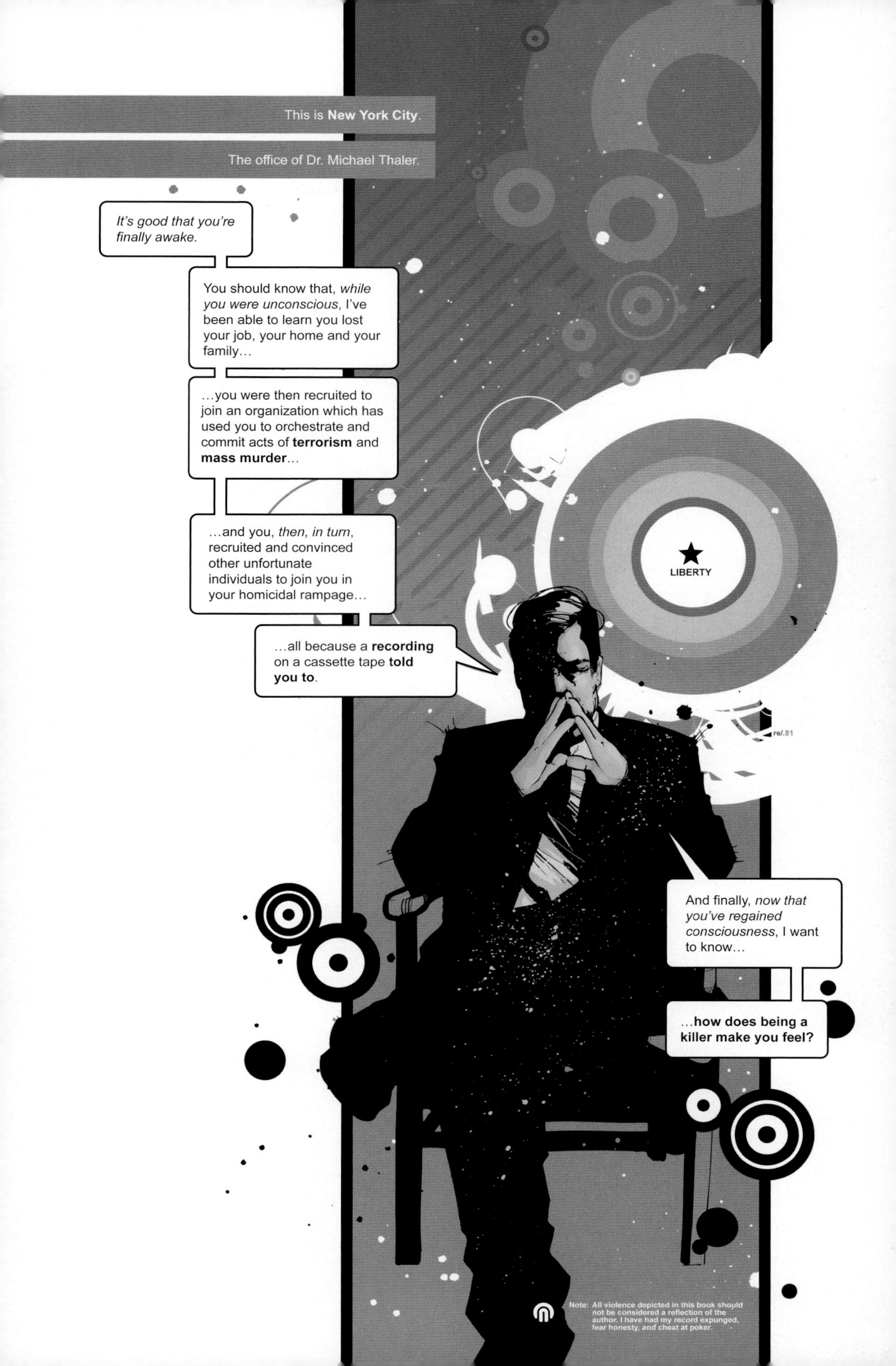
This is **New York City**.
The office of Dr. Michael Thaler.
It's good that you're finally awake.
You should know that, *while you were unconscious*, I've been able to learn you lost your job, your home and your family…
…you were then recruited to join an organization which has used you to orchestrate and commit acts of **terrorism** and **mass murder**…
…and you, *then, in turn*, recruited and convinced other unfortunate individuals to join you in your homicidal rampage…
…all because a **recording** on a cassette tape **told you to**.
LIBERTY
re/.81
And finally, *now that you've regained consciousness*, I want to know…
…**how does being a killer make you feel?**
Note: All violence depicted in this book should not be considered a reflection of the author. I have had my record expunged, fear honesty, and cheat at poker.

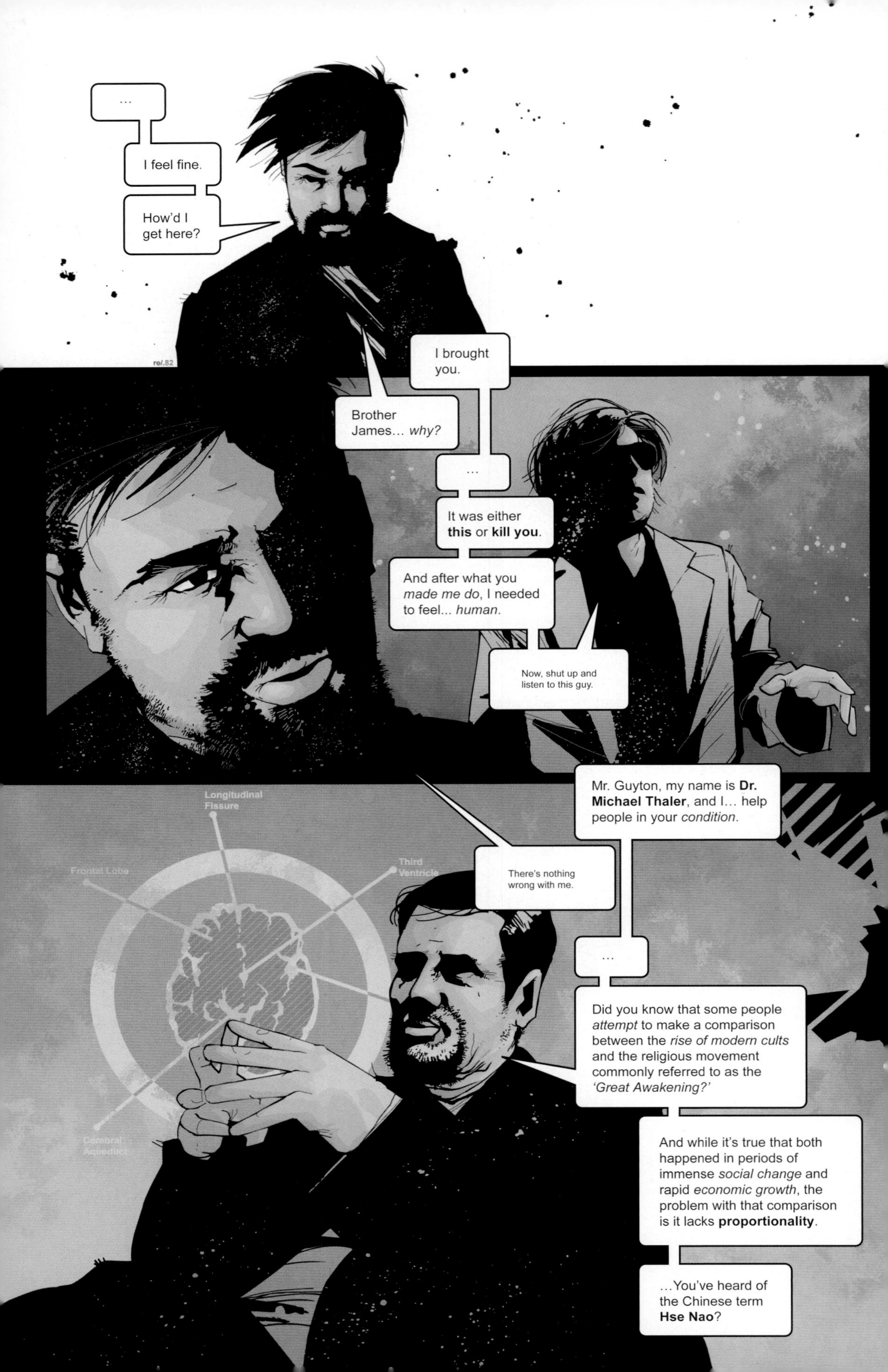

…
I feel fine.
How'd I get here?
Brother James… *why?*
I brought you.
…
It was either **this** or **kill you**.
And after what you *made me do*, I needed to feel... *human*.
Now, shut up and listen to this guy.
Longitudinal Fissure
Frontal Lobe
Third Ventricle
Cerebral Aqueduct
Mr. Guyton, my name is **Dr. Michael Thaler**, and I… help people in your *condition*.
There's nothing wrong with me.
…
Did you know that some people *attempt* to make a comparison between the *rise of modern cults* and the religious movement commonly referred to as the *'Great Awakening?'*
And while it's true that both happened in periods of immense *social change* and rapid *economic growth*, the problem with that comparison is it lacks **proportionality**.
…You've heard of the Chinese term **Hse Nao**?

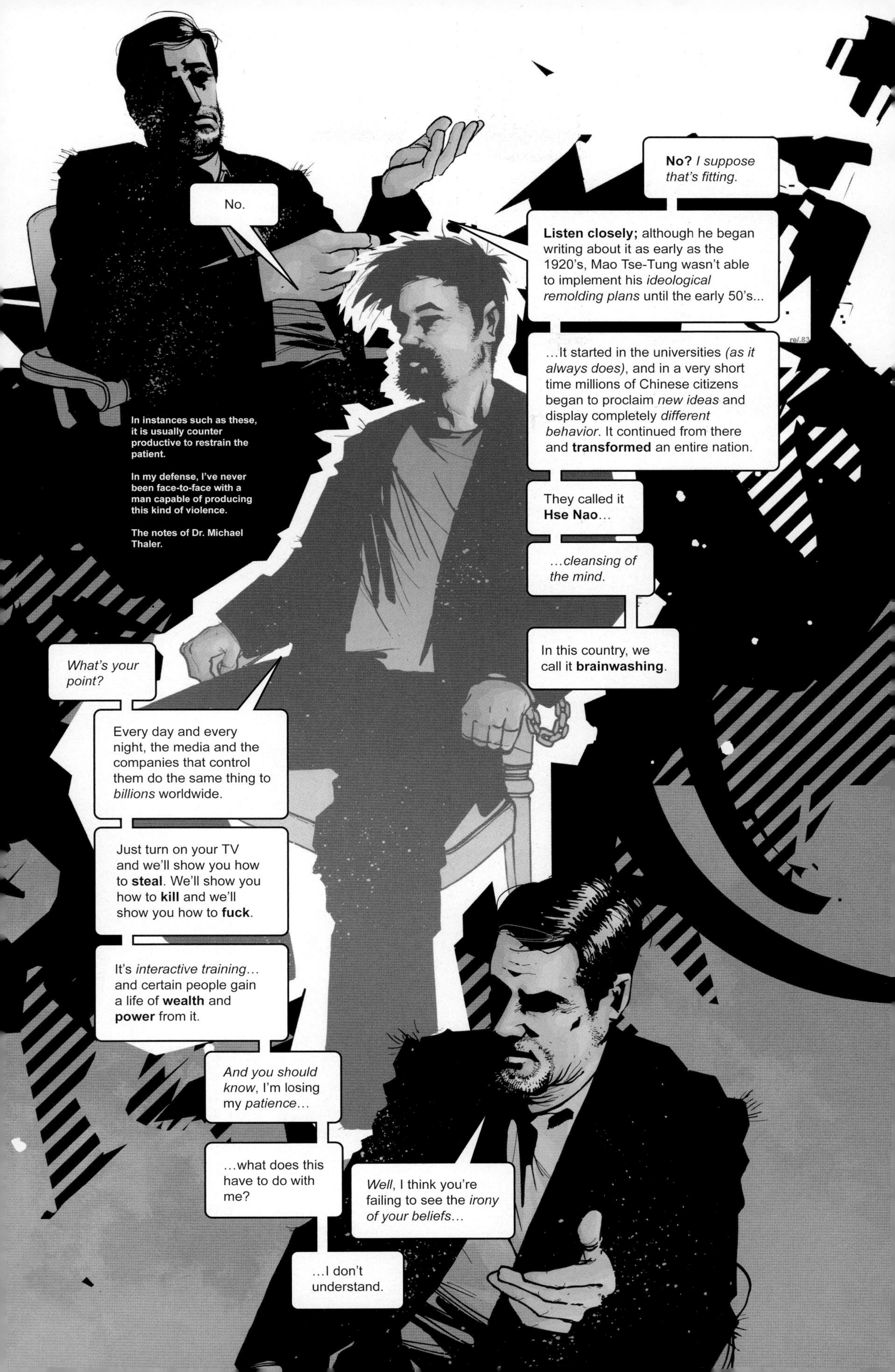

No.
No? *I suppose that's fitting.*
Listen closely; although he began writing about it as early as the 1920's, Mao Tse-Tung wasn't able to implement his *ideological remolding plans* until the early 50's...
...It started in the universities *(as it always does)*, and in a very short time millions of Chinese citizens began to proclaim *new ideas* and display completely *different behavior*. It continued from there and **transformed** an entire nation.
They called it **Hse Nao**...
...cleansing of the mind.
In this country, we call it **brainwashing**.
In instances such as these, it is usually counter productive to restrain the patient.
In my defense, I've never been face-to-face with a man capable of producing this kind of violence.
The notes of Dr. Michael Thaler.
What's your point?
Every day and every night, the media and the companies that control them do the same thing to *billions* worldwide.
Just turn on your TV and we'll show you how to **steal**. We'll show you how to **kill** and we'll show you how to **fuck**.
It's *interactive training*... and certain people gain a life of **wealth** and **power** from it.
And you should know, I'm losing my *patience*...
...what does this have to do with me?
Well, I think you're failing to see the *irony of your beliefs*...
...I don't understand.

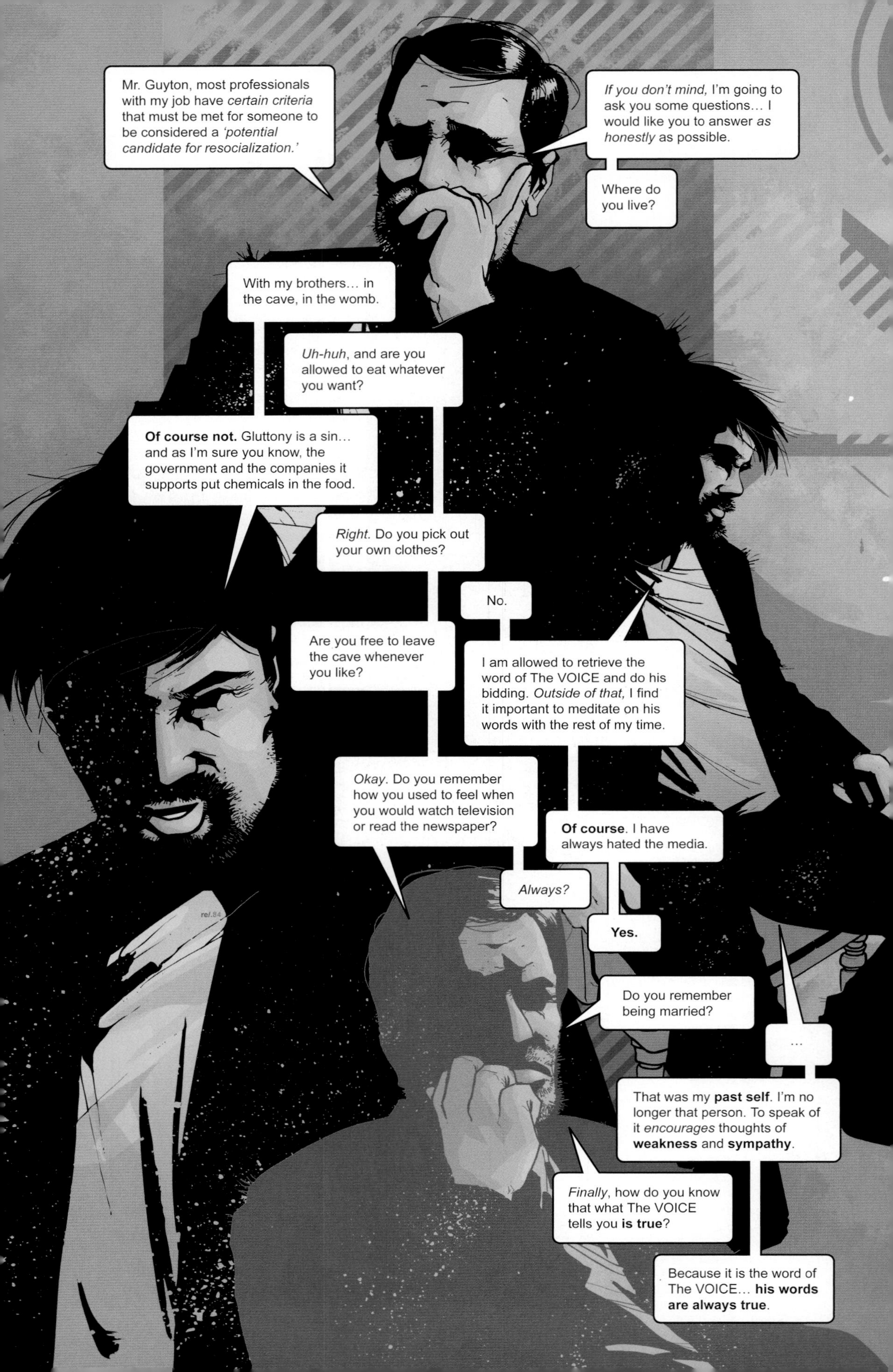

Mr. Guyton, most professionals with my job have *certain criteria* that must be met for someone to be considered a *'potential candidate for resocialization.'*
If you don't mind, I'm going to ask you some questions… I would like you to answer *as honestly* as possible.
Where do you live?
With my brothers… in the cave, in the womb.
Uh-huh, and are you allowed to eat whatever you want?
Of course not. Gluttony is a sin… and as I'm sure you know, the government and the companies it supports put chemicals in the food.
Right. Do you pick out your own clothes?
No.
Are you free to leave the cave whenever you like?
I am allowed to retrieve the word of The VOICE and do his bidding. *Outside of that,* I find it important to meditate on his words with the rest of my time.
Okay. Do you remember how you used to feel when you would watch television or read the newspaper?
Of course. I have always hated the media.
Always?
Yes.
Do you remember being married?
…
That was my **past self**. I'm no longer that person. To speak of it *encourages* thoughts of **weakness** and **sympathy**.
Finally, how do you know that what The VOICE tells you **is true**?
Because it is the word of The VOICE… **his words are always true**.

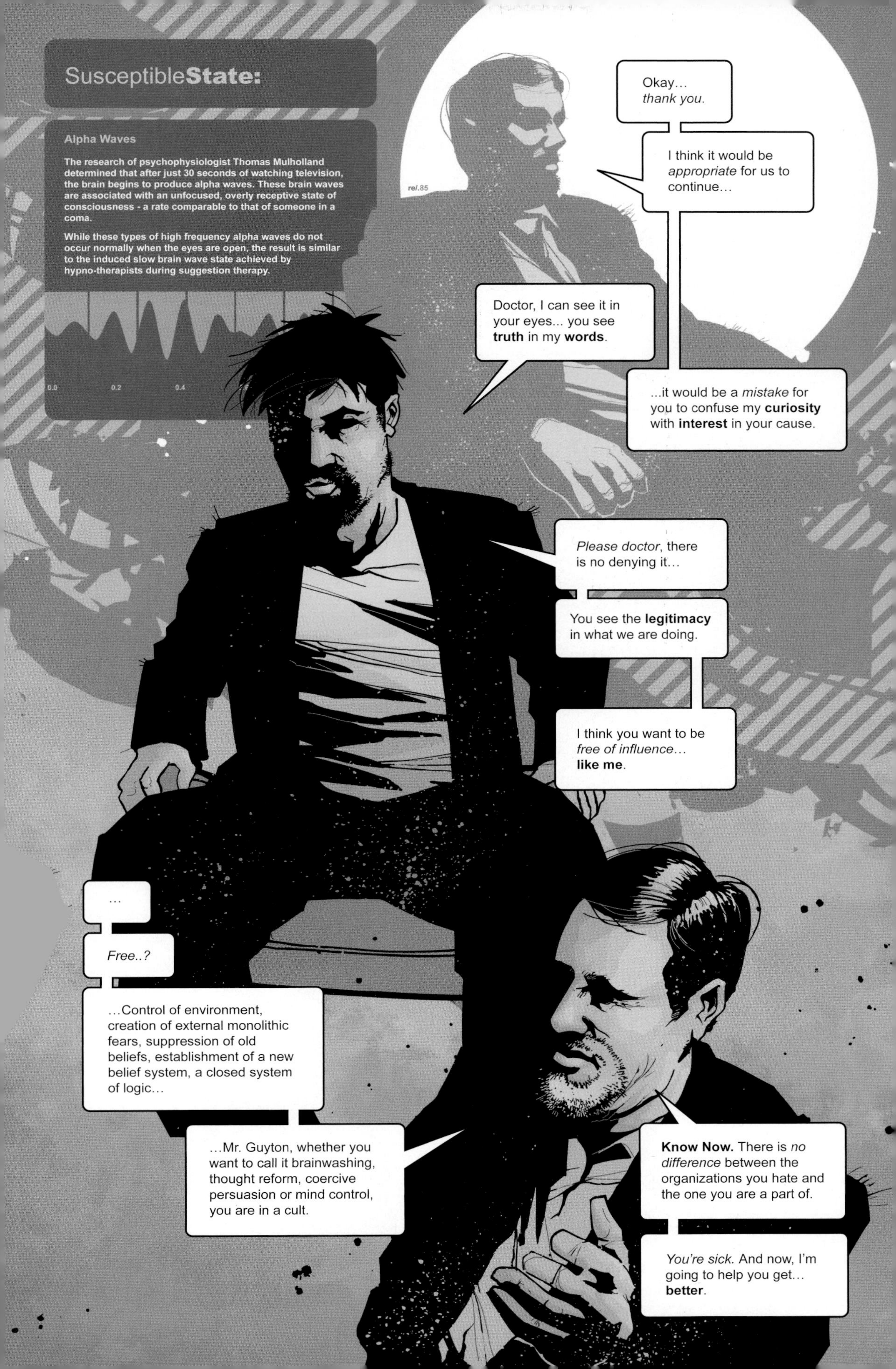

SusceptibleState:
Alpha Waves
The research of psychophysiologist Thomas Mulholland determined that after just 30 seconds of watching television, the brain begins to produce alpha waves. These brain waves are associated with an unfocused, overly receptive state of consciousness - a rate comparable to that of someone in a coma.
While these types of high frequency alpha waves do not occur normally when the eyes are open, the result is similar to the induced slow brain wave state achieved by hypno-therapists during suggestion therapy.
0.0
0.2
0.4
rel/.85
Okay... *thank you.*
I think it would be *appropriate* for us to continue...
Doctor, I can see it in your eyes... you see **truth** in my **words**.
...it would be a *mistake* for you to confuse my **curiosity** with **interest** in your cause.
Please doctor, there is no denying it...
You see the **legitimacy** in what we are doing.
I think you want to be *free of influence*... **like me**.
...
Free..?
...Control of environment, creation of external monolithic fears, suppression of old beliefs, establishment of a new belief system, a closed system of logic...
...Mr. Guyton, whether you want to call it brainwashing, thought reform, coercive persuasion or mind control, you are in a cult.
Know Now. There is *no difference* between the organizations you hate and the one you are a part of.
You're sick. And now, I'm going to help you get... **better**.

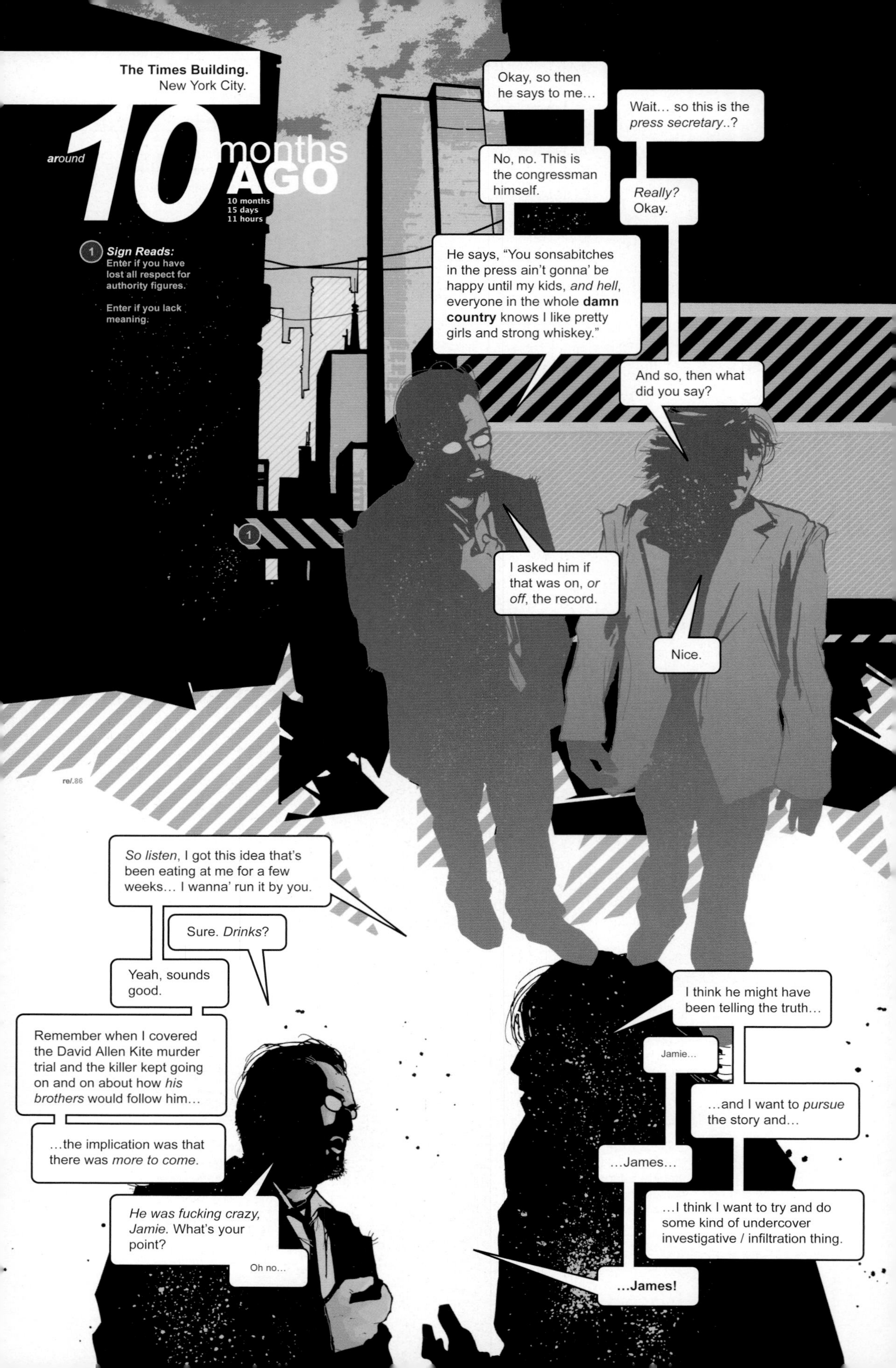
The Times Building.
New York City.
around 10 months AGO
10 months
15 days
11 hours
1 Sign Reads:
Enter if you have lost all respect for authority figures.
Enter if you lack meaning.
Okay, so then he says to me…
No, no. This is the congressman himself.
Wait… so this is the press secretary..?
Really? Okay.
He says, "You sonsabitches in the press ain't gonna' be happy until my kids, and hell, everyone in the whole damn country knows I like pretty girls and strong whiskey."
And so, then what did you say?
I asked him if that was on, or off, the record.
Nice.
re/.86
So listen, I got this idea that's been eating at me for a few weeks… I wanna' run it by you.
Sure. Drinks?
Yeah, sounds good.
Remember when I covered the David Allen Kite murder trial and the killer kept going on and on about how his brothers would follow him…
…the implication was that there was more to come.
He was fucking crazy, Jamie. What's your point?
Oh no…
I think he might have been telling the truth…
Jamie…
…and I want to pursue the story and…
…James…
…I think I want to try and do some kind of undercover investigative / infiltration thing.
…James!

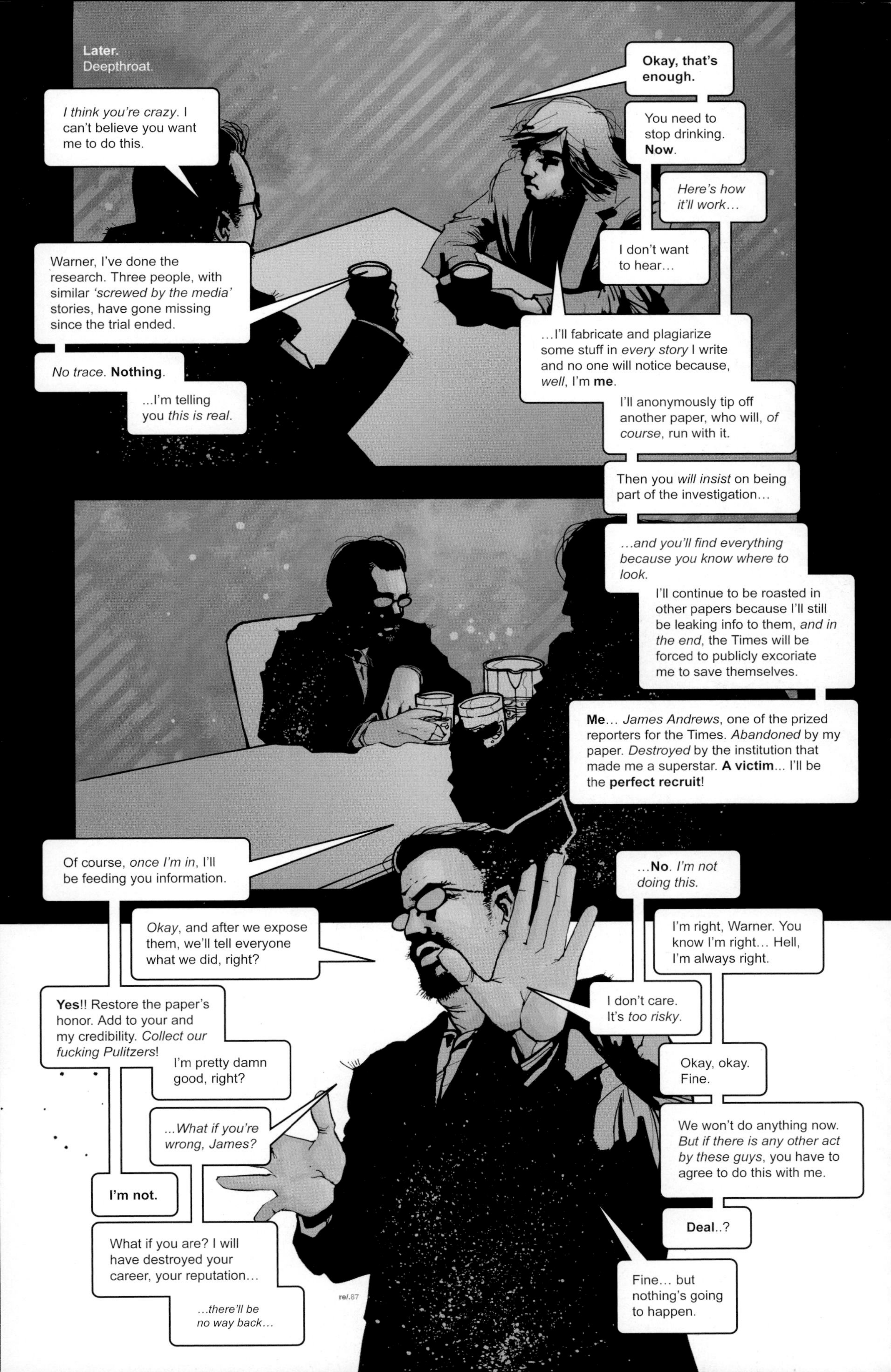

Later.
Deepthroat.
I think you're crazy. I can't believe you want me to do this.
Warner, I've done the research. Three people, with similar *'screwed by the media'* stories, have gone missing since the trial ended.
No trace. **Nothing**.
...I'm telling you *this is real*.
Okay, that's enough.
You need to stop drinking. **Now**.
Here's how it'll work…
I don't want to hear…
…I'll fabricate and plagiarize some stuff in *every story* I write and no one will notice because, *well*, I'm **me**.
I'll anonymously tip off another paper, who will, *of course*, run with it.
Then you *will insist* on being part of the investigation…
…and you'll find everything because you know where to look.
I'll continue to be roasted in other papers because I'll still be leaking info to them, *and in the end*, the Times will be forced to publicly excoriate me to save themselves.
Me… *James Andrews*, one of the prized reporters for the Times. *Abandoned* by my paper. *Destroyed* by the institution that made me a superstar. **A victim**... I'll be the **perfect recruit**!
Of course, *once I'm in*, I'll be feeding you information.
…**No**. *I'm not doing this.*
Okay, and after we expose them, we'll tell everyone what we did, right?
I'm right, Warner. You know I'm right… Hell, I'm always right.
Yes!! Restore the paper's honor. Add to your and my credibility. *Collect our fucking Pulitzers*!
I don't care. It's *too risky*.
I'm pretty damn good, right?
Okay, okay. Fine.
...What if you're wrong, James?
We won't do anything now. *But if there is any other act by these guys*, you have to agree to do this with me.
I'm not.
Deal..?
What if you are? I will have destroyed your career, your reputation…
…there'll be no way back…
Fine… but nothing's going to happen.

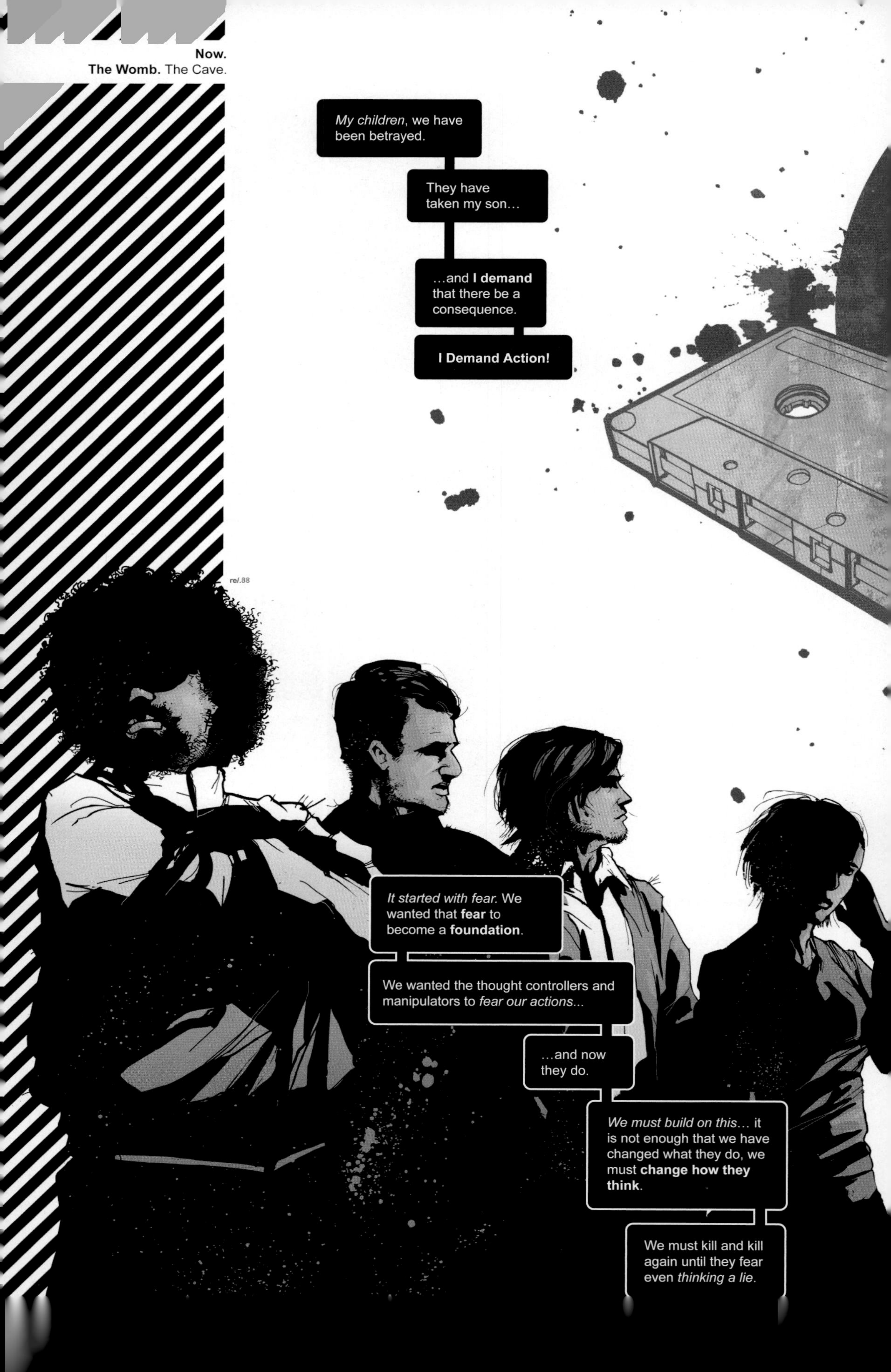
Now.
The Womb. The Cave.
My children, we have been betrayed.
They have taken my son…
…and I demand that there be a consequence.
I Demand Action!
re/.88
It started with fear. We wanted that fear to become a foundation.
We wanted the thought controllers and manipulators to fear our actions...
…and now they do.
We must build on this… it is not enough that we have changed what they do, we must change how they think.
We must kill and kill again until they fear even thinking a lie.

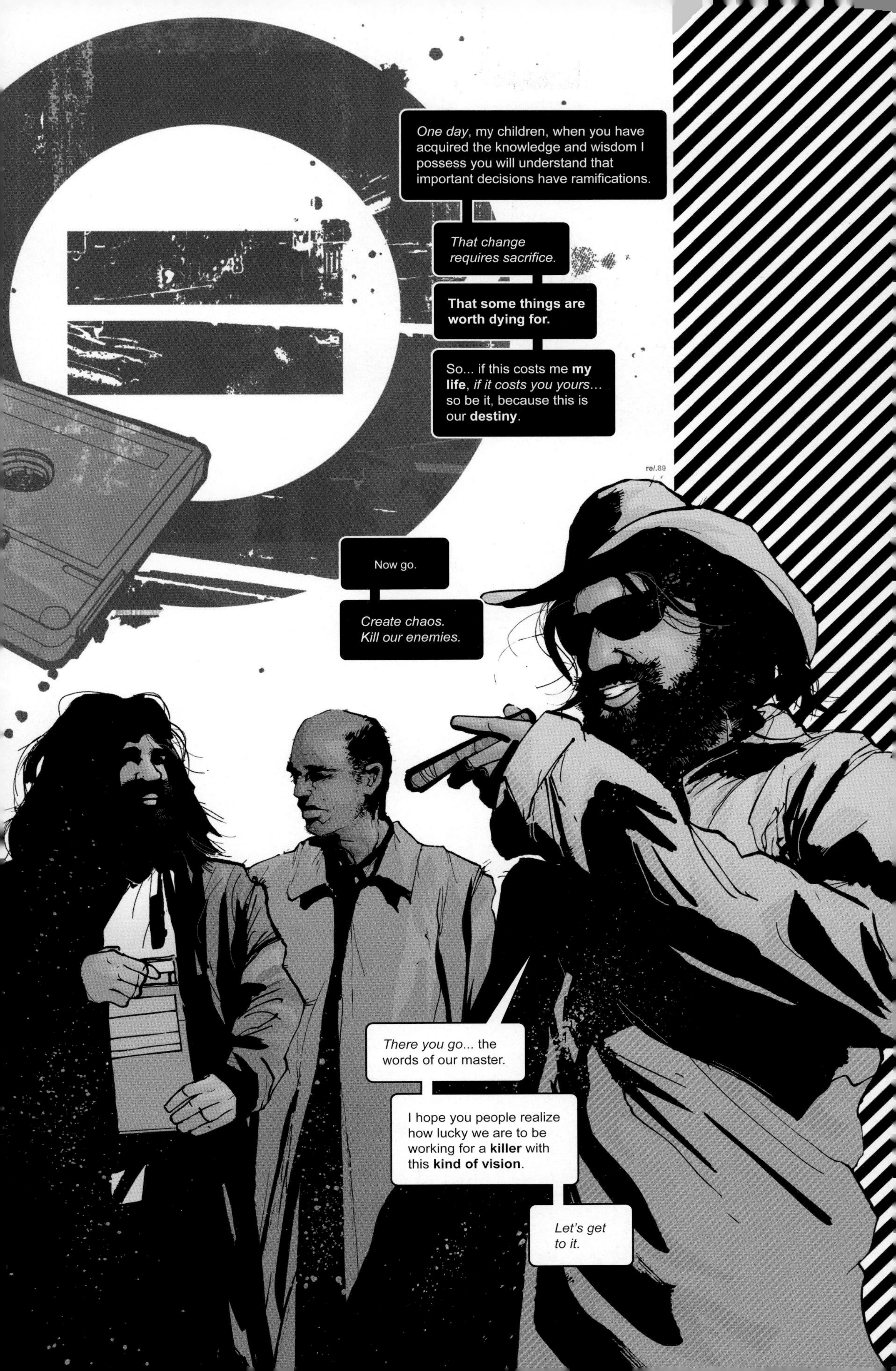

One day, my children, when you have acquired the knowledge and wisdom I possess you will understand that important decisions have ramifications.
That change requires sacrifice.
That some things are worth dying for.
So... if this costs me **my life**, *if it costs you yours*... so be it, because this is our **destiny**.
re/.89
Now go.
Create chaos. Kill our enemies.
There you go... the words of our master.
I hope you people realize how lucky we are to be working for a **killer** with this **kind of vision**.
Let's get to it.

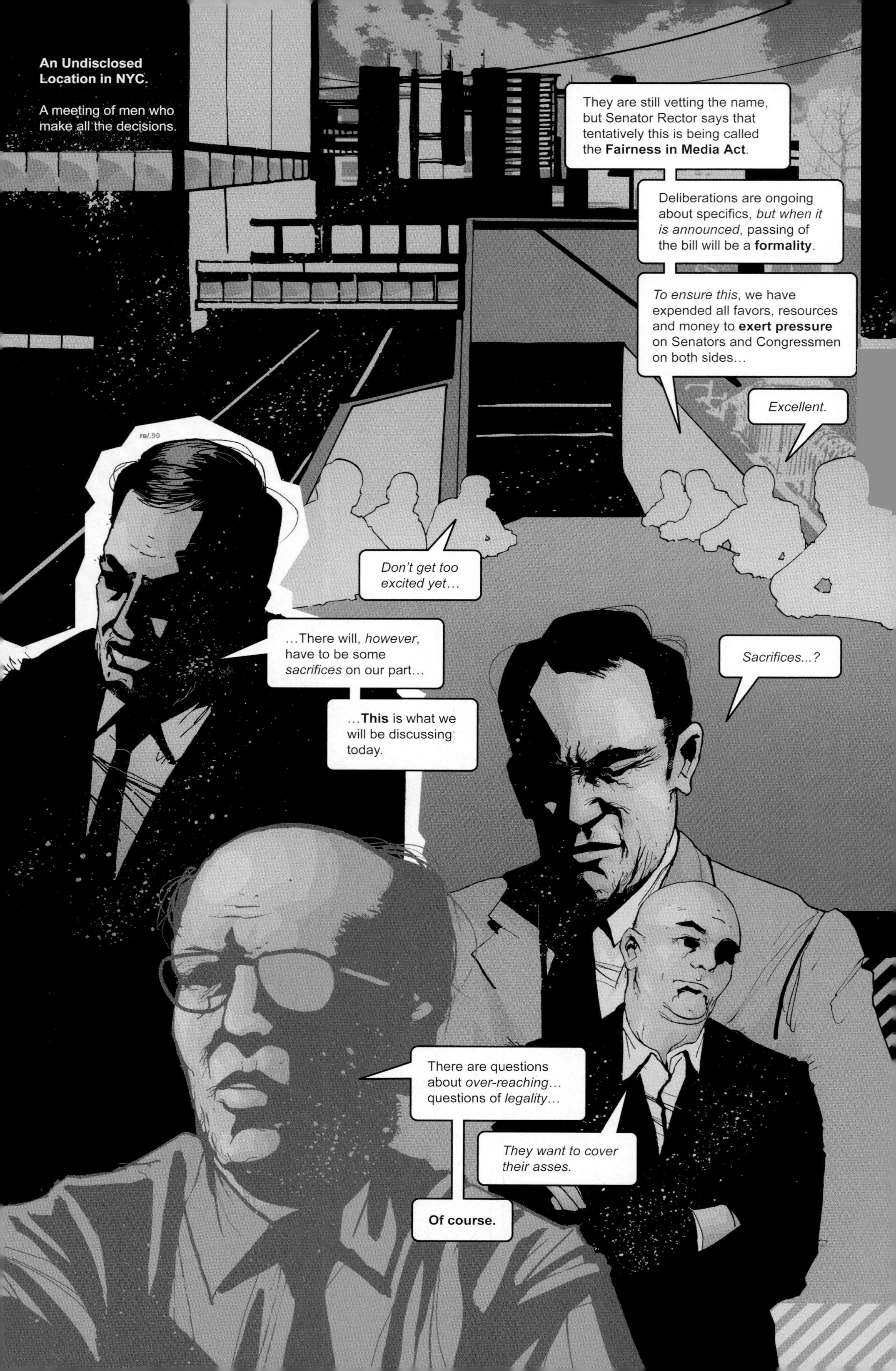
An Undisclosed Location in NYC.
A meeting of men who make all the decisions.
They are still vetting the name, but Senator Rector says that tentatively this is being called the **Fairness in Media Act**.
Deliberations are ongoing about specifics, *but when it is announced*, passing of the bill will be a **formality**.
To ensure this, we have expended all favors, resources and money to **exert pressure** on Senators and Congressmen on both sides…
Excellent.
Don't get too excited yet…
…There will, *however*, have to be some *sacrifices* on our part…
…**This** is what we will be discussing today.
Sacrifices...?
There are questions about *over-reaching*… questions of *legality*…
They want to cover their asses.
Of course.
re/.90

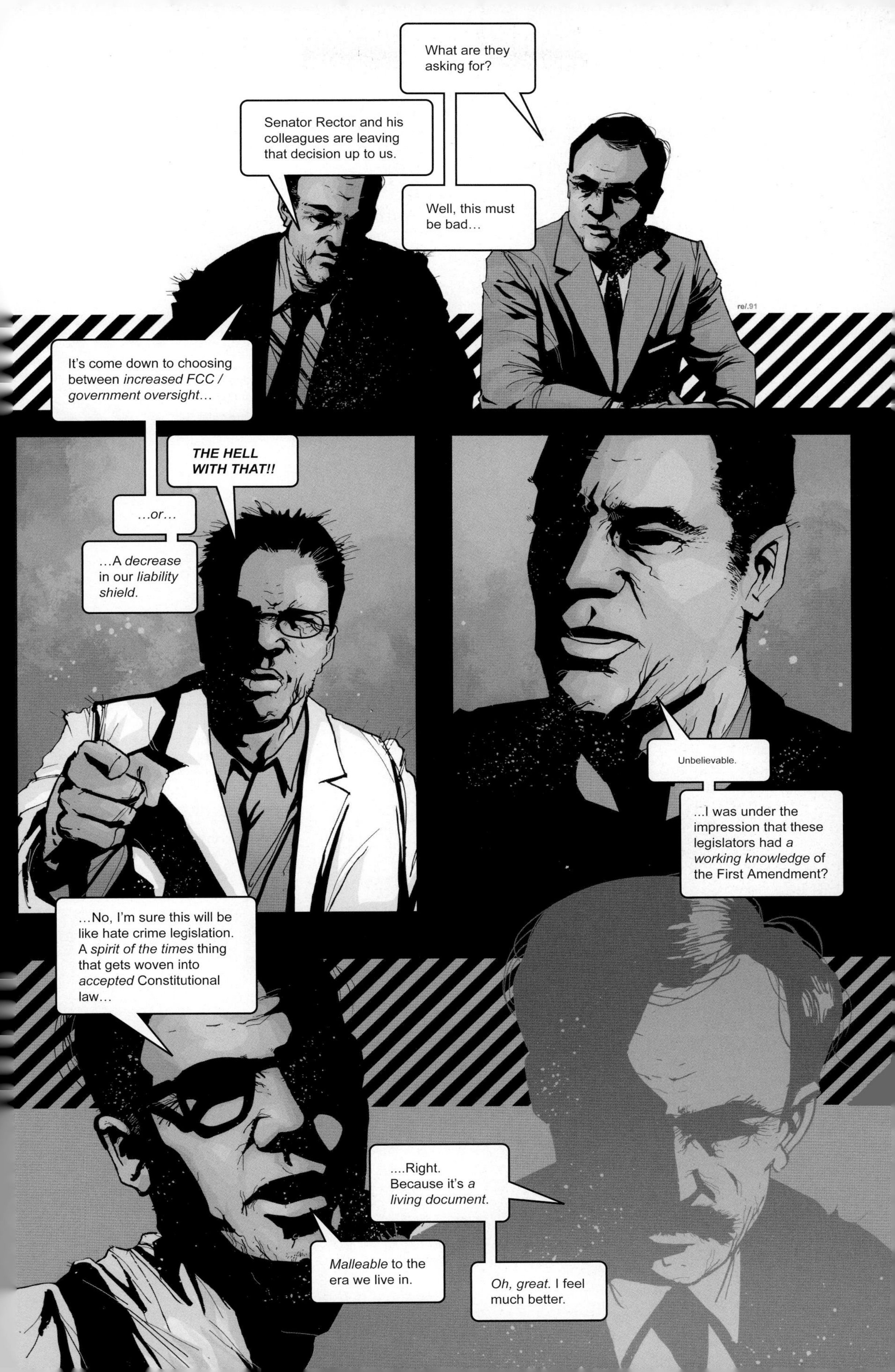
What are they asking for?
Senator Rector and his colleagues are leaving that decision up to us.
Well, this must be bad…
rel.91
It's come down to choosing between *increased FCC / government oversight*…
THE HELL WITH THAT!!
…or…
…A *decrease* in our *liability shield*.
Unbelievable.
...I was under the impression that these legislators had *a working knowledge* of the First Amendment?
…No, I'm sure this will be like hate crime legislation. A *spirit of the times* thing that gets woven into *accepted* Constitutional law…
....Right. Because it's *a living document*.
Malleable to the era we live in.
Oh, great. I feel much better.

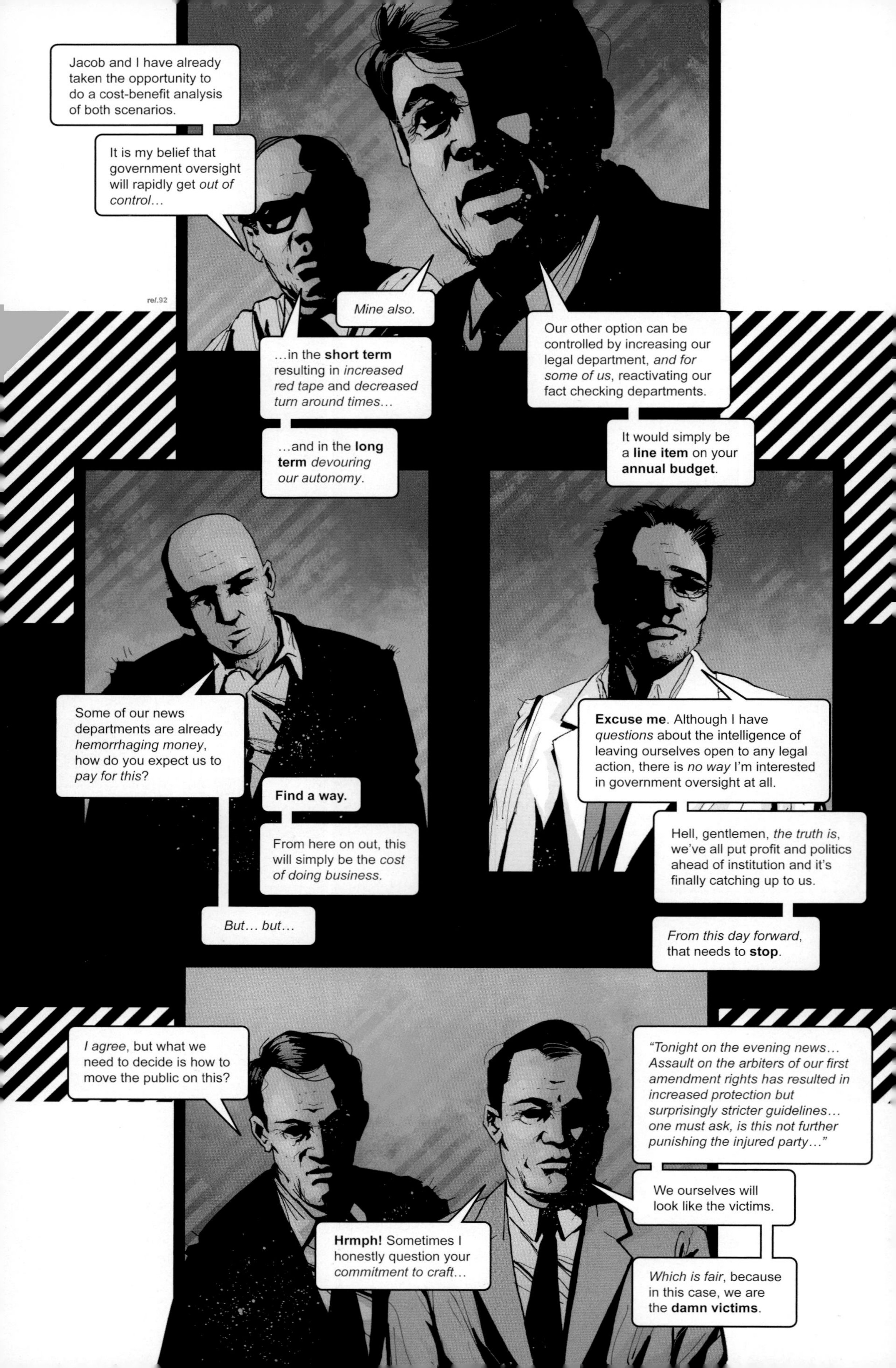
Jacob and I have already taken the opportunity to do a cost-benefit analysis of both scenarios.
It is my belief that government oversight will rapidly get *out of control*…
Mine also.
…in the **short term** resulting in *increased red tape* and *decreased turn around times*…
…and in the **long term** *devouring our autonomy*.
Our other option can be controlled by increasing our legal department, *and for some of us*, reactivating our fact checking departments.
It would simply be a **line item** on your **annual budget**.
Some of our news departments are already *hemorrhaging money*, how do you expect us to *pay for this*?
Find a way.
From here on out, this will simply be the *cost of doing business*.
But… but…
Excuse me. Although I have *questions* about the intelligence of leaving ourselves open to any legal action, there is *no way* I'm interested in government oversight at all.
Hell, gentlemen, *the truth is*, we've all put profit and politics ahead of institution and it's finally catching up to us.
From this day forward, that needs to **stop**.
I agree, but what we need to decide is how to move the public on this?
"Tonight on the evening news… Assault on the arbiters of our first amendment rights has resulted in increased protection but surprisingly stricter guidelines… one must ask, is this not further punishing the injured party…"
We ourselves will look like the victims.
Hrmph! Sometimes I honestly question your *commitment to craft*…
Which is fair, because in this case, we are the **damn victims**.

rel.92

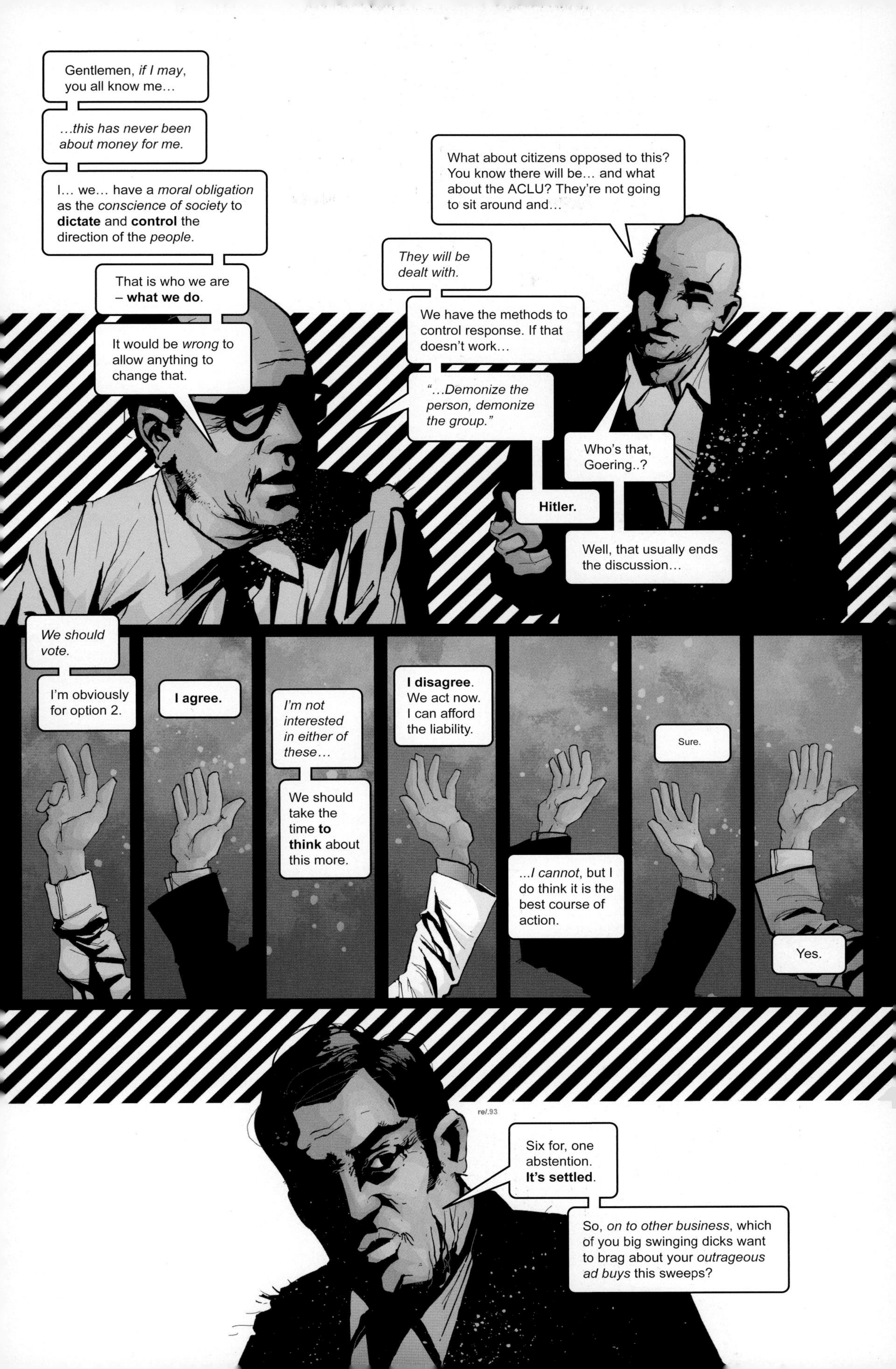
Gentlemen, *if I may*, you all know me…
…this has never been about money for me.
I… we… have a *moral obligation* as the *conscience of society* to **dictate** and **control** the direction of the *people*.
That is who we are – **what we do**.
It would be *wrong* to allow anything to change that.
What about citizens opposed to this? You know there will be… and what about the ACLU? They're not going to sit around and…
They will be dealt with.
We have the methods to control response. If that doesn't work…
"…Demonize the person, demonize the group."
Who's that, Goering..?
Hitler.
Well, that usually ends the discussion…
We should vote.
I'm obviously for option 2.
I agree.
I'm not interested in either of these…
We should take the time **to think** about this more.
I disagree. We act now. I can afford the liability.
…I cannot, but I do think it is the best course of action.
Sure.
Yes.
Six for, one abstention. **It's settled**.
So, *on to other business*, which of you big swinging dicks want to brag about your *outrageous ad buys* this sweeps?

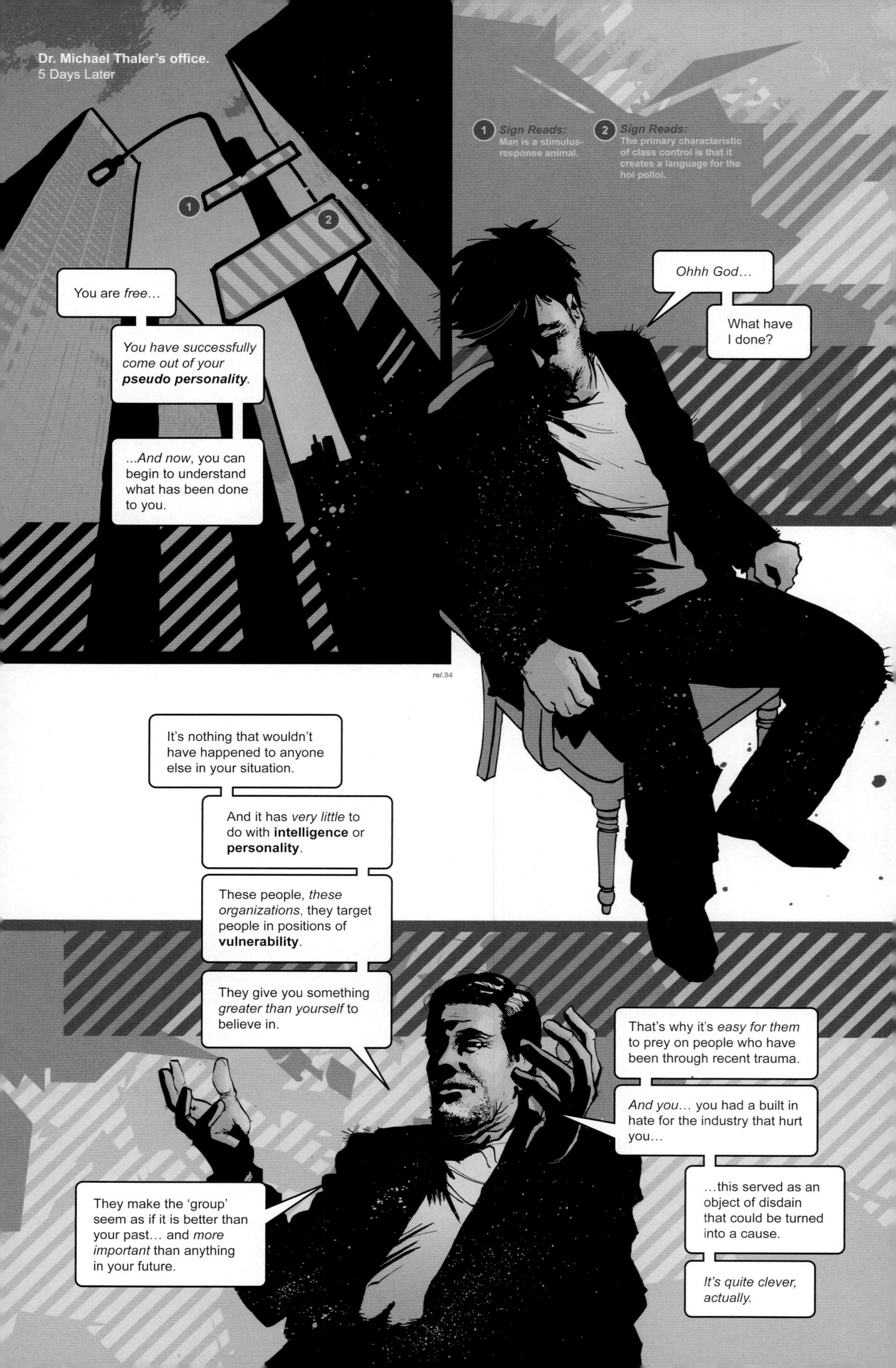

Dr. Michael Thaler's office.
5 Days Later
1 Sign Reads: Man is a stimulus-response animal.
2 Sign Reads: The primary characteristic of class control is that it creates a language for the hoi polloi.
You are *free*…
You have successfully come out of your ***pseudo personality****.*
...And now, you can begin to understand what has been done to you.
Ohhh God…
What have I done?
It's nothing that wouldn't have happened to anyone else in your situation.
And it has *very little* to do with **intelligence** or **personality**.
These people, *these organizations*, they target people in positions of **vulnerability**.
They give you something *greater than yourself* to believe in.
They make the 'group' seem as if it is better than your past… and *more important* than anything in your future.
That's why it's *easy for them* to prey on people who have been through recent trauma.
And you… you had a built in hate for the industry that hurt you…
…this served as an object of disdain that could be turned into a cause.
It's quite clever, actually.

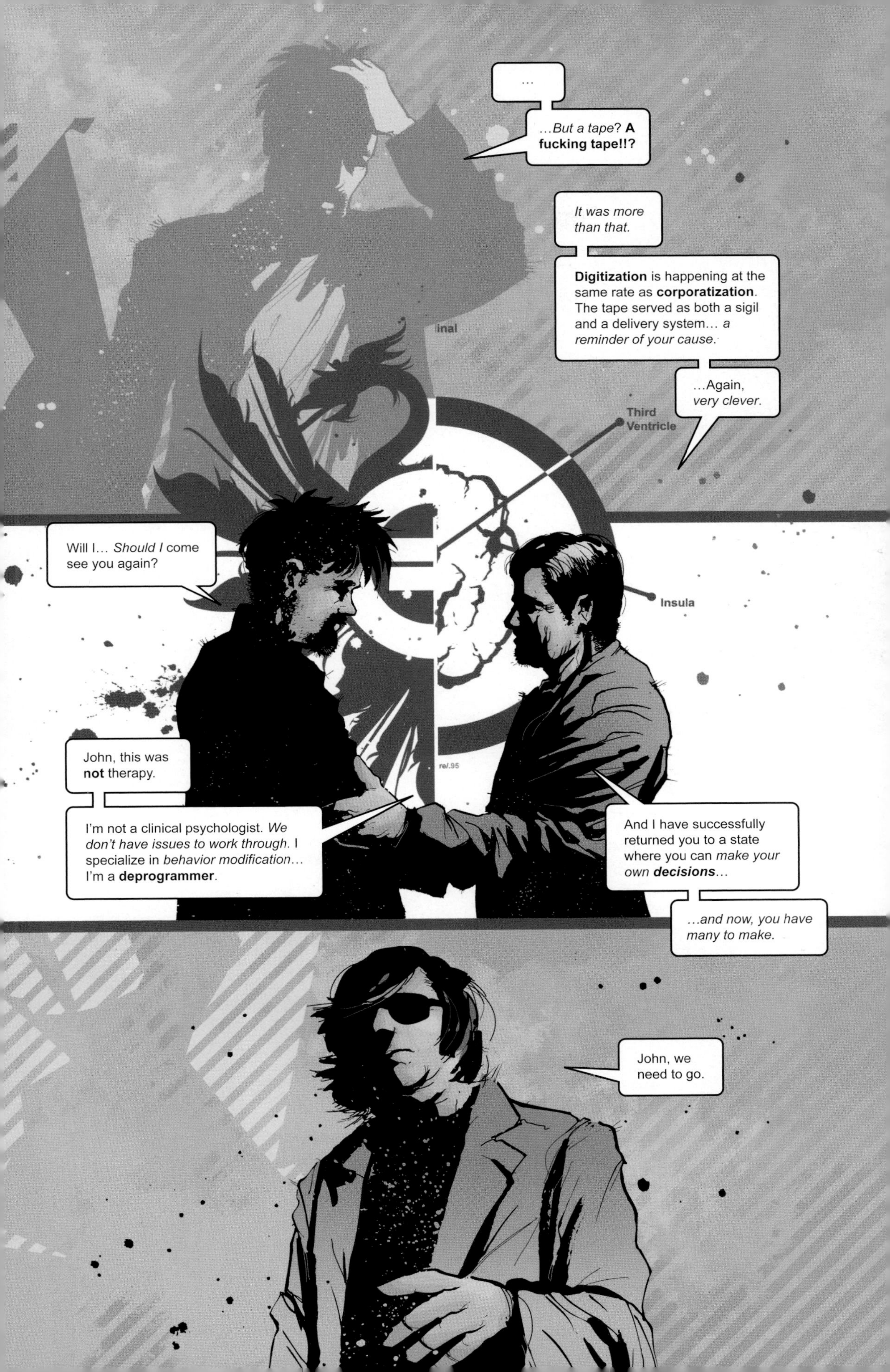

...
...But a tape? **A fucking tape!!?**
It was more than that.
Digitization is happening at the same rate as **corporatization**. The tape served as both a sigil and a delivery system... *a reminder of your cause*.
...Again, *very clever*.
inal
Third Ventricle
Will I... *Should I* come see you again?
Insula
John, this was **not** therapy.
I'm not a clinical psychologist. *We don't have issues to work through*. I specialize in *behavior modification*... I'm a **deprogrammer**.
re/.95
And I have successfully returned you to a state where you can *make your own* ***decisions***...
...and now, you have many to make.
John, we need to go.

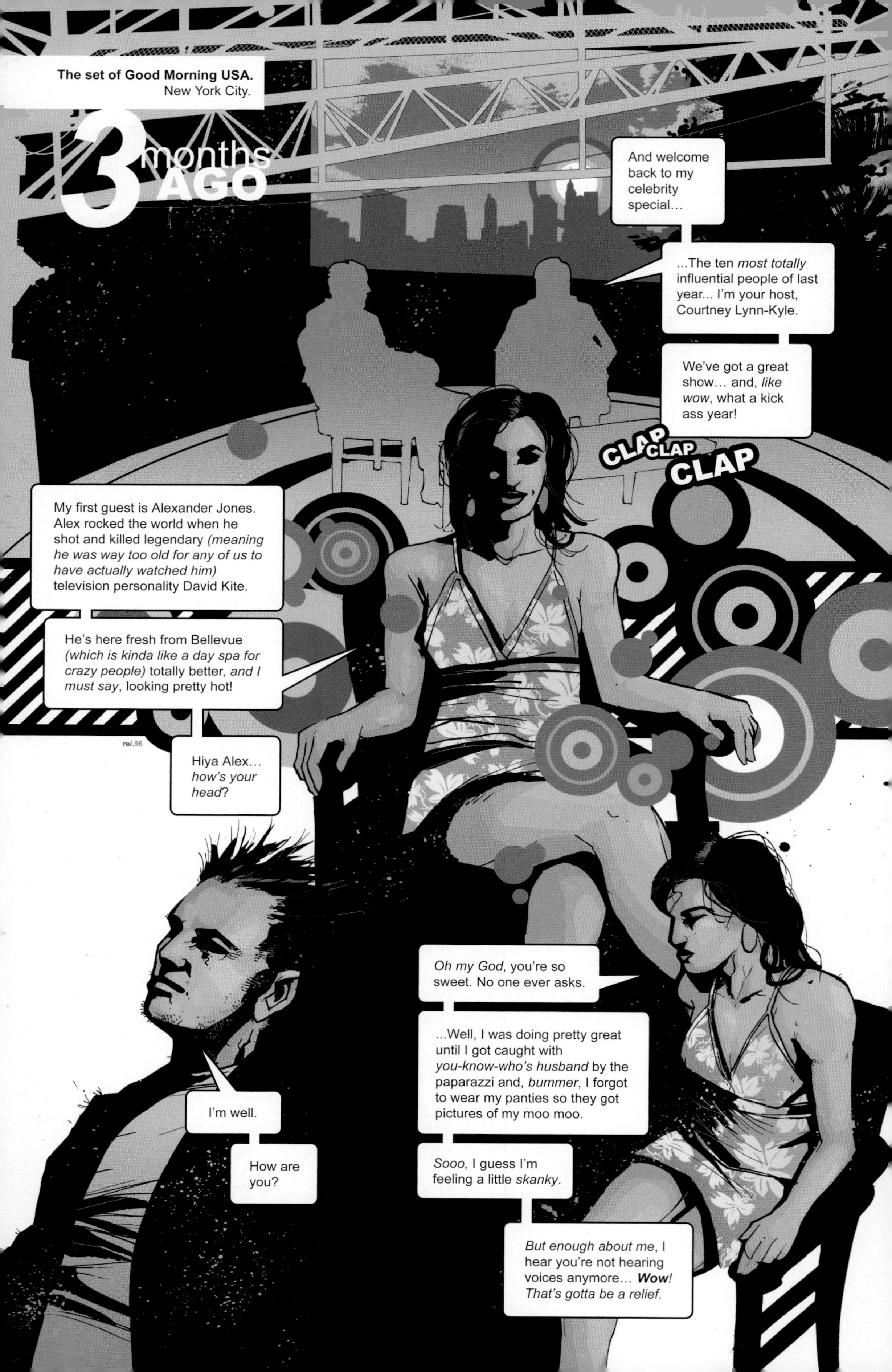

The set of Good Morning USA. New York City.
3 months AGO
And welcome back to my celebrity special...
...The ten most totally influential people of last year... I'm your host, Courtney Lynn-Kyle.
We've got a great show... and, like wow, what a kick ass year!
CLAP CLAP CLAP
My first guest is Alexander Jones. Alex rocked the world when he shot and killed legendary (meaning he was way too old for any of us to have actually watched him) television personality David Kite.
He's here fresh from Bellevue (which is kinda like a day spa for crazy people) totally better, and I must say, looking pretty hot!
Hiya Alex... how's your head?
I'm well.
How are you?
Oh my God, you're so sweet. No one ever asks.
...Well, I was doing pretty great until I got caught with you-know-who's husband by the paparazzi and, bummer, I forgot to wear my panties so they got pictures of my moo moo.
Sooo, I guess I'm feeling a little skanky.
But enough about me, I hear you're not hearing voices anymore... Wow! That's gotta be a relief.

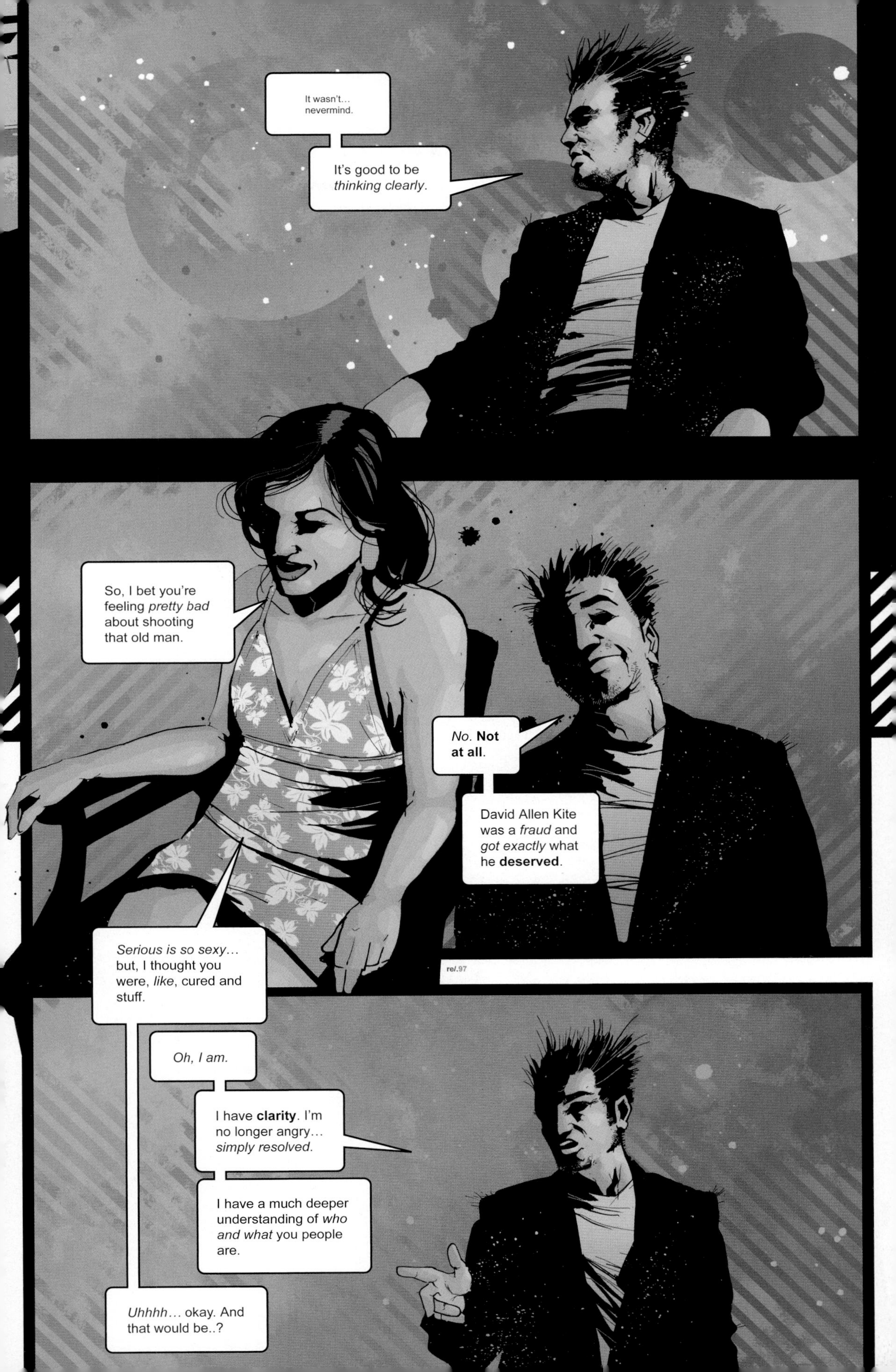
It wasn't… nevermind.
It's good to be *thinking clearly*.
So, I bet you're feeling *pretty bad* about shooting that old man.
No. **Not at all**.
David Allen Kite was a *fraud* and *got exactly* what he **deserved**.
Serious is so sexy… but, I thought you were, *like*, cured and stuff.
Oh, I am.
I have **clarity**. I'm no longer angry… *simply resolved*.
I have a much deeper understanding of *who and what* you people are.
Uhhhh… okay. And that would be..?

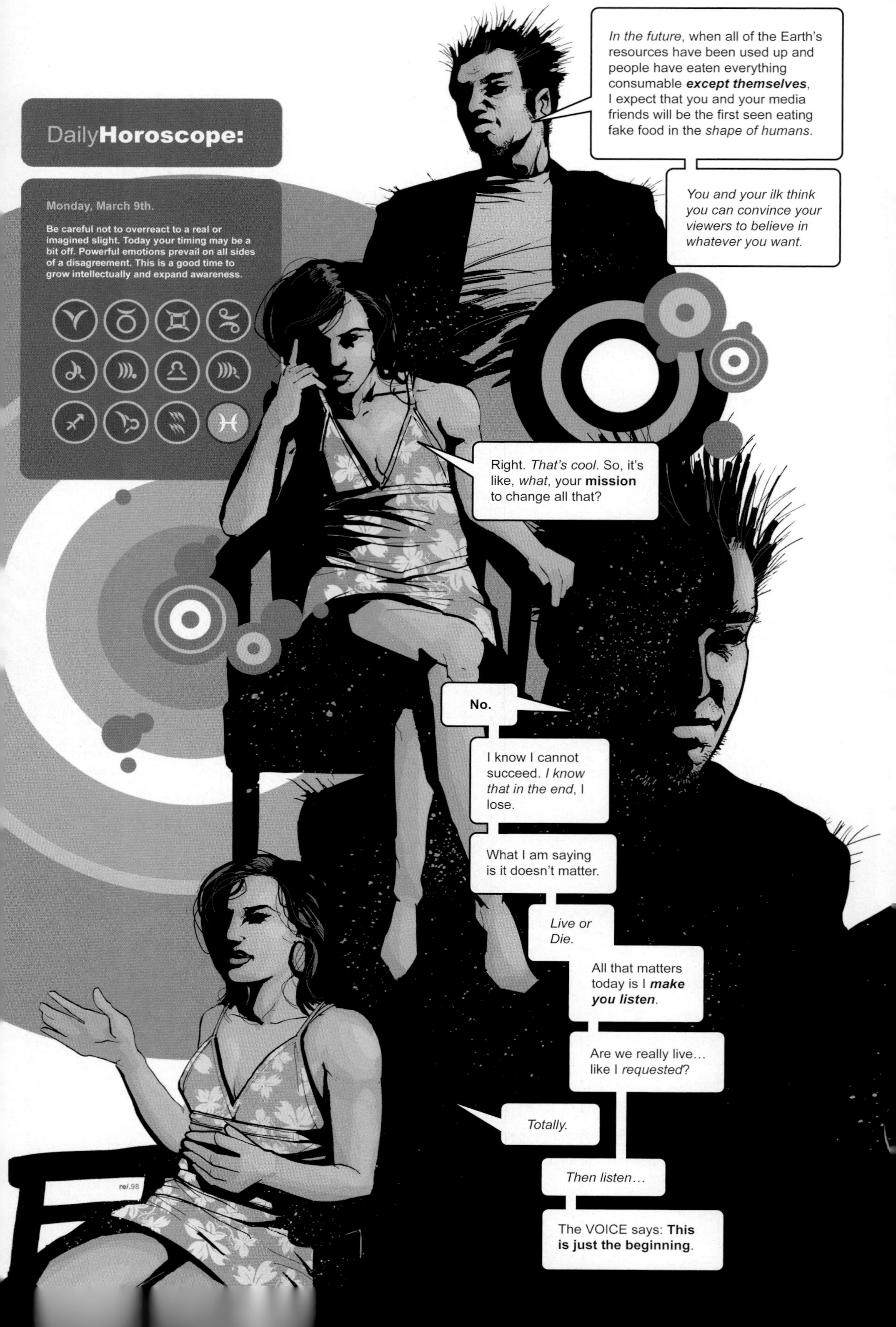
DailyHoroscope:
Monday, March 9th.
Be careful not to overreact to a real or imagined slight. Today your timing may be a bit off. Powerful emotions prevail on all sides of a disagreement. This is a good time to grow intellectually and expand awareness.
In the future, when all of the Earth's resources have been used up and people have eaten everything consumable ***except themselves***, I expect that you and your media friends will be the first seen eating fake food in the *shape of humans*.
You and your ilk think you can convince your viewers to believe in whatever you want.
Right. *That's cool.* So, it's like, *what*, your **mission** to change all that?
No.
I know I cannot succeed. *I know that in the end*, I lose.
What I am saying is it doesn't matter.
Live or Die.
All that matters today is I ***make you listen***.
Are we really live… like I *requested*?
Totally.
Then listen…
The VOICE says: **This is just the beginning**.
re/.98

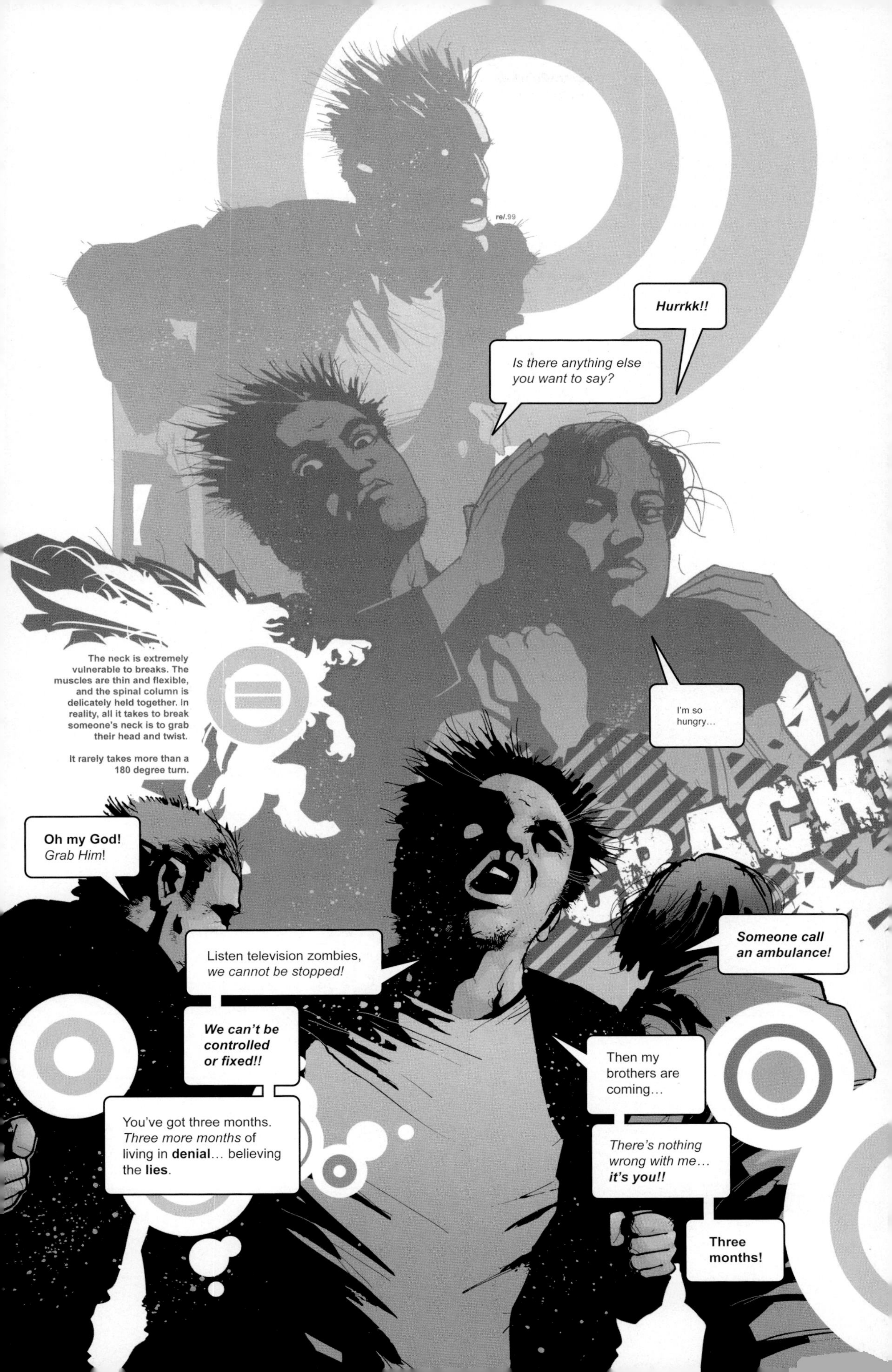

re/.99
Hurrkk!!
Is there anything else you want to say?
I'm so hungry…
The neck is extremely vulnerable to breaks. The muscles are thin and flexible, and the spinal column is delicately held together. In reality, all it takes to break someone's neck is to grab their head and twist.
It rarely takes more than a 180 degree turn.
Oh my God! *Grab Him*!
Listen television zombies, *we cannot be stopped!*
We can't be controlled or fixed!!
You've got three months. *Three more months* of living in **denial**… believing the **lies**.
Someone call an ambulance!
Then my brothers are coming…
There's nothing wrong with me… ***it's you!!***
Three months!

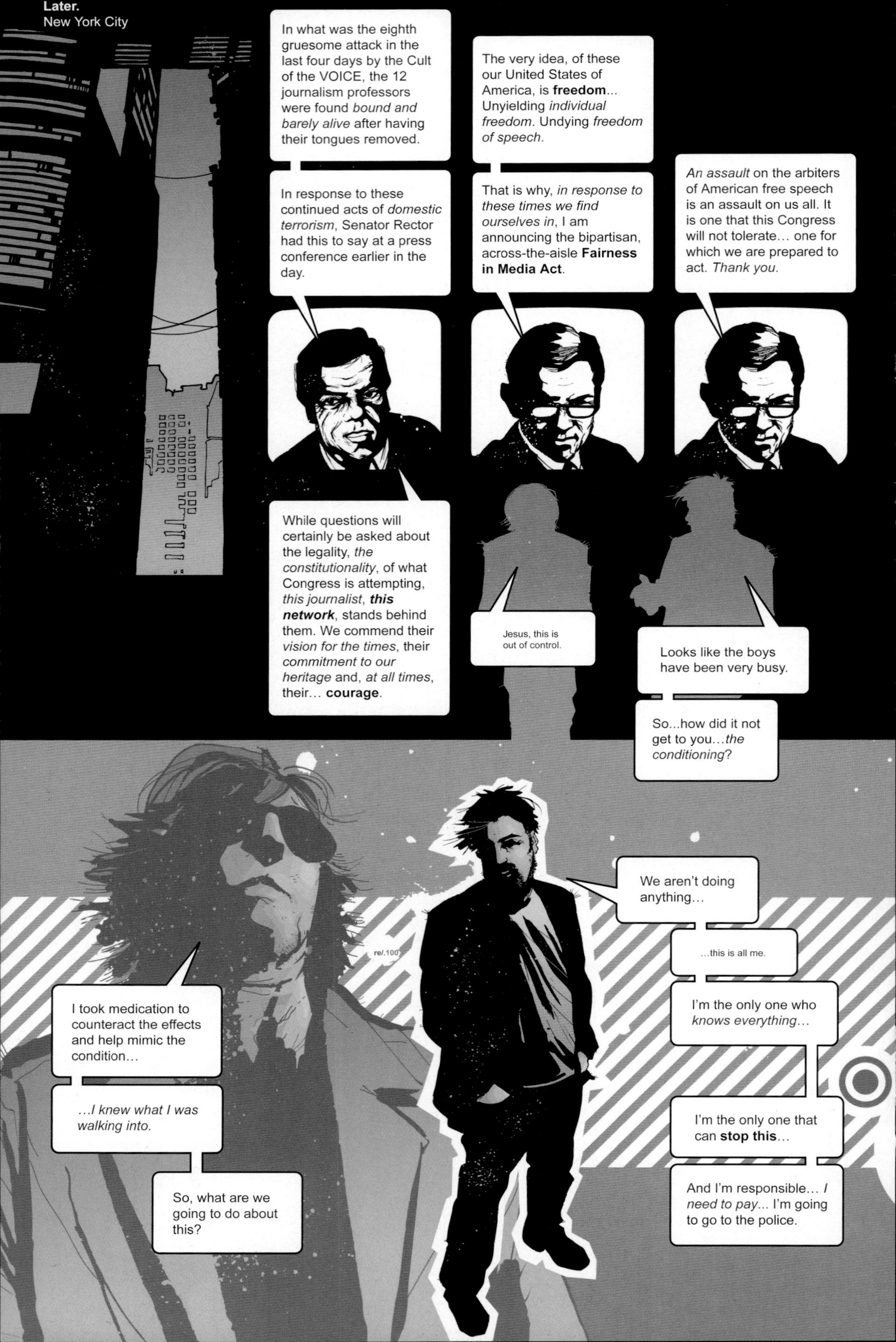

Later.
New York City
In what was the eighth gruesome attack in the last four days by the Cult of the VOICE, the 12 journalism professors were found bound and barely alive after having their tongues removed.
In response to these continued acts of domestic terrorism, Senator Rector had this to say at a press conference earlier in the day.
The very idea, of these our United States of America, is freedom... Unyielding individual freedom. Undying freedom of speech.
That is why, in response to these times we find ourselves in, I am announcing the bipartisan, across-the-aisle Fairness in Media Act.
An assault on the arbiters of American free speech is an assault on us all. It is one that this Congress will not tolerate… one for which we are prepared to act. Thank you.
While questions will certainly be asked about the legality, the constitutionality, of what Congress is attempting, this journalist, this network, stands behind them. We commend their vision for the times, their commitment to our heritage and, at all times, their… courage.
Jesus, this is out of control.
Looks like the boys have been very busy.
So...how did it not get to you…the conditioning?
We aren't doing anything…
…this is all me.
I'm the only one who knows everything…
I took medication to counteract the effects and help mimic the condition…
…I knew what I was walking into.
So, what are we going to do about this?
I'm the only one that can stop this…
And I'm responsible… I need to pay... I'm going to go to the police.

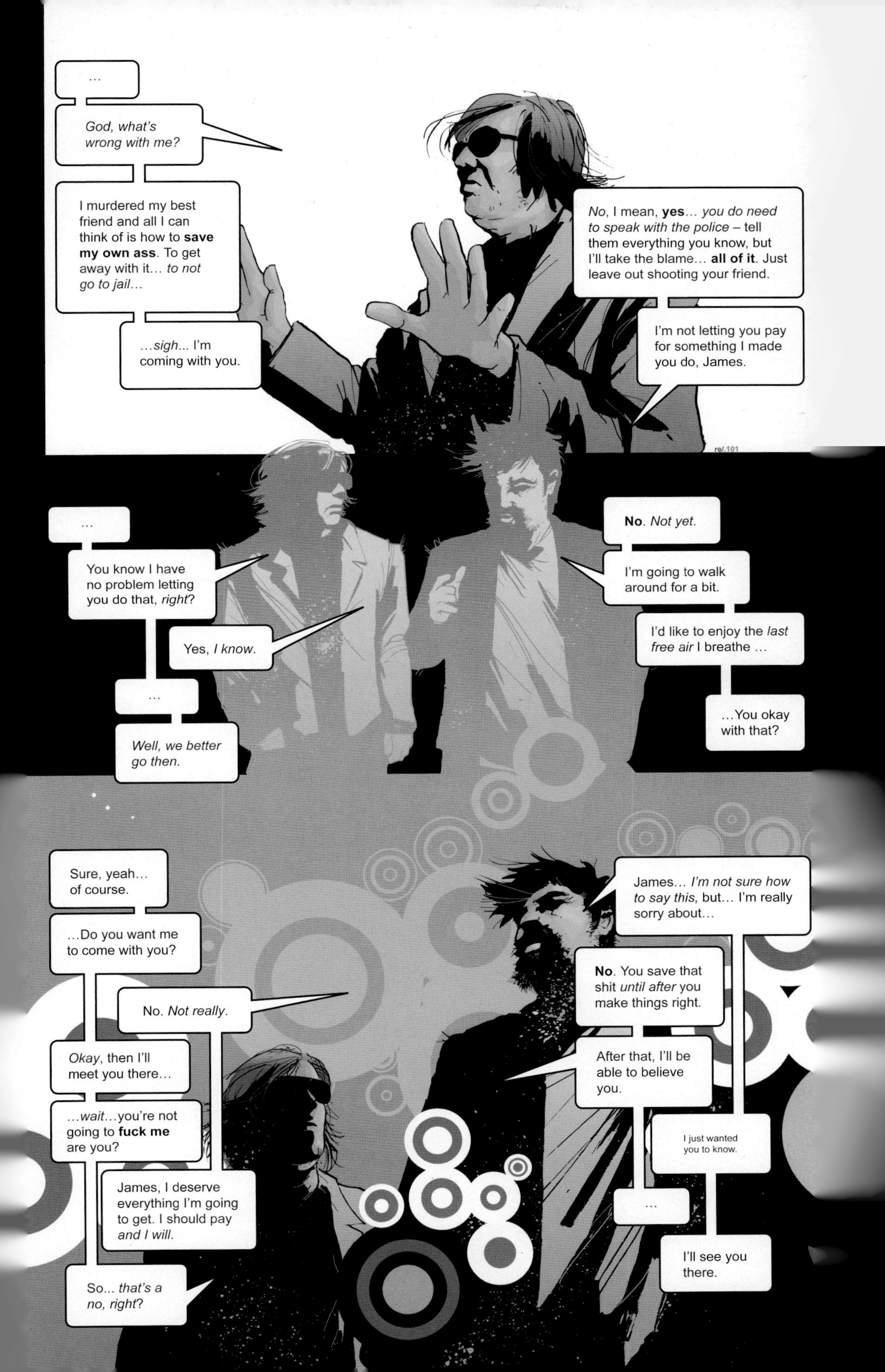

…
God, what's wrong with me?
I murdered my best friend and all I can think of is how to **save my own ass**. To get away with it… *to not go to jail…*
…sigh… I'm coming with you.
No, I mean, **yes**… *you do need to speak with the police* – tell them everything you know, but I'll take the blame… **all of it**. Just leave out shooting your friend.
I'm not letting you pay for something I made you do, James.
re/.101
…
You know I have no problem letting you do that, *right*?
Yes, *I know.*
…
Well, we better go then.
No. *Not yet.*
I'm going to walk around for a bit.
I'd like to enjoy the *last free air* I breathe …
…You okay with that?
Sure, yeah… of course.
…Do you want me to come with you?
No. *Not really.*
Okay, then I'll meet you there…
…*wait*…you're not going to **fuck me** are you?
James, I deserve everything I'm going to get. I should pay *and I will.*
So... *that's a no, right*?
James… *I'm not sure how to say this,* but… I'm really sorry about…
No. You save that shit *until after* you make things right.
After that, I'll be able to believe you.
I just wanted you to know.
…
I'll see you there.

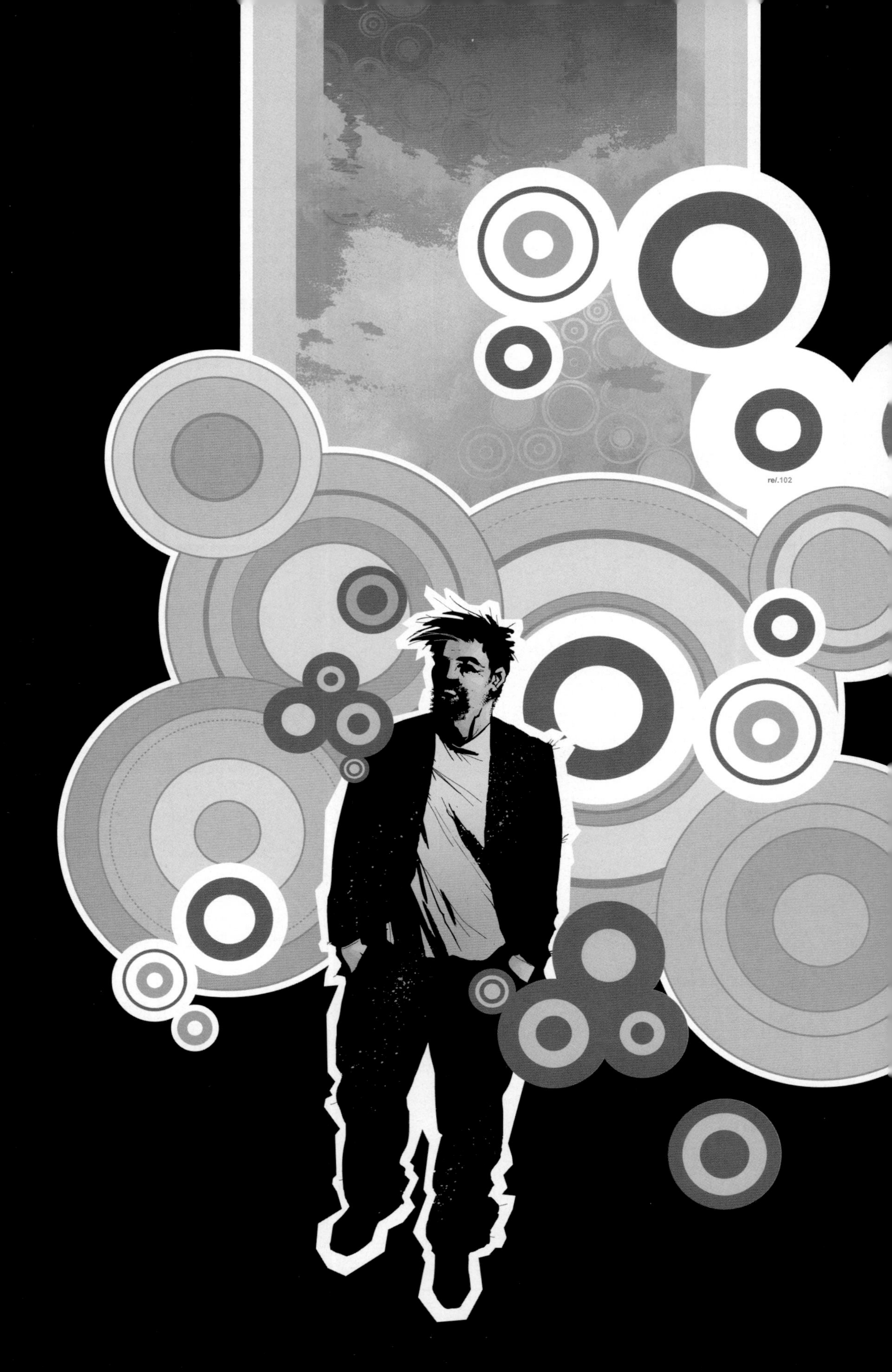
re/.102

I remember now the man I used to be – a husband, *a father*.

I understood morality, and *even though* I mostly fell short of it, I knew that it was a worthy way to try and live.

I know now that person is gone.

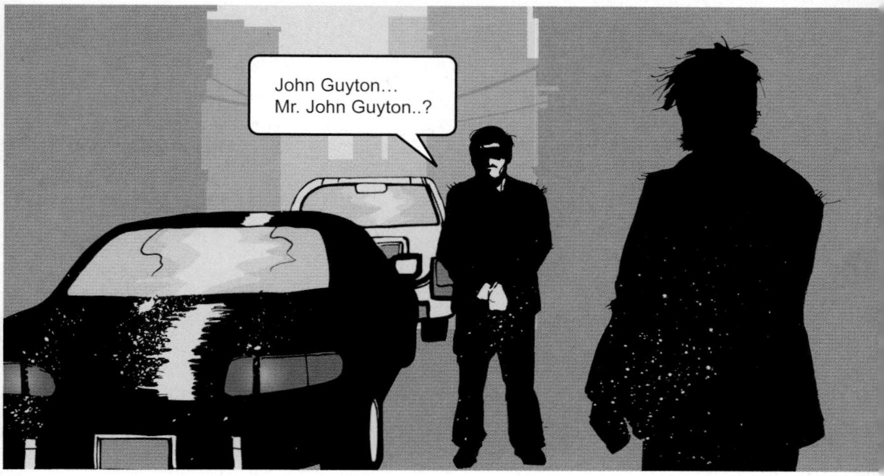
John Guyton…
Mr. John Guyton..?

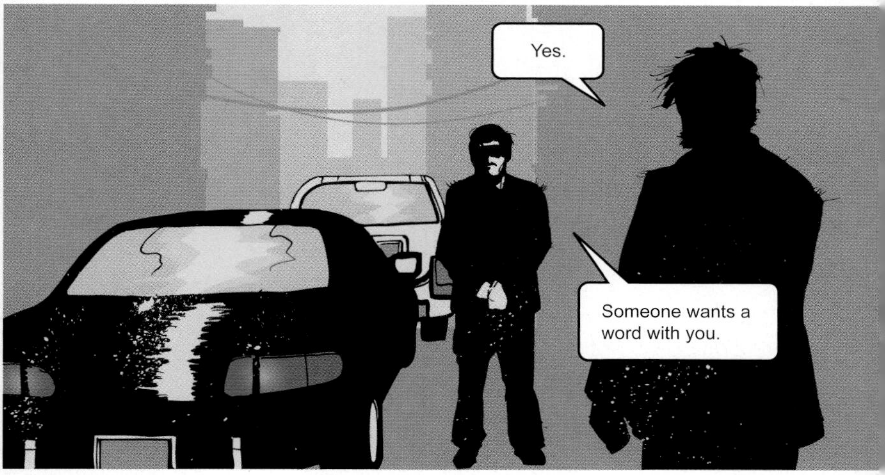
Yes.
Someone wants a word with you.

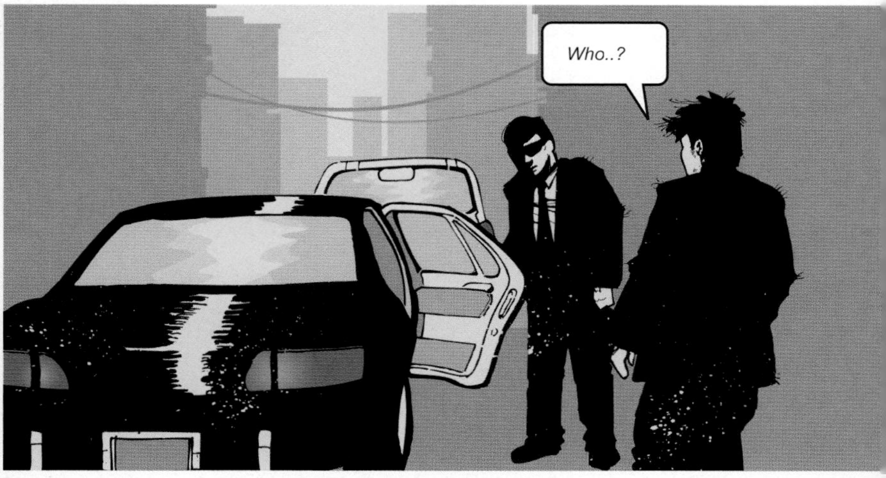
Who..?

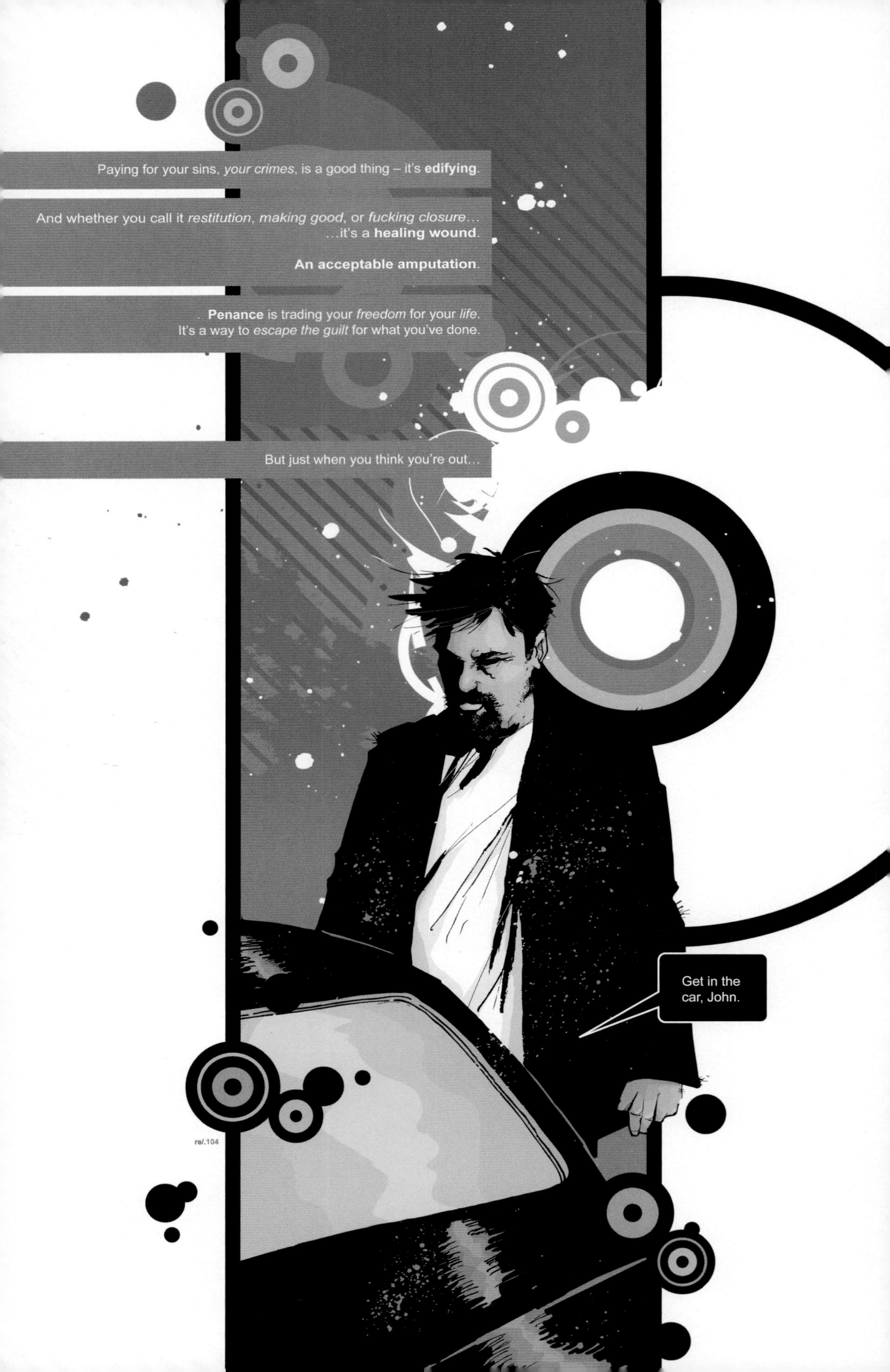
Paying for your sins, *your crimes*, is a good thing – it's **edifying**.
And whether you call it *restitution*, *making good*, or *fucking closure*… …it's a **healing wound**.
An acceptable amputation.
Penance is trading your *freedom* for your *life*. It's a way to *escape the guilt* for what you've done.
But just when you think you're out…
Get in the car, John.

END_CHAPTER 04

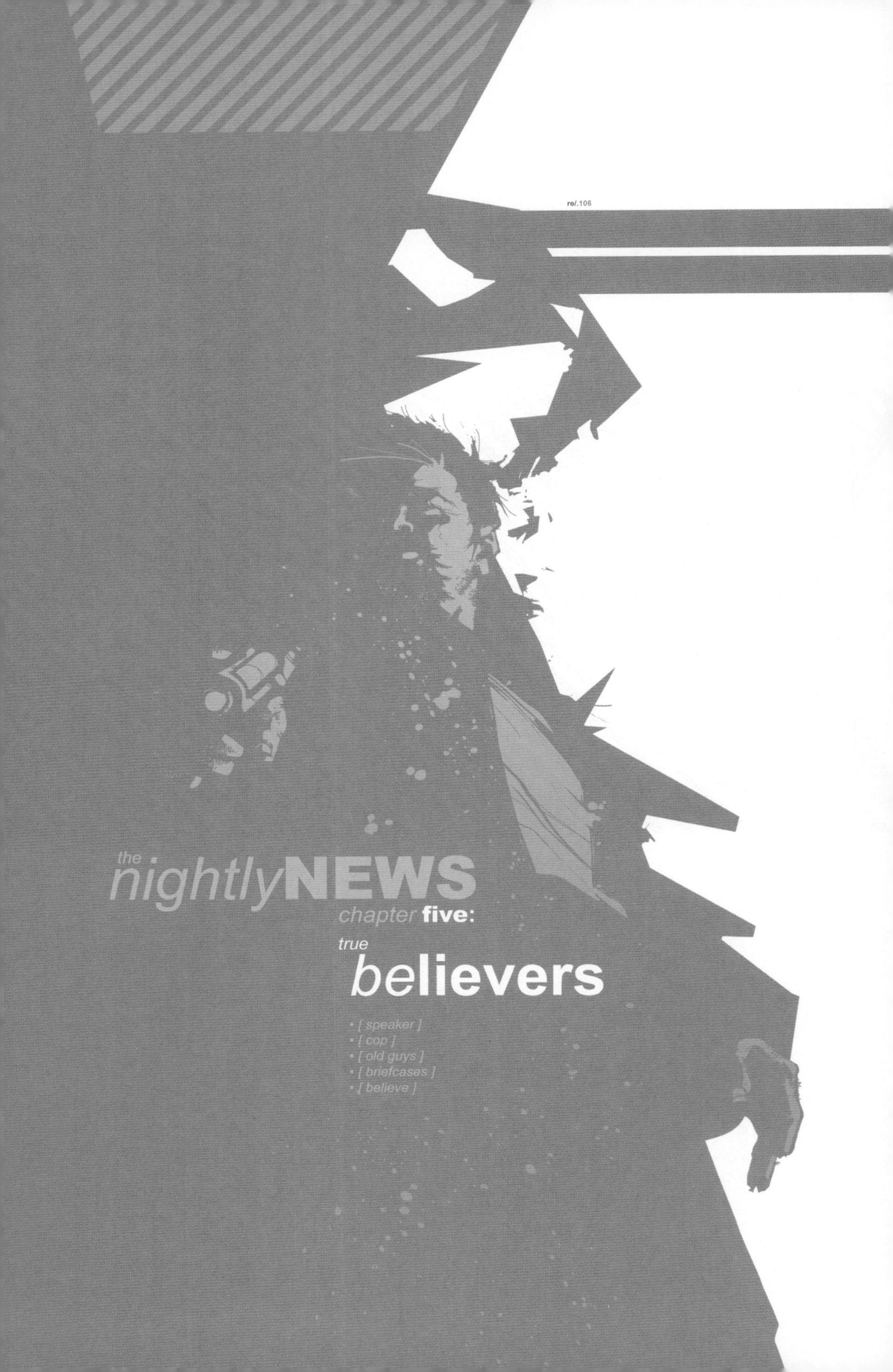
re/.106
the nightlyNEWS
chapter five:
true believers
• [speaker]
• [cop]
• [old guys]
• [briefcases]
• [believe]

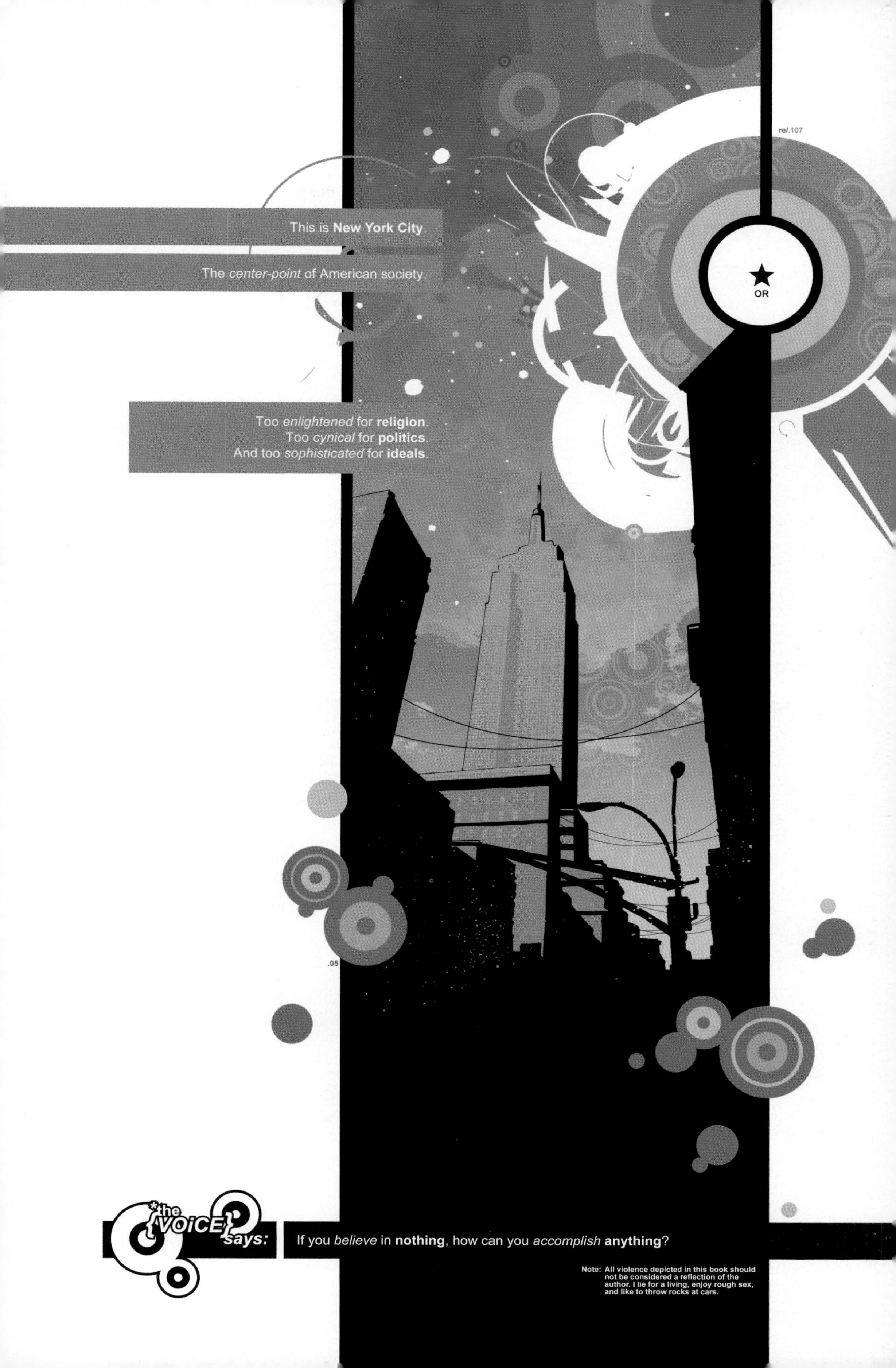

re/.107
This is **New York City**.
The *center-point* of American society.
OR
Too *enlightened* for **religion**.
Too *cynical* for **politics**.
And too *sophisticated* for **ideals**.
.05
*the {VOiCE} says:
If you *believe* in **nothing**, how can you *accomplish* **anything**?
Note: All violence depicted in this book should not be considered a reflection of the author. I lie for a living, enjoy rough sex, and like to throw rocks at cars.

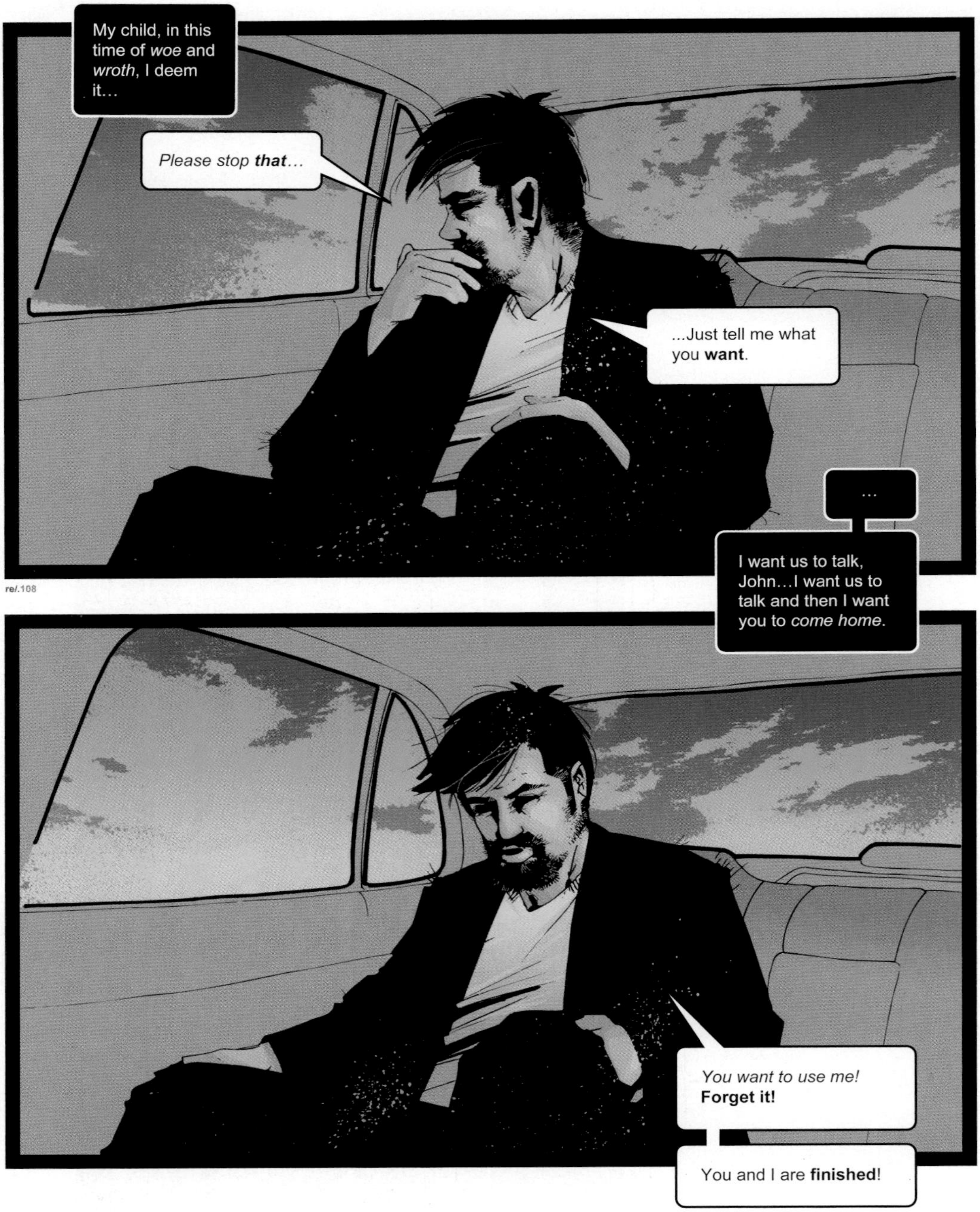
My child, in this time of *woe* and *wroth*, I deem it…
*Please stop **that**…*
...Just tell me what you **want**.
…
I want us to talk, John…I want us to talk and then I want you to *come home*.
You want to use me! **Forget it!**
You and I are **finished**!

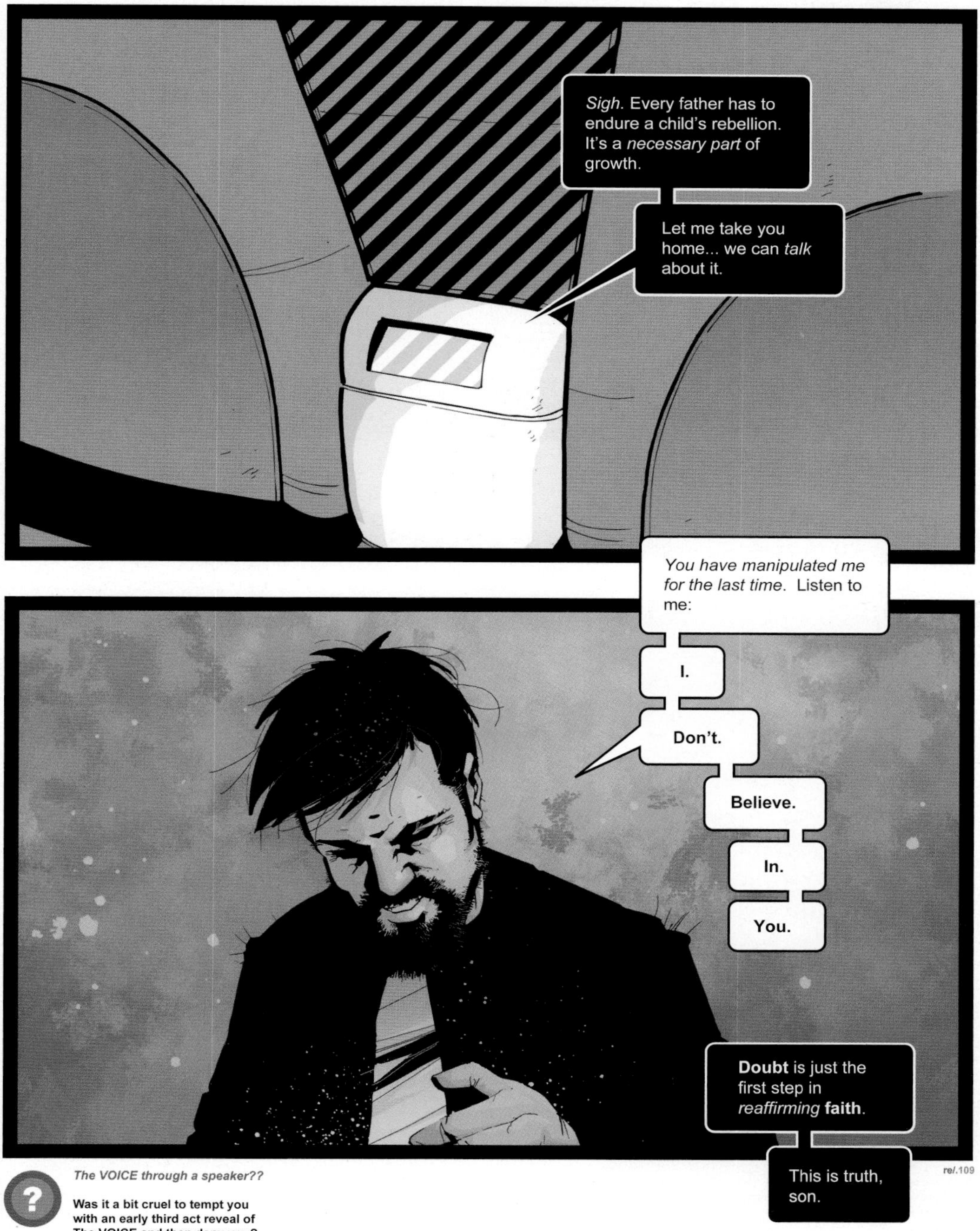
Sigh. Every father has to endure a child's rebellion. It's a *necessary part* of growth.
Let me take you home... we can *talk* about it.
You have manipulated me for the last time. Listen to me:
I.
Don't.
Believe.
In.
You.
Doubt is just the first step in *reaffirming* **faith**.
This is truth, son.

?

The VOICE through a speaker??

Was it a bit cruel to tempt you with an early third act reveal of The VOICE and then deny you?

***Probably so*, but plot demands that we prolong this dance just a little longer.**

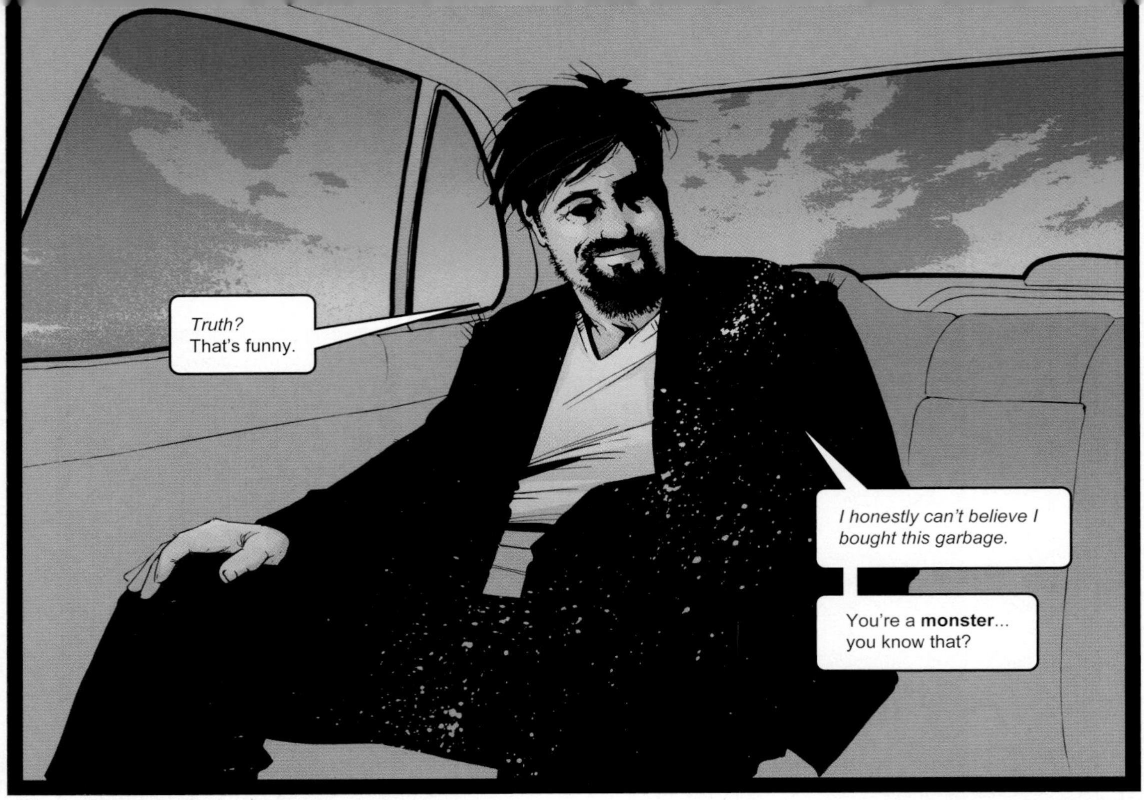
Truth?
That's funny.
I honestly can't believe I bought this garbage.
You're a **monster**... you know that?

To find out more about how journalists feel about themselves, read below. However, if you're like me and only care about watching them get blown up, keep reading on the next page!

*media report: ***striking the balance***

A survey conducted by the Committee of Concerned Journalists and the Pew Research Center has found that:

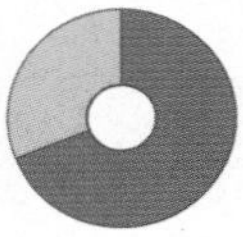

Sixty-Nine Percent

69% of the American people believe that the distinction between reporting and commentary has seriously eroded.

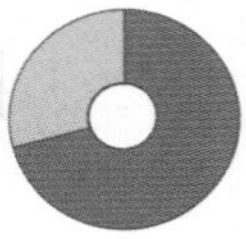

Seventy-One Percent

71% believe that too little attention is paid to complex issues.

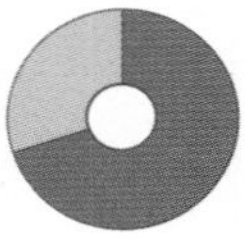

Seventy Percent

70% say news media have blurred the lines between news & entertainment and that the culture of argument is overwhelming the culture of reporting.

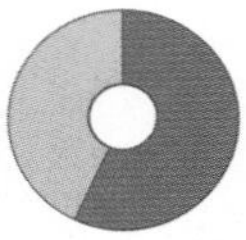

Fifty-Seven Percent

57% believe that journalists have become out of touch with their audience.

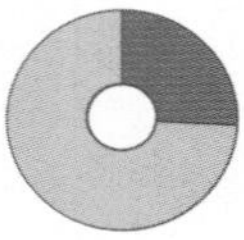

Twenty-Six Percent

26% of the public believe polls are right most or all of the time.

They**Say:**

- More than two-thirds of the print media say that providing an interpretation of the news is a core principle.
- Journalists see themselves caught in a self-defeating spiral, reacting to financial pressures in ways that lower quality, which leads to more business problems, which leads to more misguided changes in the news product.
- Journalists most often cite that citizens are overloaded with information, but this directly contradicts what the public itself believes.
- Journalists believe they are more than just communicators - they are watchdogs. "We are a very important part of this society's system of checks & balances."
- Not only is the public increasingly disaffected by the press, journalists now agree that something is wrong with their profession.

You**Say:**

The top ten reasons why you say competition with cable news media has made journalism worse:

1. Need to compete lowers standards
2. More interest in getting it first than right
3. Too eager to be first
4. Mistakes due to speed
5. Ratings take precedent over quality
6. Sensationalism/scandal/shock value
7. Careless/sloppy/thoughtless reporting
8. Using unreliable/unverifiable sources
9. Lower quality/standards
10. Repetitive reporting/pack journalism

TheFinal**Word:**

The survey concludes:

People don't trust journalists the way they used to, and they have good reason not to.

Two-thirds of Americans say the press doesn't care about the people it covers.

People don't like journalists...don't trust journalists...and don't believe journalists.

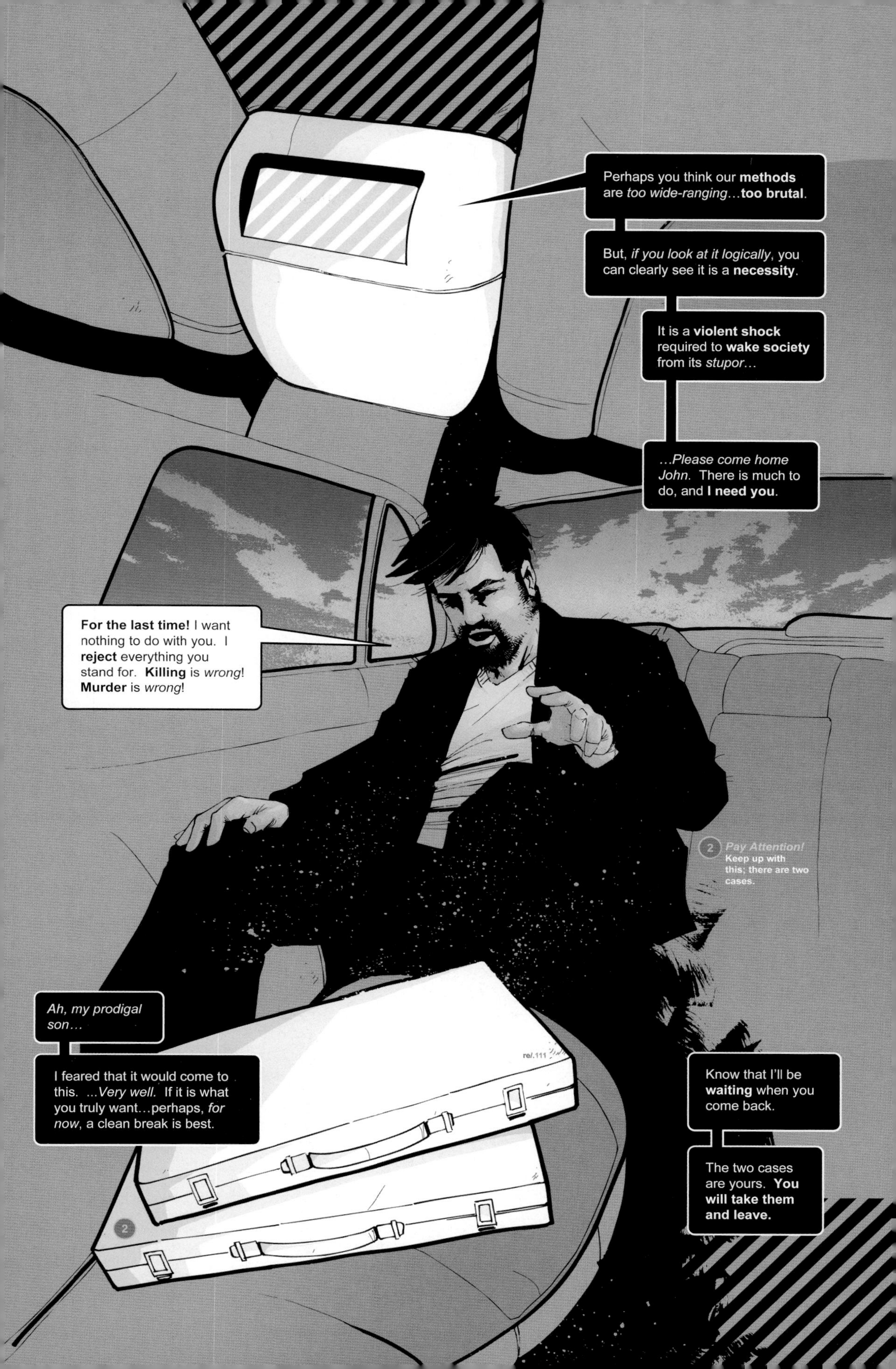

Perhaps you think our **methods** are *too wide-ranging*…**too brutal**.
But, *if you look at it logically*, you can clearly see it is a **necessity**.
It is a **violent shock** required to **wake society** from its *stupor*…
…*Please come home John*. There is much to do, and **I need you**.
For the last time! I want nothing to do with you. I **reject** everything you stand for. **Killing** is *wrong*! **Murder** is *wrong*!
2 *Pay Attention!* **Keep up with this; there are two cases.**
Ah, my prodigal son…
I feared that it would come to this. …*Very well.* If it is what you truly want…perhaps, *for now*, a clean break is best.
Know that I'll be **waiting** when you come back.
The two cases are yours. **You will take them and leave.**

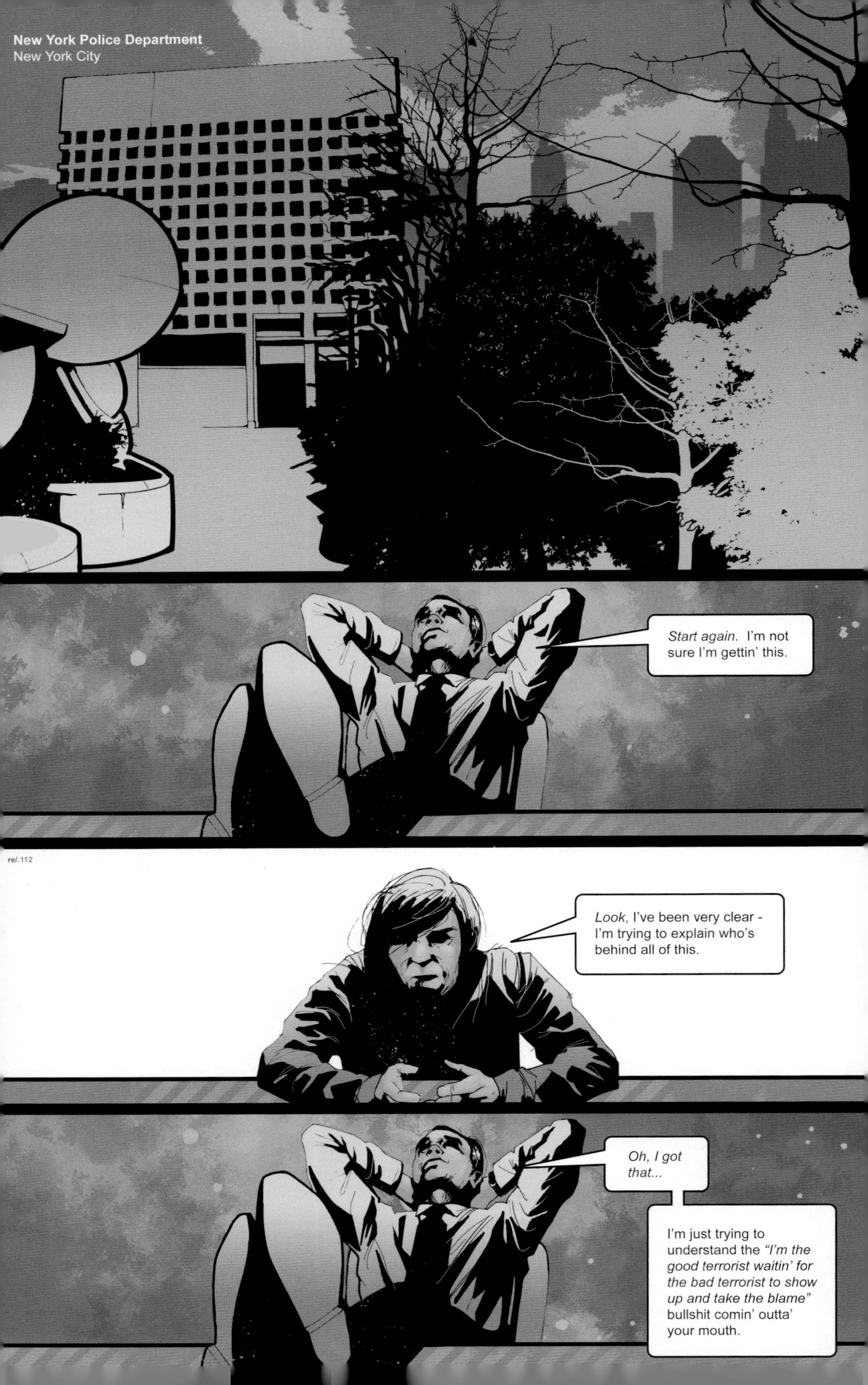
New York Police Department
New York City
Start again. I'm not sure I'm gettin' this.
re/.112
Look, I've been very clear - I'm trying to explain who's behind all of this.
Oh, I got that...
I'm just trying to understand the *"I'm the good terrorist waitin' for the bad terrorist to show up and take the blame"* bullshit comin' outta' your mouth.

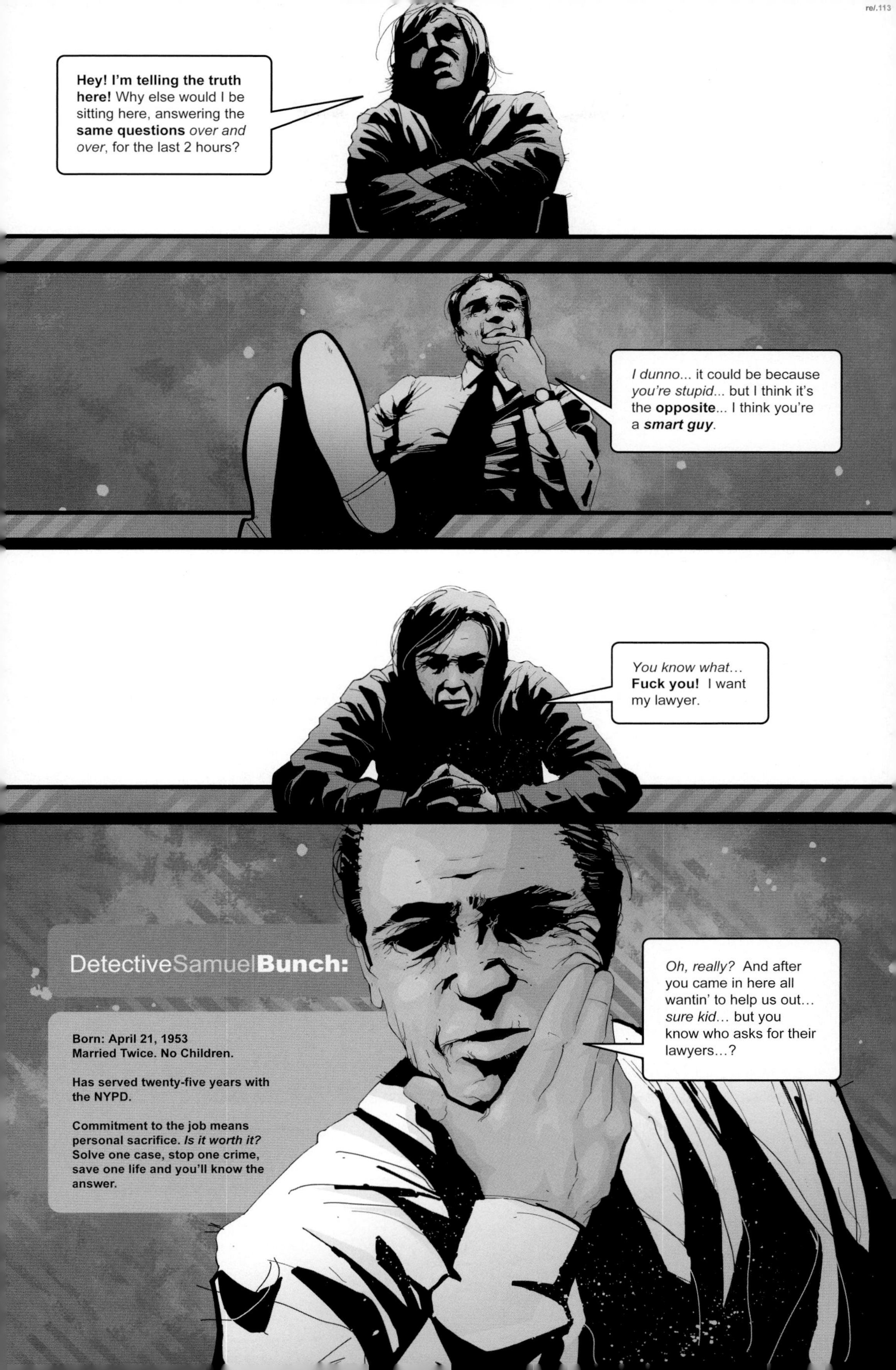
Hey! I'm telling the truth here! Why else would I be sitting here, answering the same questions over and over, for the last 2 hours?
I dunno... it could be because you're stupid... but I think it's the opposite... I think you're a smart guy.
You know what... Fuck you! I want my lawyer.
DetectiveSamuelBunch:
Born: April 21, 1953
Married Twice. No Children.
Has served twenty-five years with the NYPD.
Commitment to the job means personal sacrifice. Is it worth it? Solve one case, stop one crime, save one life and you'll know the answer.
Oh, really? And after you came in here all wantin' to help us out... sure kid... but you know who asks for their lawyers...?

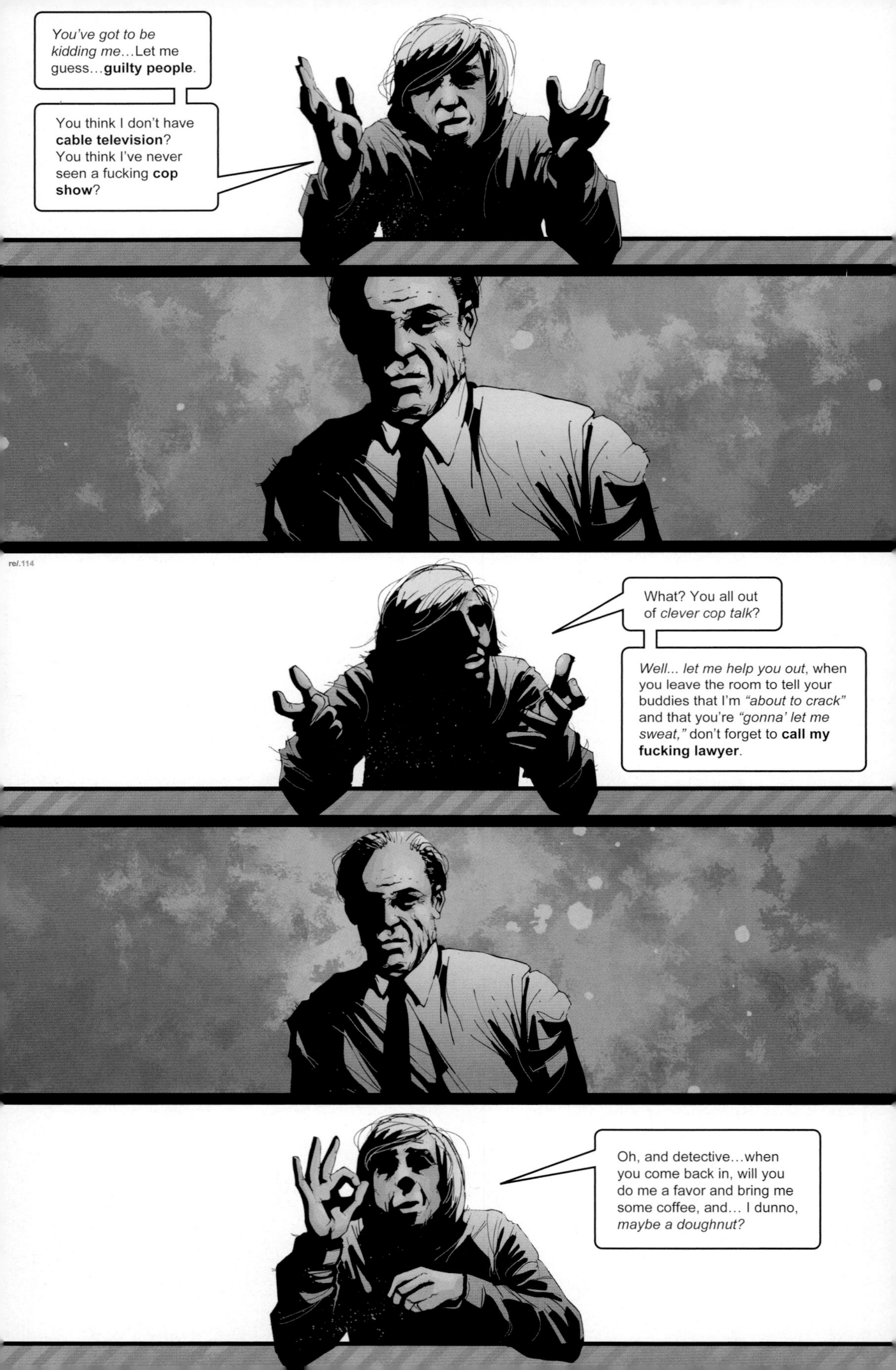
You've got to be kidding me…Let me guess…**guilty people**.
You think I don't have **cable television**? You think I've never seen a fucking **cop show**?
re/.114
What? You all out of *clever cop talk*?
Well... let me help you out, when you leave the room to tell your buddies that I'm *"about to crack"* and that you're *"gonna' let me sweat,"* don't forget to **call my fucking lawyer**.
Oh, and detective…when you come back in, will you do me a favor and bring me some coffee, and… I dunno, *maybe a doughnut?*

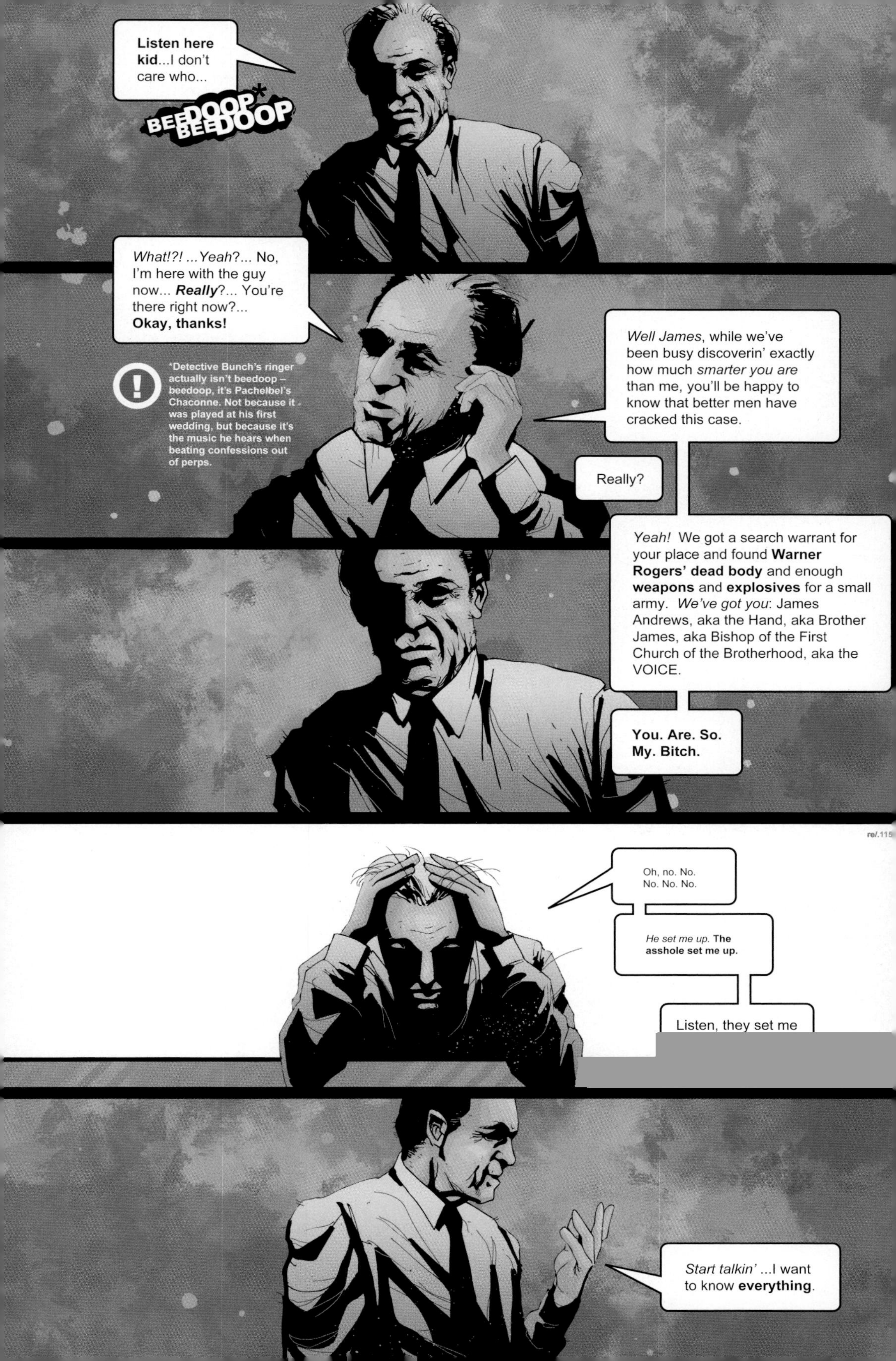
Listen here kid...I don't care who...
BEEDOOP* BEEDOOP
What!?! ...Yeah?... No, I'm here with the guy now... Really?... You're there right now?... Okay, thanks!
*Detective Bunch's ringer actually isn't beedoop – beedoop, it's Pachelbel's Chaconne. Not because it was played at his first wedding, but because it's the music he hears when beating confessions out of perps.
Well James, while we've been busy discoverin' exactly how much smarter you are than me, you'll be happy to know that better men have cracked this case.
Really?
Yeah! We got a search warrant for your place and found Warner Rogers' dead body and enough weapons and explosives for a small army. We've got you: James Andrews, aka the Hand, aka Brother James, aka Bishop of the First Church of the Brotherhood, aka the VOICE.
You. Are. So. My. Bitch.
re/.115
Oh, no. No. No. No. No.
He set me up. The asshole set me up.
Listen, they set me
Start talkin' ...I want to know everything.

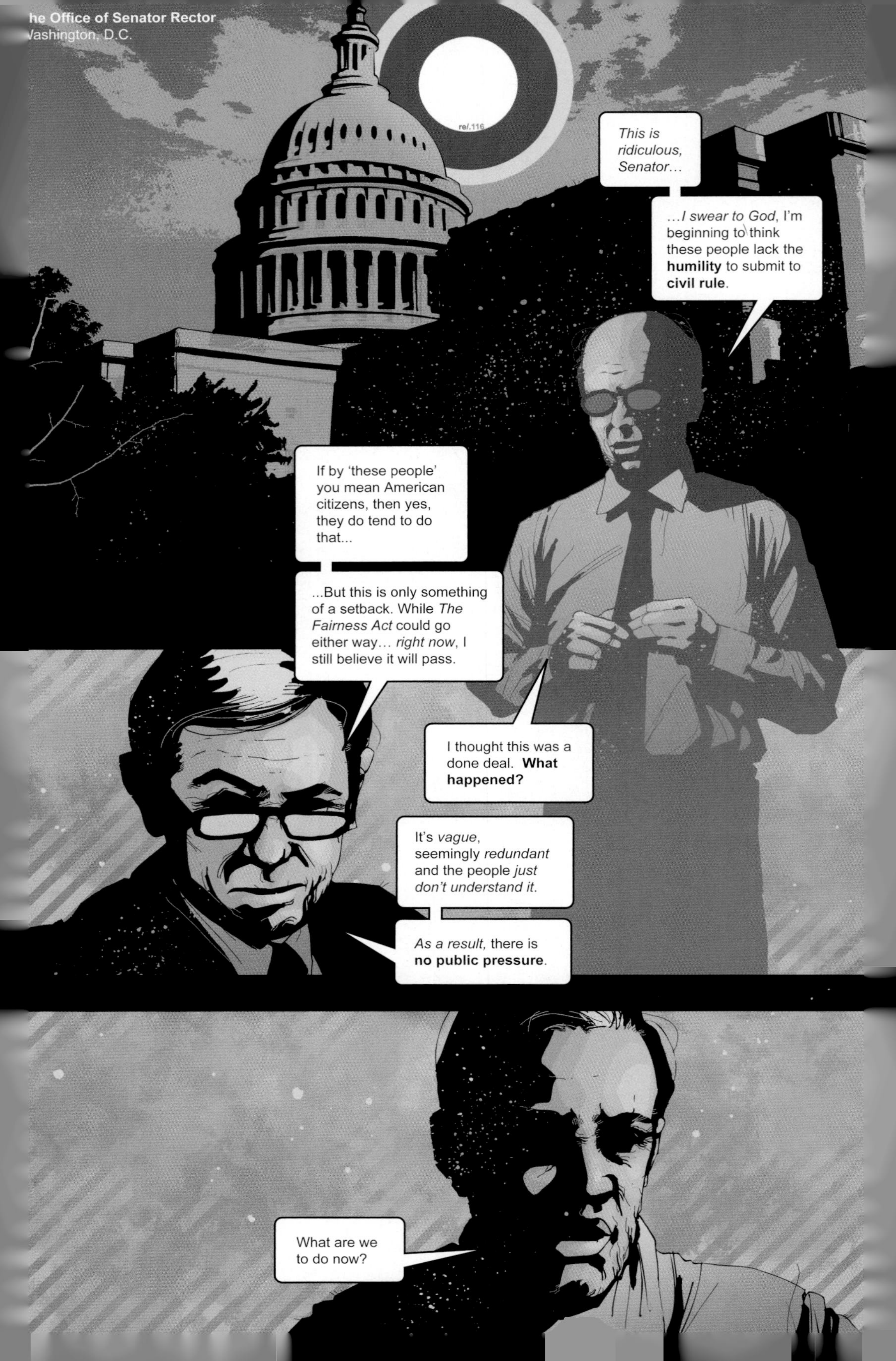

he Office of Senator Rector
Vashington, D.C.
rel.116
This is ridiculous, Senator…
…*I swear to God*, I'm beginning to think these people lack the **humility** to submit to **civil rule**.
If by 'these people' you mean American citizens, then yes, they do tend to do that...
...But this is only something of a setback. While *The Fairness Act* could go either way… *right now*, I still believe it will pass.
I thought this was a done deal. **What happened?**
It's *vague*, seemingly *redundant* and the people *just don't understand it*.
As a result, there is **no public pressure**.
What are we to do now?

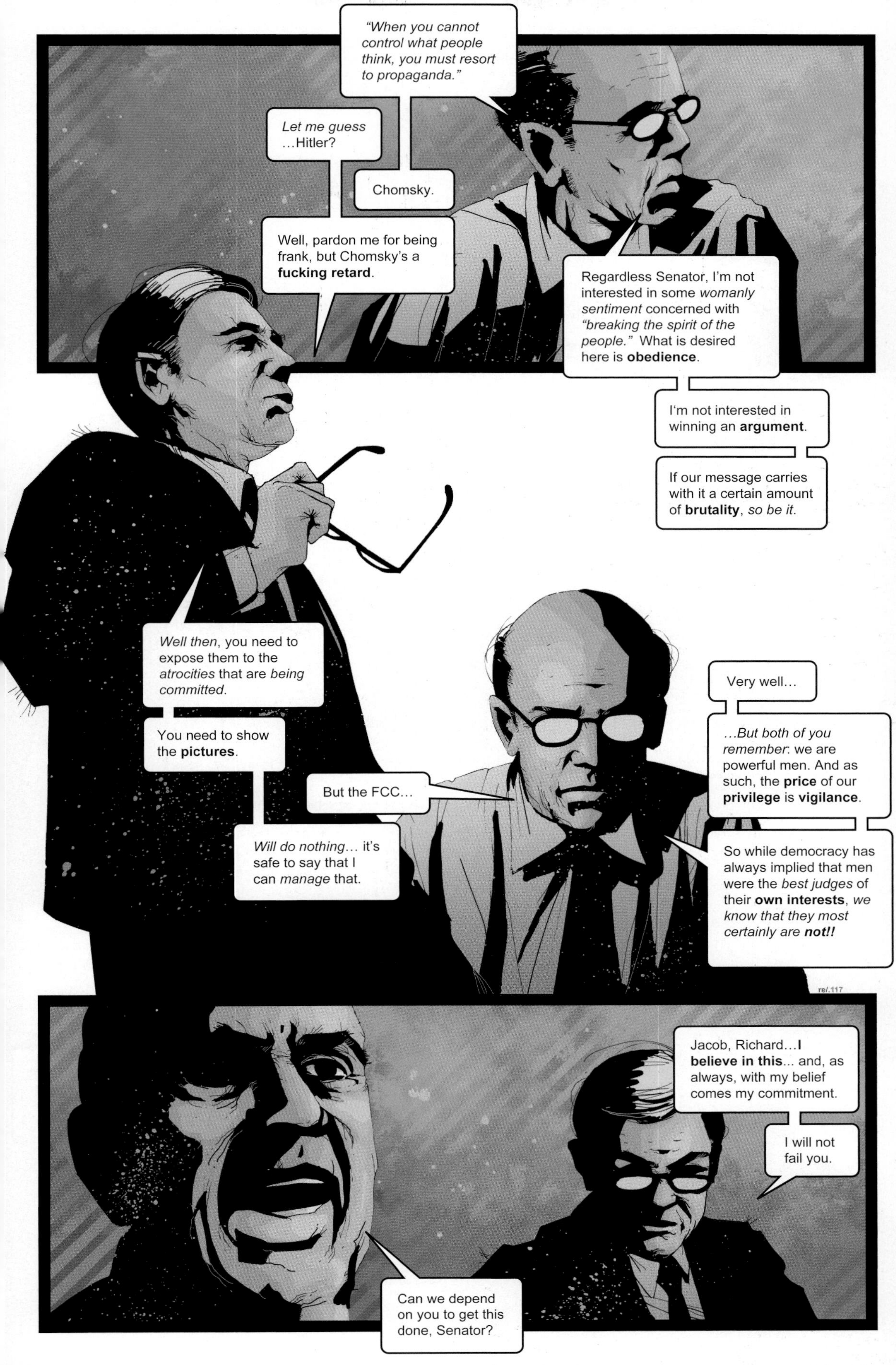
"When you cannot control what people think, you must resort to propaganda."
Let me guess ...Hitler?
Chomsky.
Well, pardon me for being frank, but Chomsky's a **fucking retard**.
Regardless Senator, I'm not interested in some *womanly sentiment* concerned with *"breaking the spirit of the people."* What is desired here is **obedience**.
I'm not interested in winning an **argument**.
If our message carries with it a certain amount of **brutality**, *so be it*.
Well then, you need to expose them to the *atrocities* that are *being committed*.
You need to show the **pictures**.
But the FCC...
Will do nothing... it's safe to say that I can *manage* that.
Very well...
...But both of you remember: we are powerful men. And as such, the **price** of our **privilege** is **vigilance**.
So while democracy has always implied that men were the *best judges* of their **own interests**, *we know that they most certainly are* ***not!!***
Jacob, Richard... **I believe in this**... and, as always, with my belief comes my commitment.
I will not fail you.
Can we depend on you to get this done, Senator?

Five Blue Oysters
New York City

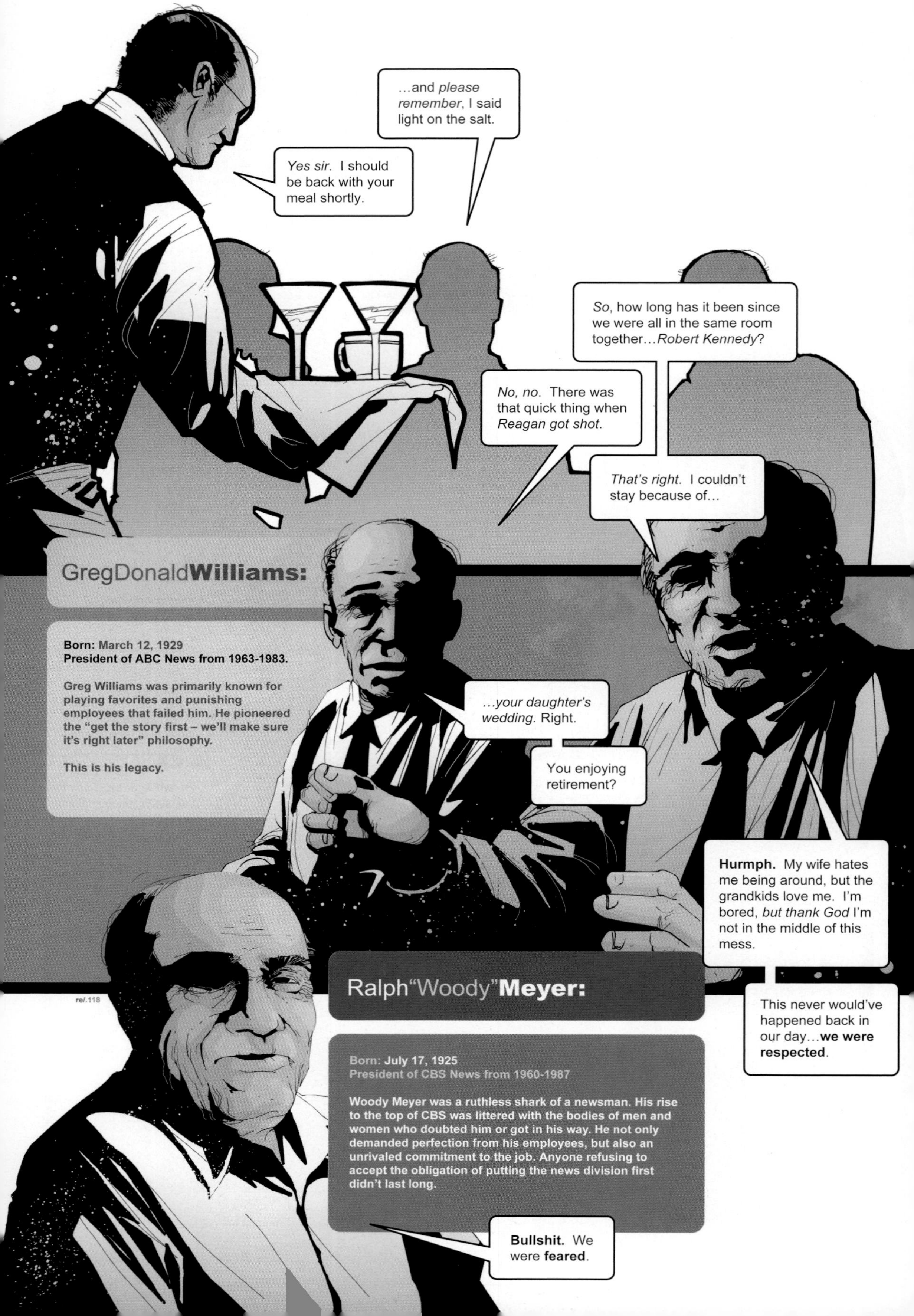
Yes sir. I should be back with your meal shortly.
...and please remember, I said light on the salt.
So, how long has it been since we were all in the same room together...Robert Kennedy?
No, no. There was that quick thing when Reagan got shot.
That's right. I couldn't stay because of...
GregDonaldWilliams:
Born: March 12, 1929
President of ABC News from 1963-1983.
Greg Williams was primarily known for playing favorites and punishing employees that failed him. He pioneered the "get the story first – we'll make sure it's right later" philosophy.
This is his legacy.
...your daughter's wedding. Right.
You enjoying retirement?
Hurmph. My wife hates me being around, but the grandkids love me. I'm bored, but thank God I'm not in the middle of this mess.
Ralph"Woody"Meyer:
Born: July 17, 1925
President of CBS News from 1960-1987
Woody Meyer was a ruthless shark of a newsman. His rise to the top of CBS was littered with the bodies of men and women who doubted him or got in his way. He not only demanded perfection from his employees, but also an unrivaled commitment to the job. Anyone refusing to accept the obligation of putting the news division first didn't last long.
This never would've happened back in our day...we were respected.
Bullshit. We were feared.

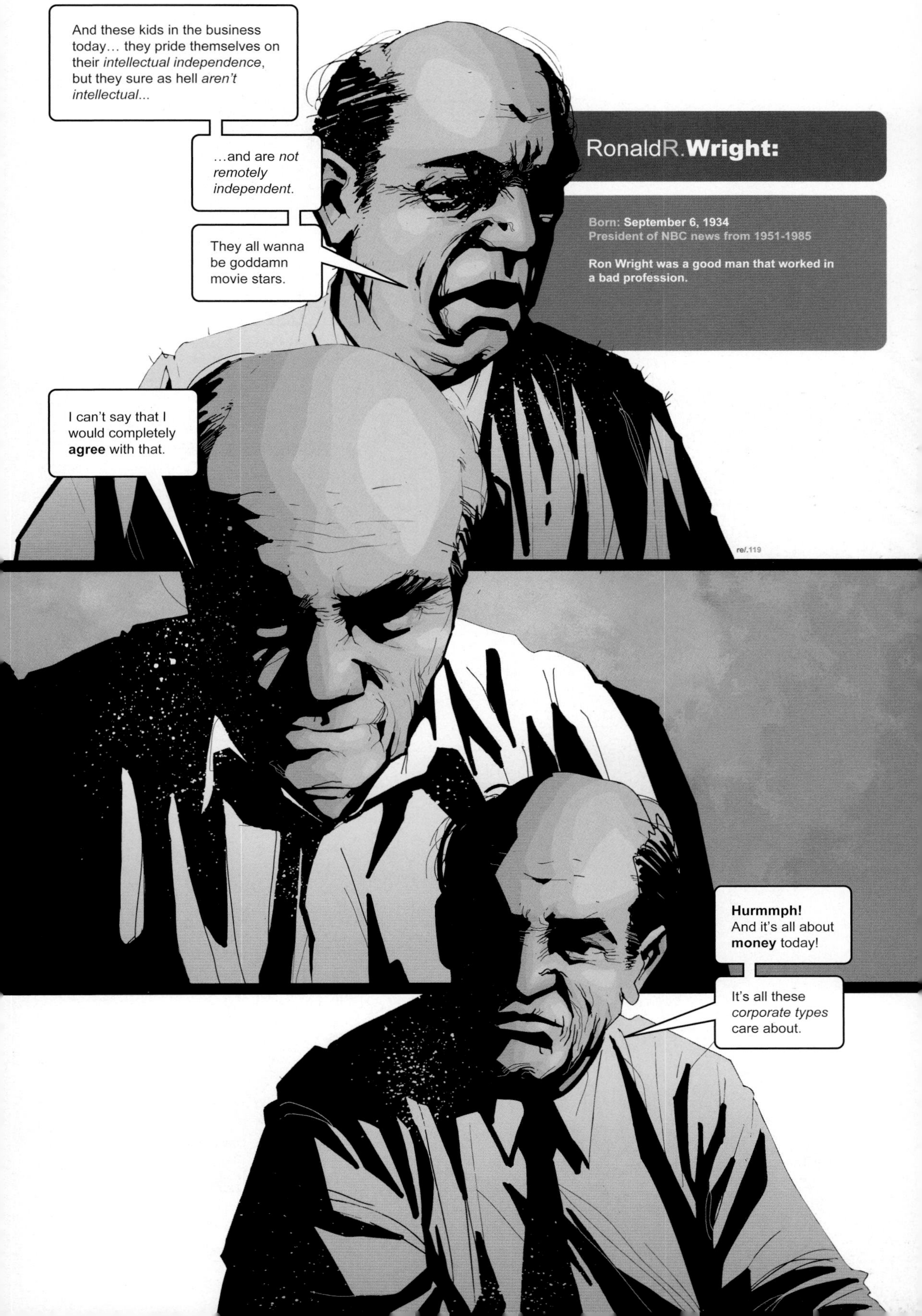

And these kids in the business today… they pride themselves on their *intellectual independence*, but they sure as hell *aren't intellectual*...
…and are *not remotely independent*.
They all wanna be goddamn movie stars.
RonaldR.**Wright:**
Born: **September 6, 1934**
President of NBC news from 1951-1985
Ron Wright was a good man that worked in a bad profession.
I can't say that I would completely **agree** with that.
re/.119
Hurmmph! And it's all about **money** today!
It's all these *corporate types* care about.

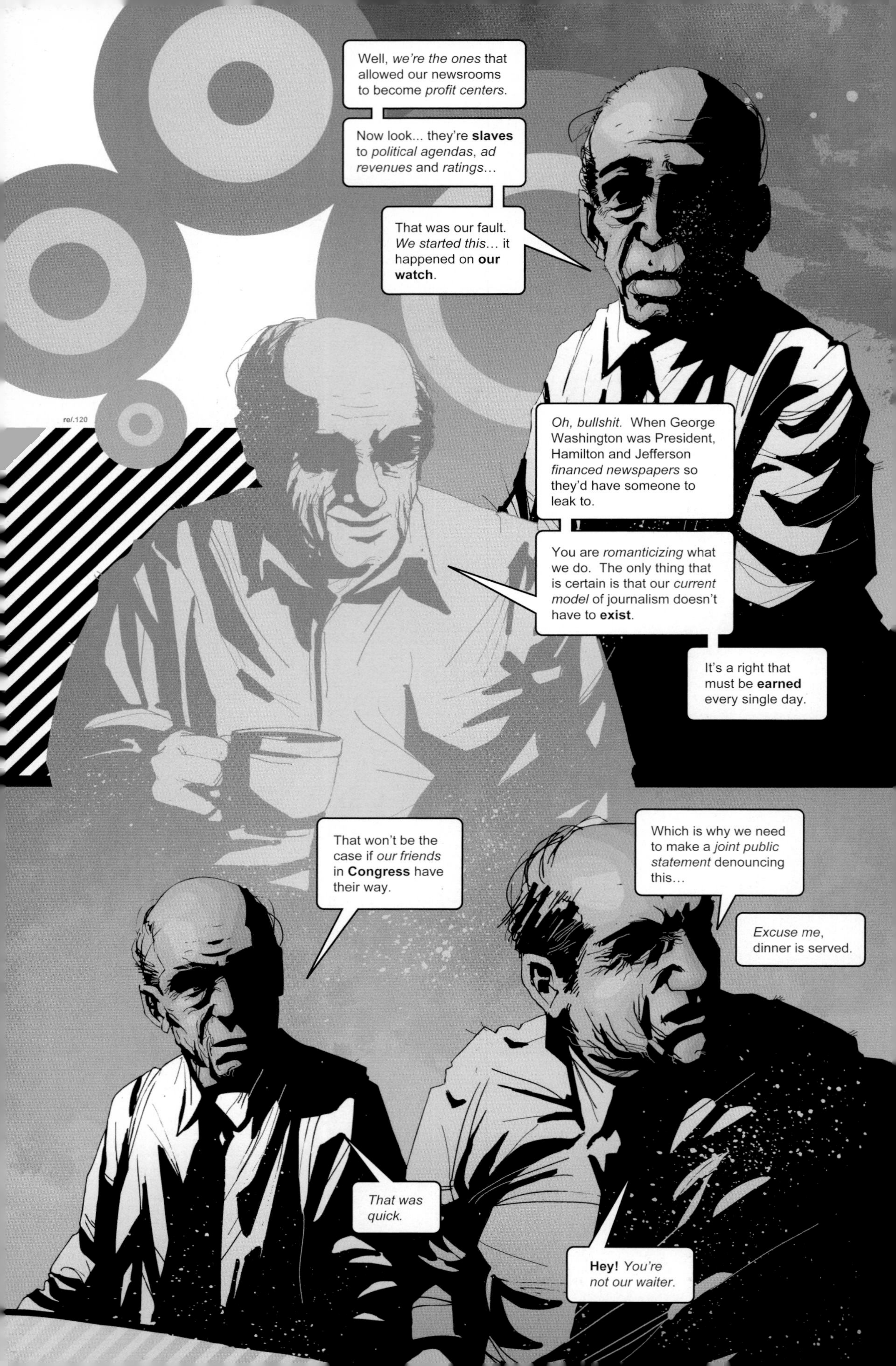
Well, *we're the ones* that allowed our newsrooms to become *profit centers*.
Now look... they're **slaves** to *political agendas*, *ad revenues* and *ratings*…
That was our fault. *We started this…* it happened on **our watch**.
Oh, bullshit. When George Washington was President, Hamilton and Jefferson *financed newspapers* so they'd have someone to leak to.
You are *romanticizing* what we do. The only thing that is certain is that our *current model* of journalism doesn't have to **exist**.
It's a right that must be **earned** every single day.
That won't be the case if *our friends* in **Congress** have their way.
Which is why we need to make a *joint public statement* denouncing this…
Excuse me, dinner is served.
That was quick.
Hey! *You're not our waiter.*

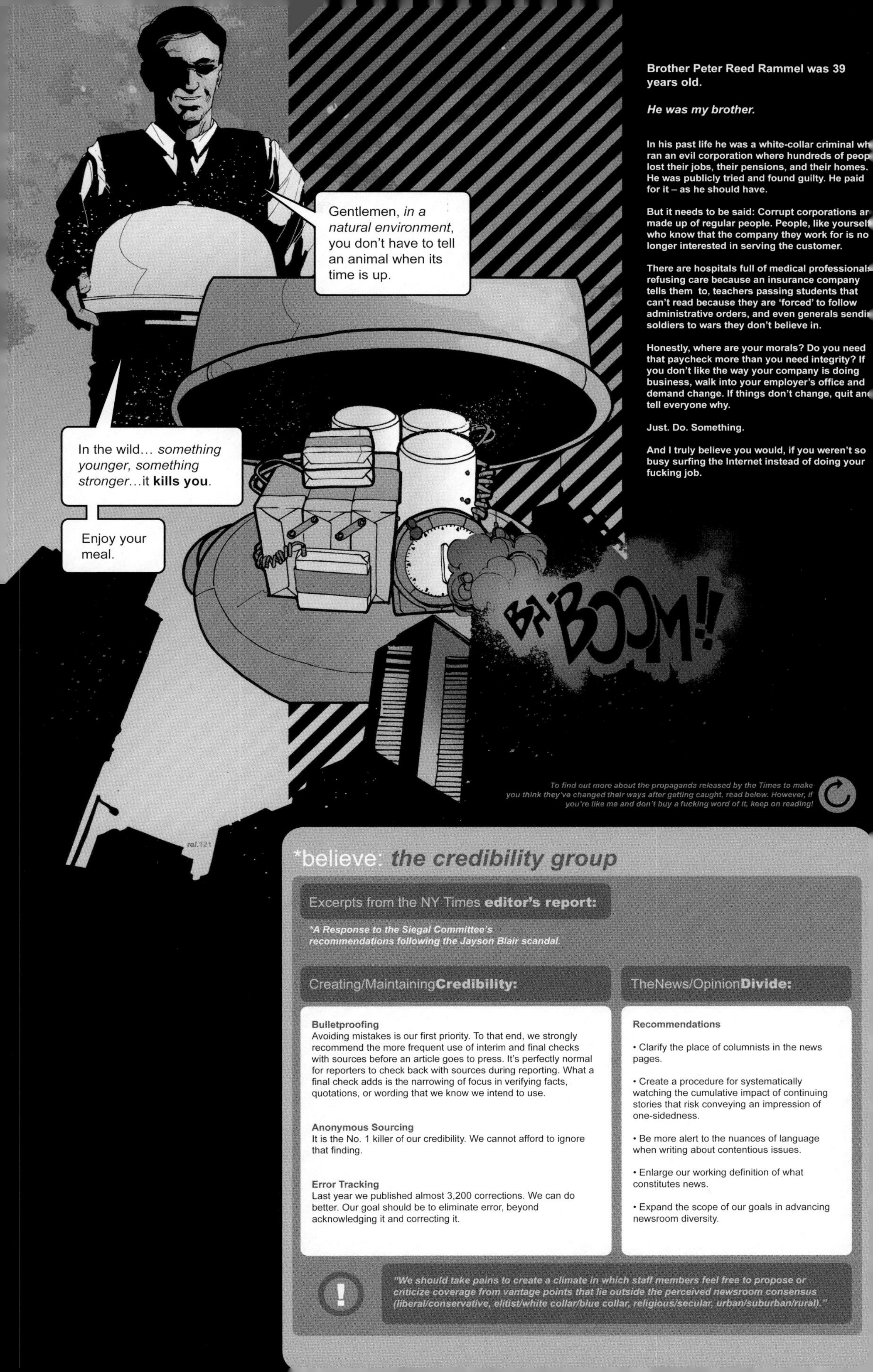

Gentlemen, *in a natural environment*, you don't have to tell an animal when its time is up.
In the wild… *something younger, something stronger*…it **kills you**.
Enjoy your meal.
BA-BOOM!!

Brother Peter Reed Rammel was 39 years old.

He was my brother.

In his past life he was a white-collar criminal wh ran an evil corporation where hundreds of peop lost their jobs, their pensions, and their homes. He was publicly tried and found guilty. He paid for it – as he should have.

But it needs to be said: Corrupt corporations ar made up of regular people. People, like yourself who know that the company they work for is no longer interested in serving the customer.

There are hospitals full of medical professionals refusing care because an insurance company tells them to, teachers passing students that can't read because they are 'forced' to follow administrative orders, and even generals sendi soldiers to wars they don't believe in.

Honestly, where are your morals? Do you need that paycheck more than you need integrity? If you don't like the way your company is doing business, walk into your employer's office and demand change. If things don't change, quit an tell everyone why.

Just. Do. Something.

And I truly believe you would, if you weren't so busy surfing the Internet instead of doing your fucking job.

To find out more about the propaganda released by the Times to make you think they've changed their ways after getting caught, read below. However, if you're like me and don't buy a fucking word of it, keep on reading!

*believe: *the credibility group*

Excerpts from the NY Times **editor's report:**

****A Response to the Siegal Committee's recommendations following the Jayson Blair scandal.***

Creating/Maintaining**Credibility:**

Bulletproofing
Avoiding mistakes is our first priority. To that end, we strongly recommend the more frequent use of interim and final checks with sources before an article goes to press. It's perfectly normal for reporters to check back with sources during reporting. What a final check adds is the narrowing of focus in verifying facts, quotations, or wording that we know we intend to use.

Anonymous Sourcing
It is the No. 1 killer of our credibility. We cannot afford to ignore that finding.

Error Tracking
Last year we published almost 3,200 corrections. We can do better. Our goal should be to eliminate error, beyond acknowledging it and correcting it.

TheNews/Opinion**Divide:**

Recommendations

• Clarify the place of columnists in the news pages.

• Create a procedure for systematically watching the cumulative impact of continuing stories that risk conveying an impression of one-sidedness.

• Be more alert to the nuances of language when writing about contentious issues.

• Enlarge our working definition of what constitutes news.

• Expand the scope of our goals in advancing newsroom diversity.

!

"We should take pains to create a climate in which staff members feel free to propose or criticize coverage from vantage points that lie outside the perceived newsroom consensus (liberal/conservative, elitist/white collar/blue collar, religious/secular, urban/suburban/rural)."

Bellevue
New York City

2 weeks AGO

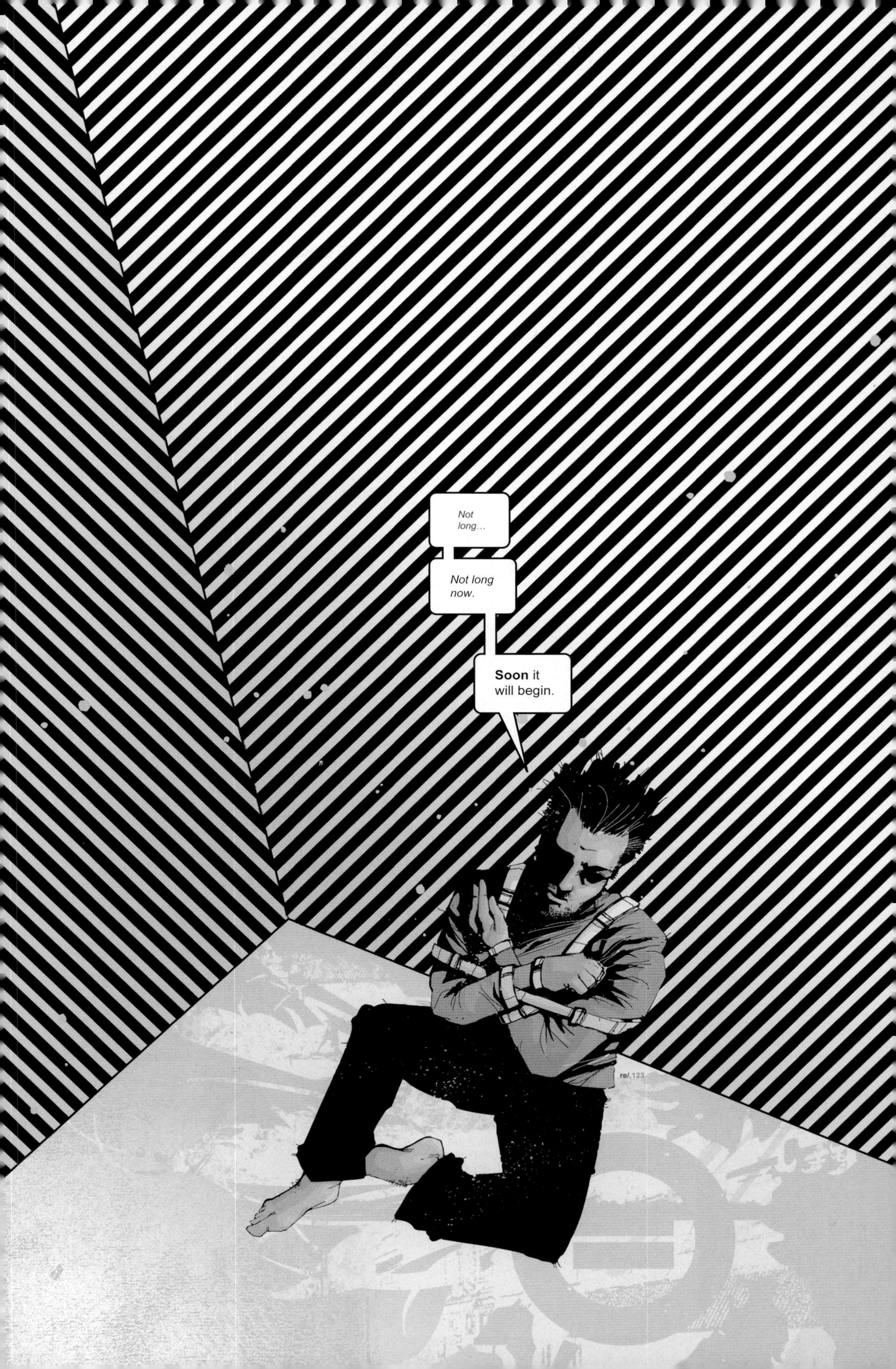

Not long…
Not long now.
Soon it will begin.

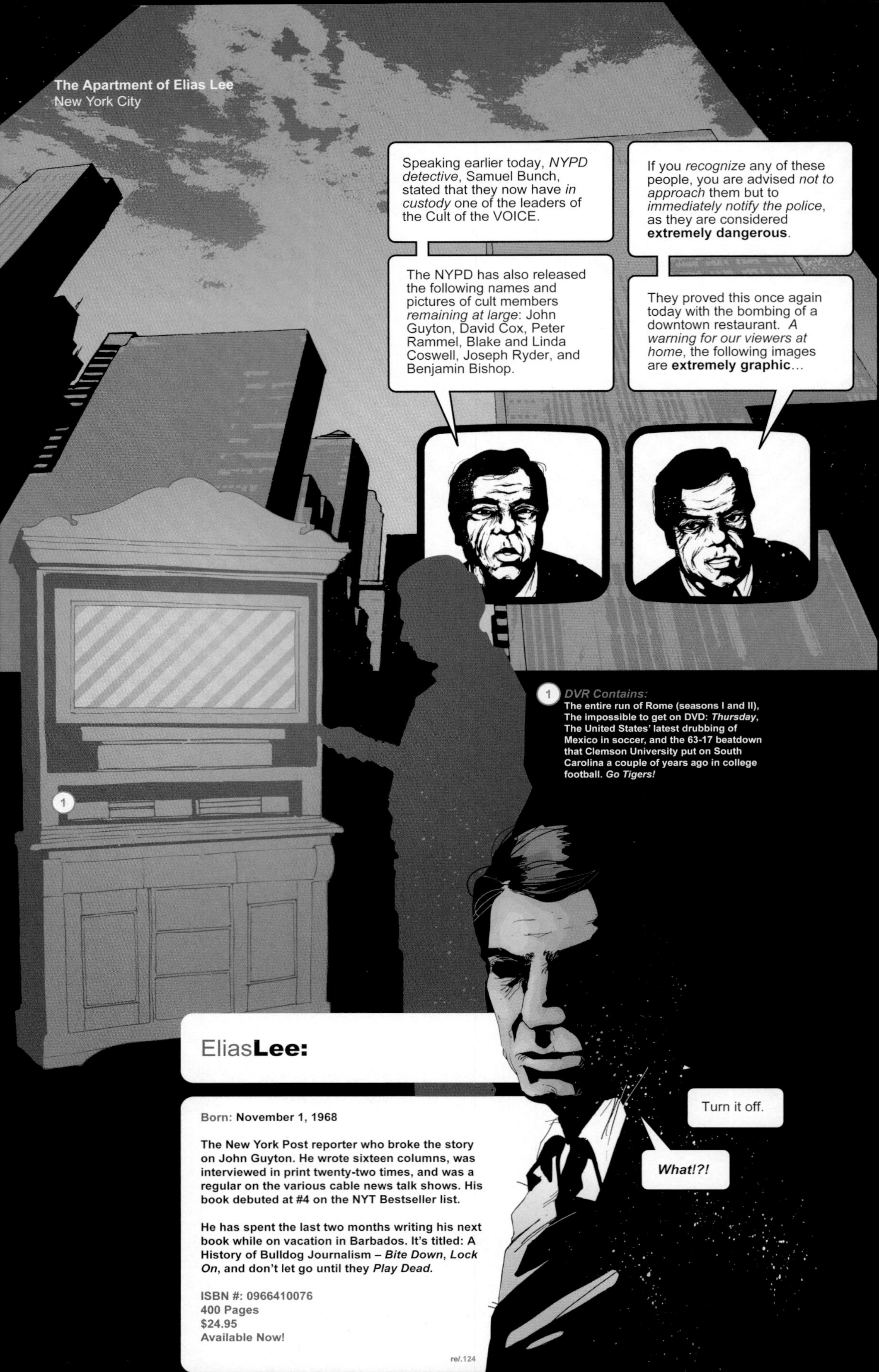

The Apartment of Elias Lee
New York City
Speaking earlier today, *NYPD detective*, Samuel Bunch, stated that they now have *in custody* one of the leaders of the Cult of the VOICE.
The NYPD has also released the following names and pictures of cult members *remaining at large*: John Guyton, David Cox, Peter Rammel, Blake and Linda Coswell, Joseph Ryder, and Benjamin Bishop.
If you *recognize* any of these people, you are advised *not to approach* them but to *immediately notify the police*, as they are considered **extremely dangerous**.
They proved this once again today with the bombing of a downtown restaurant. *A warning for our viewers at home*, the following images are **extremely graphic**…
1
1 *DVR Contains:*
The entire run of Rome (seasons I and II), The impossible to get on DVD: *Thursday*, The United States' latest drubbing of Mexico in soccer, and the 63-17 beatdown that Clemson University put on South Carolina a couple of years ago in college football. *Go Tigers!*
Elias**Lee:**
Born: November 1, 1968
The New York Post reporter who broke the story on John Guyton. He wrote sixteen columns, was interviewed in print twenty-two times, and was a regular on the various cable news talk shows. His book debuted at #4 on the NYT Bestseller list.
He has spent the last two months writing his next book while on vacation in Barbados. It's titled: A History of Bulldog Journalism – *Bite Down*, *Lock On*, and don't let go until they *Play Dead*.
ISBN #: 0966410076
400 Pages
$24.95
Available Now!
rel.124
Turn it off.
What!?!

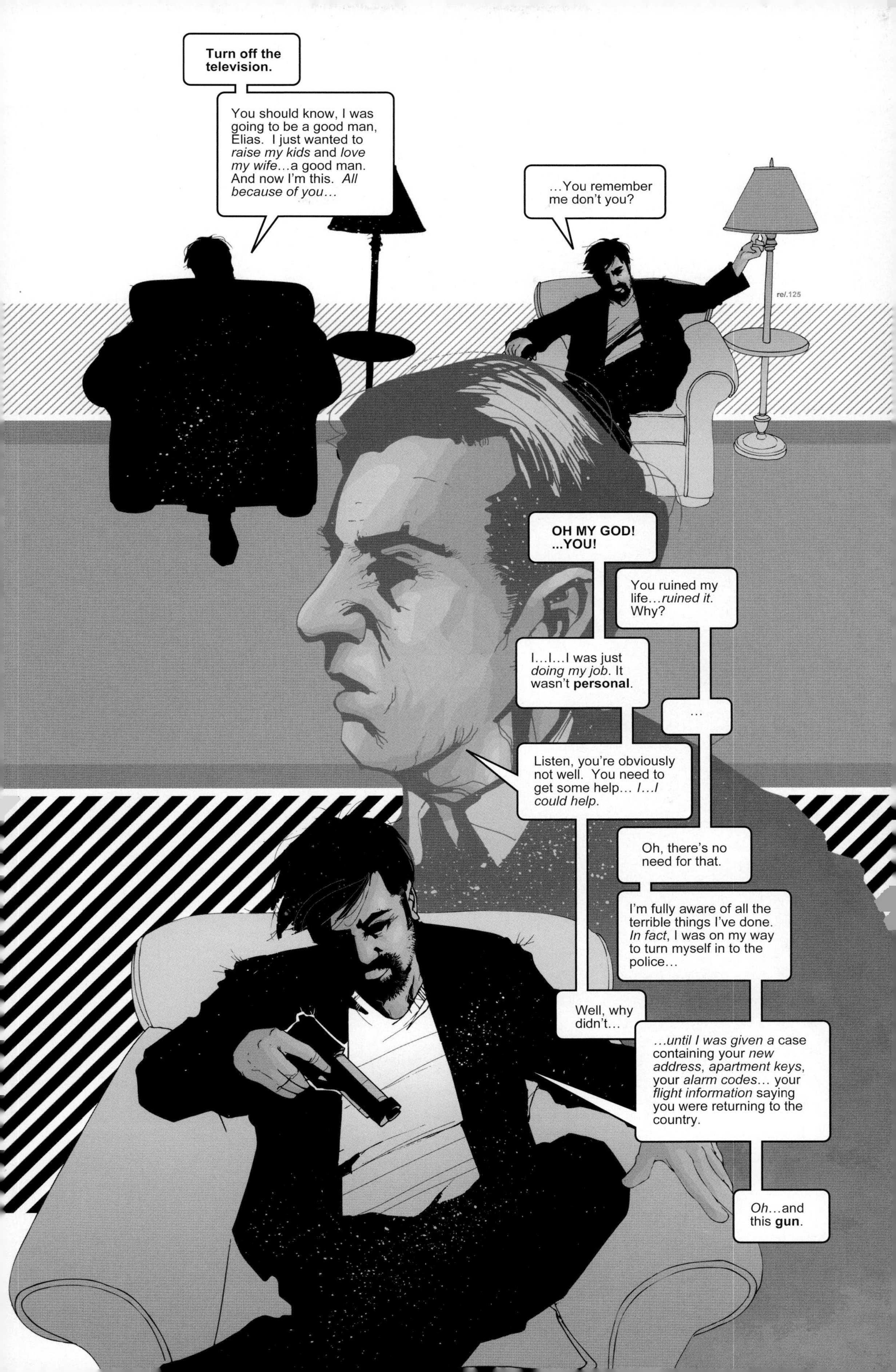
Turn off the television.
You should know, I was going to be a good man, Elias. I just wanted to *raise my kids* and *love my wife*…a good man. And now I'm this. *All because of you…*
…You remember me don't you?
rel.125
OH MY GOD! ...YOU!
You ruined my life…*ruined it*. Why?
I…I…I was just *doing my job*. It wasn't **personal**.
…
Listen, you're obviously not well. You need to get some help… *I…I could help.*
Oh, there's no need for that.
I'm fully aware of all the terrible things I've done. *In fact*, I was on my way to turn myself in to the police…
Well, why didn't…
…until I was given a case containing your *new address*, *apartment keys*, your *alarm codes*… your *flight information* saying you were returning to the country.
Oh…and this **gun**.

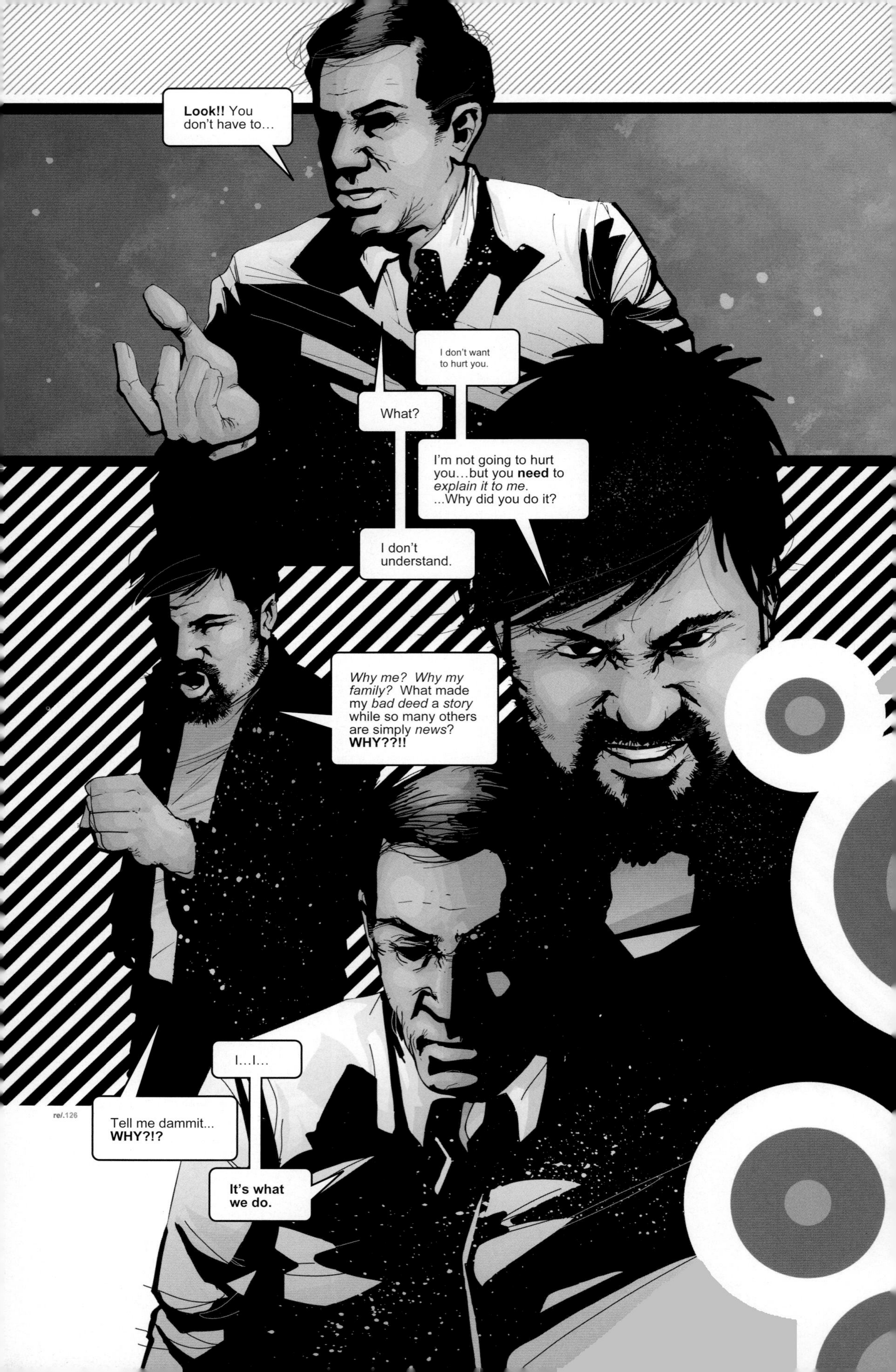
Look!! You don't have to…
I don't want to hurt you.
What?
I'm not going to hurt you…but you **need** to *explain it to me.* ...Why did you do it?
I don't understand.
Why me? Why my family? What made my *bad deed* a *story* while so many others are simply *news*? **WHY??!!**
I…I…
Tell me dammit... **WHY?!?**
It's what we do.

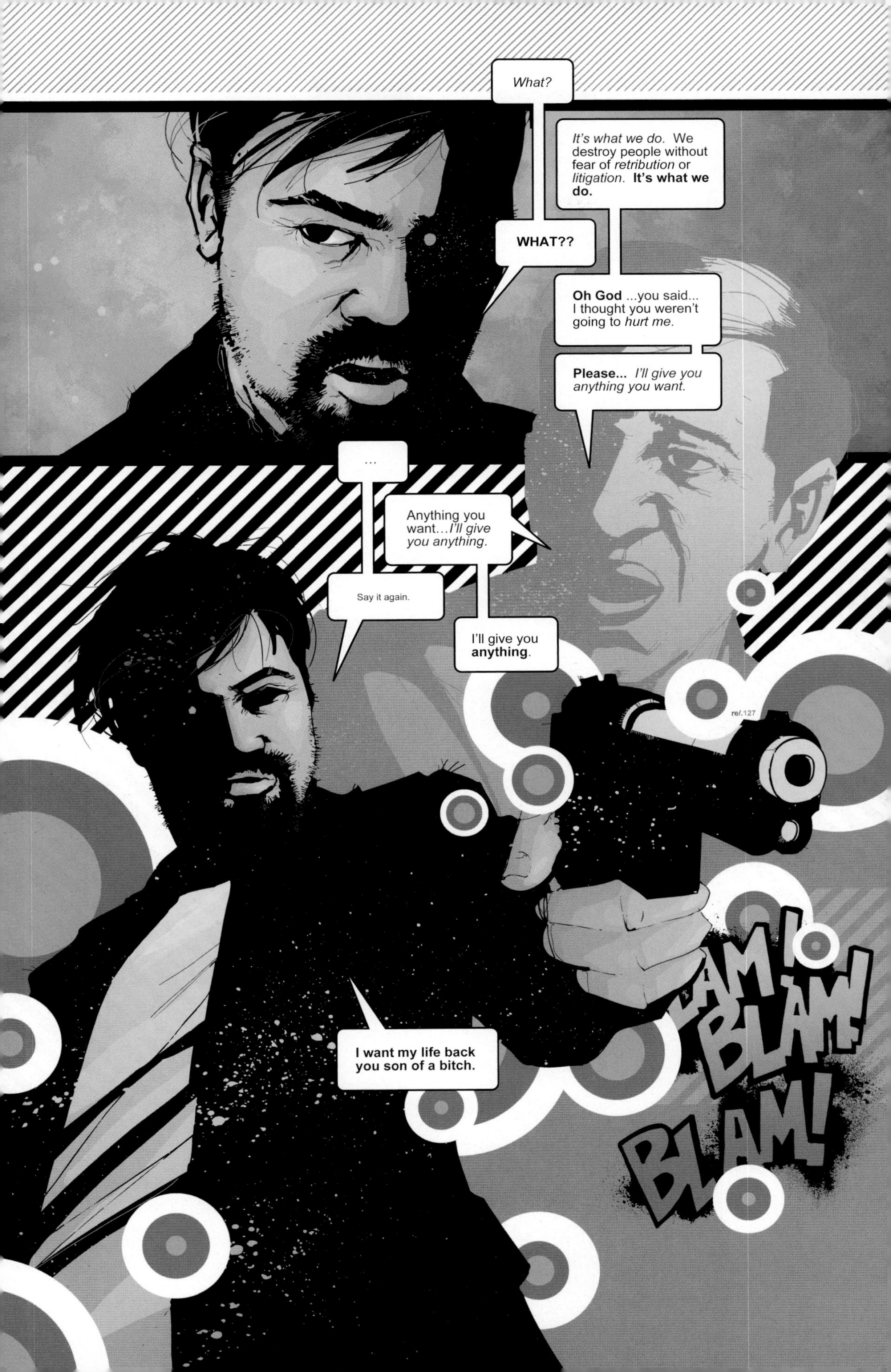
What?
It's what we do. We destroy people without fear of retribution or litigation. It's what we do.
WHAT??
Oh God ...you said... I thought you weren't going to hurt me.
Please... I'll give you anything you want.
...
Anything you want...I'll give you anything.
Say it again.
I'll give you anything.
rel.127
I want my life back you son of a bitch.
LAM!
BLAM!
BLAM!

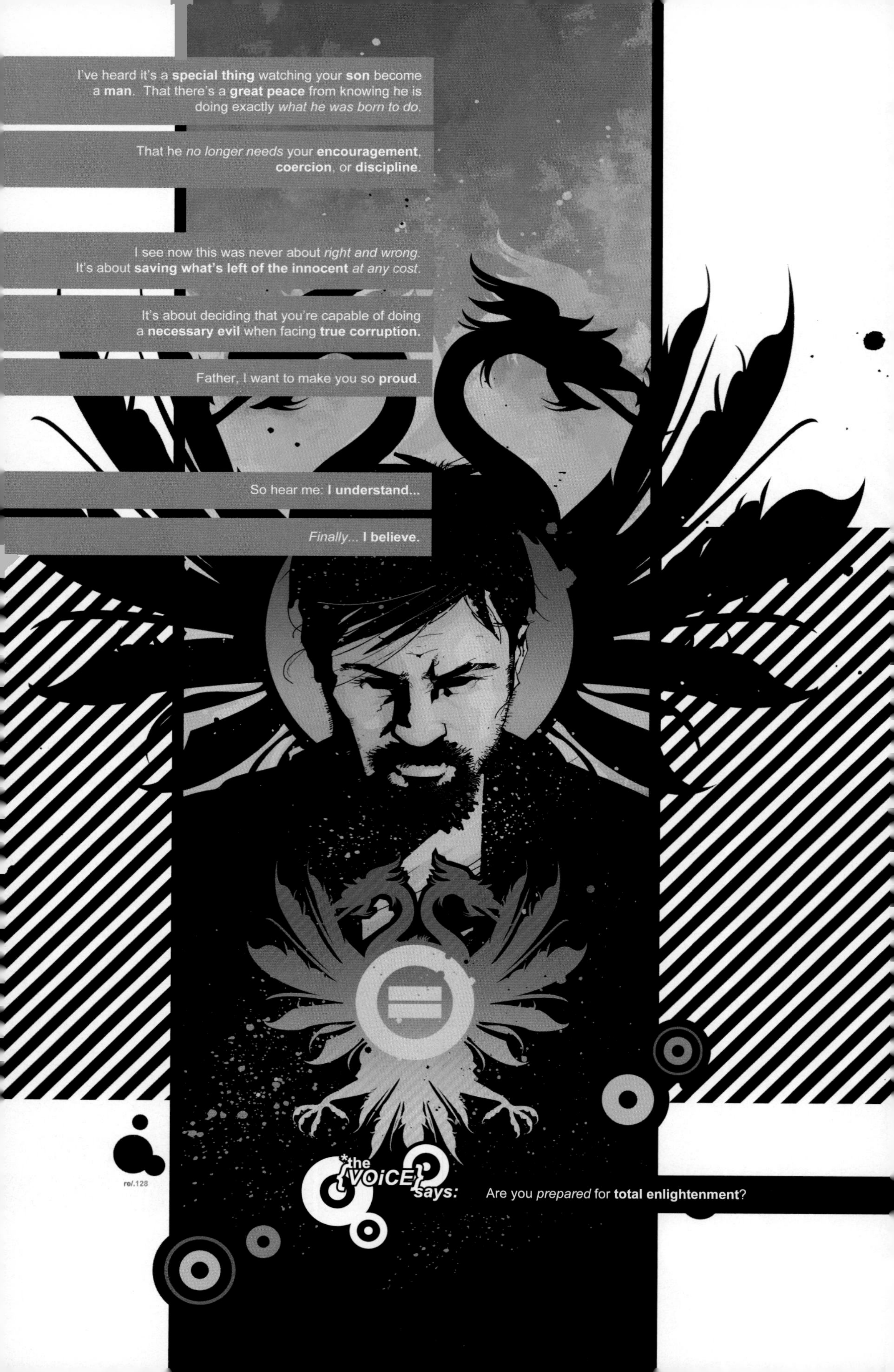
I've heard it's a **special thing** watching your **son** become a **man**. That there's a **great peace** from knowing he is doing exactly *what he was born to do*.
That he *no longer needs* your **encouragement**, **coercion**, or **discipline**.
I see now this was never about *right and wrong*. It's about **saving what's left of the innocent** *at any cost*.
It's about deciding that you're capable of doing a **necessary evil** when facing **true corruption.**
Father, I want to make you so **proud**.
So hear me: **I understand...**
Finally... **I believe.**
re/.128
*the {VOiCE} says:
Are you *prepared* for **total enlightenment**?

END_CHAPTER 05

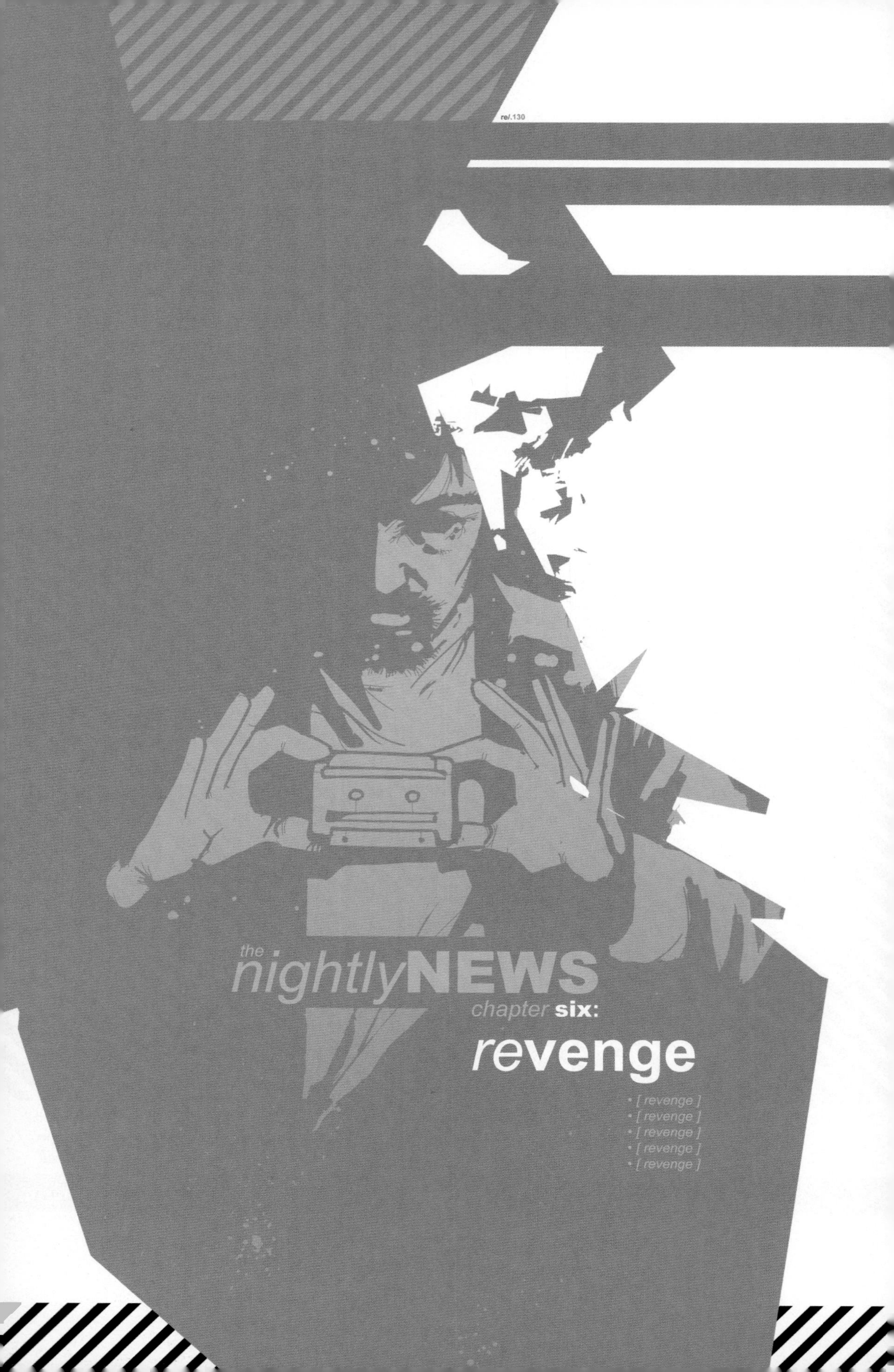
re/.130
the nightlyNEWS
chapter six:
revenge
• [revenge]
• [revenge]
• [revenge]
• [revenge]
• [revenge]

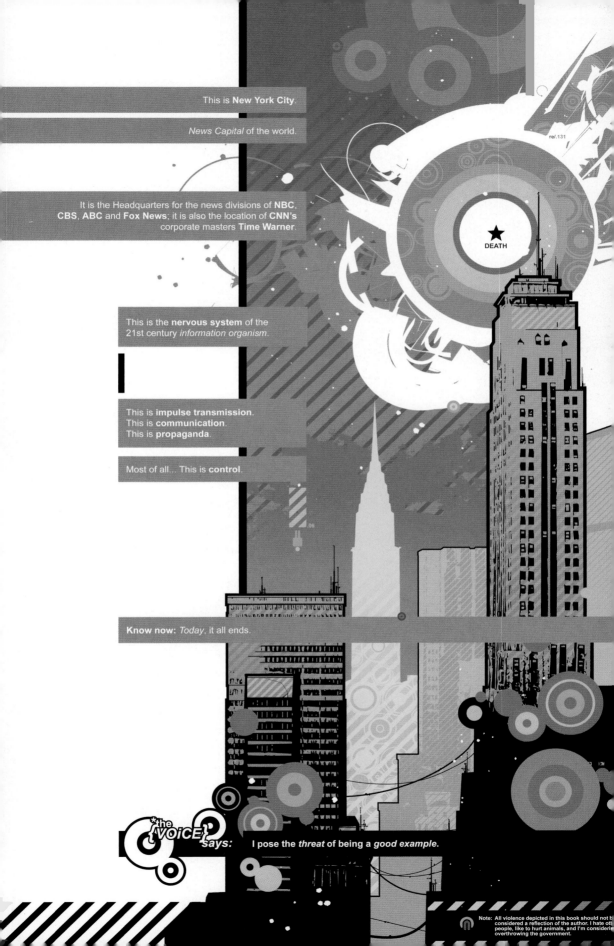

This is **New York City**.

News Capital of the world.

It is the Headquarters for the news divisions of **NBC**, **CBS**, **ABC** and **Fox News**; it is also the location of **CNN's** corporate masters **Time Warner**.

This is the **nervous system** of the 21st century *information organism*.

This is **impulse transmission**.
This is **communication**.
This is **propaganda**.

Most of all... This is **control**.

Know now: *Today*, it all ends.

re/.131

★
DEATH

the **voice** *says:* I pose the *threat* of being a *good example*.

Note: All violence depicted in this book should not be considered a reflection of the author. I hate oth people, like to hurt animals, and I'm consideri overthrowing the government.

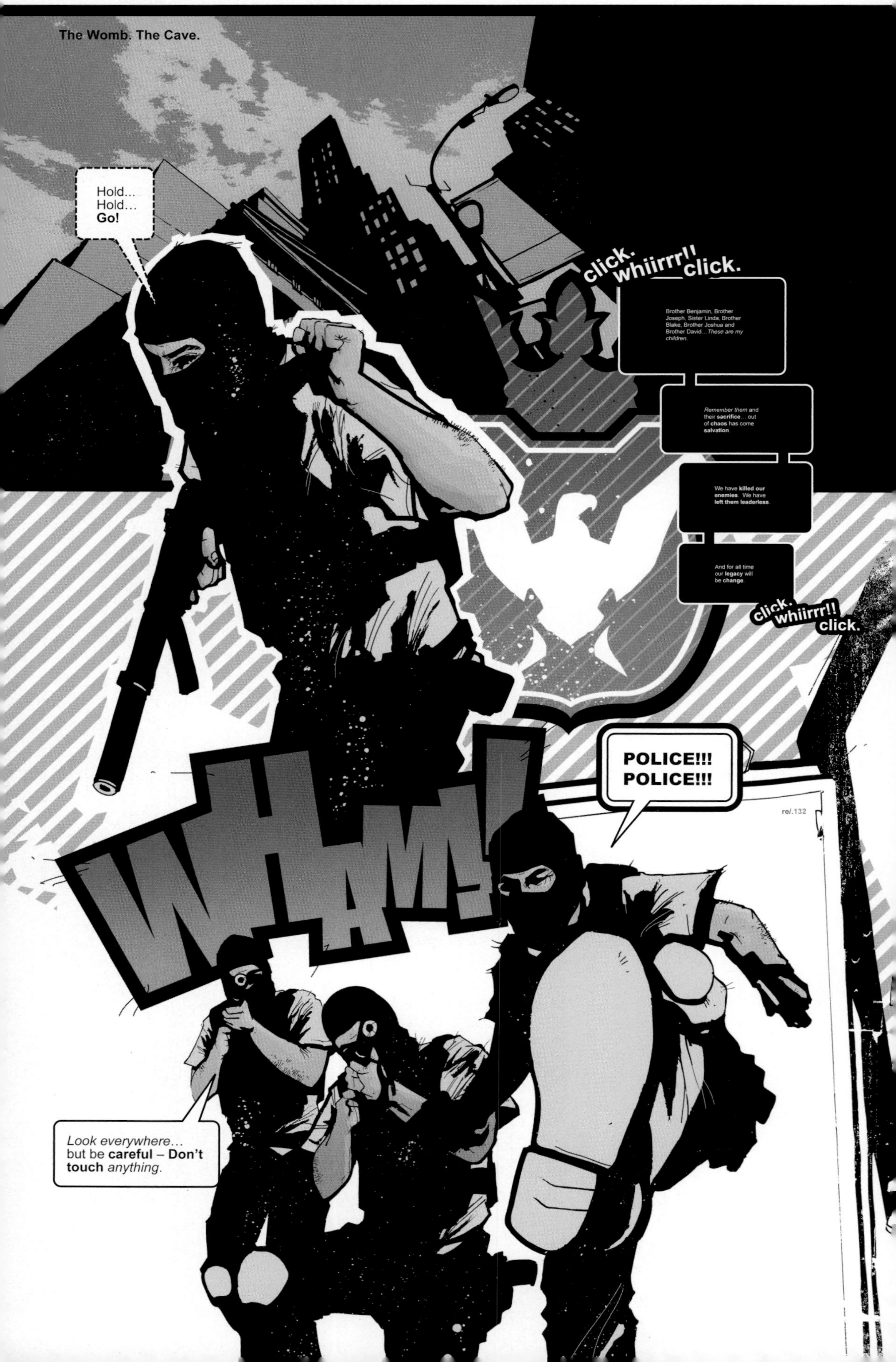

The Womb. The Cave.
Hold... Hold... **Go!**
click. whiirrr!! click.
Brother Benjamin, Brother Joseph, Sister Linda, Brother Blake, Brother Joshua and Brother David... *These are my children.*
Remember them and their **sacrifice**... out of **chaos** has come **salvation**.
We have **killed our enemies**. We have **left them leaderless**.
And for all time our **legacy** will be **change**.
click. whiirrr!! click.
WHAM!
POLICE!!! POLICE!!!
re/.132
Look everywhere... but be **careful** – **Don't touch** *anything*.

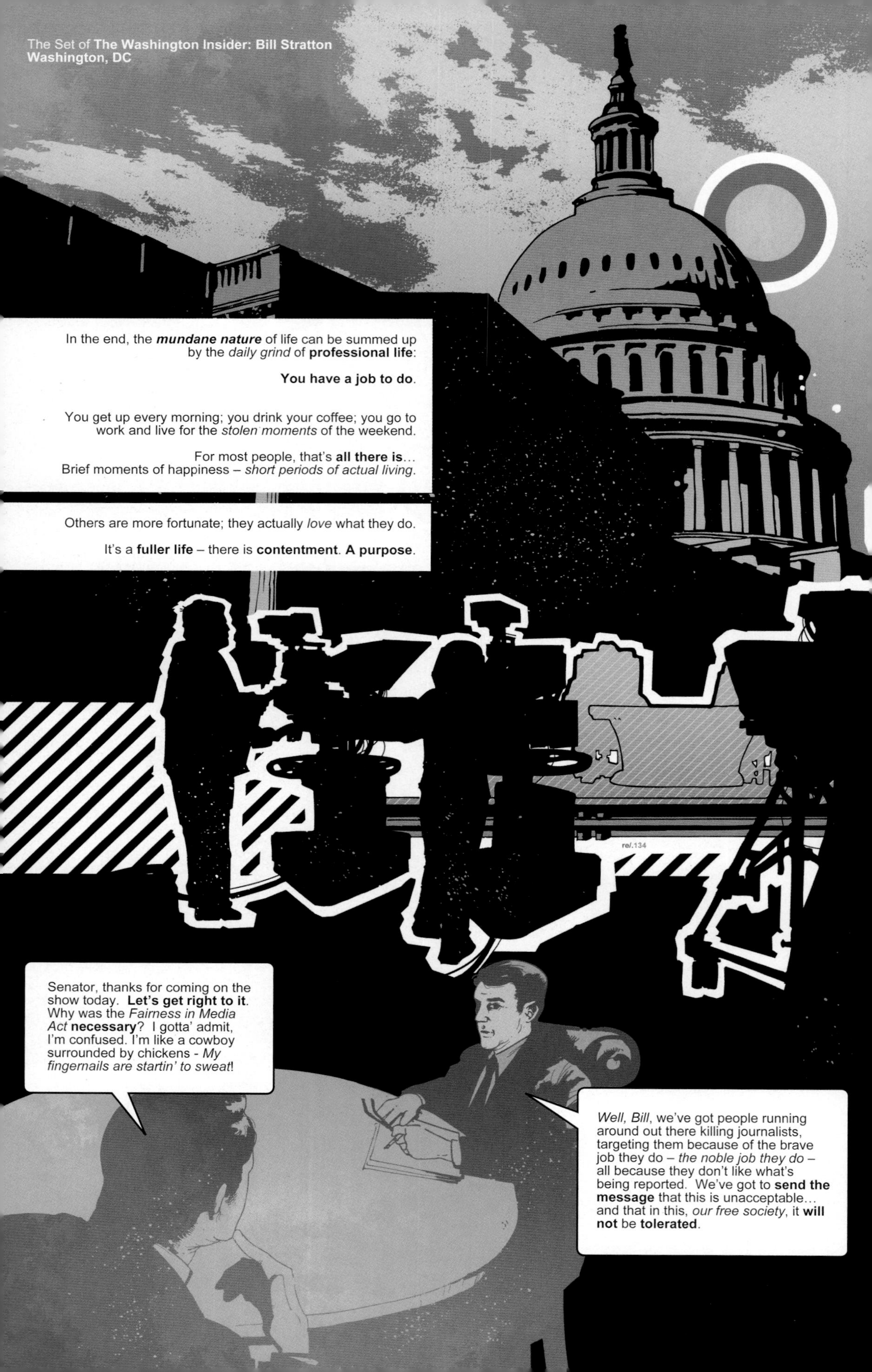

The Set of **The Washington Insider: Bill Stratton**
Washington, DC
In the end, the ***mundane nature*** of life can be summed up by the *daily grind* of **professional life**:
You have a job to do.
You get up every morning; you drink your coffee; you go to work and live for the *stolen moments* of the weekend.
For most people, that's **all there is**… Brief moments of happiness – *short periods of actual living*.
Others are more fortunate; they actually *love* what they do.
It's a **fuller life** – there is **contentment**. **A purpose**.
re/.134
Senator, thanks for coming on the show today. **Let's get right to it**. Why was the *Fairness in Media Act* **necessary**? I gotta' admit, I'm confused. I'm like a cowboy surrounded by chickens - *My fingernails are startin' to sweat*!
Well, Bill, we've got people running around out there killing journalists, targeting them because of the brave job they do – *the noble job they do* – all because they don't like what's being reported. We've got to **send the message** that this is unacceptable… and that in this, *our free society*, it **will not** be **tolerated**.

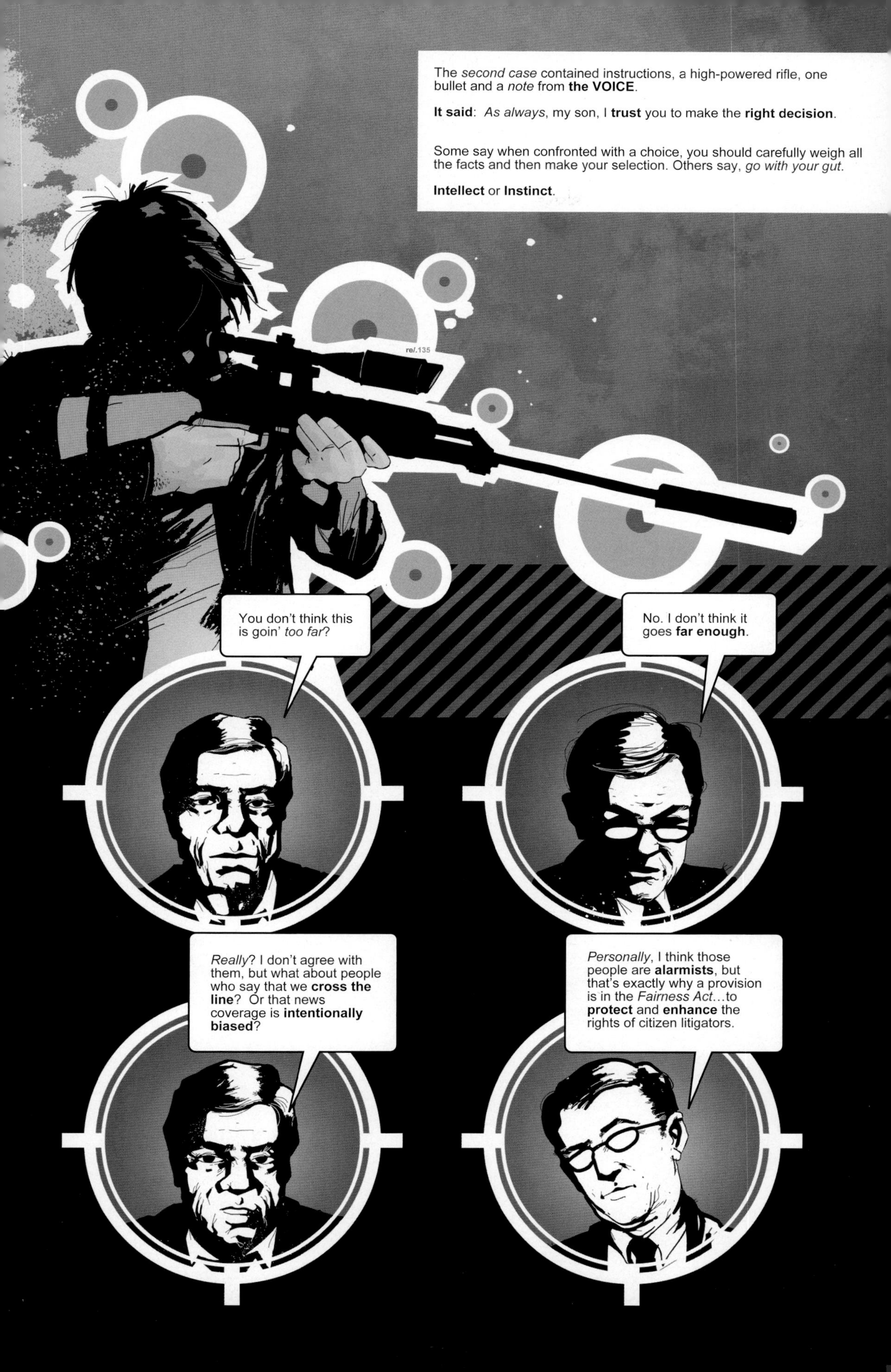
The *second case* contained instructions, a high-powered rifle, one bullet and a *note* from **the VOICE**.
It said: *As always*, my son, I **trust** you to make the **right decision**.
Some say when confronted with a choice, you should carefully weigh all the facts and then make your selection. Others say, *go with your gut*.
Intellect or **Instinct**.
re/.135
You don't think this is goin' *too far*?
No. I don't think it goes **far enough**.
Really? I don't agree with them, but what about people who say that we **cross the line**? Or that news coverage is **intentionally biased**?
Personally, I think those people are **alarmists**, but that's exactly why a provision is in the *Fairness Act*...to **protect** and **enhance** the rights of citizen litigators.

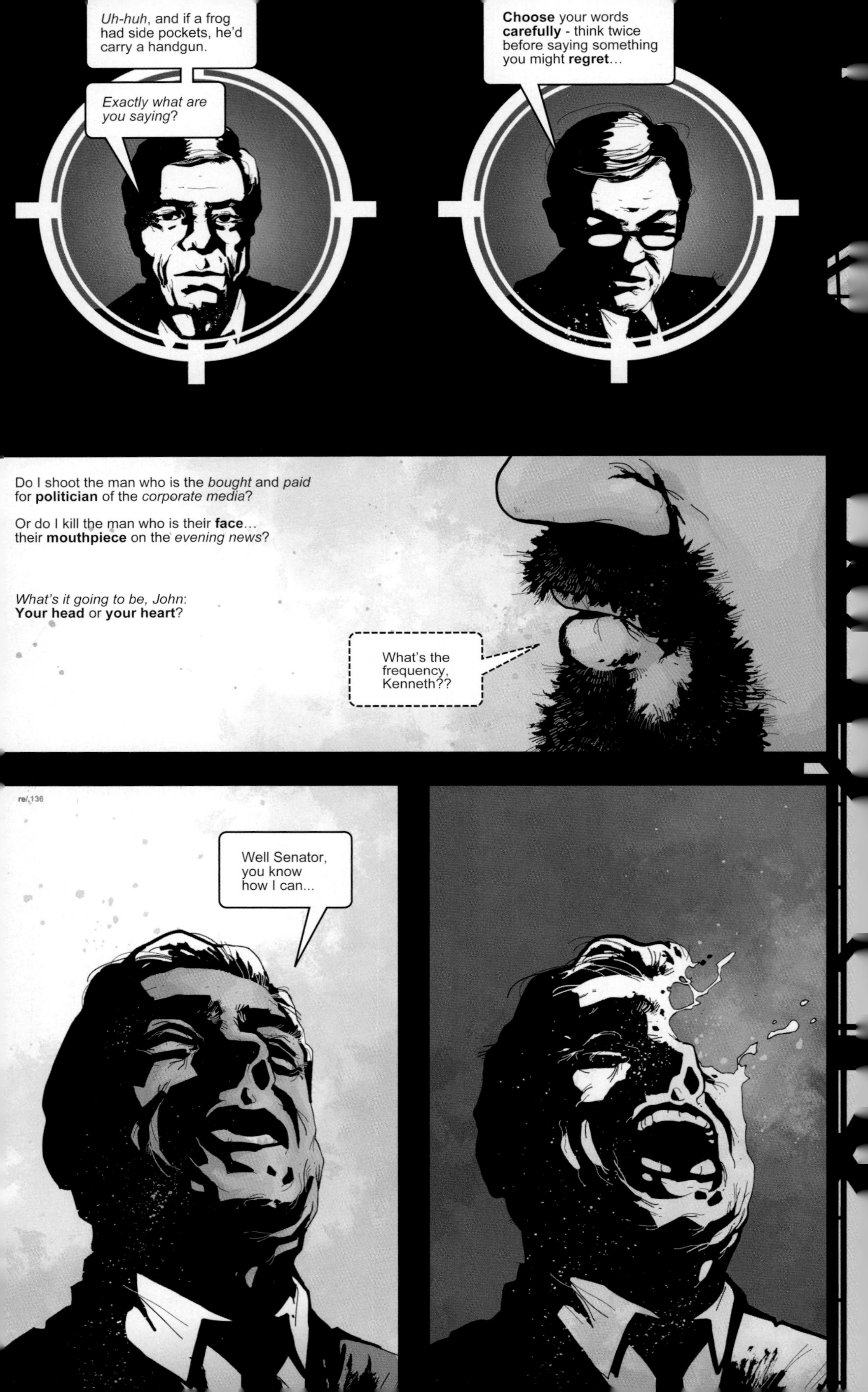
Uh-huh, and if a frog had side pockets, he'd carry a handgun.
Exactly what are you saying?
Choose your words carefully - think twice before saying something you might regret…
Do I shoot the man who is the bought and paid for politician of the corporate media?
Or do I kill the man who is their face… their mouthpiece on the evening news?
What's it going to be, John: Your head or your heart?
What's the frequency, Kenneth??
re/.136
Well Senator, you know how I can...

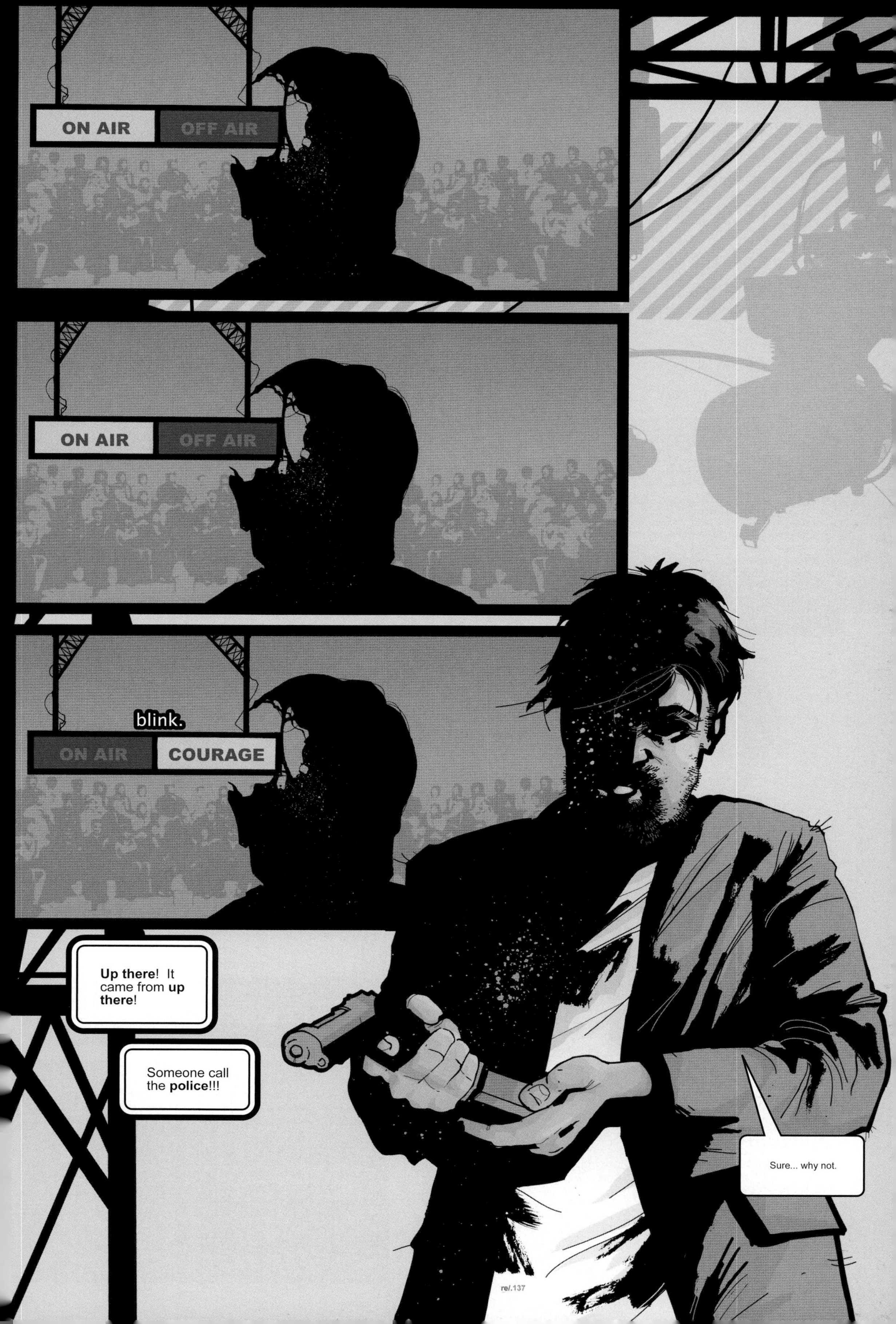
ON AIR
OFF AIR
ON AIR
OFF AIR
blink.
ON AIR
COURAGE
Up there! It came from up there!
Someone call the police!!!
Sure... why not.

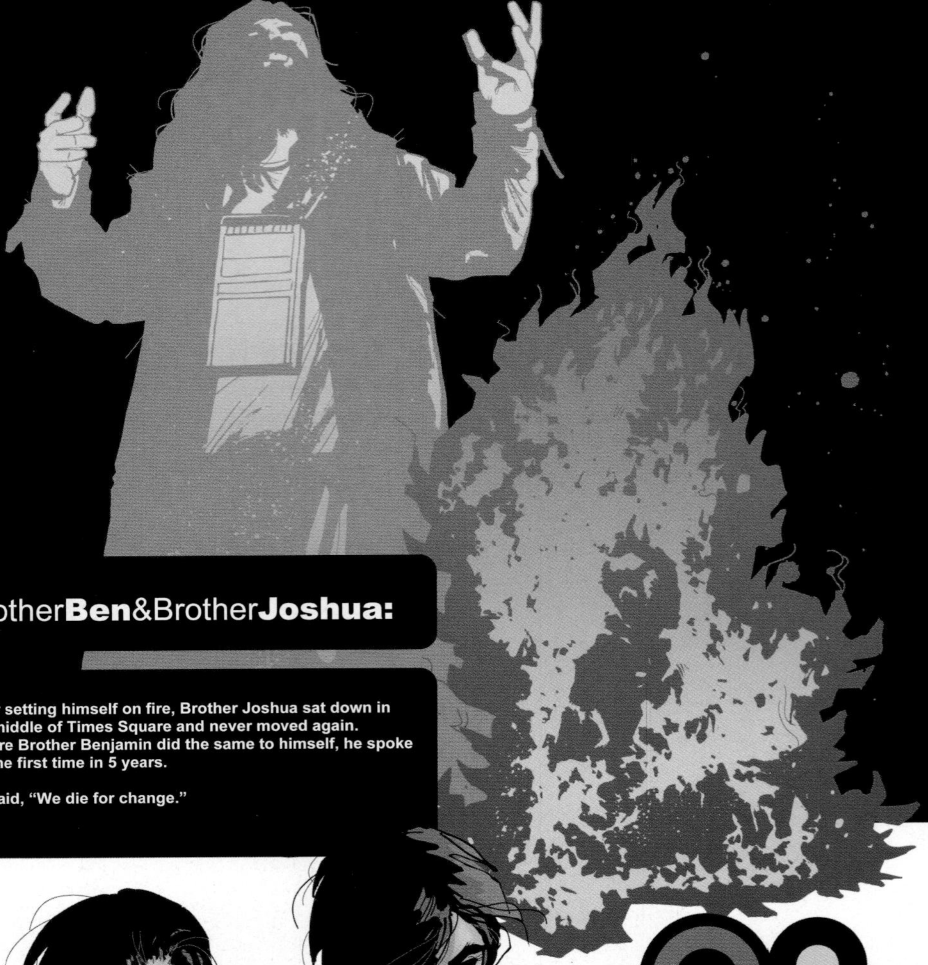

BrotherBen&BrotherJoshua:

After setting himself on fire, Brother Joshua sat down in the middle of Times Square and never moved again. Before Brother Benjamin did the same to himself, he spoke for the first time in 5 years.

He said, "We die for change."

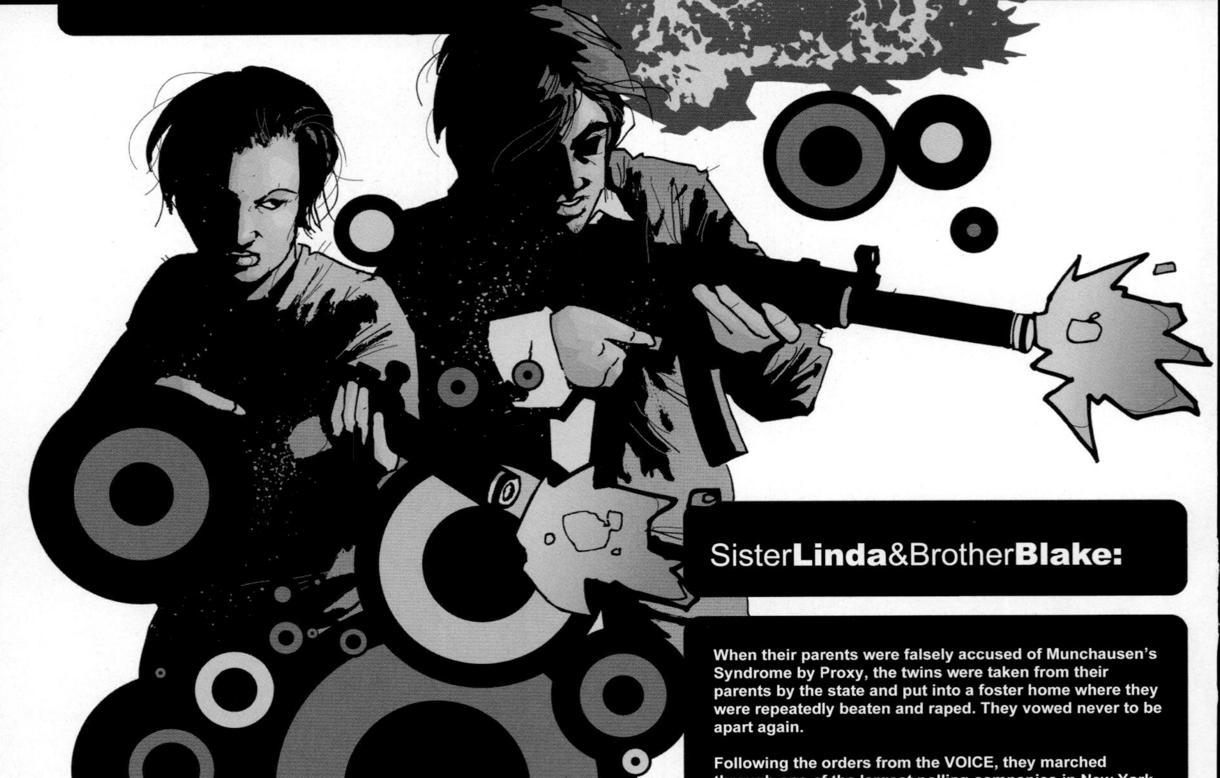

SisterLinda&BrotherBlake:

When their parents were falsely accused of Munchausen's Syndrome by Proxy, the twins were taken from their parents by the state and put into a foster home where they were repeatedly beaten and raped. They vowed never to be apart again.

Following the orders from the VOICE, they marched through one of the largest polling companies in New York killing 3 of every 5 employees.

After the Police arrived, and the ensuing gunfight, it was only fitting that they died in each other's arms.

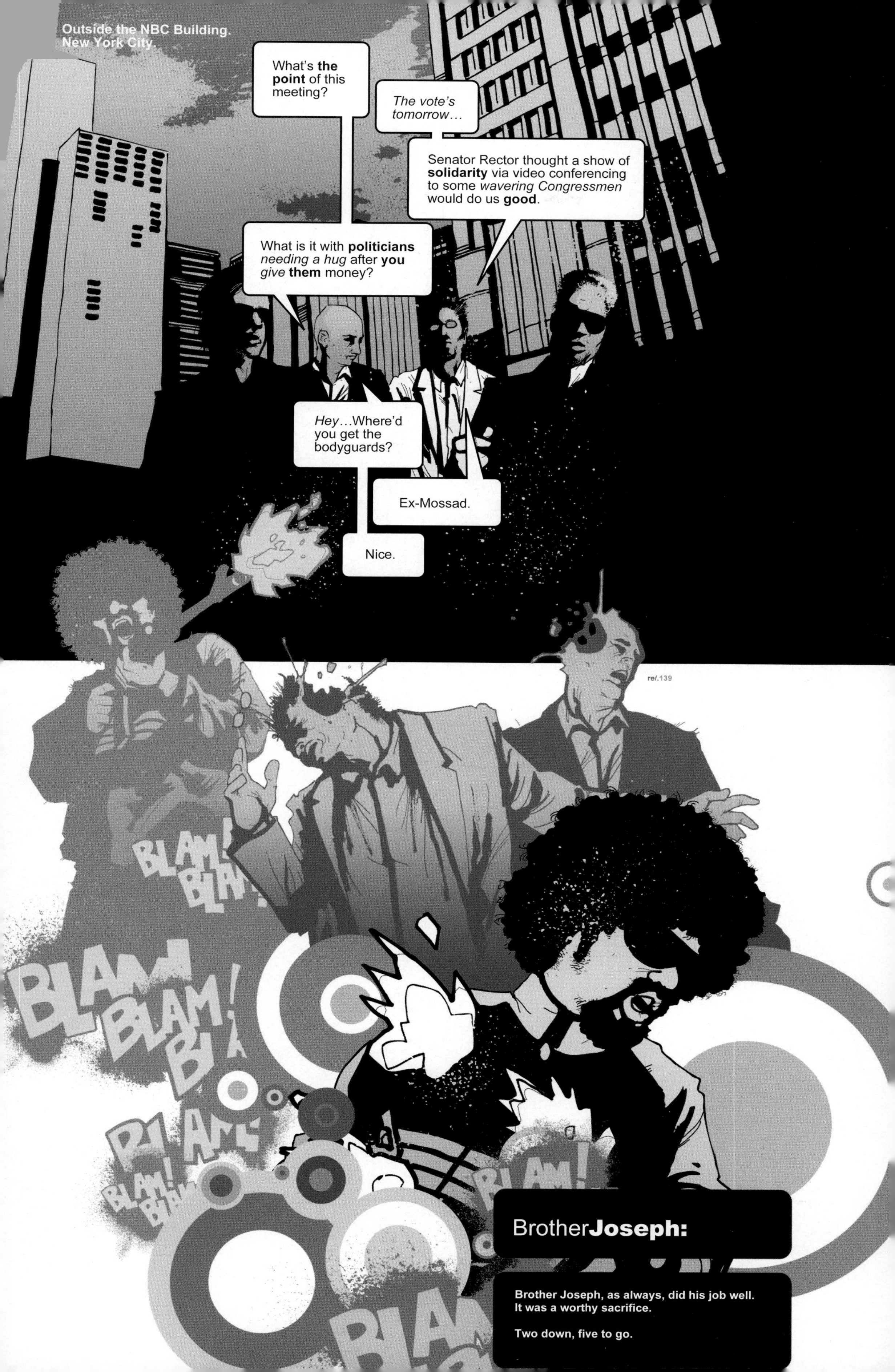
Outside the NBC Building. New York City.
What's the point of this meeting?
The vote's tomorrow…
Senator Rector thought a show of solidarity via video conferencing to some wavering Congressmen would do us good.
What is it with politicians needing a hug after you give them money?
Hey…Where'd you get the bodyguards?
Ex-Mossad.
Nice.
BLAM! BLAM!
BLAM BLAM!
BLAM!
BLAM!
BrotherJoseph:
Brother Joseph, as always, did his job well.
It was a worthy sacrifice.
Two down, five to go.

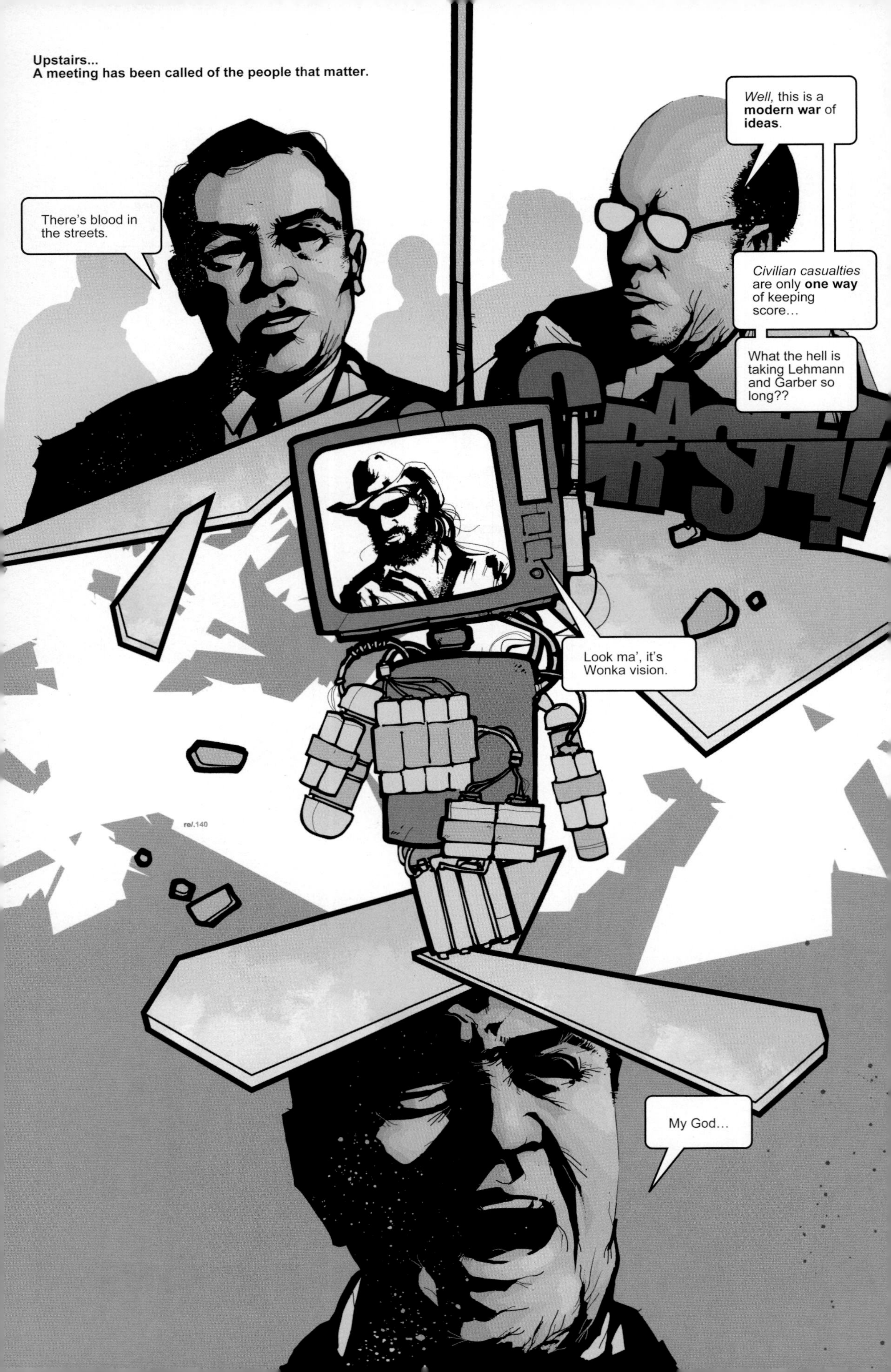
Upstairs...
A meeting has been called of the people that matter.
There's blood in the streets.
Well, this is a modern war of ideas.
Civilian casualties are only one way of keeping score…
What the hell is taking Lehmann and Garber so long??
Look ma', it's Wonka vision.
My God…

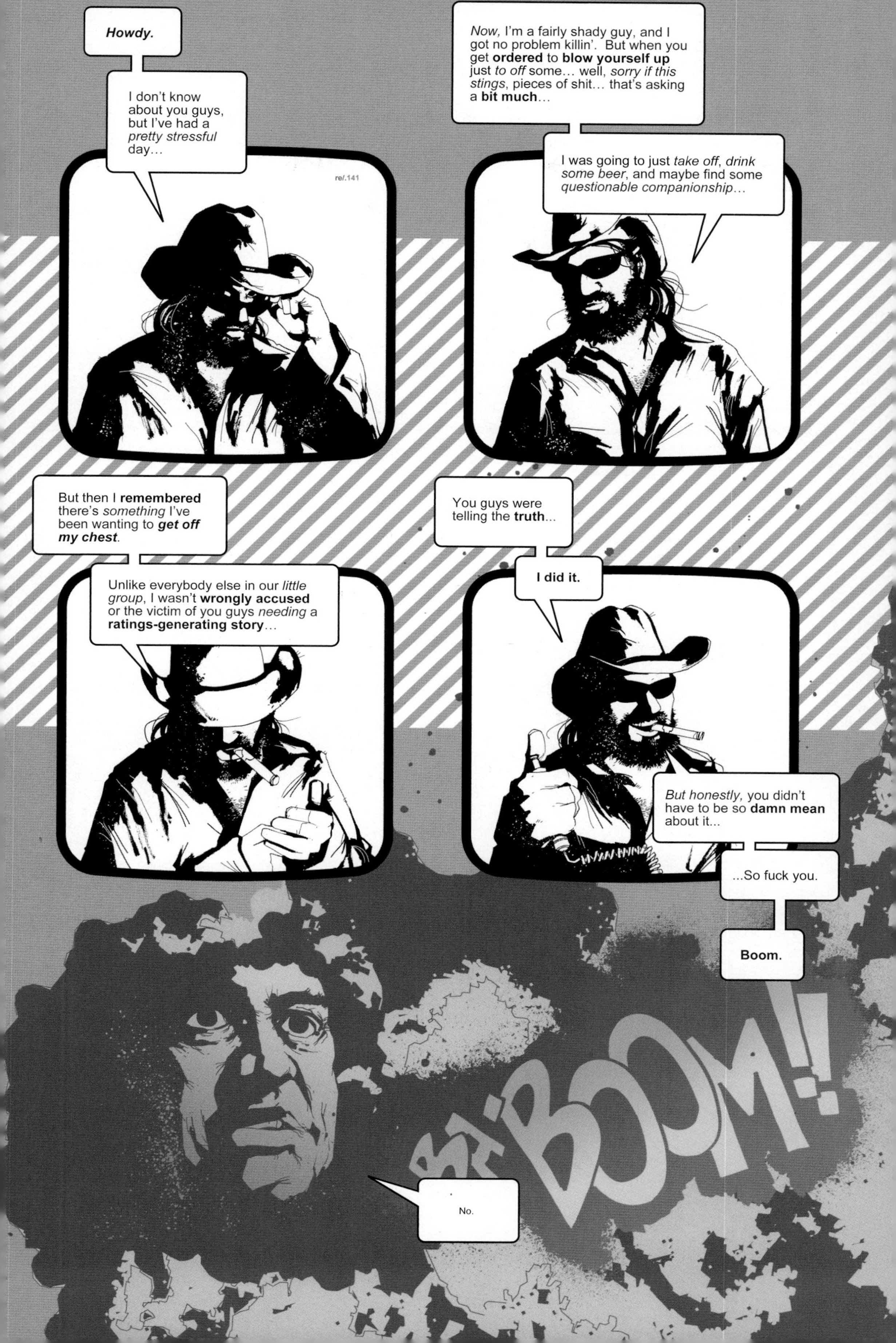
Howdy.
I don't know about you guys, but I've had a *pretty stressful* day…
re/.141
Now, I'm a fairly shady guy, and I got no problem killin'. But when you get **ordered** to **blow yourself up** just *to off* some… well, *sorry if this stings*, pieces of shit… that's asking a **bit much**…
I was going to just *take off*, *drink some beer*, and maybe find some *questionable companionship*…
But then I **remembered** there's *something* I've been wanting to ***get off my chest***.
Unlike everybody else in our *little group*, I wasn't **wrongly accused** or the victim of you guys *needing* a **ratings-generating story**…
You guys were telling the **truth**...
I did it.
But honestly, you didn't have to be so **damn mean** about it...
...So fuck you.
Boom.
BOOM!!
No.

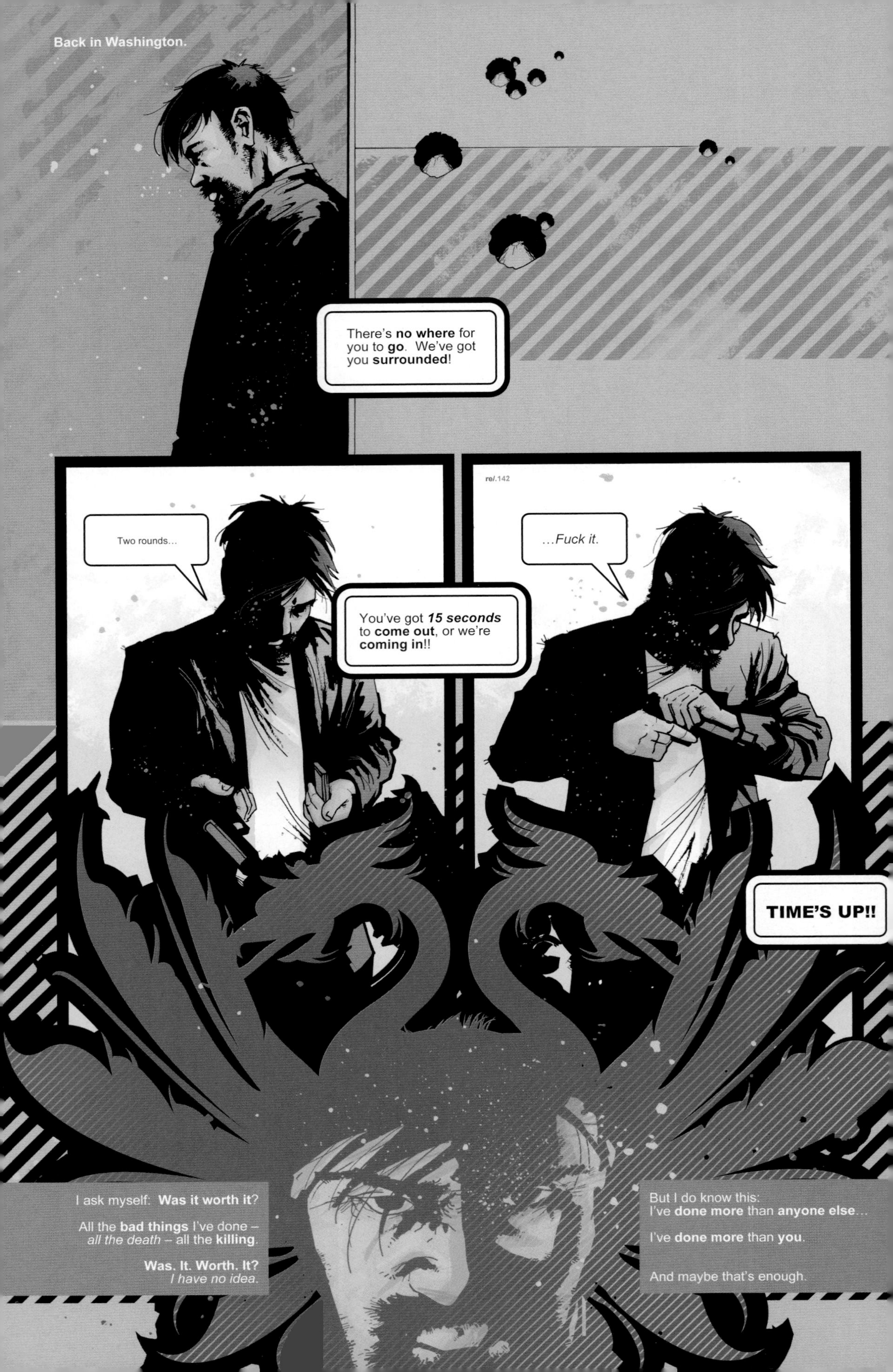

Back in Washington.
There's **no where** for you to **go**. We've got you **surrounded**!
Two rounds...
You've got ***15 seconds*** to **come out**, or we're **coming in**!!
re/.142
...*Fuck it.*
TIME'S UP!!
I ask myself: **Was it worth it**?
All the **bad things** I've done – *all the death* – all the **killing**.
Was. It. Worth. It? *I have no idea.*
But I do know this: I've **done more** than **anyone else**...
I've **done more** than **you**.
And maybe that's enough.

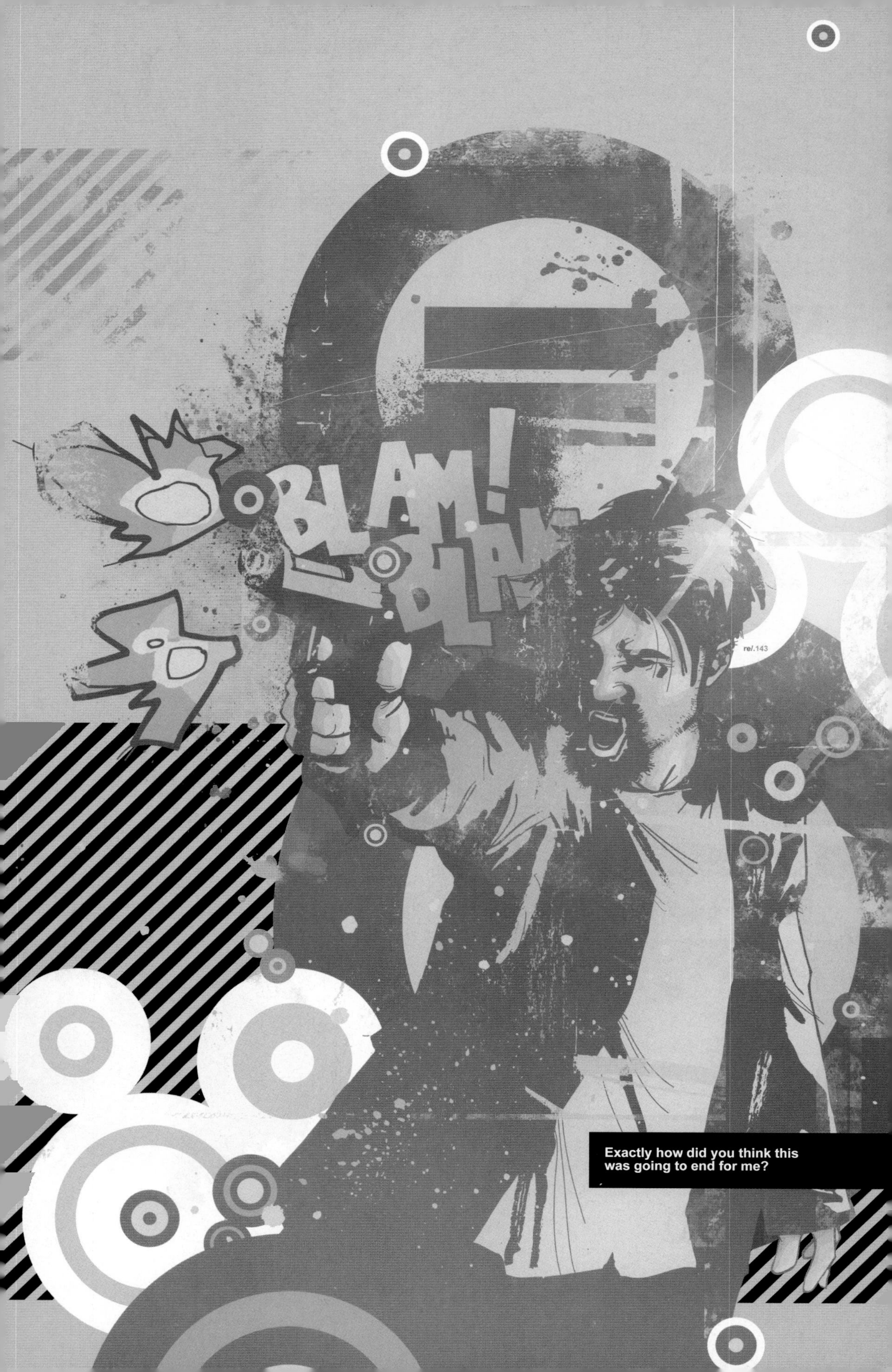
BLAM!
re/.143
Exactly how did you think this was going to end for me?

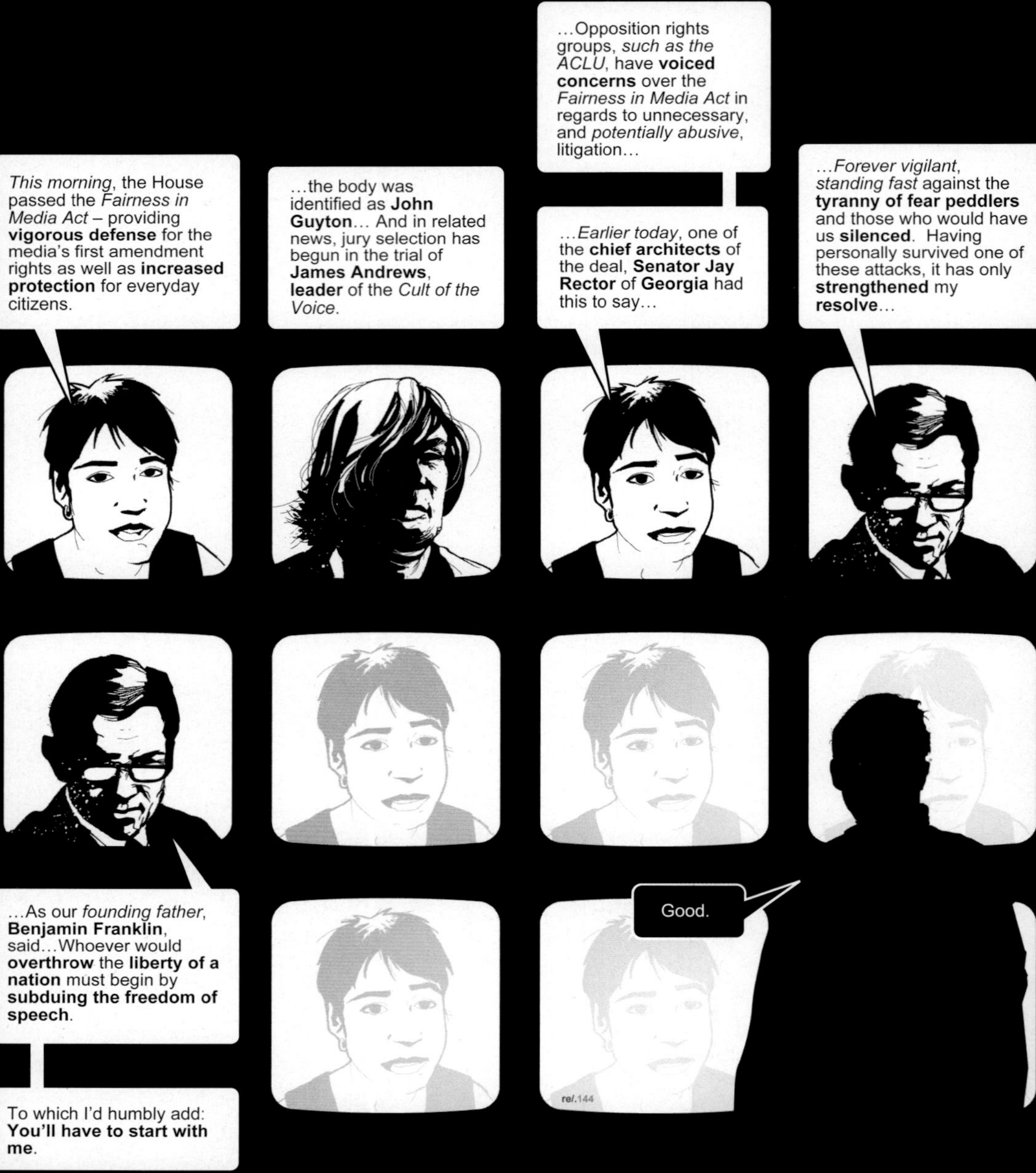
This morning, the House passed the *Fairness in Media Act* – providing **vigorous defense** for the media's first amendment rights as well as **increased protection** for everyday citizens.
...the body was identified as **John Guyton**... And in related news, jury selection has begun in the trial of **James Andrews**, **leader** of the *Cult of the Voice*.
...Opposition rights groups, *such as the ACLU*, have **voiced concerns** over the *Fairness in Media Act* in regards to unnecessary, and *potentially abusive*, litigation...
...*Earlier today*, one of the **chief architects** of the deal, **Senator Jay Rector** of **Georgia** had this to say...
...*Forever vigilant*, *standing fast* against the **tyranny of fear peddlers** and those who would have us **silenced**. Having personally survived one of these attacks, it has only **strengthened** my **resolve**...
...As our *founding father*, **Benjamin Franklin**, said...Whoever would **overthrow** the **liberty of a nation** must begin by **subduing the freedom of speech**.
To which I'd humbly add: **You'll have to start with me**.
Good.
re/.144

TWO MONTHS **LATER** ref.145

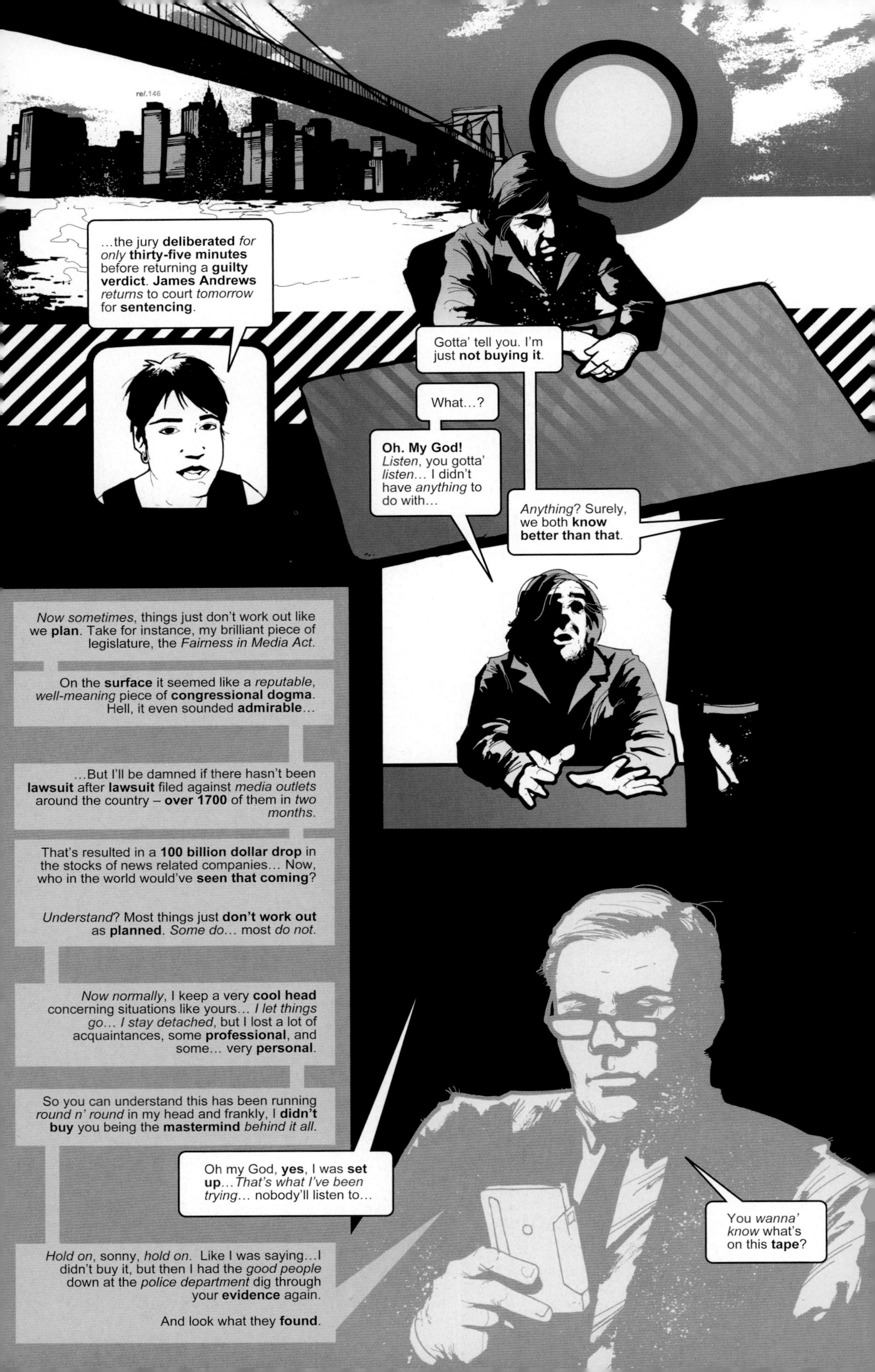

rel.146
...the jury **deliberated** *for only* **thirty-five minutes** before returning a **guilty verdict**. **James Andrews** *returns* to court *tomorrow* for **sentencing**.
Gotta' tell you. I'm just **not buying it**.
What...?
Oh. My God! *Listen*, you gotta' *listen*... I didn't have *anything* to do with...
Anything? Surely, we both **know better than that**.
Now sometimes, things just don't work out like we **plan**. Take for instance, my brilliant piece of legislature, the *Fairness in Media Act*.
On the **surface** it seemed like a *reputable*, *well-meaning* piece of **congressional dogma**. Hell, it even sounded **admirable**...
...But I'll be damned if there hasn't been **lawsuit** after **lawsuit** filed against *media outlets* around the country – **over 1700** of them in *two months*.
That's resulted in a **100 billion dollar drop** in the stocks of news related companies... Now, who in the world would've **seen that coming**?
Understand? Most things just **don't work out** as **planned**. *Some do*... most *do not*.
Now normally, I keep a very **cool head** concerning situations like yours... *I let things go*... *I stay detached*, but I lost a lot of acquaintances, some **professional**, and some... very **personal**.
So you can understand this has been running *round n' round* in my head and frankly, I **didn't buy** you being the **mastermind** *behind it all*.
Oh my God, **yes**, I was **set up**... *That's what I've been trying*... nobody'll listen to...
Hold on, sonny, *hold on*. Like I was saying...I didn't buy it, but then I had the *good people* down at the *police department* dig through your **evidence** again.
And look what they **found**.
You *wanna' know* what's on this **tape**?

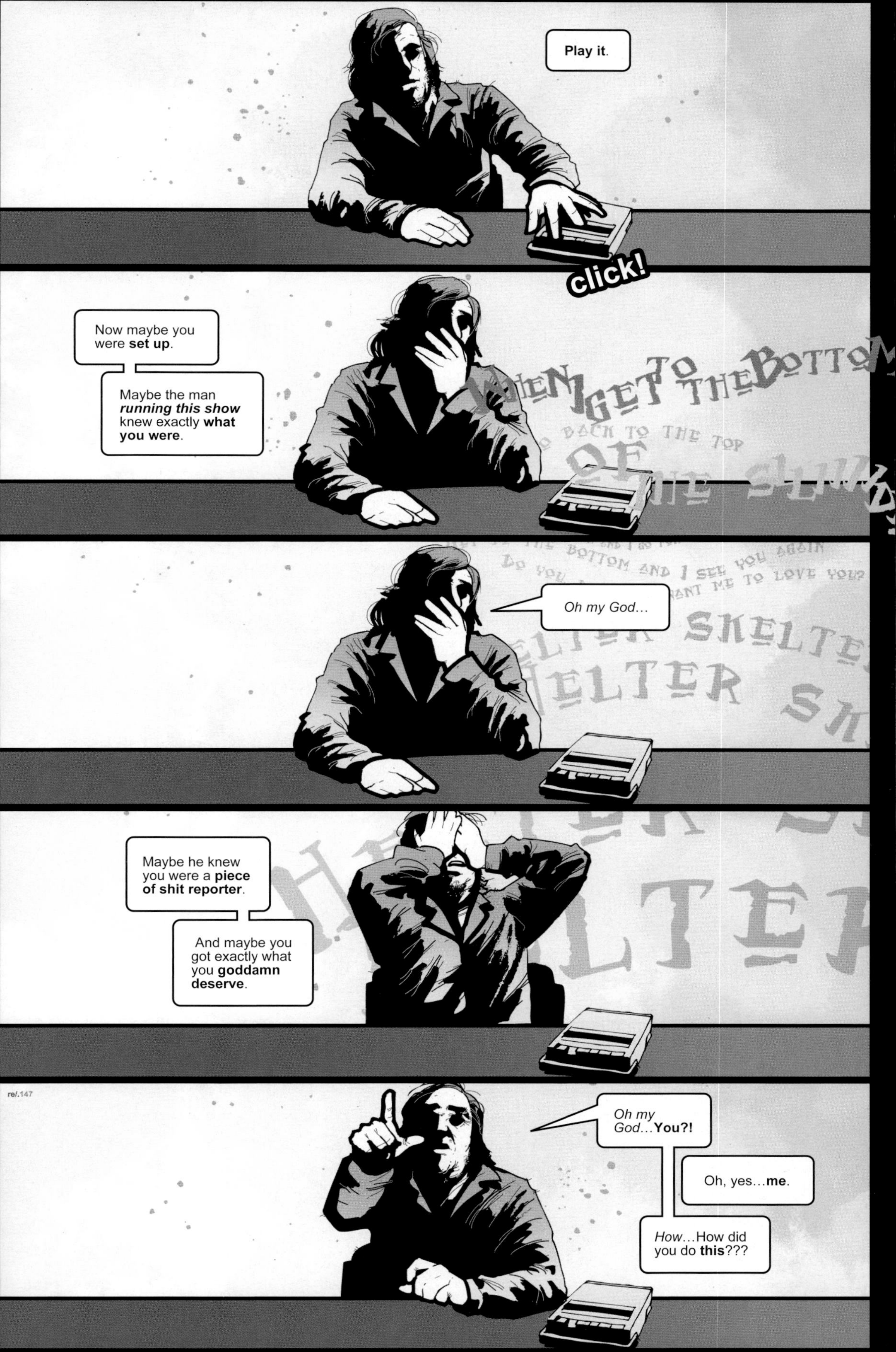
Play it.
click!
Now maybe you were set up.
Maybe the man running this show knew exactly what you were.
GET TO THE BOTTOM
BACK TO THE TOP
OF
BOTTOM AND I SEE YOU AGAIN
Oh my God…
SKELTER
ELTER
Maybe he knew you were a piece of shit reporter.
And maybe you got exactly what you goddamn deserve.
Oh my God…You?!
Oh, yes…me.
How…How did you do this???

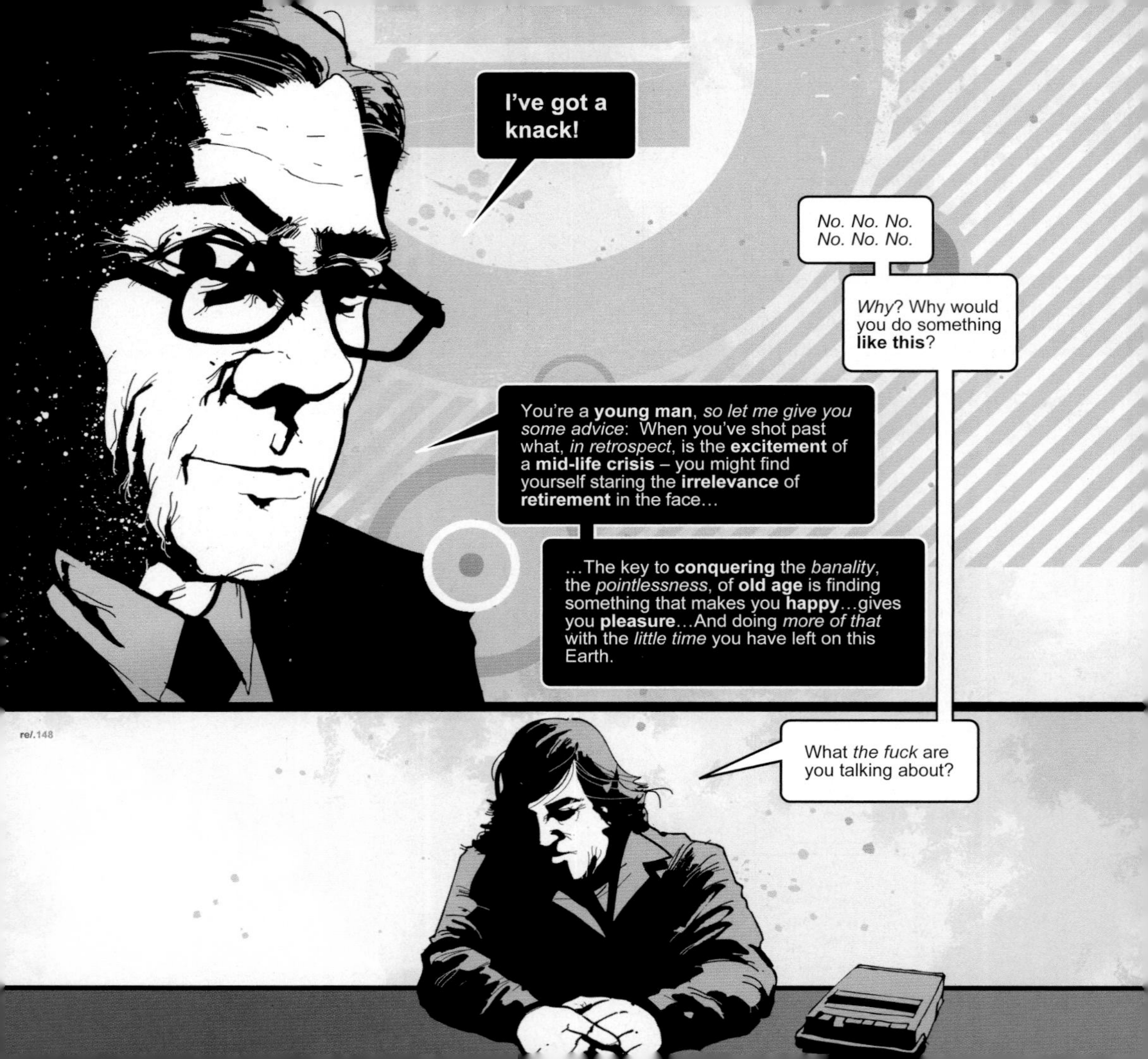

I've got a knack!
No. No. No. No. No. No.
Why? Why would you do something **like this**?
You're a **young man**, *so let me give you some advice*: When you've shot past what, *in retrospect*, is the **excitement** of a **mid-life crisis** – you might find yourself staring the **irrelevance** of **retirement** in the face…
…The key to **conquering** the *banality*, the *pointlessness*, of **old age** is finding something that makes you **happy**…gives you **pleasure**…And doing *more of that* with the *little time* you have left on this Earth.
What *the fuck* are you talking about?

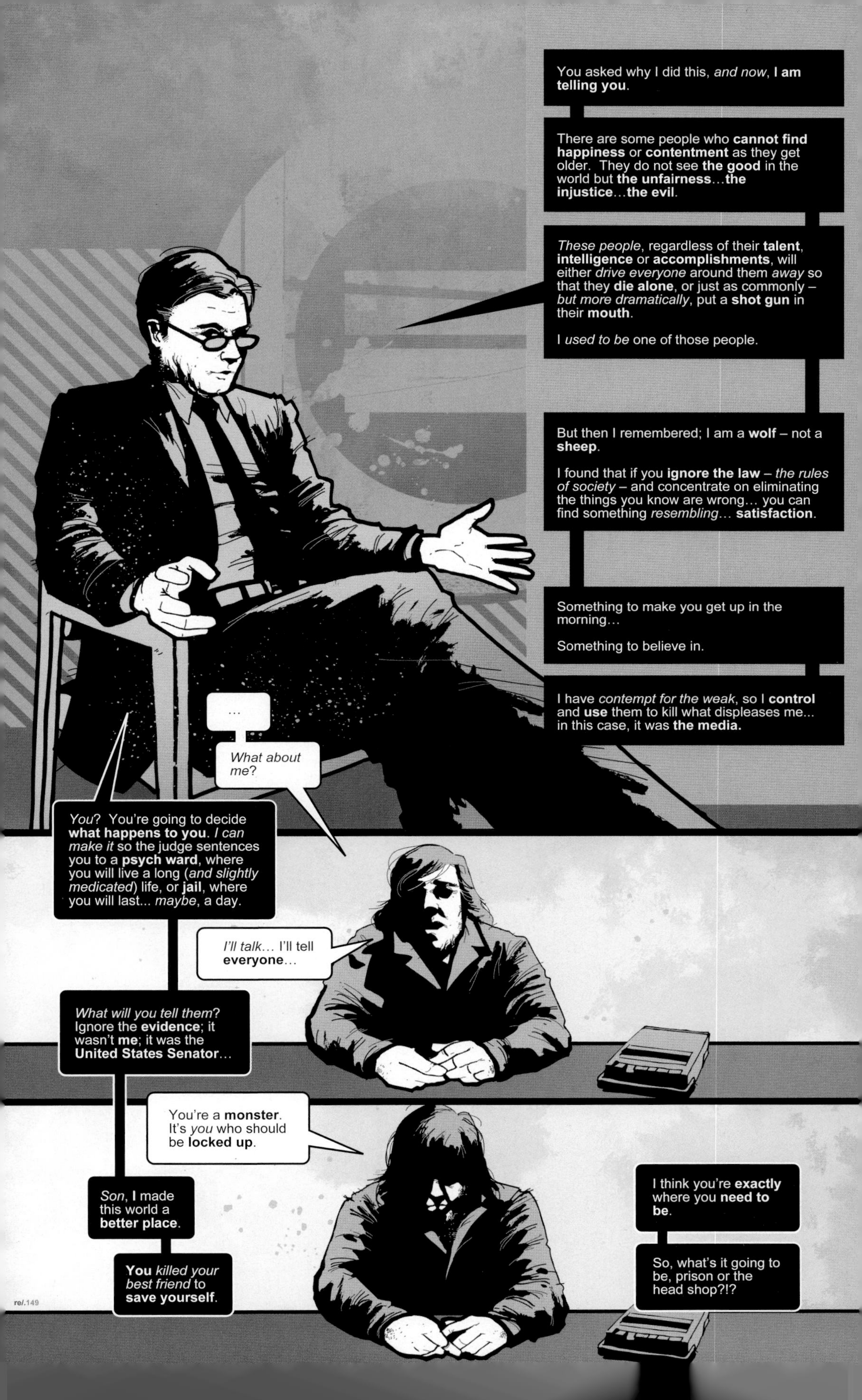
You asked why I did this, *and now*, **I am telling you**.
There are some people who **cannot find happiness** or **contentment** as they get older. They do not see **the good** in the world but **the unfairness**…**the injustice**…**the evil**.
These people, regardless of their **talent**, **intelligence** or **accomplishments**, will either *drive everyone* around them *away* so that they **die alone**, or just as commonly – *but more dramatically*, put a **shot gun** in their **mouth**.
I *used to be* one of those people.
But then I remembered; I am a **wolf** – not a **sheep**.
I found that if you **ignore the law** – *the rules of society* – and concentrate on eliminating the things you know are wrong… you can find something *resembling*… **satisfaction**.
Something to make you get up in the morning…
Something to believe in.
I have *contempt for the weak*, so I **control** and **use** them to kill what displeases me... in this case, it was **the media.**
…
What about me?
You? You're going to decide **what happens to you**. *I can make it* so the judge sentences you to a **psych ward**, where you will live a long (*and slightly medicated*) life, or **jail**, where you will last... *maybe*, a day.
I'll talk… I'll tell **everyone**…
What will you tell them? Ignore the **evidence**; it wasn't **me**; it was the **United States Senator**…
You're a **monster**. It's *you* who should be **locked up**.
Son, **I** made this world a **better place**.
You *killed your best friend* to **save yourself**.
I think you're **exactly** where you **need to be**.
So, what's it going to be, prison or the head shop?!?

SIX MONTHS **LATER** ref.150

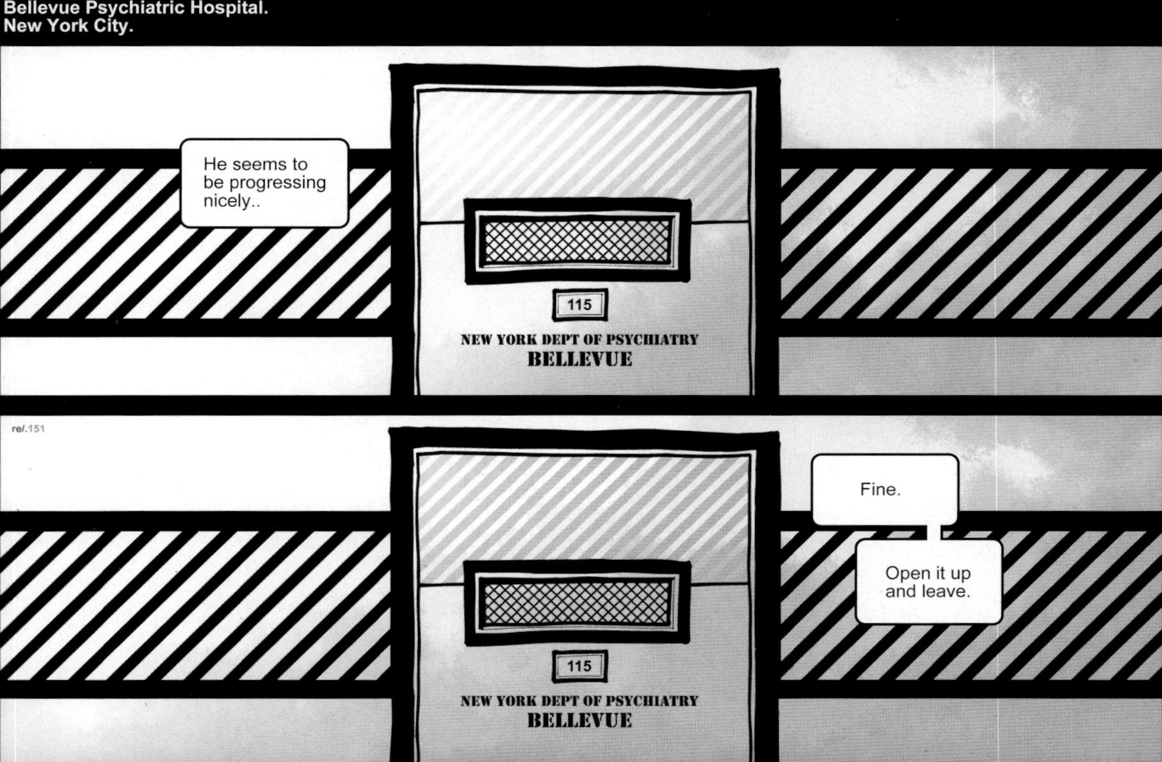
Bellevue Psychiatric Hospital.
New York City.
He seems to be progressing nicely..
115
NEW YORK DEPT OF PSYCHIATRY
BELLEVUE
rel.151
Fine.
Open it up and leave.
115
NEW YORK DEPT OF PSYCHIATRY
BELLEVUE

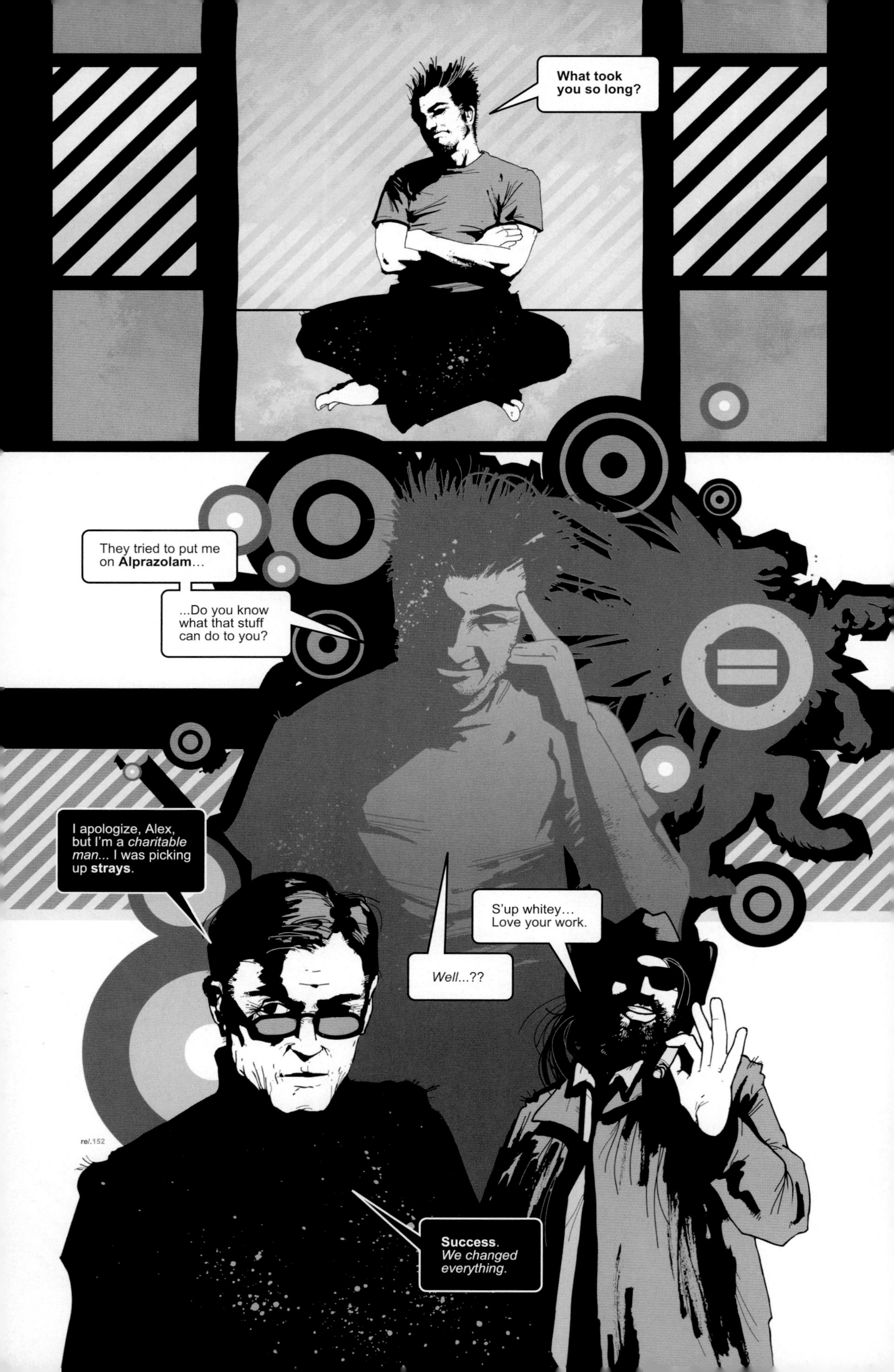

What took you so long?
They tried to put me on **Alprazolam**...
...Do you know what that stuff can do to you?
I apologize, Alex, but I'm a *charitable man...* I was picking up **strays**.
Well...??
S'up whitey... Love your work.
Success. *We changed everything*.

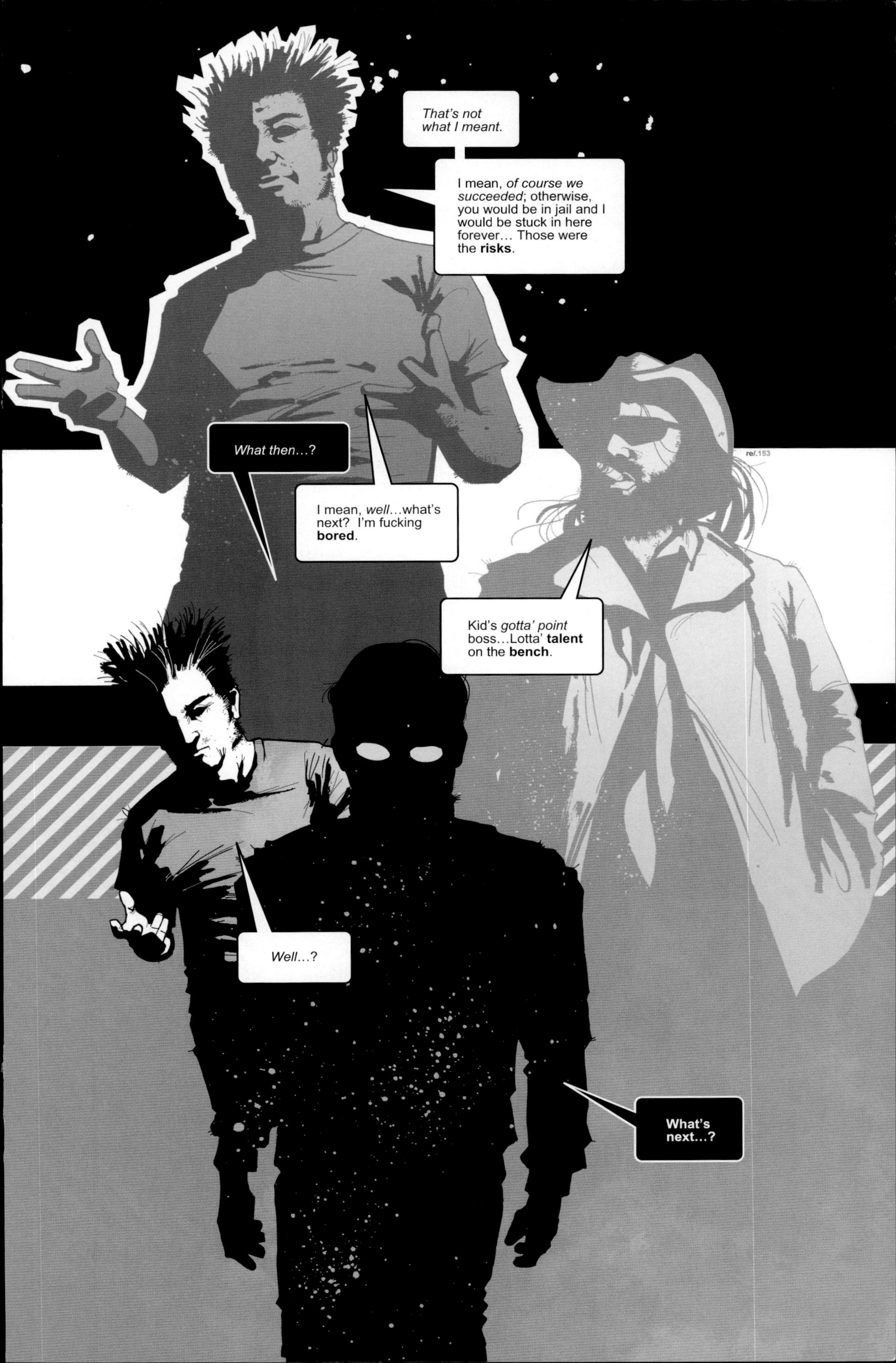
That's not what I meant.
I mean, of course we succeeded; otherwise, you would be in jail and I would be stuck in here forever… Those were the risks.
What then…?
I mean, well…what's next? I'm fucking bored.
Kid's gotta' point boss…Lotta' talent on the bench.
Well…?
What's next…?

re/.153

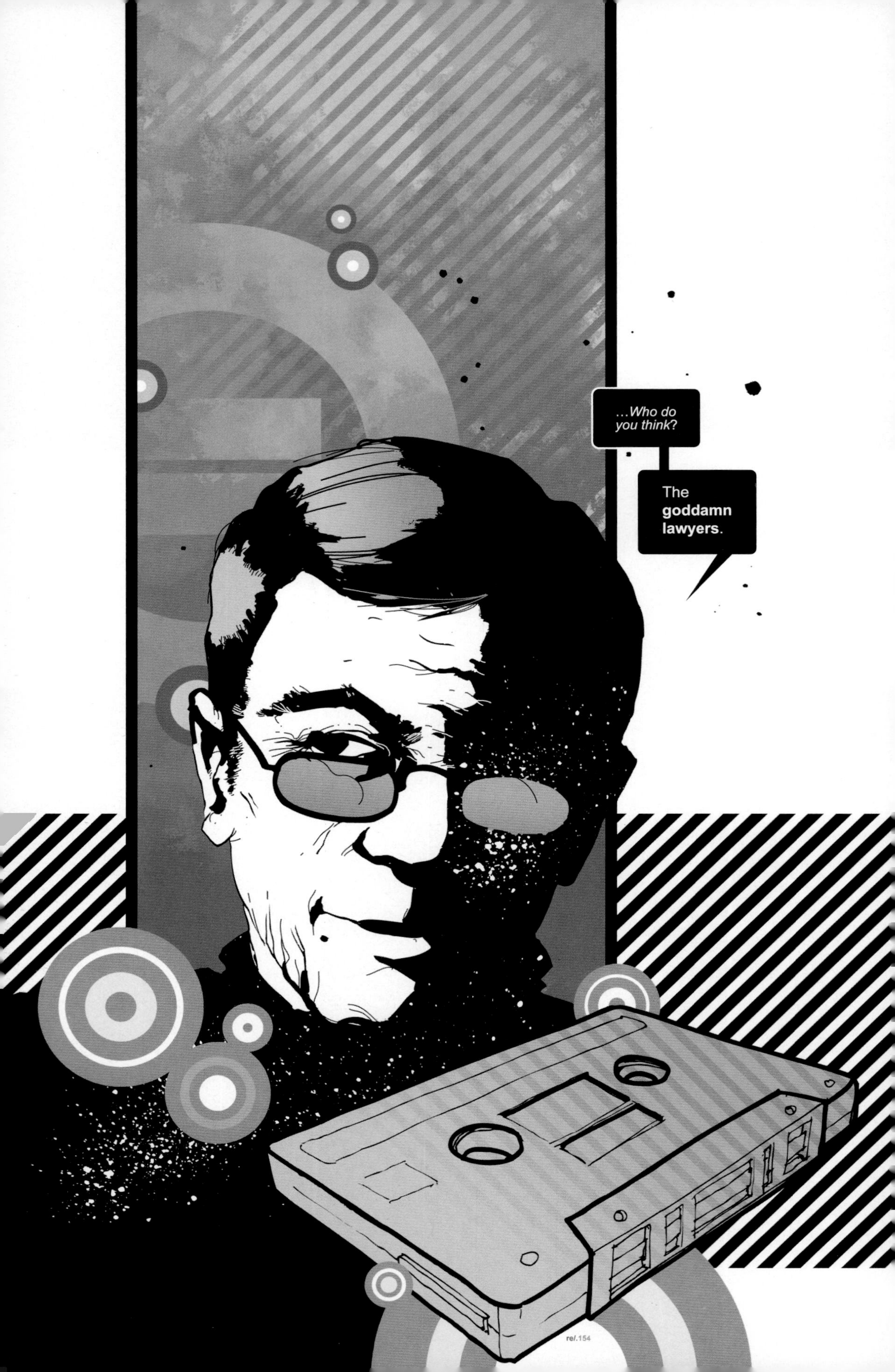
...Who do you think?
The goddamn lawyers.

END

AFTE

Jonathan Hickman
South Carolina
7.4.07

Do you feel better?

I get asked this in interviews a lot - *as if* there was something I desperately needed to get off my chest. It's usually accompanied by: Why are you so angry? (I'm not.) Do you identify with the protagonist? (No.) Is this a call to arms or is it time to get militant? (*Please.*) What is the NIGHTLY NEWS really about? (We'll get back to that.) Needless to say, *I've heard it all.*

So, let me clear one thing up: ***The NIGHTLY NEWS isn't personal socio-political therapy.***

Are there things about the story that I believe? Sure. Are there things that I completely disagree with? Abso-fucking-lutely. Are there truths masquerading as lies and vice-versa? Well, that's kind of the point... I'm telling a story.

And it's one I expected more of you would **hate**.

First, there was the concept and its execution. I thought there was absolutely zero chance that people who identify strongly with the two-party system weren't going to ruin it by weaving their own beliefs into the fabric of the story. That's guaranteed to happen in this current political climate, *right?*

What about the art? A mash-up of graphic design and comic art leaving behind (for the most part) the underlying structure of panels and page breaks – unreadable, *right?*

Plus, when you create an intentionally divisive book like The NIGHTLY NEWS, there's an expected volume level of response. Bold choices mixed with touchy topics usually ensure that people won't be indifferent. Love and hate assured, *right?*

Man, was I **wrong**.

I like to think I'm so clever. I deluded myself by thinking that if you were distracted with multiple plot lines, numerous themes, a large (intentionally ambiguous) cast, information graphics, iconic design elements and over-saturated, monochromatic color schemes you wouldn't be aware of what was really going on – **that I was putting on a show**.

And you saw right through me.

All I've ever wanted to do is tell stories – *it's what I was meant to do*. I know this because I spent 10 years trying to convince myself I'd be happy doing other things. And from the initial fan reaction to the peer recognition to the press acceptance straight on through to the series' conclusion, all of it confirmed what I believed: I was home.

So, what is the NIGHTLY NEWS about?

Let me start by saying, I don't believe in telling stories that give answers. I don't know what that accomplishes besides serving up a big 'ole helping of didactic pap. What I do believe in is telling stories that ask questions. Concerning the NIGHTLY NEWS, for me it's about believing in something so much you have to do it regardless of the cost. I'm sure you feel differently, which is the point. Enjoy the NIGHTLY NEWS for what it is to you. That's how it should be – **it's yours now**.

As to the first question – *Do I feel better?*

Top of the world.

SOURC

ES

Manufacturing Consent
Herman S. Edward and Noam Chomsky

Cults in Our Midst
Margaret Thaler Singer

Hard News
Seth Mnookin

Striking the Balance Survey
Pew Research and CCJ

New York Times Editor's Trust Report
The Credibility Group

The State of the News Media
An Annual Report on American Journalism
Journalism.org

The Scorecard on Development:
25 Years of Diminished Progress
Mark Weisbrot, Dean Baker & David Rosnick

Media Anger Management
Tom Rosenstiel and Bill Kovach

Media Ownership: Who Owns What?

Monopoly Money
Dan Kennedy

All Power to the Barons
Ivan Brisco

Global Media, Neoliberalism and Imperialism
Robert W. McChesney

What Makes Mainstream Media Mainstream
Noam Chomsky

Necessary Illusions
Noam Chomsky

The Underground History of American Education
John Taylor Gatto

Good Clean Fun
Clive Thompson

Psychopolitics
Lavrent Pavlovich Beria

Everything You Know is Wrong
Edited by: Russ Kick

Psychiatric Drugging of Children for Behavioral Control
Peter Breggin, M.D.

The Senator's Ashes
Douglas Valentine

Burn the Olive Tree, Sell the Lexus
Greg Palast and Oliver Shykles

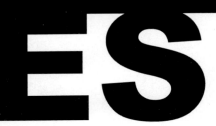

NOTE

These are the explanations, origins and random musings regarding the process and development of creating the NIGHTLY NEWS.

In front of each comment is the page number to which it applies. While the page numbers are found in different places on each page, they are uniform in appearance and should be easily located.

re/.01

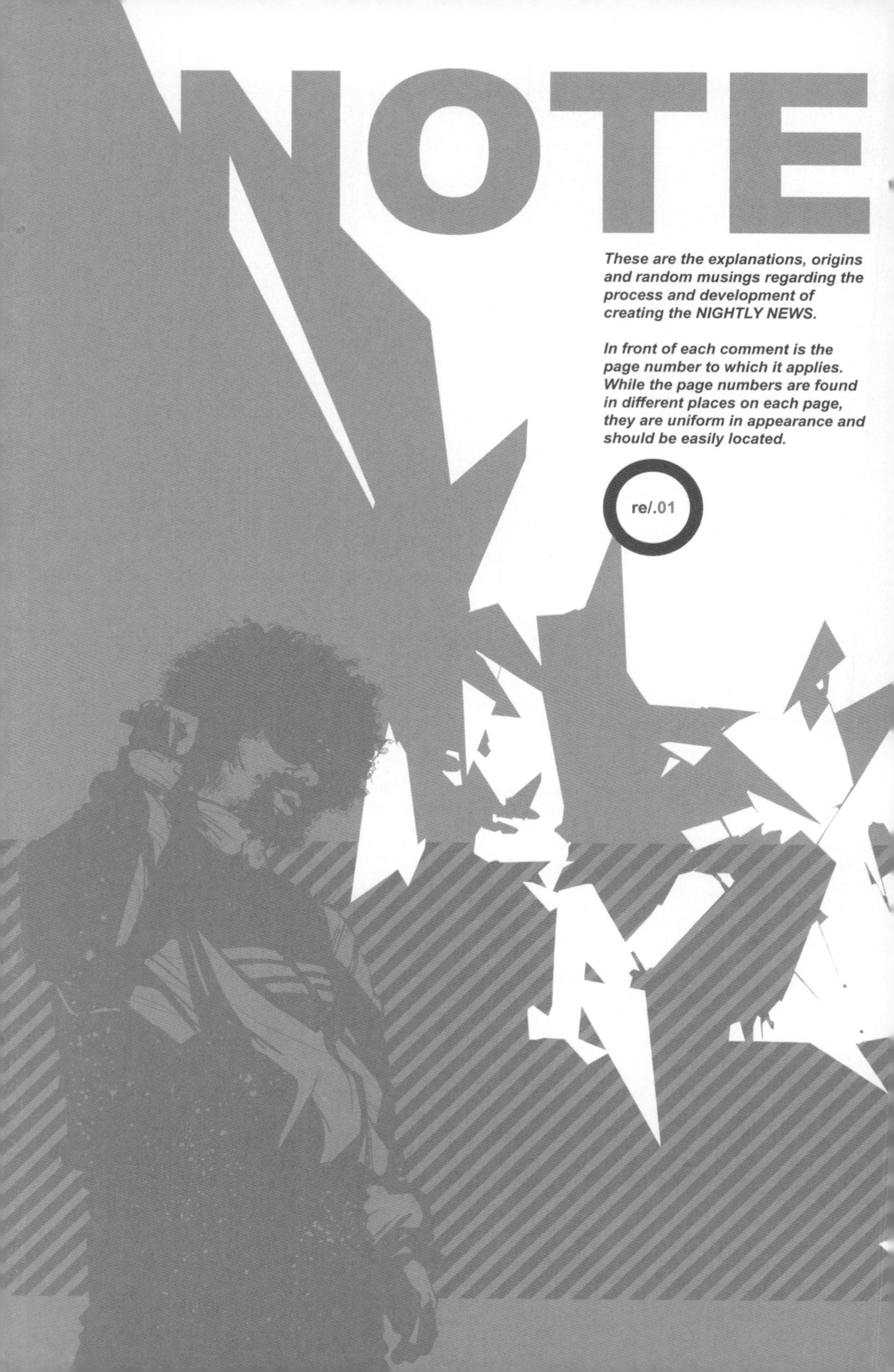

START

Chapter One:

1 – The straight-from-LA, buy-Hollywood-buy, high-concept pitch for the Nightly News was Reservoir Dogs meets Network, which while ridiculous gets the point across. The title of the first chapter "**I'm mad as hell and I'm not going to take this anymore**" is, naturally, Chayefsky. I was going to go with "The whole song is a metaphor for big dicks," but it lacked a certain something.

1 – Yes, New Yorkers, I know the image here has been reversed. It looked better this way.

1 – The idea of the news as an **information organism**, a living thing, (in this instance) implies that it is something to be domesticated or controlled.

1 – And speaking of **control,** it's an idea that keeps popping up lately in a lot of popular fiction. I believe some of this is a reaction to the increasingly pronounced leader-follower relationships throughout western culture, but (and let's be honest here) most of it is blowback from the freedoms we concede to others in exchange for comfort.

2 – Much of the **globalization** information comes from an article I read by Greg Palast (see sources). This is probably one of those areas where even though the information is interesting, accurate and timely, I should be clear and say that I don't believe that the end product of globalization is inherently evil or wrong; but it's fair to say, almost all bureaucratic and monetary systems attract people with questionable morals. Flies to shit and all that.

2 – **Conscientious objectors, protestors, activists**… I hate the way people continually rename things when they become uncomfortable with the connotation of a commonly defined word.

3 – Speaking on that kind of ilk, this idea that being a protestor is not just a noble activity but is a righteous work done by the enlightened is some type of reality-warped, romanticized notion of the sixties. For the most part, this is nothing more than public therapy by part-timers. Their focus isn't actually on changing the world; it's on making a public display, a cathartic offering, out of guilt that they live in an opulent society. There is nothing more pussy than sitting around and doing chants and singing songs pretending like that is going to change the world. Nothing. It's an embarrassing charade by the wealthy.

3 – And that, of course, leads directly into **what are you willing to do**. It's a call to arms by the VOICE to do whatever is necessary to change a system and it completely flies in the face of fake examples of commitment. I'm not an advocate for violence – far from it, but the world has been shaped by violent men who have taken what they wanted. Pretending otherwise doesn't make it less so.

4 – Brother John is quoting from **Might is Right** by Ragnar Redbeard, which Anton LeVay plagiarized when he wrote the Satanic Bible. The point here is I'm letting you know we're dealing with people of questionable morals. I'm letting you know, in my own obscure kind of way, it's a cult.

4 – If it hasn't been clear already, I believe the children of the sixties (on the right and the left) grew up to be the worst generation of Americans ever.

5 – The line, **"When killing activists, never shoot for the head, always aim for the heart"** is probably what sold the book.

6 – The **SWAT logo** is the first example of using iconography to visually identify a character, or a character's purpose, in The Nightly News. It's one of the *rules of design* I created for the book.

7 – The idea of displaying people on the **television screen** only in **black and white** is about the binary nature of the medium. The current environment in the United States is one where a two-party system permeates everything. There is only left or right, right or wrong, black or white.

7 – Blanket regurgitated statements like **"all men are rapists"** are the kind of over-the-top demagoguery that is celebrated as intellectual insight by 60's refugees and their progeny. Its bastard child is message board machismo. While I wish ill on no one, the fact that Marilyn French got esophageal cancer should be a lesson to all over-posturing agitators.

7 – Just to clarify, the feminist movement was needed and historically is one of the more interesting things to have happened in the last 60 years in the US. I think the only place where some feminists really get it wrong is confusing 'equal' with 'same'. i.e. While men and women are equal, they most certainly are not the same. And about sex…

7 – **Not being allowed to have sex** is the first very clear, very prominent sign that we're dealing with a cult.

8 – Refusing to call a sniper a sniper is another example of putting a nice face on the ugly things we want to believe in. A perfect example of this is the President of the United States. Here's an individual that no matter who it is or what party they come from, when they leave office it's as a murderer. It's a prerequisite for the job. It never gets talked about in debates, but we expect it. (It's the real reason why the military question is so important, we secretly want to know that a candidate's going to kill, kill, kill for his country) It makes me laugh whenever people talk about the long hours, the demanding schedule, being why Presidents look so much older when they leave office. These are haunted men who will never again sleep the sleep of the just. They willingly go to Hell for the safety of the American people and there will be no atonement. It's the reason why a decent and good man like Jimmy Carter was a terrible President. He lacked the proper amount of blood in his mouth to do the job.

10 – All of the stories with each member of the cult are derivatives of actual real world events. **Brother Hassan Nidal's story** is based on that of Iyad K. Hilal.

11 – "It's about revenge" is the first time that I clue you in to the overall theme of the entire work, which is people that were done wrong getting even.

11 – The idea of an established persona – that you are the sum of all of your experiences, decisions and feelings – is false. We are, in fact, quite malleable to new experiences, peer influence and tragedy. Adaptability, humanity's evolutionary strength, is also one of its greatest weaknesses.

12 – This is the introduction of the second color scheme. The concept is that current time would be in the reds, oranges and yellows and any other time, either in the past or in the future, would be in blues.

15 – Brother Alex offering John what he really wants and John turning around and saying his cold cup of coffee is **"the best cup of coffee I've ever had"** is obviously a derivative of the old Klingon proverb.

17 – The main news anchor here should not be considered to be Dan Rather, but rather an amalgam of all the evening news guys. **He just talks like Dan.**

18 – David Allen Kite is obviously based on Walter Cronkite. The speech that he gives is basically excerpts from an actual one.

18 – Indoctrination disguised as education is a theme that gets visited heavily in chapter 3.

18 – The crux of the speech by David Allen Kite is that the hoi polloi, the common people, are not intelligent enough to make decisions and therefore the **responsibility of their education** falls on the shoulders of journalists. Do you think it's an honest depiction of a sentiment that exists?

19 – The idea that when you are at war the **rules of society** are not abandoned is something we like to believe is true. We live in a time where we trust that such a thing as perfectly sanitized, enemy combatant only, no collateral damage warfare is possible - and it isn't. All wars are horrible; all wars are evil.

20 – Everything human is **biased**. Journalists are not the only people on the planet capable of separating themselves from their work.

"It's a testament to *the willingness* of the government to actively engage in human programming."

8 – The idea behind there being **3 shooters** is triangulation, i.e. there is nowhere to hide.

9 – The statistics about **firing ratios in the military** are accurate (see sources). It's almost unbelievable that in roughly a 25-year period of time there was a 75% jump in the willingness of an individual to shoot their weapon to kill another man. It's a testament to the willingness of the government to actively engage in human programming. If you think this is limited to the military sector, you're kidding yourself.

12 – Blackrock is the coolest name ever for a building.

13 – The **job posting** for the First Church of the Brotherhood of the VOICE was a pathetic way of sneaking in my web address. It's **www.pronea.com** by the way.

14 – Perfect hair and rotten mouths is the perfect description of people who appear on the evening news.

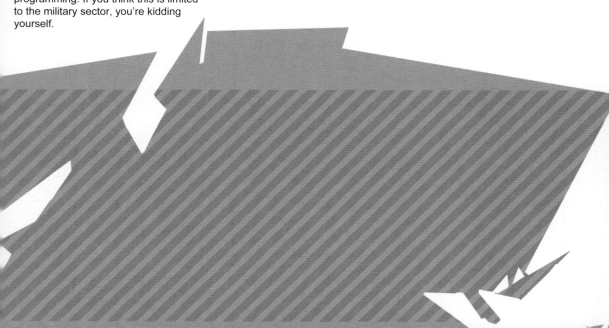

"Expecting anything beyond lowest common denominator *stereotyping* is a waste of time."

23 - As **consolidation** continues and fewer companies own more of the business, the idea that everyone is in bed with each other is assured. The idea that a news organization wouldn't want to investigate a story because it might affect a company they do business with is a reality.

23 – **The back-story for the Senator** is that he was a presidential frontrunner until he got caught up in a sex scandal. Imagine how painful it must have been for Gary Hart to watch Bill Clinton become president. That is Senator Rector.

24 - Just want to go on record as saying that, in fact, fat jokes do not equal wife-cheating jokes. You should never try and escalate the verbal smack in this manner. Fisticuffs are inevitable.

26 - I love writing these **quasi-inspirational/religious speeches**. Note this is a first person "testimony" type of speech, not at all like the speeches by the VOICE.

27 – **The Fedex slip** with the tracking number on it, 8560 3206 6920, is from my submission of the Nightly News to Image Comics. You can still type it in at Fedex.com and it'll show that Eric Stephenson signed for it.

28 – If there was someway that I could guarantee that I wouldn't go to jail for tax evasion, I would totally start a **501c3 tax-exempt non-profit organization** – the Church of Me or The Reunified Brotherhood of the Second Apostolic Goatherders. Whatever.

Chapter Two:

31 – **The truth is analog**… I'm certainly not a paralyzed-by-choice, moral relativist, but this idea of things only being right or wrong has always bothered me.

31 – Let's be honest. **Cassette tapes** look infinitely cooler than vinyl, cds or dvds.

32 – **The VOICE** is a creation of Senator Rector and as such, the language he uses is just as artificial as his persona. All the speeches by the VOICE are mash-ups of Margaret Thaler Singer and Lavrent Pavlovich Beria – A marriage of modern day cultic indoctrination and soviet era pychopolitics. Some of it is rote regurgitation.

34 – Make sure you check out that **YouTube video of Larry King** and Starr Jones. Funny stuff.

35 – If this were an actual cult, **the children would not be left alone**. One of the first things that would happen would be incorporating the entire family into the organization.

37 – The idea of the **Constitution** as nothing more than an overly precious document serving the interest of the elite is something we are going to hear more of in the near future. If the Supreme Court continues to behave as if the rights of citizens are something akin to land being claimed on the frontier, prepare to embrace a siege mentality.

38 – Alex is pretending to be carrying on two conversations. One with himself, and the other with anyone who will listen.

39 – On a second reading, it should be pretty apparent that Alex is working the system.

40 – The 'shop talk' at **the fundraiser** pretends to show an interesting look at capitalism. From disdain for unionized labor (workers' rights), to portraying partakers of entertainment as consumers, to national defense as a profit center - I tried to hit every platitude possible in order to make the following point: party talk is boring predictable pap. Expecting anything beyond lowest common denominator stereotyping is a waste of time. i.e. I love parties.

42 – The **homicide statistics** come from the FBI. The idea that America remains the Wild West should be branded into every kid's ass when they get to grade school.

43 – Knowing that Senator Rector is the VOICE makes reading **"Tell them a story"** one truly sinister statement. He knows that if the media companies broadcast only feel-good stories, much of the societal angst would dissipate (as we are natural receivers). Having felt it's full weight, the Senator understands the power of the media better than the media moguls. He is, in fact, giving his acquaintances one last chance.

Chapter Three:

44 – On theft. In a global economy, intellectual property should be protected as fiercely as actual goods and services. Unfortunately, I do not believe this to be an achievable goal as long as foreign governments actively participate in screwing over inventors, artists and storytellers.

> "Victims of *viral ideas* revert to a type of human behavior tolerated in the West only before the Age of Reason. It reeks of apocalyptic *religious intolerance*."

45 – On plagiarism. While it is becoming more of a gray area as commentary on commentary has become acceptable art, it remains predominately a home of procrastinators and the lazy.

47 – The aplomb with which **Jayson Blair** was destroyed by other news organizations is laughable. They, of course, would never employ lazy plagiarizing reporters.

49 – Warner's speech about **working at the New York Times** is based on the first chapter of Seth Mnookin's book **Hard News**. Great author - great book, but the self-congratulatory, implied pedigree of being a *Timesman* is pretty accurate. It reminds me of the way Microsoft employees used to talk about themselves.

51 – It should go without saying, but any bartender, waiter or waitress that actually **serves one of these drinks** and emails me the reporter's name is getting seriously rewarded. Additionally, the *societal debt* to Chuck Palahniuk for Project Mayhem will never be fully repaid.

52 – No John, it actually is **terrorism**.

54 – We don't need no education. When arguing with myself (which, despite sounding crazy, is a lot like single player chess [except louder]) the non-emotional, intellectual side of me usually wins. Which never happens in the real world.

55 – Any ideas of educational institutions being **work programs for adults** are completely valid and, in my opinion, one of the chief culprits of the failure of the American educational system. You have to be able to fire outdated, passionless teachers in order to hire good ones, especially as kids are already handicapped by an inane curriculum.

55 – Subordination to a hierarchical system is the desired end product of any institution.

56 – Methylphenidate is Ritalin.

56 – This reality of institutional programming in conjunction with the **intentional drugging of children** is the one issue in the Nightly News I consider myself passionate about. If it is true – that you can judge a society by how they treat their children – we are failures all.

57 – Much of the information about the **nature of education** comes from my reading of John Taylor Gatto. Check the source page and read his stuff.

57 – Emily Dickinson was chosen at random. There is no particular bone to pick.

58 – The **education worth equation** was inspired by a book full of fun math like this. I didn't buy the book the day I saw it, and now am unable to find it anywhere; so if anyone knows this book, drop me an email and let me know the name so I can order it.

59 – The only thing you should ever learn from school is that you don't belong. I'm definitely going to be a hit at PTA meetings and God help the poor educator that has a parent / teacher conference with me.

60 – Victims of **viral ideas** revert to a type of human behavior tolerated in the West only before the Age of Reason. It reeks of apocalyptic religious intolerance. The man-made global warming crowd is a good example of this. After every tornado, hurricane, drought or snowstorm: They point to the sky and say it's a sign… these are the end times, our last days. Heretics be damned, for our cause is righteous and salvation only comes from repentance and the changing of your ways! These people may be right, but their behavior marks them as Jesuits all.

62 – On originality. I'm so bored with the attempt by individuals to distinguish themselves from others by 'difference branding.' You got a new tattoo, how original. Oh, a new piercing – You. Fucking. Rebel.

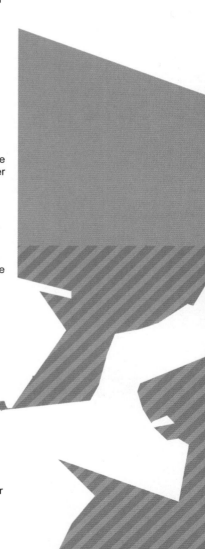

63 – **Inner decay, outer decay**… I've always thought that one reflects the other.

64 – **The Matrix** was the best science fiction movie of the last 15 years.

65 – It's been sad watching **Katie Couric** get old.

66 – **MediaKill** sounds like a great name for a first person shooter doesn't it?

67 – The idea of disseminating **the marriage of porn and news** online is redundant. It's like trying to distinguish something like chocolate covered chocolate, or soap scented soap from the rest of the market.

69 – The **Chomsky, Goebbels,** and later, Hitler gag running through the series is, I concede, way over the top. But the payoff quote at the beginning of this collected edition is totally worth it.

71 – I threw the **crossing the threshold** out there to mess with story archetype lovers. I would argue there is no hero's journey contained within the Nightly News. I suppose a case could be made for Brother John, but I wouldn't buy it. Maybe I could be convinced… somebody should write a term paper.

"Maybe I could be convinced… somebody should write a *term paper*."

75 – What drives **James to finally shoot Warner** is his fear that he might 'give him up', it's rationalized self-preservation.

76 – **Brother David** loves attention, and as such, gives great speeches.

78 – **Enough lessons, enough preaching**… This was a note to myself going forward to ratchet up the beats – to move the plot forward faster as the story built.

Chapter Four:

80 – Margaret Thaler Singer's seminal work, **Cults in Our Midst**, is the title of this chapter and one of the inspirations for this book. Dr. Singer's work in this field deserves merit not only because it was groundbreaking, inspired and timely, but also because it was courageous – *a thing of bravery*. Despite abandonment by her peers, harassment by brainwashers and lawsuits by groups with agendas and deep pockets, she pursued publishing her research. Margaret Thaler Singer died in 2003 at the age of 82.

81 – **Dr. Thaler** is obviously named after Dr. Singer.

82 – The correlation I'm making between **religion, education and information** shouldn't be overlooked. In fact, one of the main points I'm making in the Nightly News is the following: Distilled down to their essence, there is no psychological difference in the information provider/information receiver relationship when comparing the corporate news and its audience with religious cult leaders and their followers.

84 – As a defense mechanism or personality reinforcement, many people like to reconstruct their memories of the past to fit their current vision of the present. In a cult this is intentionally done to separate a candidate from any previously existing support structure.

85 – You have become what you hate is something heard too often.

86 – If I could redo parts of the Nightly News it would be situations like this where, because of page constraints, I was forced to cram events into fewer pages so other parts in each issue could breathe. It's not that the page is overly wordy and therefore visually confusing (Hell, this argument could be made about the entire series), but that this section might be seen as less relevant because of the page count when, in fact, nothing could be less true.

89 – Create chaos… guerilla warfare 101.

90 – The idea behind the **Fairness in Media Act** is that of a Trojan horse, legislation crafted by the Senator to destroy the established structure of 'the Press' in the US.

95 – Digitization is actually on a steeper acceleration curve than **corporatization**. I'm sure there's a valid argument to be made for the eventual digitization of everything.

95 – The graphic behind Brother John and the doctor symbolizes a meeting of the minds. Deep stuff, I know.

96 – Courtney Lynn-Kyle is a composite of all the ridiculous 'dirty teens' paraded on TV that wear a temporary celebrity crown. Whether it's the applause that vestal virgins like Britney and Jessica get as they sex it up or the oh-how-daring, fake shock directed towards pretend whores like Christina, the response these brainless tarts receive is completely manufactured.

98 – My birthday is **March ninth**. I share it with Mickey Spillane, Bobby Fischer and Yuri Gagarin.

101 – Once again, James' sense of self-preservation dominates his thinking. Even though he said on the previous page "[he] knew what [he] was walking into," he refuses to accept any guilt from his actions.

102 – The idea behind this page was to make the reader stop and breathe, a pause before the climax and final act.

103 – It's a universal truth that the only way to have the good life is to live a life that is good. There is no **real forgiveness** for anything without personal change or restitution. It's not a hard concept to grasp and it certainly doesn't extend beyond any man's reach.

"Number 1 – Chicken fettuccine alfredo (The *secret* is using honey and blackened seasoning)"

90 – The idea behind the **corporate heads** was based on the original 12 Angry Men (And monthly issue collectors will remember this as the answer to the second Nightly News contest).

92 – And speaking of contest, the two gentlemen in panels two and three are the first Nightly News contest winners. As promised, their heads are blown off in chapter six. Congratulations, boys!

99 – I'm so hungry. My desert island, all-time, top five favorite foods: Number 5 – (tie) Steak fajitas or Bojangles fries. Number 4 – General Tso's chicken with white rice. Number 3 – Bacon-wrapped filet with mushrooms and bernese sauce. Number 2 – A bloomin' onion from Outback steakhouse. Number 1 – Chicken fettuccine alfredo (The secret is using honey and blackened seasoning)

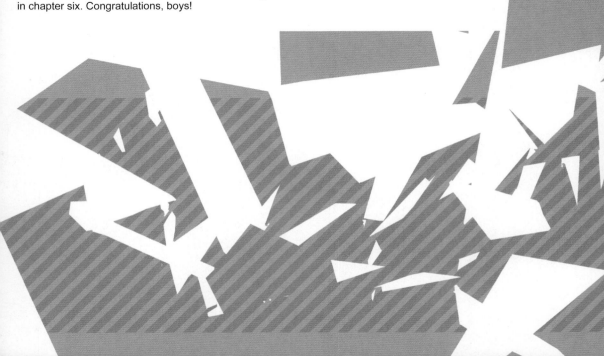

Chapter Five:

106 – True Believers. The good and the bad, or it's not always about drinking the Kool-aid.

107 – If you believe in nothing, how can you accomplish anything? There's an evolving brand of militant atheist that continually parrots science as the defined answer to every question – as if science isn't about evolving truth in the face of newly discovered errors. Some of the things that historically, and so very clearly, define us (wanderlust, compassion, love) have very little to do with science. And while spirituality has lost credibility in the face of religion, to believe is human. So do choose carefully, but believe in something.

108 – There comes a time when a father can no longer talk to his son as if he is still a child. Chapter five of the Nightly News is the story of the Prodigal Son.

109 – Doubt and faith are different points along the same line. One almost always leads to the other; they give each other their power.

110 – Striking the Balance (see sources) is a blanket indictment of everything that is wrong about American journalism today and the problems it will face going forward. People don't like journalists… don't trust journalists… and don't believe in journalists. Research for this report was done by the Committee of Concerned Journalists and the Pew Research Center, which makes the report all the more damning.

114 – I think the key to turning an interesting scene is flipping the conventional.

115 – What is implied here is that yet again James' sense of self-preservation kicked in and he immediately revealed everything he knew. This leads to the police raid at the beginning of chapter six.

116 – The common people lacking the humility to submit to civil rule is a paragon of Chomsky propaganda speech. When the political bases on both the right and the left are constantly seen as an irritant to elected representatives, the time for wholesale abandonment of a generation of politicians is at hand. Viva scabs!

118 – The three old newsmen concept came late in the book. There's a no-nonsense thing that most elderly men have when reflecting on their lives and the idea of them looking back on when and how it went wrong added a certain weight to the story.

120 – The thing about **Hamilton and Jefferson** financing papers is completely true and lets you know how ingrained the insular nature of Washington, D.C. is.

121 – The idea of **corporate corruption** falling solely on the head of the employer obviously doesn't resonate with me. Sure, we all sellout to a certain extent for a paycheck, but pretending that the prevalence of employee theft not impacting the morality of a corporation is naive. Whether it's not working when you're being paid to, the gaming of travel and business expenses, or playing around on the Internet, it all comes back on the ethics of the business and the abuse of the consumer.

122 – Caution! This page and the next will induce nausea and vomiting if stared at for 10 minutes or longer. Prolonged exposure can result in erectile dysfunction or the onset of genital warts.

124 – On the DVR. A couple things here: One, I'm a graduate of Clemson and as such I will never apologize for making a University of South Carolina joke (sorry, I just won't); and two, I'm a damned patriot when it comes to the US Men's soccer team, so the filthy donkey-fucking El Tri can suck a big one (and they often do: 2-0).

127 – It's what we do… this is a derivative of what was said in the Page Six scandal a couple of years ago.

> **"There's an evolving brand of *militant atheist* that continually parrots science as the defined answer to every question – as if science isn't about *evolving truth* in the face of *newly discovered errors*."**

128 – We sons are always trying to please and gain the praise of our fathers. I've always wondered if the reason that men crave male children is not that they want someone to carry on the family legacy, but that they want to finally be the receiver of such adoration.

Chapter Six:

130 – **Revenge.** I'll concede, there are times when I might be a bit direct.

131 – **I pose the threat of being a good example** is a take on an OxFam quote about Nicaragua's relationship with the United States.

133 – **The reel-to-reel** surrounded by pictures and candles is a homage to the mental ceremonial methodology relating to Japanese Kamikaze pilots. This is their last mission - to return would be failure.

134 – **You have a job to do** is probably the most autobiographical text in the Nightly News. You can read more about this in the section "Fully Committed," but the short version is this: Some people exist, some people live – be the latter.

135 – **Intellect or Instinct.** My friends and I have this argument a lot. You hear it phrased different ways, but it basically boils down to making decisions with your head or your heart. My problem is I'm analytical to a fault (plus I'm a grass is greener on the other side kind of guy) so being an instinctual person looks pretty appealing to me. But relating to the story…

136 – The VOICE knew that John would always go for the symbolic victory. Sure, the Senator is a bit fucking nuts, but in this moment he felt no fear. Even if he was wrong and John killed him, his plan was almost guaranteed to succeed – at worst, he's a martyr. In the end, John remained a guy that simply wanted to get even with people in the news. The Senator was comfortable with his calculations. While he had come to a mental conclusion and John had come to an emotional one, he knew they were the same. Plus, there was no way he was going to miss this asshole getting his head blown off.

136 – I refuse to explain, **"what's the frequency, Kenneth?"** – google it.

137 – The visual gag of the **on air/off air sign** flashing 'courage' through the hole in the anchor's head was the first image that popped in my head when I was first coming up with the Nightly News. Courage, of course, is the ridiculously pretentious manner in which Dan Rather signed off.

139 – As promised, contestant winners' heads go explodey.

140 – I always thought Mike Teevee was the most interesting kid in **Willy Wonka and the Chocolate Factory**. To Hell with Veruca and Charlie, give me a kid with a pistol every time. Brother David was always envisioned as the screwed up adult version of Mike.

141 – **You didn't have to be so damn mean** about it is, I believe, the foundation of society's problem with the media.

143 – In a book full of statements by people who have been deceived, struggled with their sins, and had their lives destroyed, **'exactly how did you think this was going to end for me'** might be the saddest line in the story.

144 – The last wave of violence was an emotional trigger for the populace. All the Senator had to do was make people feel a certain way.

146 – The way the Senator toys with James is not only evidence of the contempt with which he holds journalists, but also a demonstration of how completely detached he is. His casual manner on this and the next 3 pages suggests that he's a sociopath.

148 – When asked how he got all those girls to do what he wanted, Charlie Manson replied, **"I've got a knack."** This is the payoff for the joke on the previous page – Helter Skelter.

149 – The argument could be made that James did commit the greater sin as his was a personal betrayal.

152 – **Alprazolam** is Xanax.

154 – I came up with the ending for the Nightly News when I was taking my morning shower the day after I started working on the book. I smiled the rest of the day.

OTES
/END

fully COMMIT

or how I broke into comics and am refusing to leave.
or tips in some essential areas if you want to make a go of this.

(First, let me apologize. This is primarily from an American to Americans, which is, after all, my experience… so ignore the offending, or irrelevant bits accordingly you whiney subhuman foreigners.)

You gotta' get in first.

Despite what you've heard, this is much, much easier than advertised. It's simple really; all you have to do is be better than most everyone else.

No problem, right?

Artists, there is a new shit reality you have to face: the big companies in the US are searching everywhere for talent. Writing American comics is, for all intents and purposes, limited to westerners – drawing or painting comics is not. So while, yes, it has been traditionally true that it's easier to break in as an artist, the sample size you're competing against is now somewhere north of 5 Billion.

(And here's another little bit specifically for the artists – most of you can't compete with foreign talent. They will kick your ass because they're hungry for success in a way your pampered, western rear will never be.)

What's my point?

It's tough. I tried very hard to get in ten years ago and failed miserably. Sure, part of it was creative and personal immaturity, but it's also just so damned difficult. So, what's my one piece of advice on getting in?

Do something that's different. Whether it looks different or sounds different, do not (under the constant pain of rejection) submit derivative books. Otherwise, it's a waste of time.

Oh, and a second one: Follow the submission guidelines. You do not impress anyone by wasting time doing an entire graphic novel that no one wants to publish in the first place. Yes, that's the voice of experience.

So, adjust your attitude accordingly and get to work.

Be a Professional:

This is easy and bullet-pointable.

1. Work everyday.
2. Exercise everyday.
3. Make a realistic budget.
4. Understand what budget actually means.
5. Stick to said budget.
6. Turn in your work in a timely fashion.
7. Have good hygiene .
8. Have good manners.
9. Don't be a computer/internet/messageboard zombie.
10. Have actual relationships.

TTED

Personal Commitment:

It was October 2nd, 2004. I was sitting alone, bawling my eyes out, in a little Greek restaurant about half a block from the hotel where I was attending a Robert McKee seminar. I was reading Steven Pressfield's book, THE WAR OF ART.

It's a book about overcoming obstacles that stand in the way of creative undertakings. It's about realizing the only thing preventing you from succeeding is yourself. It's about becoming the person you are meant to be.

Here's an excerpt:
"We don't even know what hit us. I never did. From age twenty-four to thirty-two, Resistance kicked my ass from East Coast to West Coast and back thirteen times and I never knew it existed. I looked everywhere for the enemy and failed to see it right in front of my face."

From twenty-four to thirty-two... **I was that guy**.

Pressfield uses the word resistance to identify that thing within every creative person that keeps us from actually creating: Doubt, procrastination, fear, etc.

You know what I'm talking about.

A couple months earlier I'd decided to try and make a go of making comics, but it was that night I stopped being a *dabbler* and became a *creator*. I went back to my hotel, sat down and wrote myself a reminder. Now, I read it everyday before I start work:

I am my own Enemy,
Resistance is my Nature.

I am aware of **Resistance**
And it prevents me from achieving the life I am *Meant To Have*.

Resistance is Self-Generated, Self-Perpetuated.
It Lies and Seduces. Its goal is my Utter Destruction.
Every day is a battle for my soul.

This Moment, This Day,
I change my life.

Help me to defeat myself,
And realize fate.

Now, is all of this a little too spiritual? Is it too much new age, feel good, self-actualization?

Maybe, but am I committed?

Absolutely.

Jonathan Hickman is the visionary talent behind such works as The NIGHTLY NEWS issue 1, The NIGHTLY NEWS issue 3 and The NIGHTLY NEWS issue 6. His upcoming books *PAX ROMANA*, *A RED MASS FOR MARS* and *TRANSHUMAN* are all expected to eclipse his earlier work, *like The NIGHTLY NEWS issue 2*, as he plans on making full use of the spell-checker.

His twin brother, Marc, plays professional soccer for the Shimizu S-Pulse in Japan, which just happens to be the *second coolest job* on the planet. Hi Marc, your apartment is smaller than my closet. **Suck it.**

Jonathan lives in South Carolina surrounded by immediate family and in-laws, which he plans on leaving unless they start showering him with the love and affection he deserves.

This includes his wife.

You can visit his website:*www.pronea.com*, or email him at:*jonathan@pronea.com*.

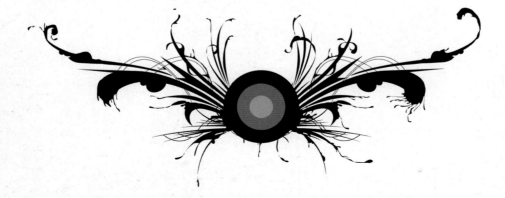